ESSENTIALS OF MANAGERIAL ACCOUNTING

(As per UGC Guidelines)

ESSENTIALS OF MANAGERIAL ACCOUNTING

(As per UGC Guidelines)

Prof. JAWAHAR LAL
Department of Commerce
Delhi School of Economics,
University of Delhi.
Delhi.

Himalaya Publishing House

MUMBAI • NEW DELHI • NAGPUR • BENGALURU • HYDERABAD • CHENNAI • PUNE
LUCKNOW • AHMEDABAD • ERNAKULAM • BHUBANESWAR • INDORE • KOLKATA • GUWAHATI

First Edition : 2005
Reprint : 2013

Published by : Mrs. Meena Pandey for **Himalaya Publishing House Pvt. Ltd.**,
"Ramdoot", Dr. Bhalerao Marg, Girgaon, **Mumbai - 400 004.**
Phone: 022-23860170/23863863, Fax: 022-23877178
E-mail: himpub@vsnl.com; Website: www.himpub.com

Branch Offices :

New Delhi : "Pooja Apartments", 4-B, Murari Lal Street, Ansari Road, Darya Ganj, New Delhi - 110 002. Phone: 011-23270392, 23278631; Fax: 011-23256286

Nagpur : Kundanlal Chandak Industrial Estate, Ghat Road, Nagpur - 440 018. Phone: 0712-2738731, 3296733; Telefax: 0712-2721215

Bengaluru : No. 16/1 (Old 12/1), 1st Floor, Next to Hotel Highlands, Madhava Nagar, Race Course Road, Bengaluru - 560 001. Phone: 080-32919385; Telefax: 080-22286611

Hyderabad : No. 3-4-184, Lingampally, Besides Raghavendra Swamy Matham, Kachiguda, Hyderabad - 500 027. Phone: 040-27560041, 27550139; Mobile: 09390905282

Chennai : No. 8/2, Modley 2nd Street, Ground Floor, T. Nagar, Chennai - 600 017. Phone: 044-28144004/28144005; Mobile: 09345345051

Pune : First Floor, "Laksha" Apartment, No. 527, Mehunpura, Shaniwarpeth (Near Prabhat Theatre), Pune - 411 030. Phone: 020-24496323/24496333; Mobile: 09370579333

Lucknow : House No. 731, Sehkhupura Colony, Near B.D. Convent School, Lucknow -226024. Mobile : 09307501549

Ahmedabad : 114, "SHAIL", 1st Floor, Opp. Madhu Sudan House, C.G. Road, Navrang Pura, Ahmedabad - 380 009. Phone: 079-26560126; Mobile: 09377088847

Ernakulam : 39/104 A, Lakshmi Apartment, Karikkamuri Cross Rd., Ernakulam, Cochin - 622011, Kerala. Phone: 0484-2378012, 2378016; Mobile: 09344199799

Bhubaneswar : 5 Station Square, Bhubaneswar - 751 001 (Odisha). Phone: 0674-2532129, Mobile: 09338746007

Indore : Kesardeep Avenue Extension, 73, Narayan Bagh, Flat No. 302, IIIrd Floor, Near Humpty Dumpty School, Indore - 452 007 (M.P.). Mobile: 09301386468

Kolkata : 108/4, Beliaghata Main Road, Near ID Hospital, Opp. SBI Bank, Kolkata - 700 010, Phone: 033-32449649, Mobile: 09910440956

Guwahati : House No. 15, Behind Pragjyotish College, Near Sharma Printing Press, P.O. Bharalumukh, Guwahati - 781009, (Assam). Mobile: 09883055590, 09883055536

Printed at : Shri Krishna offset Press Delhi-93

IN MEMORY OF MY PARENTS

PREFACE

Management accounting deals with the development and use of accounting information by different organisations for the purpose of decision making, planning, control, product costing and performance evaluation. The field of management accounting has been influenced greatly by the competitive and complex business environment. This requires that management accounting as a discipline should help the managers who are faced with managerial accounting issues and managerial problems in their organisations. Managers of Indian companies need to make business decisions with sound knowledge and understanding of the use of accounting information for the efficient and profitable functioning of their enterprises.

The text 'Managerial Accounting' focuses on the uses of managerial accounting information to resolve different managerial issues emerging in different organisations. The book makes a comprehensive coverage of important topics, current trends in management accounting and presents the concepts, techniques and use of accounting information in a clear, concise and logical manner.

The book is structured into nine chapters: Scope of Managerial Accounting, Statement of Changes in Financial Position (SCFP), Financial Statement Analysis, Cost Classifications, Marginal (Variable) Costing, Differential Analysis and Decision Making, Budgeting, Responsibility Accounting, Standard Costing.

The book contains many features to give a balanced blend of conceptual framework, managerial accounting techniques and practical use of accounting information. Some of the features are:

- Comprehensive and up-to-date coverage of the subject.
- Clear, concise and readable presentation.
- Real-world illustrative problems included in the chapters for better understanding of managerial accounting principles and techniques.
- Inclusion of charts, diagrams and figures to help in understanding the discussion easily and quickly.
- Thought-provoking and real-life theory questions given at the end of all chapters.
- Numerical problems given in an easy to complex manner to help the students in better learning and understanding of the material.

The book is designed on the UGC Model Curriculum prepared by them for the benefit of Indian universities and covers fully the syllabus suggested in the Model Curriculum.

The book would be useful for the students pursuing M.Com., MBA, and Bachelor of Commerce courses in universities and management institutes.

I wish to express many thanks to academic colleagues and friends for their helpful comments and suggestions.

I am grateful to my family members, my wife Pratibha; children Sanjay, Seema, Rajnish and daughter-in-law Pragati for their encouragement, moral support and understanding in completing this project.

Prof. JAWAHAR LAL

CONTENTS

Preface

Chapter 1. Scope of Managerial Accounting 1 - 6

Chapter 2. Statement of Changes in Financial Position (SCFP) 7 - 49

Chapter 3. Financial Statement Analysis 50 - 75

Chapter 4. Cost Classifications 76 - 90

Chapter 5. Marginal (Variable) Costing 91 - 169

Chapter 6. Differential Analysis and Decision Making 170 - 210

Chapter 7. Budgeting 211 - 263

Chapter 8. Responsibility Accounting 264 - 275

Chapter 9. Standard Costing 276 - 345

Chapter 1

SCOPE OF MANAGERIAL ACCOUNTING

Managerial accounting is that field of accounting which deals with providing information including financial accounting information to managers for their use in planning, decision-making, performance evaluation, control, management of costs and cost determination for financial reporting. Managerial Accounting contains reports prepared to fulfil the needs of various levels of management.

CIMA (UK) defines the term managerial accounting in the following manner:

"Management accounting is an integral part of management concerned with identifying, presenting and interpreting information used for:

(*i*) Formulating strategy

(*ii*) Planning and controlling activities

(*iii*) Decision taking

(*iv*) Optimising the use of resources

(*v*) Disclosure to shareholders and others external to the entity.

(*vi*) Disclosure to employees and

(*vii*) Safeguarding assets."

Thus, managerial accounting is concerned with data collection from internal and external sources, analysing, processing, interpreting and communicating the information for use within the organisation so that management can more effectively plan, make decisions and control operations.

Cost Accounting and Managerial Accounting

Cost accounting is mainly concerned with the ascertainment of product costs and the techniques of product costing and deals with only cost and price data. It is limited to product costing procedures and related information processing. It helps the management in planning and controlling costs relating to both production and distribution activities.

Inspite of the differing parameters of cost accounting and managerial accounting, cost accounting is generally indistinguishable from what is known as management or managerial accounting. Both these accounting systems are closely linked as they use common basic data and reports to a material degree. Much of the information used to prepare accounting statements and reports in cost accounting are also used in managerial accounting reports. Cost accounting largely uses data about production, sales, wages and overhead services. Managerial accounting utilises the same (and also additional) data to prepare budgets, performance reports, control reports and data analyses for decision-making purposes. Special decision methods, use of highly quantitative methods, behavioural techniques, information systems and budgeting are areas of managerial accounting.

MANAGEMENT PROCESS AND ROLE OF MANAGERIAL ACCOUNTING

The Management process implies the four basic functions of (1) Planning, (2) Organising, (3) Controlling, and (4) Decision-making. Managerial accounting plays a vital role in these managerial functions performed by managers.

(1) Planning: Planning is formulating both short-term and long-term plans and actions to achieve a particular end. The long-term plan indicates management's expectation of the future during the next three to five years or perhaps even longer. A budget is financial planning showing how resources are to be acquired and used over a specified time interval.

Managerial accounting is closely interwoven in planning at two levels because it provides information for decision making and because the entire budgeting process is developed around accounting – related reports. It also helps managers in planning by providing reports which estimate the effects of alternative actions on an enterprise's ability to achieve desired goals. For example, if a business enterprise determines a target profit for a year, it should also determine how to reach that target. For example, what products are to be sold at what prices?

(2) Organising: Organising is a process of establishing an organisational framework and assigning responsibility to people working in an organisation for achieving business goals and objectives. Organising requires clarity about each manager's responsibility and lines of authority. The various departments and units are interrelated in a hierarchy, with a formal communication structure in which information and instructions are passed downwards to the lower level management and upwards to the top management level.

Managerial accounting helps managers in organising by providing reports and necessary information to regulate and adjust operations and activities in the light of changing conditions. For example, the reports under managerial accounting can be prepared on product lines on which basis managers can decide whether to add or eliminate a product line in the current product mix.

(3) Controlling: Control is the process of monitoring, measuring, evaluating and correcting actual results to ensure that a business enterprise's goals and plans are achieved. Control is accomplished with the use of feedback. Feedback allows managers to decide to let the operations and activity continue as they are, take remedial actions to put some actions back in harmony with the original plan and goals or do some rearranging and replannings at the midstream level.

Managerial accounting helps in the control function by producing performance reports and control reports which highlight variances between expected and actual performances. Such reports serve as a basis for taking necessary corrective action to control operations. The use of performance and control reports follows the principle of management by exception. In case of significant differences between budgeted and actual results, a manager will usually investigate to determine what is going wrong and possibly which subordinates or units might need help.

(4) Decision-making: Decision-making is a process of choosing among competing alternatives. Decision making is inherent in each of three management functions described above namely, planning, organising and controlling. A manager cannot plan without making decisions and has to choose among competing objectives and methods to carry out the chosen objectives. Only one of the different competing plans can be selected by a manager. Similarly in organising, managers need to decide on an organisational structure and on specific actions to be taken on day-to-day operations. In control function, managers have to decide whether variances are worth investigating.

Managerial accounting plays a critical role in the decision-making process. This accounting system contains a storehouse of valuable information for predicting the results of various courses of action. Thus managerial accounting can assist the management in formally structuring decision problems as well as placing the alternatives and their consequences in a form that will be easier for the management to evaluate.

FINANCIAL ACCOUNTING

Financial Accounting is concerned with providing information to external users. It refers to the preparation of general purpose reports for use by persons outside a business enterprise, such as shareholders (existing and potential), creditors, financial analysts, labour unions, government authorities and the like. Financial accounting is oriented towards the preparation of financial statements which summarise the results of operations for selected periods of time and show the financial position of the business at particular dates. The following points are important to understand the scope and nature of financial accounting:

Contents

The end products of the financial accounting process are the financial statements that communicate useful information to decision-makers. There are three primary financial statements for a profit-making entity in India, viz., the Income Statement (statement of revenues, expenses and profit), the Balance Sheet (statement of assets, liabilities and owners'equity) and cash flow statement.

Accounting System

The accounting system includes various techniques and procedures used by the accountant (preparer) in measuring, describing and communicating financial data to users. Journals, ledgers and other accounting techniques used in processing financial accounting information depend upon the concept of the double-entry system. This technique includes Generally Accepted Accounting Principles (GAPP) which encompass the conventions, rules and procedures necessary to define accepted accounting practice at a particular time.

Measurement Unit

Financial accounting is primarily concerned with the measurement of economic resources and obligations and changes in them. Financial accounting measures in terms of monetary units of a society in which it operates. For example, the common denominator or yardstick used for accounting measurement is the rupee in India and dollar in the US. The assumption is that the rupee or the dollar is a useful measuring unit.

Users of Financial Accounting Information

As stated earlier, financial accounting information is intended primarily to serve external users. Financial accounting information is used by a variety of groups and for diverse purposes. Some users have direct interest in reported information. Examples of such users are owners, creditors and suppliers, potential owners, suppliers, management, tax authorities, employees and customers. Some users need financial accounting information to help those who have direct interest in a business enterprise. Example of such users are financial analysts and advisers, stock exchanges, financial press and reporting agencies, trade associations and labour unions. These users groups having direct/indirect interest have different objectives and diverse informational needs. The emphasis in financial accounting has been in general-purpose information which obviously is not intended to satisfy any specialised needs of individual users or specific user groups.

Limitations of Financial Accounting

Financial accounting suffers from the following limitations which have been responsible for the emergence of cost and managerial accounting:

(*i*) It does not provide detailed cost information for different departments, processes, products, or jobs in the production divisions. Similarly separate cost data are not available for different services and functions in the administration division.

(*ii*) Financial accounting does not set up a proper system of controlling materials and supplies. Undoubtedly, if material and supplies are not controlled in a manufacturing concern, they will lead to losses on account of misappropriation, misutilisation, scrap, defectives etc.

(*iii*) The recording and accounting for wages and labour is not done for different jobs, processes, products or departments. This creates problems in analysing the cost associated with different activities.

(*iv*) It is difficult to know the behaviour of costs in financial accounting as expenses are not assigned to the product at each stage of production. Expenses are not classified into direct and indirect and therefore cannot be classified as controllable and uncontrollable.

(*v*) Financial accounting does not possess an adequate system of standards to evaluate the performance of departments and employees working in the departments. Standards need to be developed for materials, labour and overheads so that a firm can compare the work of labourers, workers, supervisors and executives with what should have been done in an allotted period of time.

(*vi*) It contains historical cost information which is accumulated at the end of the accounting period. This accounting does not provide day-to-day information about costs and expenses. This is the reason why much dissatisfaction has been shown with external financial reporting.

(*vii*) Financial accounting does not provide cost data to determine the price of the product being manufactured or the service being rendered to the consumers. It is also not possible to prepare detailed cost reports for the purpose of comparison and analysis between two periods of time within an enterprise and also for making inter-firm comparison.

Differences Between Managerial Accounting and Financial Accounting

Managerial accounting and financial accounting differ from each other in the following respects:

1. Primary users of information: The users of financial accounting statements are mainly external to the business enterprise. These financial statements are relevant to various levels of management but are not adequate for the purpose of planning, control and decision-making. External users include shareholders, creditors, financial analysts, government authorities, stock exchanges, labour unions etc.

Management accounting aims at preparing reports and supplying information to the management for planning, controlling and decision-making. The information generated under the accounting system is used by members of management at different levels.

2. Accounting method: Financial accounting follows the double-entry system for recording, classifying and summarising business transactions. This accounting process results in aggregate balances of all accounts maintained in a firm's books. Managerial accounting is not based on the double-entry system. The data under managerial accounting may be gathered for small or large segments or activities of an organisation and monetary as well as other measures can be used for different activities in the firm.

3. Accounting principles: Financial accounting data is primarily meant for external users. The 'generally accepted accounting principles' are important in financial accounting and are used extensively while recording, classifying, summarising and reporting business transactions.

On the contrary, managerial accounting is not bound to use the 'generally accepted accounting principles.' It can use any accounting technique or practice which generates useful information.

4. Unit of measurement: All information under financial accounting is in terms of money, i.e., transactions measured in terms of money have already occurred. In comparison, managerial accounting applies any measurement unit that is useful in a particular situation. Besides the monetary units, the management accountant may find it necessary to use such measures as number of labour hours, machine hours and product units for the purpose of analysis and decision-making.

5. Time Span: Financial accounting data and statements are developed for a definite period, usually a year or six months. It requires that financial statements be developed and presented at regular time intervals. Company annual reports may be prepared semi-annually or quarterly but the important point is that they are prepared on a regular basis.

Management accounting reports and statements are prepared whenever needed. Reports may be prepared on a monthly, weekly or even on a daily basis. Frequency of reports is determined by particular planning, controlling and decision-making needs.

6. General Purpose Report Vs Specific Purpose Report: Financial accounting produces information and reports which are general purpose reports in order to serve the informational needs of many external users such as shareholders, creditors, potential investors, customers, suppliers, regulatory authorities, employees and the general public.

On the contrary, the reports and data developed in managerial accounting are known as specific purpose reports designed for a particular user (manager) or particular decision. Management accounting uses internal reports to evaluate the performance of entities, product lines, departments and managers.

7. Historical Vs Futuristic Data: Financial accounting has a historical orientation and records and reports of what has happened. Managerial accounting has a futuristic orientation and concentrates on what is likely to happen in the future. This is due to the fact that management accounting emphasises on developing information for planning, control and decision-making purposes.

8. Detailed and aggregated information: Managerial accounting provides detailed and disaggregated information about products, individual activities, divisions, plants, operations, tasks or any other responsibility centres. On the other hand, financial accounting focuses on the company as a whole. Sometimes, in financial accounting, some information is given about different products or lines of activity due to financial reporting requirements as provided in the Companies Act/Other Rules and Regulations.

RESPONSIBILITIES OF MANAGEMENT ACCOUNTANT

The management accountant, often referred to as the controller, is the manager of accounting information used in planning, control and decision-making areas. He is responsible for collecting, processing and reporting information that will help managers and decision-makers in their planning, controlling and decision-making activities. He participates in all accounting activities within the organisation. He performs many vital responsibilities and functions within an organisation such as:

(*i*) Providing help in the design of an accounting information system,

(*ii*) Collecting data,

(*iii*) Helping in the maintenance of accounting records, preparation of financial statements,

(*iv*) Helping in the budget preparation,

(*v*) Preparation of performance reports, control reports, special managerial reports/analyses for planning, control and decision-making,

(*vi*) Coordinating budget-making and report preparation activities,

(*vii*) Interpreting accounting data based on the particular requirements of a manager in a given situation and

(*viii*) Ensuring that the accounting information system is adequate and useful in accordance with the budgets, plans, policies and decision-related requirements.

THEORY QUESTIONS

1. Define managerial accounting. Explain its importance.
2. Discuss the scope of management accounting.
3. What are the steps involved in the managerial decision-making process. What role does management accounting play in that process.
4. "The best management accounting system is one that provides managers with all the information they would like to have." Do you agree with this statement. Give reasons.
5. Why is financial accounting subject to more strict rules and regulations than management accounting.
6. "A management accountant is both an information provider and a part of management." Explain.
7. What are the four basic functions of the management process. How does management accounting help in this process.
8. "Management accounting is an extension of financial accounting techniques for special uses." Explain this statement with suitable illustrations.
9. "The emphasis of financial accounting and management accounting differ." Explain.
10. Explain the role and responsibilities of a management accountant in a large scale business enterprise.
11. Explain the difference between financial accounting and management accounting. What is the role of a management accounting in a business firm.
12. Explain the nature and scope of management accounting. In what ways do the roles and responsibilities of management accountants differ from those of financial accountants.

Chapter 2

STATEMENT OF CHANGES IN FINANCIAL POSITION (SCFP)

CONCEPT OF SCFP

Financial statements of a business enterprise, i.e. income statement and balance sheet are important statements to judge the results of business operation and financial position at the beginning and end of the year. The income statement sets forth the enterprise's revenues, expenses, gains and losses. It shows the resources generated and consumed in business operations. The balance sheet portrays the overall financial position of a business enterprise at a specific date during the recurring cycles of investment, recovery of investment and reinvestment. The income statement, however, does not show the effects of all the events which affected an enterprise's liquidity — its ability to meet its cash obligations on time — nor does it reflect all the flows of resources into or out of the enterprise during the period.

A statement of changes in financial position (funds statement) helps us to understand how and why the financial position of a business enterprise has changed during a period. This statement summarises the organisation's activities for a period by showing how it acquired its resources and what those resources were used for.

The statement of changes in financial position summarises the long-term financing and investing activities of an enterprise; it shows where the financial sources (funds) have come from and where they have gone. With this understanding of how funds have flowed into the business and how these funds have been used, we can answer many important questions such as: Do the normal operations of the business generate sufficient funds to enable the company to pay regular dividends? Has the company been forced to borrow to pay for the new plant and other fixed assets? Has the company been able to generate the funds from its current operation? Is the business becoming more solvent or less solvent? Perhaps the most puzzling question: How can a profitable business be running low on cash and working capital? Even though a business operates profitably, its working capital may decline and the business may even become insolvent. The statement of changes in financial position gives us answers to these questions, because it shows in detail the amount of funds received from each source and the amount of funds used for each purpose throughout the year. Statement of changes in financial position is particularly helpful in appraising financial policies of the past and in planning financial activities of the future.

CONCEPT OF FUNDS

A statement of changes in financial position can be prepared using different concepts of funds as a basis. For instance, statement of changes in financial position may focus on changes in working capital, cash, or total financial resources of a business enterprise. Accordingly, this chapter discusses the preparation of the following types of statement of changes in financial position:

(*i*) Statement of changes in working capital, popularly known as Funds Flow Statement or Statement of Sources and Applications of Funds,

(*ii*) Statement of Changes in Cash, popularly known as Cash Flow Statement, and

(*iii*) Statement of Changes in Total Financial Resources.

FUNDS DEFINED AS WORKING CAPITAL

Working capital is defined as current assets minus current liabilities and thus is a broader definition of funds than is cash. The basic objective of the statement of changes in financial position and working capital basis is to explain the changes in the working capital for a specified period of time. In the process of achieving this objective, the statement should enable the user to identify the changes as they relate to three basic causes:

- Amount of changes in working capital associated with the operating activities of the firm.
- Long term financing or other sources that cause an increase in the working capital, and
- Long term investment activities or other uses that cause a reduction in the working capital.

SOURCES AND USES OF WORKING CAPITAL

Any transaction that increases the amount of working capital is a source of working capital. For example, the sale of merchandise at a price greater than its cost is a source of working capital, because the increase in cash or receivable from the sale is greater than the decrease in inventory. Any transaction that decreases working capital is a use of working capital. For example, either incurring current liability to acquire a non-current asset or using cash to pay expenses represents a decrease in working capital.

The principal sources and uses of working capital are listed below:

Sources of Working Capital

The sources of working capital are:

1. Funds from Business Operations: If the inflow of funds from sales exceeds the outflow of funds to cover the cost of merchandise purchases and expenses of doing business, current operations will provide a net source of funds. If the inflow of funds from sales is less than these outflows, operation will result in the net use of funds. Working capital provided by operations is the net increase or decrease in working capital resulting from the normal business activities of earning revenue and paying expenses. There are many similarities between the providing of working capital by operations and the earning of net income. For example, earning revenue increases net income and the related inflow of cash and receivables increases working capital. However, not all the expenses require the use of funds in the current period: therefore the amount of funds provided by operations is not the same as the amount of net income earned during the period. The following points explain this situation:

(*i*) Some expenses do not reduce working capital. Expenses such as depreciation and amortisation of intangible assets reduce net income but have no immediate effect on the amount of working capital provided by operations, i.e. these items do not reduce working capital. The net income figure therefore understates the amount of working capital provided by operations by amount of depreciation expense recorded during the period. One objective of the statement of changes in financial position is to explain any differences between net income and the amount of working capital provided by operations. Thus funds provided by operations would be computed in the following manner:

Funds from Operations:

Net income	—
Add: Depreciation expense	—
Funds provided by operations	—

(*ii*) Some items increase income but do not increase working capital — specifically some items in the income statement increase net income without increasing working capital; such items must be deducted from net income in arriving at working capital provided by operations.

(*iii*) Non-operating gains and losses, if material in amount, should be eliminated from net income in order to show the working capital provided by 'normal' operations. For example, assume that a plant costing Rs. 1,00,000 is sold at Rs. 1,20,000 at a net gain of Rs. 20,000. In the statement of changes in financial position, the entire Rs. 1,20,000 as proceeds from sale will be reported as funds provided by the sale of the plant. The Rs. 20,000 non-operating gain, however, is included in the net income for the period. In determining the amount of working capital provided by operations, this Rs. 20,000 non-operating gain must be deducted from the net income figure because the entire proceeds from sale of the plant are reported elsewhere in the statement of changes in financial position.

As a separate example, assume that the same plant is sold for Rs. 90,000; then the non-operating loss of Rs. 10,000 should be added back to the net income to arrive at working capital provided by operations and the working capital provided through the sale of the plant should be reported at Rs. 90,000.

Briefly, the procedure of computing funds provided by operations can be summarised as follows:

Funds from Operations

Net profit (or loss) as per the profit and loss account:

Add: (*i*) Depreciation expense.

(*ii*) Amortisation of goodwill, patents and other intangible assets.

(*iii*) Amortisation of extraordinary losses occurred in previous periods.

(*iv*) Amortisation of discount on debentures.

(*v*) Loss on sale of non-current assets such as plant, equipment etc.

Less: (*i*) Gain on sale of the non-current assets such as plant, equipment etc.

(*ii*) Profit or revaluation surplus of non-current assets.

(*iii*) Dividends and interest on investments (earned but not received) and

(*iv*) Amortisation of premium received on debentures

= Funds from Business Operations

2. Sales of Non-current Assets: A business may obtain working capital by selling non-current assets, such as plant and equipment or long-term investments, in exchange for current assets. As long as current assets are received, the sale is a source of funds regardless of whether the non-current assets are sold at a gain or loss. For example, assume that a business firm sells for Rs. 2,50,000 a plant which costs Rs. 3,00,000. Although the plant was sold at a loss, the firm has increased its current assets by Rs. 250,000 by selling the plant. Thus, the transaction is a source of working capital.

3. Long-term borrowing: Long-term borrowing, such as issue of debentures and bonds result in an increase in current assets, thereby increasing working capital. Short-term borrowing, however, does not increase working capital. When a company borrows cash on short term credit or by signing a short-term note payable, working capital is unchanged because the increase in current assets is offset by an increase in current liabilities of the same amount.

4. Issue of additional equity capital: The issue of additional equity shares results in an inflow of current assets, thereby increasing working capital. In a similar manner, additional investments of current assets by owners represent source of funds in single proprietorship and partnership.

Uses of Working Capital

The following are the uses of working capital:

1. Declaration of cash dividend: The declaration of a cash dividend results in a current liability (dividend payable) and is therefore the use of funds. It should be understood that it is the declaration of dividend, rather than the payment of the dividend which is the use of funds. Actual payment of the dividend reduces current assets and current liabilities by the same amount and thus has no effect upon the amount of working capital. Issue of shares in lieu of dividend does not involve any distribution of assets and, therefore, are not use of funds.

2. Purchase of non-current assets: Purchases of non-current assets, such as plant and equipment, reduce current assets or increase current liabilities. In either case, working capital is reduced.

3. Repayment of long-term debt: Working capital is decreased when current assets are used to repay long-term debt. However, repayment of short-term debt is not a use of funds, since current assets and current liabilities decrease by the same amount.

EFFECT OF TRANSACTIONS ON WORKING CAPITAL

In preparing a statement of changes in financial position, on working capital basis, it is convenient to classify business transactions into three categories:

1. Transactions Affecting only Current Asset or Current Liability Accounts: These transactions produce changes in working capital accounts but do not change the amount of working capital. For example, the purchase of merchandise increases inventory and accounts payable but has no effect on working capital; it may therefore be ignored in preparing a statement of changes in financial position. Similarly, paying accounts payable affects cash, so this transaction would be reflected in the cash basis statement of changes in financial position. However, the transaction has no effect on working capital since a current asset (cash) and a current liability (accounts payable) decrease by the same amount. Hence, the transaction would not be reflected as a source or use in a working capital basis statement of changes in financial position. Other transactions like collection of receivables, short-term borrowing, purchase of short-term government securities also fall in this category of transactions. Thus, when funds are defined as working capital, there is no need to show the details of the more or less continuous movement of resources between current liabilities and current assets which results from the manufacture and sale of goods and the collection of receivables from customers. Indeed, the focus is on the usually more significant flows affecting non-current assets (i.e. long-term investments) and permanent capital, the name given to the sum of long-term liabilities and owners' equity.

Thus the funds statement, i.e. Statement of Changes in Financial Position based on changes in working capital position is a better and useful tool for highlighting the changes that have taken place in the financial operations between two balance sheet dates.

2. Transactions Affecting Current Asset or Current Liability Account and a Non-Working Capital (Non-current) Account: These transactions bring about either an increase or decrease in the amount of working capital. The issue of long-term bonds, for example, increases current assets and increases loan on bonds, a non-working capital account; therefore the issue of bonds is a source of working capital. Similarly, when the bonds approach maturity, they are transferred to the current liability classification in the balance sheet. This causes a reduction (a use) of working capital. If changes in non-working capital accounts are analysed, these events are brought to light, and their effect on working capital will be reported in the statement of changes in financial position.

3. Transactions Affecting only Non-current Accounts: These transactions have no direct effect on the amount of working capital. The entry to record depreciation is an example of such a transaction. Other transactions in this category, such as issue of share capital in exchange for plant assets, are called *exchanged transactions* involving only non-current accounts and are viewed as both a source and a use of working capital, but do not change the amount of working capital. Alternatively, such exchange transactions may not be considered in preparing a statement of changes in financial position on working capital basis.

MAIN STEPS IN PREPARING THE STATEMENT

In order to prepare a statement of changes in financial position on a working capital basis, it is necessary to have balance sheets at two points in time and an income statement covering that span of time. The steps involved in preparing the statement are as follows:

(*i*) Determine the change (increase or decrease) in working capital.

(*ii*) Determine the adjustments account to be made to net income for items.

(*iii*) For each non-current-account on the balance sheet, establish the increase or decrease in that account. Analyse the change to decide whether it is a source (increase) or use (decrease) of working capital and

(*iv*) Be sure the total of all sources including those from operations minus the total of all uses equals the change found in working capital in step 1.

General Rules for Preparing Funds Flow Statement

The following general rules should be observed while preparing funds flow statement:

(*i*) Increase in a current asset means increase (plus) in working capital.

(*ii*) Decrease in a current asset means decrease (minus) in working capital.

(*iii*) Increase in a current liability means decrease (minus) in working capital.

(*iv*) Decrease in a currrent liability means increase (plus) in working capital.

(*v*) Increase in current asset and increase in current liability does not affect working capital.

(*vi*) Decrease in current asset and decrease in current liability does not affect working capital and

(*vii*) Changes in fixed (non-current) assets and fixed (non-current) liabilities affects working capital.

SCHEDULE OF CHANGES IN WORKING CAPITAL

Many business enterprises prefer to prepare another statement, known as schedule of changes in working capital, while preparing a funds flow statement, on a working capital basis. This schedule of changes in working capital provides information concerning the changes in each individual current assets and current liabilities accounts (items). This schedule is a part of the funds flow statement and increase (decrease) in working capital indicated by the schedule of changes in working capital will be equal to the amount of changes in working capital as found by funds flow statement. The schedule of changes in working capital can be prepared by comparing the current assets and current liabilities at two periods. The format of schedule of changes in working capital is as follows:

Schedule of Changes in Working Capital

Items	*As on*	*As on*	*Changes*	
			Increase	*Decrease*
A. *Current Assets:*				
Cash balance				
Bank balance				
Accounts receivable (Debtors)				
Marketable Securities				
Stock				
Prepaid expenses				
B. *Current liabilities:*				
Bank overdraft				
Accounts payables (creditors)				
Outstanding expenses				
Total				
Net increase/decrease in working capital				

Format of Funds Flow Statement

A funds flow statement can be prepared in statement form or 'T' form. Both the formats are being given below:

Funds Flow Statement (Statement Form)

A. Sources of Funds:	
(*i*) Funds from business operations	
(*ii*) Sale of fixed asset	
(*iii*) Issue of shares	
(*iv*) Issue of debentures	
(*v*) Long-term borrowings	
Total Sources	
B. Application of Funds:	
(*i*) Loss from business operations	
(*ii*) Payment of dividend	
(*iii*) Payment of tax	
(*iv*) Purchase of fixed assets	
(*v*) Payment of long-term loans	
(*vi*) Redemption of debentures	
(*vii*) Redemption of preference shares	
Total Use	—
Net increase/decrease in working capital (Total sources Minus Total uses)	—

Funds Flow Statement ('T' Form)

Source of Funds	*Rs.*	*Application of Funds*	*Rs.*
(*i*) Funds from business operations		(*i*) Loss from business operations	
(*ii*) Sale of fixed assets		(*ii*) Payment of dividend	
(*iii*) Issue of shares		(*iii*) Payment of tax	
(*iv*) Issue of debentures		(*iv*) Purchase of fixed assets	
(*v*) Long-term borrowings		(*v*) Payment of long-term loans	
(*vi*) Decrease in working capital		(*vi*) Redemption of debentures	
(*vii*) (If application amount is more than the sources amount)		(*vii*) Redemption of preference shares	
		(*viii*) Increase in working capital (if sources are more than the application amount)	
Total		Total	

TREATMENT OF PROVISION FOR TAXATION AND PROPOSED DIVIDENDS

Provision for Taxation

There are two possible treatments about the provision for taxation:

(1) Provision for taxation can be treated as a current liability and it will decrease the working capital in the schedule of changes in working capital. However, payment of tax does not affect working capital because it involves both current asset and current liability account, i.e. payment decreases cash or bank balance on the one hand and decreases the current liability (tax provision) by the equivalent amount on the other hand.

(2) Provision for taxation may be considered as an appropriation of profit, i.e. like internal reserve. Such a treatment does not change working capital position. Provisions made for taxation during the current year is transferred to adjusted profit and loss account. The amount paid as tax is shown as an application of fund.

Proposed Dividends

There are also two treatments about the proposed dividend:

(*i*) Proposed dividends can be considered as current liability and hence will decrease working capital in the schedule of changes in working capital. However, when dividends are paid, it is not treated as uses of funds and

(*ii*) Proposed dividend can be treated as an appropriation of profits. In this case, proposed dividend for the current year is added back to the current year's profit in order to find out funds from operations if such amount of dividend has already been charged to profit. Then payment of dividend will be shown as application of funds.

Example: Compute funds from Operations from the following income statement:

Income Statement

	Rs.		*Rs.*
To Salaries	10,000	By G/P b/d	2,000
To Rent	4,000	By Rent	10,000
To Depreciation	2,000	By Interest amount	8,000
To Preliminary expenses	4,000	By Net loss	10,000
To Loss on sale of furniture	10,000		
	30,000		30,000

Solution:

Funds from Operations

Net loss as per Income statement		(10,000)
Add: Items which do not decrease funds:		
Depreciation	Rs. 2,000	
Preliminery expenses	Rs. 4,000	
Loss on sale of furniture	Rs. 10,000	16,000
Funds from operations		6,000

Notes: Rent and interest on investment, alternatively can be considered as non-operating income and in such a case, they will have to be excluded (deducted) while calculating funds from operations. Also, then these items will be shown under 'non-operating income' in the funds flow statement.

Example: From the following balance sheets for the years 2001 and 2002, find out funds from operations

	2001 (Rs.)	*2002 (Rs.)*
General reserve	10,000	12,500
Goodwill	5,000	2,500
Provision for depreciation on plant	5,000	6,000
Preliminary expenses	3,000	2,000
Profit and losses appropriation A/c	15,000	20,000

Solution:

Funds from Operations

	Rs.
Profit and loss appropriation account as an December 31, 2002	20,000
Add: Items not decreasing funds:	
Transfer to general reserve	2,500
Goodwill written off	2,500
Provision for depreciation on Plant	1,000
Preliminary expenses written off	1,000
	27,000
Less: Profit and loss appropriation account balance as on December 31, 2001	15,000
Funds from operations	12,000

The funds from operations can also be found by preparing adjusted profit and loss account as given below:

Adjusted Profit and Loss Account

	Rs.		*Rs.*
To Transfer to general reserve	2,500	By balance b/d	15000
To Goodwill written off	2,500	By funds from operations (balancing figure)	12000
To Preliminary expenses Written off	1,000		
To Provision for depreciation	1,000		
To Balance c/d	2,000		
	27,000		27,000

Example 1

The following are the balance sheet of a company for the years 2001 and 2002 and income statement for the year 2002.

Balance Sheets as on December 31, 2001 and December 31, 2002

	Dec. 31, 2002 Rs.	*Dec. 31, 2001* Rs.	*Increase (decrease)* Rs.
Assets:			
Current assets:			
Cash	19,000	17,400	1,600
Debtors	24,600	24,000	600
Inventory	33,000	34,000	(1,000)
Prepaid insurance	4,000	3,600	400
Long-term assets:			
Machinery	3,60,000	3,50,000	10,000
Less: Accumulated depreciation	(1,68,800)	(1,66,000)	(2,800)
Total assets	2,71,800	2,63,000	8,800
Liabilities and Equity			
Current liabilities:			
Creditors	33,600	32,400	1,200
Salaries payable	600	1,000	(400)
Income taxes payable	4,400	3,400	1,000
Long-term loan	46,000	40,000	6,000
Equity Capital	1,00,000	1,00,000	
Retained earnings	87,200	86,200	1,000
Total Liabilities	2,71,800	2,63,000	8,800

Income Statement for the year ending 2002

	Rs.
Sales	63,800
Expenses:	
Cost of goods sold	45,600
Salaries	8,400
Rent	1,200
Depreciation	2,800
Insurance	600
Interest	400
Income tax	1,000
Total expenses	60,000
Net Income	3,800

Statement of Retained Earnings	Rs.
Retained earnings for the year 2001	86,200
Add: Net income for the year 2002	3,800
	90,000
Less: Dividends	2,800
	87,200

You are required to prepare a Funds Flow Statement on a working capital basis.

Solution:

Funds Flow Statement
(Working Capital Basis)

		Rs.	Rs.	Rs.
(A) Sources of Funds:				
(*i*)	Funds from operations:			
	Net income	3,800		
Add:	Non-cash charges:			
	Depreciation	2,800		
	Funds provided by operations		6,600	
(*ii*)	Other sources:			
	Long-term borrowings		6,000	12,600
(B) Uses of funds:				
(*i*)	Purchase of machinery		10,000	
(*ii*)	Dividends		2,800	
	Total uses			12,800
	Changes in Working Capital			(200)

The above statement presentation is a two-part statement; the sources are first detailed and then totalled, followed by the detail information and total for uses. The difference between the sources and uses must equal the change in working capital.

It can be noticed that sources of funds (working capital) is sub-divided into two parts; the first part is concerned with sources from operations and the second part deals with other sources.

Uses of working capital in the above statement do not include any uses for operations, such as salaries and rent, because these have been included automatically by starting the funds flow statement with the net income rather than with revenue. Generally, the most common uses of funds shown are for the firm's investment activities such as the purchase of the new equipment, declaration of dividends or payment of long-term liabilities.

Using the figures given in Problem 1, the Schedule of Changes in Working capital can be prepared as follows:

Schedule of Changes in Working Capital (Changes in Current Assets and Current Liabilities)

	December 31, 2002	*December 31, 2001*	*Increase (Decrease)*
Current assets:			
Cash	Rs. 19,000	Rs. 17,400	Rs. 1,600
Accounts receivable	24,600	24,000	600
Inventory	33,000	34,000	(1,000)
Prepaid insurance	4,000	3,600	400
Total current assets	80,600	79,000	1,600
Current liabilities:			
Accounts payable	33,600	32,400	1,200
Salaries payable	600	1,000	(400)
Income taxes payable	4,400	3,400	1,000
Total current liabilities	38,600	36,800	1,800
Working capital	42,000	42,200	(200)

Example 2

From the following Balance Sheets of M/s Wilson & Co. for the year ending 31st December 2001 and 2002, prepare a statement showing sources and application of funds:

Liabilities	*2001* *Rs.*	*2002* *Rs.*	*Assets*	*2001* *Rs.*	*2002* *Rs.*
Share Capital	4,00,000	5,75,000	Plant	75,000	1,00,000
Trade Creditors	1,06,000	70,000	Stock	1,21,000	1,36,000
P & L A/c	14,000	31,000	Debtors	1,81,000	1,70,000
			Cash	1,43000	2,70,000
Total	5,20,000	6,76,000		5,20,000	6,76,000

Solution:

Statement of Sources and Applications of Funds for the year ended 31st December, 1983

Sources	*Rs.*	*Applications*	*Rs.*
Issue of Shares Capital	1,75,000	Purchases of Plant	25,000
Funds from Operation	17,000	Increase in Working Capital	1,67,000
	1,92,000		1,92,000

Schedule of Changes in Working Capital

	2001 *Rs.*	*2002* *Rs.*	*Increase* *Rs.*	*Decrease* *Rs.*
Current Assets:				
Stock	1,21,000	1,36,000	15,000	
Debtors	1,81,000	1,70,000		11,000
Cash	1,43,000	2,70,000	1,27,000	
Total (A)	4,45,000	5,76,000		
Current Liabilities				
Trade Creditors	1,06,000	70,000	36,000	
Total (B)	1,06,000	70,000		
Working Capital (A-B)	3,39,000	5,06,000		
Increase in Working Capital	1,67,000			1,67,000
	5,06,000	5,06,000	1,78,000	1,78,000

Adjusted Profit & Loss A/c

	Rs.		Rs.
To Balance c/d	31,000	By Balance b/d	14,000
		By Funds from operation	17,000
	31,000		31 00

Plant A/c

	Rs.		Rs.
To Balance b/d	75,000	By Balance c/d	1,00,000
To Bank A/c (balancing figure)	25,000		
	1,00,000		1,00,000

Example 3

Balance Sheets of M/s Black and White as on 1 January, 2001 and 31 December, 2001 were as follows:

Balance Sheets

Liabilities	*1 Jan.*	*31 Dec.*	*Assets*	*1 Jan*	*31 Dec.*
Creditors	40,000	44,000	Cash	10,000	7,000
Mr. White's			Debtors	30,000	50,000
Loan	25,000	—	Stock	35,000	25,000
Loan from P.N. Bank	40,000	50,000	Machinery	80,000	55,000
Capital	1,25,000	1,53,000	Land	40,000	40,000
			Building	35,000	60,000
	2,30,000	2,47,000		2,30,000	2,47,000

During the year, machine costing Rs. 10,000 (accumulated depreciation Rs. 3,000) was sold for Rs. 5,000. The provision for depreciation against machinery as on 1 January 2001 was Rs. 25,000 and on 31 December 2001 Rs. 40,000. Net profit for the year 2001 amounted to Rs. 45,000. You are required to prepare Funds (Working Capital) Flow Statement.

Solution:

Funds Flow Statement for the year ending 31 December 2001

	Rs.
Sources:	
Loan from P.N. Bank	10,000
Sale of Plant	5,000
Funds from operations (See Working Note 2)	65,000
Total Sources	80,000
Applications:	
White's Loan repaid	25,000
Partner's Drawings	17,000
Purchase of Land	10,000
Purchase of Building	25,000
Total Applications	77,000
Increase in Working Capital	3,000

Working Notes:

1. Schedule of Changes in Working Capital

	Increase Rs.	*Decrease* Rs.
Cash		3,000
Debtors	20,000	
Stock		10,000
Creditors		4,000
	20,000	17,000
Increase in Working Capital	3,000	

2. Funds from Operations

	Profits made during the year	45,000
Add:	Loss on sale of Machine sold	2,000
	Depreciation on Machinery	18,000
		65,000

3. Machinery Account

To Balance b/d	1,05,000	By provision for depreciation on machinery sold	3,000
		By Bank	5,000
		By Loss on machinery sold	2,000
		By Balance c/d	95,000
	1,05,000		1,05,000

4. Provision for Depreciation on Machinery

To Machinery A/c	3,000	By Balance b/d	25,000
To Balance c/d	40,000	By P. and L. A/c (Depreciation provided during the year — Balancing figure)	18,000
	43,000		43,000

Example 4

Following are the summarised Balance Sheets of A Co. Ltd. as on 31st December, 2001 and 2002:

Liabilities	*2001* *Rs.*	*2002* *Rs.*	*Assets*	*2001* *Rs.*	*2002* *Rs.*
Share Capital	2,00,000	2,50,000	Land & Buildings	2,00,000	1,90,000
General Reserve	50,000	60,000	Machinery & Plant	1,50,000	1,69,000
Profit & Loss A/c	30,500	30,600	Stock	1,00,000	74,000
Bank loan	70,000	—	Sundry debtors	80,000	64,200
Sundry Creditors	1,50,000	1,35,200	Cash	500	600
Provision for taxation	30,000	35,000	Bank	—	8,000
			Goodwill	—	5,000
	5,30,500	5,10,000		5,30,500	5,10,800

Additional information supplied:

During the year ended 31st December, 2002:

(*a*) Dividend of Rs. 23,000 was paid:

(*b*) Assets of another company were purchased for a consideration of Rs. 50,000 payable in shares. The following assets were purchased: Stock Rs. 20,000, Machinery Rs. 25,000.

(*c*) Machinery was purchased for Rs. 8,000.

(*d*) Depreciation written off: Building Rs. 10,000, Machinery Rs. 14,000.

(*e*) Income tax paid during the year: Rs. 28,000. Provision of Rs. 33,000 was charged to profit and loss A/c.

Prepare a Statement of Sources and Applications of funds for the year ended 31st December, 2002.

Solution:

Statement of Sources and Applications of Funds

Sources	*Rs.*	*Applications*	*Rs.*
Issue of shares	20,000	Dividend paid	23,000
Funds from operation	90,100	Purchase of Machinery	8,000
		Income tax paid	28,000
	1,10,100	Bank loan paid	70,000
Decrease in working capital (as per statement)	18.900		
	1,29,000		1,29,000

Statement of Changes in Working Capital

	2001 Rs.	*2002 Rs.*	*Increase Rs.*	*Decrease Rs.*
Current Assets:				
Stock	1,00,000	74,000	26,000	
Sundry debtors	80,000	64,200	15,800	
Cash	500	600	100	
Bank	—	8,000	8,000	
Total (A)	1,80,500	1,46,800		
Current Liabilities:				
Sundry Creditors	1,50,000	1,35,200	14,800	
Total (B)	1,50,000	1,35,200		
Working Capital (A – B)	—	18,900	18,900	
	30,500	30,500	41,800	41,800

Adjusted Proft & Loss A/c

	Rs.		*Rs.*
To Depreciation Land & Building	10,000	By Balance b/d	30,500
To Depreciation Machinery	14,000	By Funds from operation (balancing figures)	90,100
To General Reserve	10,000		
To Dividend	23,000		
To Provision for tax	33,000		
To Balance c/d	30,600		
	1,20,600		1,20,600

Share Capital A/c

	Rs.		*Rs.*
To Balance c/d	2,50,000	By Balance b/d	2,00,000
		By Machinery purchase	25,000
		By Stock	20,000
		By Goodwill (balancing figure)	5,000
	2,50,000		2,50,000

Machinery A/c

To Balance b/d	1,50,000	By Depreciation	14,000
To Share Capital (purchase)	25,000	By Balance c/d	1,69,000
To Cash (purchase)	8,000		
	1,83,000		1,83,000

Provision for Income Tax

To Cash (tax paid)	28,000	By Balance b/d	30,000
To Balance c/d	35,000	By P & L A/c	33,000
	63,000		63,000

Example 5

The summarised Balance Sheets of P Ltd. as on 31 December, 2001 and 2002 are as follows:

	December 31, 2001 *Rs.*	*December 31, 2002* *Rs.*
Fixed Assets: At cost	16,00,000	19,00,000
Less: Depreciation	4,60,000	5,80,000
	11,40,000	13,20,000
Trade Investments	2,00,000	1,60,000
Current Assets	5,60,000	6,60,000
Preliminary Expenses	40,000	20,000
	19,40,000	21,60,000
Share Capital	6,00,000	8,00,000
Capital Reserves	—	20,000
General Reserve	3,40,000	4,00,000
Profit and Loss Account	1,20,000	1,50,000
Debentures	4,00,000	2,80,000
Liabilities for goods and services	2,40,000	2,60,000
Provision for income tax	1,80,000	72,000
Proposed dividend	60,000	72,000
Unpaid dividend	—	800
	19,40,000	21,60,000

During 2002, the company

(*i*) Sold one machine for Rs. 50,000; the cost of machine was Rs. 1,28,000 and the depreciation provided for it amounted to Rs. 70,000.

(*ii*) Provided Rs. 1,90,000 as depreciations,

(*iii*) Redeemed 30% of debenture @ 103;

(*iv*) Sold some trade investments at profit credited to capital reserve; and

(*v*) Decided to value the stock at cost, whereas previously the practice was to value stock at cost less 10%. The stock according to books on 31.12.2001 was Rs. 1,08,000; the stock on 31.12.2002 Rs. 1,50,000 was correctly valued at cost.

You are required to prepare the Funds Flow Statement during 2002 complying requirements of Accounting Standard 3. Working should form part of your answer.

Solution:

Statement of sources and uses of working capital for the year ended December 31, 2002

Sources:	
Funds from Operations	5,41,700
Share Capital	2,00,000
Sale of Trade Investments	60,000
Sale of Fixed Assets	50,000
Total Sources	8,15,600
Uses:	
Purchase of Fixed Assets	4,28,000
Redemption of Debentures	1,23,600
Dividend Paid	52,000
Income Tax Paid	1,80,000
Total Uses	7,83,600
Increase in Working Capital	68.000

Working Notes

(1) Fixed Assets Account

	Rs.		Rs.
Balance B/d	16,00,000	Bank	50,000
Bank (balancing figure)	4,28,000	Loss on sale	8,000
		Deprecation	70,000
		Balance c/d	19,00,000
	20,28,000		20,28,000

(2) Provision for taxation is assumed to be a non-current item. It is also assumed that tax paid during the year is equal to the provision for tax made last year, i.e. Rs. 1,80,000.

(Adjusted) Profit and Loss Account

	Rs.		Rs.
Depreciation (1,20,000 + 70,000)	1,90,000	Balance b/d	1,20,000
Loss on sale	8,000	Increase in value of stock on 12.12.2001 $\left(1,00,000 \times \frac{100}{90} - 1,08,000\right)$	12,000
Preliminary Expenses	20,000		
Premium on Redemption of Debentures	3,600	Funds from operations (balancing figure)	5,41,600
Proposed Dividend	72,000		
Provision for tax	1,70,000		
General Reserve	60,000		
Balance c/d	1,50,000		
	6,73,600		6,73,600

Example 6

From the following balance sheets of A Ltd., make out the statement of sources and uses of funds:

Liabilities	*2001 Rs.*	*2002 Rs.*	*Assets*	*2001 Rs.*	*2002 Rs.*
Equity share capital	3,00,000	4,00,000	Goodwill	1,15,000	90,000
8% Redeemable			Land and & Bldg.	2,00,000	1,70,000
Preference shares	1,50,000	1,00,000	Plant	80,000	20,000
General Reserve	40,000	70,000	Debtors	1,60,000	2,00,000
Profit & Loss A/c	30,000	48,000	Stock	77,000	1,09,000
Proposed dividend	42,000	50,000	Bills receivable	20,000	30,000
Creditors	55,000	83,000	Cash in hand	15,000	10,000
Bill payable	20,000	16,000	Cash at bank	10,000	8,000
Provision for taxation	40,000	50,000			
	6,77,000	8,17,000		6,77,000	8,17,000

Additional information: (*i*) Depreciation of Rs. 10,000 and Rs. 20,000 have been charged on plant account and land and buildings account respectively in 2002, (*ii*) An interim dividend of Rs. 20,000 has been paid in 2002, (*iii*) Income tax Rs. 35,000 was paid during the year 2002.

Solution:

Statement of Sources and Applications of Funds for the year ended 31st December, 2002

Sources	*Rs.*	*Applications*	*Rs.*
Issue of Equity share capital	1,00,000	Redemption of preference share capital	50,000
Sale of land	10,000	Purchase of plant	1,30,000
Funds from operation	1,76,000	Dividend paid	20,000
		Income Tax	35,000
		Increase in working capital	51,000
	2,86,000		2,86,000

Schedule of Changes in Working Capital

	2001 Rs.	*2002 Rs.*	*Decrease Rs.*	*Rs.*
Current Assets:				
Cash in hand	15,000	10,000	—	5,000
Cash in Bank	10,000	8,000	—	2,000
Bills Receivable	20,000	30,000	10,000	—
Stock	77,000	1,09,000	32,000	—
Debtors	1,60,000	2,00,000	40000	—
Total (A)	2,82,000	3,57,000		
Current Liabilities:				
Creditors	55,000	83,000	—	28,000
Bill Payable	20,000	16,000	4,000	—
Total (B)	75,000	99,000		
Working Capital (A – B)	2,07,000	2,58,000		
Increase in Working capital	51,000	—	—	51,000
	2,58,000	2,58,000	86,000	86,000

Adjusted Profit and Loss Account

	Rs.		Rs.
To Goodwill	25,000	By Balance b/d	30,000
To Depreciation		By Funds from operation	1,76,000
Land & Building	20,000		
Plant	10,000		
To General Reserve	30,000		
To Proposed Dividend	28,000		
To Provision for Taxation	45,000		
To Balance c/d	48,000		
	2,06,000		2,06,000

Goodwill

	Rs.		Rs.
To Balance b/d	1,15,000	By Adjusted P & L A/c	25,000
		By Balance c/d	90,000
	1,15,000		1,15,000

Land and Buildings

	Rs.		Rs.
To Balance b/d	2,00,000	By Adjusted P & L A/c (Depreciation)	20,000
		By Bank	10,000
		By Balance c/d	1,70,000
	2,00,000		2,00,000

Plant A/c

	Rs.		Rs.
To Balance b/d	80,000	By Adjusted & P & LA/c	10,000
To Bank (balancing figure)	1,30,000	By Balance c/d	2,00,000
	70,000		70,000

General Reserve

	Rs.		Rs.
To Balance c/d	70,000	By Balance c/d	40,000
		By Adjusted P & L A/c	30,000
	70,000		70,000

Proposed Dividend

	Rs.		Rs.
To Dividend paid	20,000	By Balance b/d	42,000
To Balance c/d	50,000	By Adjusted P & L A/c	28,000
	70,000		70,000

Provision for Taxation

	Rs.		Rs.
To Income Tax	35,000	By Balance b/d	40,000
To Balance c/d	50,000	By Adjusted P & L A/c	45,000
	85,000		85,000

SIGNIFICANCE OF STATEMENT OF CHANGES IN FINANCIAL POSITION — WORKING CAPITAL BASIS

A better understanding and analysis of the affairs of a business enterprise requires the knowledge about the movements in assets, liabilities and capital which have taken place during the year and their consequent effect on its financial position. This information is not specifically disclosed by a profit and loss account and balance sheet but can be made available in working capital-based funds flow statement.

The funds flow statement is in no way a replacement for the profit and loss account and balance sheet although the information which it contains is a selection, reclassification and summarisation of information contained in these two statements. The balance sheet gives a 'snapshot' view at a point in time of the sources from which a firm has acquired its funds and the uses which the firm has made of these funds. The equities side of the balance sheet delineates these sources, and the asset side shows the uses. The income statement is a flow statement; it explains changes that occurred in the retained earnings account by summarising the increases (revenues) and decreases (expenses) in retained earnings during the accounting period. A funds flow statement explains the changes that took place in a balance sheet account or group of accounts during the period between dates of two balance sheets' 'snapshots.' It shows the manner in which the operations of an enterprise have been financed and in which its financial resources have been used. It also distinguishes the use of funds for the long-term from the short-term. For example, it distinguishes the use of funds for the purchase of new fixed assets from funds used in increasing the working capital of the company. Thus, it provides a meaningful link between the balance sheets at the beginning and at the end of a period and profit and loss account for that period. It should be understood, however, that a funds statement does not purport to indicate the requirements of a business for capital.

The concept of working capital is in conformity with normal accrual accounting procedures. Hence, a funds flow statement based on the concept of networking capital fits well with other statements. Above all, working capital is also a measure of the short-term liquidity of the firm. Therefore, an analysis of factors bringing about a change in the amount of networking capital is useful for decision-making by shareholders, creditors, lenders and management. Due to these reasons, the working capital approach to studying the changes in the financial position is superior to the cash approach.

LIMITATIONS OF STATEMENT OF CHANGES IN FINANCIAL POSITION — WORKING CAPITAL BASIS

The working capital concept of funds enlarges the problem of valuation because it includes inventory and prepaid items. Thus, the measurement of working capital flows is less precise than for cash. However, this concept further reduces the areas for window dressing, for example, the postponement of the purchase of merchandise on open account will not influence working capital flows. A fund statement based on the working capital concept is usually a brief presentation, and many significant inter-firm transactions are not dislcosed. For example, significant addition to inventories financed by short-term notes would not be shown because the two items are offset in the computation of the net change in working capital. Furthermore, transactions not affecting working capital, such as the acquisition of plant and equipment by the issuance of equity capital, would not be included in the statement. Therefore, the funds statement in this presentation would not disclose structural changes in the financial relationships in the firm or major changes in policy regarding investments in current assets and short-term financing.

CASH FLOW STATEMENT
(Or Statement of Changes in Financial Position — Cash Basis)

A cash flow statement discloses the net increase (or decrease) in cash during an accounting period. It provides information about the flow of cash into and out of a company. A balance sheet reports the financial position of a business enterprise at a point in time. But the cash flow statement explains the change in cash position from one balance sheet date to the next balance sheet date. The profit and loss account reveals the results of a business enterprise for an accounting period in the form of profit which contributes substantially to the change in cash as reported in the cash flow statement.

Classifiation of Cash Inflows and Outflows

A cash flow statement focuses on various activities and items which bring about changes in the cash balance between two balance sheet dates. This statement covers all items which increase or decrease the cash of a business enterprise. For example, this statement includes items like receipts from debtors and payments to creditors. On the contrary, this statement will not cover items which have no immediate effect on cash increase or decrease. For instance, goods purchased on credit and goods sold on credit will not be included in this statement as these transactions have no effect on inflow and cutflow of cash.

A cash flow statement aims to determine the effects on cash of different types of cash inflows and outflows. In this process, all cash flows, i.e., activities resulting into cash flows are classified into different categories. The AS3 'Cash Flow Statement' issued by ICAI has classified cash flows into three categories:

(1) Operating Activities

(2) Investing Activities and

(3) Financial Activities

(1) Operating Activities: Operating activities are those transactions which are considered in the determination of net income. Examples of cash inflows in this category are cash received from debtors for goods and services, interest and dividend received on loans and investment. Examples of cash outflows in this category are cash payments for goods and services, merchandise, wages, interest, taxes, supplies and others.

(2) Investing Activities: Investing activities include acquisition and disposal of long-term or fixed assets, acquisition and disposal of intangible assets, purchase and sale of shares, debentures and other securities, lending of money and its subsequent collection. Cash inflows from investing activities generally include cash sales of property, plant, equipment and intangible assets, cash sales of investments in shares, debentures and other securities and cash collection (loan repayments) from borrowers. Cash outflows are purchase of shares, debentures and securities of other enterprises, purchase of property, plant, equipment and other long-term assets including loan given to other firms.

(3) Financing Activities: Financing activities relate to long-term liability and equity capital. A firm engages in financing activities when it obtains resources from owners, returns resources to owners, borrows resources from creditors and repays amounts borrowed. Cash inflows include proceeds from issue of shares and short-term and long-term borrowings. Cash outflows include repayment of loans and payments to owners including cash dividends. Repayments of accounts payable or accrued liabilities are not considered repayment of loans under financing activities but are classified as cash outflows under operating activities.

FORMAT OF CASH FLOW STATEMENT

While preparing the cash flow statement, cash flows from operating activities are presented first, followed by investing activities and then financing activities. The individual inflows and outflows relating to investing and financing activities are presented separately in their respective cátegories. The operating activities section can be presented using the direct method or indirect method. In the direct method, cash flow statement is presented primarily on a cash receipt and cash payment basis, instead of on accrual basis. In the indirect method, net income is adjusted for items that affected net income but did not affect cash.

Figures 2.1 and 2.2 show respectively the direct and indirect method of preparing cash flow statement.

A cash flow statement differs from the summary of cash receipts and disbursements. A cash flow statement is prepared by a rearrangement of items on the income statement and balance sheet, rather than from entries made to the cash account. Cash flow statement may also highlight the amount of cash generated by the firm's operations. This is not reported in the statement of cash receipts and disbursements.

Furthermore, cash flow statement apparently differs from income statement. An income statement includes adjustments in respect of expenses accrued in the calculation of periodic income, whereas cash flow statement excludes such adjustments. The largest item of difference between them is the allocation of fixed assets costs as depreciation. Also the procedures adopted in the two statements are reflected in changes in balance sheet items. These would include changes in balances of trade debtors and trade creditors.

Cash Flow Statement (Direct Method)
A B C Company
For the Year Ended December 31, 2002

	Rs.	*Rs.*
(A) Cash Flow from Operating Activities:		
Cash Receipts from:		
Sales		
Interest Received		
Cash Payments for:		
Purchases		
Operating Expenses		
Interest Payments		
Income Taxes		
Net Cash Flow from Operating Activities		
(B) Cash Flows from Investing Activities		
Sale of Plant Assets		
Sale of Investments		
Purcahse of Plant Assets		
Purchase of Investments		
Net Cash Flows Used by Investing Activities		
(C) Cash Flows from Financing Activities		
Repayment of Bonds and Debentures		
Issue of Common shares		
Dividends Paid		
Net cash Flows from Financing Activities		
Net Increase (Decrease) in Cash		

Fig. 2.1: Cash Flow Statement (Direct Method)

Cash Flow Statement (Indirect Method)

ABC Company
For the Year Ended December 31, 2002

	Rs.	Rs.
(A) Cash Flows from Operating Activities		
Net Income		
Adjustments to Reconcile Net income to Net Cash provided by Operating Activities		
Depreciation		
Gain on Sale of Investments		
Loss on Sale of Plant Assets		
Decrease in Accounts Receivable		
Increase in Inventory		
Decrease in Prepaid Expenses		
Increase in Accounts Payable		
Increase in Accrued Liabilities		
Decrease in Income Taxes Payable		
Net Cash Flows from Operating Activities		
(B) Cash Flows from Investing Activities		
Sale of Plant Assets		
Sale of Investments		
Purchase of Plant Assets		
Purchase of Investments		
Net Cash Flows Used by Investing Activities		
(C) Cash Flows from Financing Activities		
Repayment of Bonds and Debentures		
Issue of common shares		
Dividends Paid		
Net Cash flows from Financing Activities		
Net Increase (Decrease) in cash		

Fig. 2.2: Cash Flow Statement (Indirect Method)

PREPARING CASH FLOW STATEMENT

Before preparing cash flow statement, first of all, the following three steps have to be completed:

(*i*) Determining cash flows from operations or operating activities.
(*ii*) Determining cash flows from investing activities and
(*iii*) Determining cash flows from financing activities.

After obtaining information regarding the above, a cash flow statement can be prepared. The three steps have been discussed below:

Cash Flow from Operations

The profit and loss account focuses on net income determination from operating activities. However, it does not show cash inflow and outflow relating to operating activities because the profit and loss account is prepared on an accrual basis. In preparing profit and loss account, revenues are recorded even though cash for them has not been received. Similarly, expenses are recorded even though they may not have been paid. Therefore, to find cash flows from operations, one needs to convert accrual basis income statement figures to cash basis by making adjustments. By way of adjustments, earned revenues will be converted into cash received from sales or customers and incurred expenses will be converted into cash expended, i.e. expenses actually paid in cash.

The conversion of accrual basis income statement to cash basis income statement along with required adjustments has been shown in Fig. 2.3.

The conversion process displayed in Fig. 2.3 can be described as follows, using a short-cut calculation:

Accrual-Basis Net Income

↓

Deduct Increase in Accounts Receivable (or Add Decrease in Accounts Receivable)
Deduct Increase in Merchandise Inventory (or Add Decrease in Merchandise Inventory)
Deduct Increase in Prepaid Expenses (or Add Decrease in Prepaid Expenses)

Add Increase in Accounts Payable (Or Deduct Decrease in Accounts Payable)
Add Increase in Accrued Expenses (or Deduct Decrease in Accrued Expenses) and
Add Depreciation and Amortization Expenses for the year.

↓

Cash-Basis Net Income

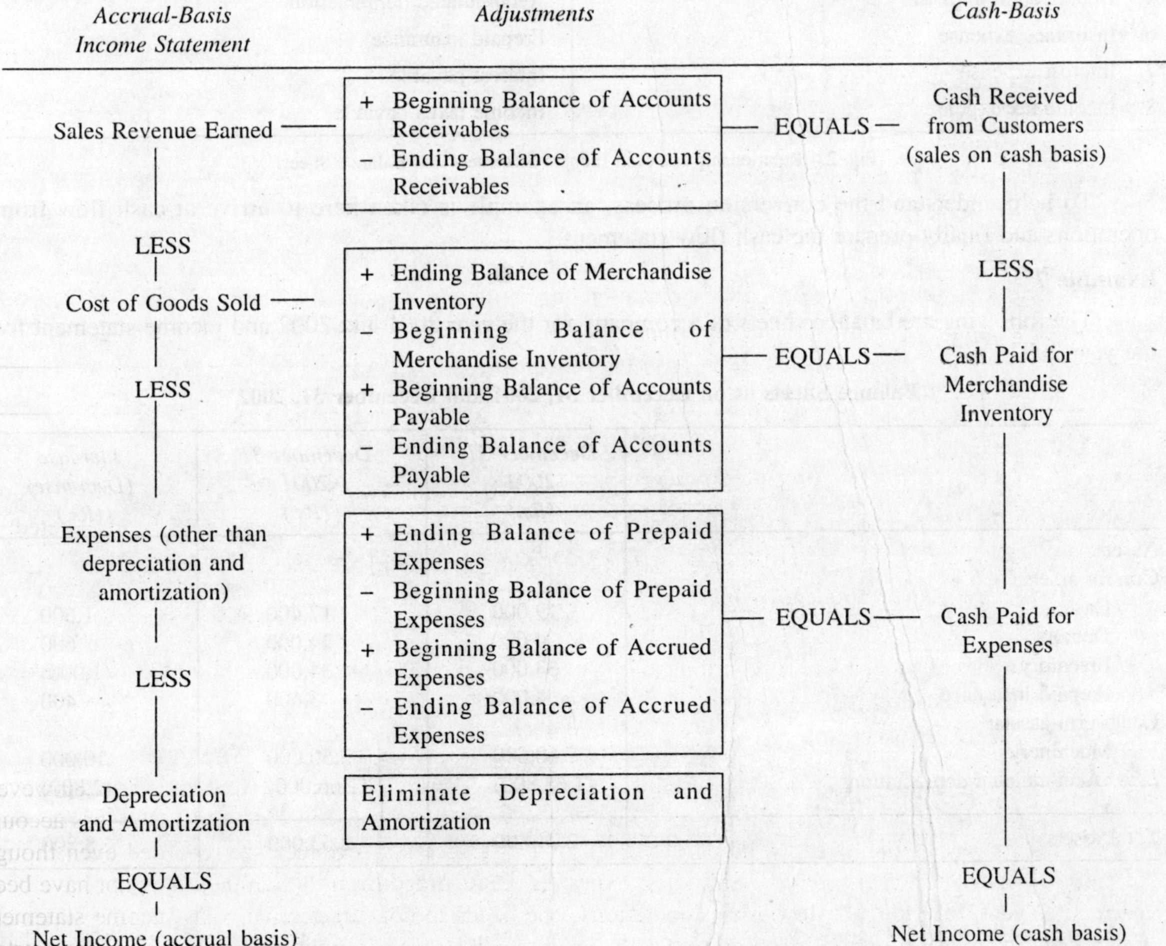

Fig 2.3: Relationship of Accrual Basis and Cash Basis of Accounting

While making conversion, one should know the relationship between income statement accounts and balance sheet changes. Each individual item on the income statement should be viewed as it relates to a balance sheet account. On the accrual basis of accounting, the explanation for the difference between the amount of sales revenue and the receipts from those sales is found in the changes in accounts receivable and debtor's account. Similarly, the difference between the amount of an expense and the amount of payments for that expense is found in the changes of its associated asset or liability, such as prepaid rent or rent payable. If there is no associated balance sheet account for an item on the income statement, it is presumed that the amount shown on the income statement resulted in a cash flow exactly equal to that revenue or expense. Fig. 2.4 shows the relationship between some income statement accounts and balance sheet accounts.

Financial Statement Relationship

Income Statement Accounts	*Related to Balance Sheet Accounts*
1. Sales	Debtors
2. Cost of goods sold	(Inventory) (Creditors)
3. Salaries Expenses	Salaries payable
4. Rent expense	Rent payable
5. Depreciation expense	Accumulated depreciation
6. Insurance expense	Prepaid insurance
7. Interest expense	Interest payable
8. Income tax expense	Income taxes payable

Fig. 2.4 Relationship between Income Statement and Balance Sheet.

To help understand the conversion process, an example is taken here to arrive at cash flow from operations and finally prepare the cash flow statement.

Example 7

The following are balance sheets of a company for the year 2001 and 2002 and income statement for the year 2002:

Balänce Sheets as on December 31, 2001 and December 31, 2002

	December 31 2002 (Rs.)	*December 31 2001 (Rs.)*	*Increase (Decrease) (Rs.)*
Assets:			
Current assets:			
Cash	19,000	17,400	1,600
Debtors	24,600	24,000	600
Inventory	33,000	34,000	(1,000)
Prepaid insurance	4,000	3,600	400
Long-term assets:			
Machinery	3,60,000	3,50,000	10,000
Less: Accumulated depreciation	(1,68,800)	(1,66,000)	(2,800)
Total assets	2,71,800	2,63,000	8,800

Liabilities and Equity			
Current liabilities:			
Creditors	33,600	32,400	1,200
Salaries payable	600	1,000	(400)
Income taxes payable	4,400	3,400	1,000
Long-term loan	46,000	40,000	6,000
Equity capital	1,00,000	1,00,000	—
Retained earnings	87,200	86,200	1,000
Total liabilities	2,71,800	2,63,000	8,800

Income Statement for the year ending 2002

	Rs.
Sales	63,800
Expenses:	
Cost of goods sold	45,600
Salaries	8,400
Rent	1,200
Depreciation	2,800
Insurance	600
Interest	400
Income tax	1,000
Total expense	60,000
Net Income	3,800
Statement of Retained Earnings	*(Rs.)*
Retained earnings for the year 2001	86,200
Add: Net income for the year 2002	3,800
	90,000
Less: dividends	2,800
	87,200

Solution

In the example, the change in cash balance is visible in the balance sheets which has increased by Rs. 1600. The cash flow statement aims to determine the factors responsible for increase (or decrease) in cash during the period.

1. Cash Receipts from Customers: Sales on account (on credit) are important factors in most business firms. The relationship between the amount of cash collected from customers and the net sales reported in the income statement depends on the change in the accounts receivable during the period. If accounts receivable have increased during the period, it means credit sales are being made faster than the cash being collected from the customers. If accounts receivable have decreased, cash is being collected faster than credit sales are being made. The relationship between net sales and cash collections from customers may be stated as follows:

$$\text{Net Sales} \begin{bmatrix} + \text{Decrease in accounts receivable or} \\ - \text{increase in accounts receivable} \end{bmatrix} = \text{Cash receipts from customers}$$

The above procedure helps in converting sales to cash basis. In the above example, cash receipts from customers during the year 2002 can be determined as follows:

Net sales	Rs. 63,800
Less: Increase in accounts receivable during the year	600
Cash receipts from customers	63,200

or

Beginning Balance + Sales on account-Ending balance = Collections

That is Rs. 24,000 + 63,000 – 24600 = Rs. 63,200

2. Cash Payments for Purchases: The relationship between the cost of goods sold for a period and the cash payments for the purchase of merchandise depends both on the change in inventory and the change in accounts payable to merchandise suppliers during the period. The relationship may be stated in two stages, as follows:

(*a*) Cost of goods sold	+ increase in inventory or decrease in inventory	= Net purchase
(*b*) Net purchases	+ decrease in accounts payable or increase in accounts payable	= Cash payments for purchases

The above procedure converts cost of goods sold to cash basis. Again referring to the above example, the cash payments for purchases during the year 2002 would be computed as follows:

Cost of goods sold	Rs.	45,600
Less: decrease in inventory	Rs.	1,000
Net purchases (accrual basis)	Rs.	44,600
Less: Increase in accounts payable	Rs.	1,200
Cash payments for purchases	Rs.	43,400

In computing cash payments for purchases, the basic problem is that the amount of the payments cannot be determined until the amount of the net purchases is known. When the net purchases information is not available, it must be determined before attempting to compute the payments. As it is known, the cost of goods sold expense has the following equation:

Beginning inventory + Purchases – Closing inventory = Cost of goods sold.

The above equation can be rearranged to reveal the amount of purchases as the unknown.

Cost of goods sold – Beginning inventory + Closing inventory = Purchases

Since the beginning inventory has a minus sign and the closing inventory a plus sign, it may be concluded that increase in inventory results from purchasing more than was sold and a decrease in the inventory results from purchasing less than was sold. Thus, to find purchases, increases in inventory are added to cost of goods sold and decreases in inventory are deducted from the cost of goods sold.

Once the amount of net purchase is known, it may be combined with the information about the accounts payable balance to find the payments. Ignoring the possibility of paying for purchases in advance, the most a business firm would pay would be the full amount of its beginning accounts payable balance plus the entire amount of net purchases for the current period. If the company has a closing balance in the accounts payable, the following equation will state the payments:

Purchase + Beginning accounts payable – Closing accounts payable = Payments

3. Cash Payments for Expenses: Relationships between the balance sheet accounts and the income statement accounts for the remaining expenses are fairly simple and easy to understand. Salaries expenses and salaries payable are associated accounts. Sometimes, an expense account has no related balance sheet account. In such cases, the amount of expense and the amount of payments (decrease in cash) must be equal. Under the accrual system of accounting, any difference between the payment for an item and the expense for that item must be reflected in a related asset or liability. If there is no associated asset or liability on the balance sheet, it can only be because the amounts of the payments and expense are the same.

Unlike most other expenses that are related to current accounts, depreciation expense is related to the non-current balance sheet account. The depreciation entry does not affect the cash balance in any way and this is why it is frequently referred to as a non-cash item.

The relationship between operating expenses and cash payments depends on changes in asset accounts representing the prepayment of expenses, and on change in accrued liability accounts. These relationships may be summarised as follows:

Expenses	[+ increase in related prepayment or – decrease in related prepayment]	and	[+ decrease in related accrued liabilities – increase in related accrued liability]	=	Cash payments for expenses

Using the data in the above example, cash payments for different operating expenses can be computed as follows:

(*i*) Payments for salary
Beginning + Current period's – Ending balance = Payments
Rs. 1,000 + 8,400-600 = Rs. 8,800

(*ii*) Payments for income tax
Beginning balance + Current Period's expense – Ending balance = Payments
3,400 + 1,000 – 4,400 = Zero

(*iii*) Payments for insurance
Write-off to + Closing balance – Beginning balance = Payments expenses
Rs. 600 + 4,000 – 3,600 = 1,000

Determining Cash Flows Relating to Investing and Financing Activities

The second step in the preparation of cash flow statement is to determine cash flows from investing activities. For this, individual accounts are examined that involve cash receipts and cash payments from investing activities. The objective is to explain the change in the account balance from one year to the next.

For the purposes of determining cash flows from financing activities, a similar procedure is followed as that of investing activities. With regard to financing activities, long-term liability accounts and equity accounts are analysed. It is to be noted that in the example given earlier, some balance sheet accounts having connection with income statement have already been analysed to know their effects on cash flow. The only change among the assets side from cash which has not been accounted for is the Rs. 10,000 increase in machinery. Increase in fixed assets are a result of purchasing additional items, and these are assumed to be cash purchases. This is usually a safe assumption because if the money for the purchase is obtained from creditors, that information will be found in the liability accounts and will be accounted for when those changes are analysed. Purchase of long-term assets for cash is a use (decrease) of cash.

Among the liabilities, only the increases in the long-term loan remains to be accounted for. Additional borrowings undoubtedly increase cash and therefore are listed as sources of cash.

The change in retained earnings is easier to analyse if the statement of retained earnings is used because it contains helpful detailed information. In the above example, increase in retained earnings by Rs. 1,000 is a result of an increase from net income of Rs. 3,800 and a decrease for dividends of Rs. 2800. The effect of the net income on cash account were determined when the income statement accounts were analysed in relation to changes in balance sheet accounts. Thus, the dividend account is only left. Since there is no dividend payable liability on the balance sheet, the dividends must have already been paid. If there are either beginning or ending balances, or both are in the liability account, the payments for dividend may be determined as follows:

Dividends declared + Beginning balance – Closing balance = Payments declared

An increase in the dividends payable balance would mean that the dividends declared were larger than dividends payments. The increase in the liability should be deducted from the amount of the dividend declaration to determine the cash payments. The reverse is true if there is a decrease in the liability. The amount of the decrease should be added to the amount of dividend declared to determine how much cash was paid.

Finally, the cash flow statement will appear as follows:

Cash Flow Statement for the year ending 2002

	(Rs.)	*(Rs.)*	*(Rs.)*
Sources of Cash			
From operations:			
Collections from customers		63,200	
Less: Payments for:			
Inventory purchases	(43,400)		
Salaries	(8,800)		
Rent	(1,200)		
Insurance	(1,000)		
Interest	(400)	(54,800)	
Total provided by operations			8,400
Other sources:			
Long-term loan			6,000
Total source			14,400
Uses of cash other than for operations:			
Purchase of machinery equipment			10,000
Payment of dividends			2,800
Total uses			12,800
Increase in cash			1,600

Example 8

Rajan, a retailer, has prepared the following balance sheets for the years ending 2001 and 2002:

Balance Sheets as on December 31, 2001 and 2002

Assets		*2002 (Rs.)*		*2001 (Rs.)*
Freehold property at cost		2,00,000		2,00,000
Furnitures	32,000		30,000	
Less depreciation	23,200	8,000	20,000	10,000
Current assets:				
Stocks		36,000		34,000
Debtors and prepayments		50,000		34,000
Cash in hand and at bank		4,000		2,000

Liabilities:		
Capital	2,54,800	2,60,000
Trade and accrued expenses	24,000	20,000
Loan Account (Sanjay)	20,000	
	2,98,800	2,80,000

Other data: The net profit for the year 2002 was Rs. 40,000. Rajan is paid a salary of Rs. 16,000. His drawing amounted to Rs. 45,200.

You are required to:

(*i*) Prepare a statement of changes in financial position on working capital basis.

(*ii*) Explain why the cash in hand and at bank has only increased by Rs. 2,000 over the year, although the net profit for the same period was Rs. 40,000.

Solution:

1. **Statement of Changes in Financial Position (Working Capital Basis) for the year ending December 31,2002**

Sources of Funds		*(Rs.)*
Profit		40,000
Add: Depreciation		3,200
Total generated from operations		43,200
Funds from other sources:		
Loan from Sanjay		30,000
		63,200
Uses of Funds		
Purchase of Furniture	2,000	
Rajan's drawings	45,200	
		47,200
Increase in working capital		16,000

Statement of Changes (Increase or Decrease) in working Capital

	Rs.
Increase in stocks	2,000
Increase in debtors	16,000
Increase in cash and bank balance	2,000
(Increase) in creditors	(4,000)
Net increase in working capital	16,000

2. In the accrual accounting system, it is not necessary that net income will be equal to liquid funds. Net profits is determined after taking into account accruals and prepayments at the beginning and end of the accounting year. Besides some items appearing in profit and loss account, e.g. profit on the sale of fixed assets, or depreciation do not affect the movement of cash. In addition, items regarded as capital, e.g. purchase of fixed assets do not appear in the profit and loss account.

In this case, the main reason why the cash at the bank and in hand increased by only Rs. 2,000, whereas the net profit has increased by Rs. 40,000 is because Rajan has drawn substantial amounts of cash out of the business during the year. Infact, Rajan would have taken an overdraft from the bank if Sanjay had not given him a loan of Rs. 20,000. Another reason is that Rajan has invested more of the business funds in working capital, largely because of an increase in the amount due from debtors.

The above vital facts have been clearly highlighted by the statement of changes in financial position which provides additional useful information more than that disclosed in the profit and loss account and balance sheet.

Example 9

The comparative balance sheets for the years 2001 and 2002 and the income statement of 2002 for ABC Company are shown below:

Balance Sheets
December 31, 2001 and December 31, 2002

Assets	*2002* *Rs.*	*2001* *Rs.*
Cash	1,15,850	1,21,850
Accounts Receivable (net)	2,96,000	3,14,500
Inventory	3,22,000	3,01,000
Prepaid Expenses	7,800	5,800
Long-term Investments	36,000	86,000
Land	1,50,000	1,25,000
Building	4,62,000	4,62,000
Accumulated Depreciation, Building	(91,000)	(79,000)
Equipment	1,59,730	1,67,230
Accumulated Depreciation, Equipment	(43,400)	(45,600)
Intangible Assets	19,200	24,000
Total Assets	14,34,180	14,82,780
Liabilities and Shareholders Equity		
Accounts Payable	133,750	2,33,750
Notes Payable (current)	75,700	1,45,700
Accrued Liabilities	5,000	—
Income Taxes Payable	20,000	—
Bonds Payable	2,10,000	3,10,000
Mortgage Payable	3,30,000	3,50,000
Ordinary Shares	3,60,000	3,00,000
Preferences Shares	90,000	50,000
Retained Earnings	2,09,730	93,330
Total Liabilities and shareholders	Rs. 14,34,180	14,82,780

Income Statement for the year ended December 31, 2002

	Rs.	*Rs.*
Sales		16,50,000
Cost of Goods Sold		9,20,000
Gross Margin		7,30,000
Operating Expenses (including Depreciation Expense of Rs. 12,000 on Buildings and Rs. 23,100 on Equipment and Amortization Expense of Rs. 4,800)		4,70,000
Operating Income		2,60,000

Other income (Expense)		
Interest Expense	(55,000)	
Dividend Income	3,400	
Gain on Sale of Investment	12,500	
Loss on Disposal of Equipment	(2,300)	(41,400)
Income Before Taxes		2,18,600
Income taxes		52,200
Net Income		1,66,400

The following additional information was taken from the company's records:

(*a*) Long-term investments that cost Rs. 70,000 were sold at a gain of Rs. 12,500; additional long-term investments were made in the amount of Rs. 20,000.

(*b*) Land was purchased for Rs. 25,000 for a parking lot.

(*c*) Equipment that cost Rs. 37,500 with accumulated depreciation of Rs. 25,300 was sold at a loss of Rs. 2,300; new equipment in the amount of Rs. 30,000 was purchased.

(*d*) Notes payable in the amount of Rs. 1,00,000 were repaid; an additional Rs. 30,000 was borrowed by signing notes payable.

(*e*) Bonds Payable in the amount of Rs. 1,00,000 were converted into 6,000 shares of common shares.

(*f*) Mortgage Payable was reduced by Rs. 20,000 during the year.

(*g*) Cash dividends declared and paid were Rs. 50,000.

Required:

(*i*) Prepare a schedule of cash flows from operating activities using the (*a*) direct method and (*b*) indirect method.

(*ii*) Prepare a statement of cash flows using the direct method.

Solution:

1. (a) Schedule of cash flows from operating activities — direct method

ABC Company

Schedule of Cash Flows from Operating Activities for the Year Ended December 31, 2002

	Rs.	*Rs.*
Cash Flows from Operating Activities		
Cash Receipts from:		
Sales	16,68,500	
Dividends Received	3,400	16,71,900
Cash Payments for:		
Purchases	10,41,000	
Operating Expenses	427,100	
Interest Payments	55,000	
Income Taxes	32,200	15,55,300
Net Cash Flows from Operating Activities		116,600

Notes:

Rs. 16,50,000 + Rs. 18,500 = Rs. 16,68,500
Rs. 920,000 + Rs. 21,000 + Rs. 100,000 = Rs. 10,41,000
Rs. 470,000 + Rs. 2,000 – Rs. 5,000 – (Rs. 12,000 + Rs. 23,100 + Rs. 4,800) = Rs. 427,100
Rs. 52,200 – Rs. 20,000 = Rs. 32,200

1. (b) Schedule of cash flows from operating activities — indirect method prepared.

A B C Company

Schedule of Cash Flows from Operating Activities for the year ended December 31, 2002

		Rs.
Net Income		1,66,400
Add: (or Deduct) Items Not Affecting Cash Flows from Operating Activities:		
Depreciation Expense, Equipment	23100	
Depreciation Expense, Buildings	12,000	
Amortization Expense, intangible Assets	4,800	
Gain on Sales of Investments	(12,500)	
Loss on Disposal of Equipment	2,300	
Decrease in Accounts Receivable	18,500	
Increase in Inventory	(21,000)	
Increase in Prepaid Expenses	(2,000)	
Decrease in Accounts Payable	(1,00,000)	
Increase in Accrued Liabilities	5,000	
Increase in Income Taxes payable	20,000	49,800
Net Cash Flows from Operating Activities		1,16,600

2. Statement of cash flows — direct method

A B C

Statement of Cash Flows

For the year Ended December 31, 2002

	Rs.	Rs.
Cash Flows from Operating Activities		
Cash Receipts from		
Sales	16,68,500	
Dividends Received	3,400	
		16,71,900
Cash Payments for		
Purchases	10,41,000	
Operating Expenses	427,100	
Interest Payments	55,000	
Income Taxes	32,200	
		15,55,300
Net Cash Flows from Operating Activities		116,600
Sale of Long-term Investments	82,500	
Purchase of Long-term Investments	(20,000)	
Purchase of Land	(25,000)	
Sales of Equipment	9,900	
Purchase of Equipment	(30,000)	
Net Cash Flows from investing Activities		17,400
Cash Flows from Financing Activities		
Repayment of Notes Payable	(100,000)	
Issuance of Notes Payable	30,000	
Reduction in Mortgage	(20,000)	
Dividends Paid	(50,000)	
Net Cash Flows Used by Financing Activities		(140,000)
Net Increase (Decrease) in Cash		(6,000)

SIGNIFICANCE OF CASH FLOW STATEMENT

Cash basis funds flow statement is important for a number of reasons:

(1) First, by focussing on cash flows, it explains the nature of the financial events which have affected the cash position. This statement explains the reason for the difference between opening and closing cash balance.

(2) The statement is important for financial planning purposes. For example, budgeted cash statements are a crucial element in the process of budget plans. These surpluses and shortfalls are expressed sequentially over the planning period and require the management to deal with the forecasted cash surplus or deficit, the former involving a short-term investment of surplus cash, the latter a short-term borrowing arrangement.

(3) This statement brings into sharp focus the enterprise's earning capacity with its spending and operating activity. Accounting contentions restrict the income statement to matching periodic revenues with the cost of earning those revenues. Statement of changes in cash is not restricted in this way; hence it provides an extended view of the financial inflows and outflows by including both capital and revenue flows. Thus, borrowings and capital additions, as well as proceeds from the realisation of assets are incorporated with the cash generated from sales to give a more complete picture of financial inflows; repayments of loans, capital expenditure, dividends and taxation are incorporated with revenue expenses to give a more complete picture of financial outflows.

(4) Cash flow statement provides an insight into the critical areas of financial management by identifying two important classes of cash flows, namely, operating cash flows and financing cash flows. This distinction draws attention to the net cash flows from operations and the net financing cash flows. The net operating cash flows classify the capability of the firm to support dividend payments to shareholders. It is these net cash flows which are of critical importance to investors and shareholders in predicting the amount of cash likely to be distributed in the future in the form of liquidation distribution or repayment of principal and in the evaluation of risk.

(5) The significance of cash flow statement lies in the increased complexity of business activity. This complexity results in a greater disparity between the time when income and expense items are reported and the time when the related cash flows occur. It may also result in a greater variability of cash flows. Inflation and major changes in the structure of the economy may also create a need for cash flow statements because these external changes and influences affect cash flows more quickly than reported income.

LIMITATIONS OF CASH FLOW STATEMENT

Cash flow can be more precisely measured than can other concepts of funds because the valuation problems of cash are not as great as for other financial resources. However, movement of cash may be easily influenced. For example, payment of liabilities may be temporarily delayed or marketable securities may be sold, increasing cash flow for a given period. This statement, since it does not cover non-cash items, is not useful in analysing changes in the financial position of an enterprise. Cash and changes in cash are not adequate to measure changes in financial position. For instance, an enterprise may possess a very satisfactory financial (cash) position during a particular month. But if the firm has to pay creditors next month or make payments for the plant purchased in the near future, the cash position of the firm will be adversely affected. In this way, the statement of changes in financial position measured through cash only has drawbacks and does not indicate accurately the changes in financial position. The statement has utility for making short-term financial planning but for long-term planning, this statement would not be useful. Because of the limited usefulness of statement of changes in cash, the preparation of statement of changes in working capital (popularly known as funds flow statement) has been suggested.

STATEMENT OF CHANGES IN TOTAL FINANCIAL RESOURCES

One of the limitations of the working capital concept of funds is that it omits a few major financial and investment transactions. Important information regarding changes in the resources of the firm and in the financial structure of the firm are omitted. Such items do not of course, affect net working capital, but if included, would certainly provide quantitative and analytical information for decision-making. For example, issuing equity shares or debentures for purchase of buildings or plant and machinery has no effect on working capital, but is a significant financial transaction that should be disclosed.

Under the total financial resources concept of funds, the statement is not limited to transactions affecting working capital but would also be extended to cover all significant financial transactions that would otherwise be omitted under the other concepts of funds. That is the total financial resources concept requires that all material financial transactions be disclosed in the statement of changes in financial position. Transactions that technically do not increase or decrease funds (regardless of the concept of funds employed) but that represent significant financing and investing activities entered into by an entity must also be disclosed within the statement. Disclosure of a significant transaction that does not increase or decrease funds is made by showing one side of the transaction as a source of funds and the other side of the transaction as a corresponding use of funds. Transactions that affect financial position but do not increase or decrease funds include the following:

(*i*) Purchase of non-current assets, e.g. property and equipment by issuing share capital or debenture or long term debt.

(*ii*) Reduction of a long-term liability by the issuance of share capital or the incurrence of another long-term liability or a reduction in a non-current asset.

The above statement would be more useful in summarising the resources from which the funds have been obtained and the uses to which they have been put. The statement can analyse sources and uses in two categories of items: (*i*) those which affect working capital and (*ii*) those which do not affect working capital. Such a statement is certainly more informative and therefore potentially more useful in disclosing the firm's financing and investing activities during the two balance sheet dates. The fact that items which do not affect working capital are separately dealt with implies that it retains all the advantages of the working capital concept and, in addition, has the additional advantage of providing a complete picture of the total financial and investment activities of the firm.

As stated earlier, this statement includes significant transactions involving flows of non-cash resources even if cash itself is not affected. To recognise changes in all resources, these transactions are reported as both sources and uses of cash.

The following illustrations explain it:

(*i*) Purchased a Rs. 5,00,000 building for Rs. 1,00,000 cash and Rs. 4,00,000 mortgage note.

Source of Cash:

Issuing Mortgage note	Rs. 4,00,000

Use of Cash:

Purchase of Building	Rs. 5,00,000

(*ii*) Issued a promissory note to acquire land at a cost of Rs. 50,000

Source of Cash:

Issuing promissory note	Rs. 50,000

Use of Cash:

Purchase of land	Rs. 50,000

(*iii*) Issued 10,000 shares in exchange for 1,000 convertible debentures with Rs. 10,000 book value and Rs. 1,00,000 face value.

Source of Cash:

Issue of Shares	Rs. 1,00,000

Use of Cash

Retirement of debentures	Rs. 1,00,000

It can be noticed that each side of the transaction has a significant impact on the company's financial position. By applying the total resources concept, the statement of changes in financial position reflect more fully these significant events.

Limitations of Statement of Changes in Financial Position, on Total Resources Basis

The statement of changes in financial position, on total resources basis, has the following limitations:

Firstly, the concept of financial resources is vague and ill-defined. The separate items included in the classification of sources and applications of funds do not necessarily represent increases and decreases of resources. Therefore, there is no direct disclosure of the extent to which the total resources of the firm have changed during the period.

Secondly, acquisitions of property in exchange for shares cannot be measured with the same degree of reliability as assets acquired for cash. Therefore, the summation of gross additions to plant and equipment for example, may result in misleading interpretations of the amount of resources required.

Preparing Funds Flow Statement — Total Resources Basis

In order to prepare funds flow statement, on total resources basis, successive balance sheets are compared and changes in each balance sheet item are recorded and further designated as a source of funds or a use of funds. The comparison of successive balance sheets will generally lead to following sources and uses of funds:

Sources of Funds

(*i*) Increase in owner's equity

(*ii*) Increase in liability and

(*iii*) Decrease in an asset.

Uses of Funds

(*i*) Decrease in owner's equity

(*ii*) Decrease in a liability and

(*iii*) Increase in an asset.

It is important to note that when funds are defined as on total resources basis, the sources of funds are equal to the uses of funds as assets are always equal to owners' equity plus liabilities. Example 10 illustrates funds flow statement on total resources basis.

Example 10

The following is the balance sheets of a company for the years 2001 and 2002 and an income statement for the year 2002.

Balance Sheets as at Dec. 31, 2001 and 2002

(Rs. '000)

	2001 *Rs.*	*2002* *Rs.*		*2001* *Rs.*	*2002* *Rs.*
Share Capital:			*Fixed Assets:*		
Equity	240	240	Gross block	1,128	1,210
Preference	100	100	Accumulated		
Reserves and surplus	360	430	depreciation	(702)	(752)
Long-term debt:			Net fixed assets	426	458
Debentures	100	100	Long-term investment	30	70
Current liabilities and provisions:			*Current Assets:*		
			Cash and bank	146	146
Loans and advances	294	262	Marketable securities	12	12
Creditors	638	660	Debtors	320	378
Provisions	126	1,398	Stock	768	710
			Other current assets	134	134
			Intangible assets	22	30
	1,858	1,930		1,058	1,930

Income Statement for the Year 2002

(Rs. '000)

Sales		1,808
Cost of goods sold:		
Materials	732	
Wages	376	
Other manufacturing expenses	320	
		1,428
Gross Profit		380
Operating expenses:		
Selling and administration	142	
Depreciation	50	
		192
Operating profit		188
Non-operating income (or expenses)		98
Net income before interest and tax		286
Interest:		
Debentures	8	
Borrowings	58	
		66
Profit before tax		220
Tax		116
Profit after tax		104
Dividend:		
Equity Capital	28	
Preference capital	6	34
Net income		70

Solution:

Before preparing funds flow statement, changes in balance sheet items are analysed.

Changes in Balance Sheet Items

	(Rs. '000)			
	2001	*2002*	*Increase*	*Decrease*
Assets:				
Net fixed assets	426	458	32	—
Long-term investments	30	70	40	—
Cash and Bank	146	146	—	—
Marketable securities	12	12	—	—
Debtors	320	378	58	—
Stock	768	710	—	58
Other current assets	134	126	—	8
Intangible assets	22	30	8	—
Equity and liabilities:				
Equity capital	120	120		
Preference capital	100	100		
Reserves and surplus	360	430	70	
Debentures	100	100		
Loans and advances	294	262	—	32
Creditors	638	660	22	
Provisions	126	138	12	

Sources and Uses of Funds for the year 2002

(Rs. '000)

Source of Funds:		
Increase in equity		
Reserve and surplus		70
Increase in liabilities:		
Creditors	22	
Provisions	12	34
Decrease in assets:		
Stocks	58	
Other current assets	8	66
Total		170
Uses of funds:		
Decrease in equity	—	—
Decrease in Liabilities:		
Loan and advances	32	32
Increase in assets:		
Net fixed assets	32	
Long-term investments	40	
Debtors	58	
Intangible assets	8	138
		170

The sources and uses of funds statement can be prepared in a different manner using the information given in income statement of the company. This is given below:

Sources and Uses of Funds Statement for the year 2002

(Rs. '000)

Sources of Funds		
Profit before tax		220
Depreciation		50
Issue of equity capital		—
Increase in liabilities:		
Creditors	22	
Provisions	12	
		34
Decrease in assets:		
Stocks	58	
Other current assets	8	
		66
Total		370
Uses of Funds		
Taxes		116
Dividends		34
Decrease in liabilities:		
Loans and advances	32	32
Increase in assets:		
Fixed asset (gross)	82	
Long-term investments	40	
Debtors	58	
Intangible assets	8	188
		370

The above funds flow statement contains more detailed information than the previous one. This statement contains the following additional information:

(*i*) Change in reserve and surplus, which is equal to net income, is expressed as follows:

Profit before tax

Less: taxes

Less: dividends

Profit before tax is a source of funds, and taxes and dividends have been, therefore, shown as uses of funds.

(*ii*) Gross increase in fixed assets has been shown as uses of funds.

(*iii*) Depreciation for the year 2002 is shown as source of funds.

THEORY QUESTIONS

1. Explain why an adequate amount of working capital is essential for the successful operation of a business enterprise.
2. What are the primary ways in which an enterprise generates working capital and the primary ways in which a firm uses working capital.
3. What information can a reader gain from a statement of changes in financial position that is not apparent from reading an income statement?

4. If you were given the option to prepare statement of changes in financial position (SCFP) either on working capital basis or cash basis which one would you prefer. Why. Explain keeping in view the objective of the financial statement of a business enterprise.
5. Explain the different concepts of funds used in the preparation of statement of changes in financial position. Which concept of funds is appropriate and under what circumstances and objectives.
6. How does a funds flow differ from a balance sheet and an income statement Distinguish between á cash basis funds flow statement and disbursement statement.
7. What additional information is required to convert a statement of sources and uses of networking capital into a statement of changes in financial position.
8. Why is cash flow statement a useful statement.
9. Identify the three major types of activities classified on a cash flow statement and give examples of cash inflow and cash outflow in each classification.
10. What limitations of funds flow statement are overcome by a cash flow statement.
11. What are the purposes of cash flow statement.
12. Discuss the procedures in preparing a funds flow statement.
13. Discuss the procedures in preparing a cash flow statement.
14. What are the three classifications of cash flows and give some examples of each.
15. Explain the statement of changes in financial position, prepared on total resources basis.
16. What are the two methods of determining cash flows from operation. Generally which of these methods is preferable?
17. Why is the change in the cash balance so important for financial reporting and managerial decisions.
18. "A cash flow statement is required to explain changes in cash account balances between balance sheet dates." Explain this statement.
19. Explain in general how the cash balance is increased or decreased by income statement transactions.
20. List the common sources and uses of cash in each activity area: operating, investing and financing.
21. What are the different meanings of funds in relation to statement of changes in financial position.
22. What are the purposes of statement of changes in financial position.
23. How does a funds flow differ from balance sheet and income statement.

PROBLEMS

1. From the following particulars, prepare the funds flow statement:

	1 January Rs.	*31 December* Rs.
Cash	4,000	3,600
Debtors	35,000	38,400
Stock	25,000	22,000
Land	20,000	30,000
Building	50,000	55,000
Machinery	80,000	86,000
	2,14,000	2,35,000
Creditors	36,000	41,000
Bank loan	30,000	45,000
Capital	1,48,000	1,49,000
	2,14,000	2,35,000

During the year, drawings by the proprietor for personal use amounted to Rs. 26,000. Provisions for depreciation on machinery stood at Rs. 27,000 on 1 January and at Rs. 36,000 on 31 December.

(**Ans:** Decrease in Working Capital Rs. 5,000)

2. From the following balance sheet of a company, you are required to prepare (*i*) a statement showing changes in the working capital and (*ii*) a statement of sources and applications of funds.

Particulars	*January* Rs.	*December* Rs.
Cash	40,000	44,400
Accounts receivable	10,000	20,700
Inventories	15,000	15,000
Land	4,000	4,000
Buildings	20,000	16,000
Equipment	15,000	17,000
Accumulated Depreciation	(5,000)	(2,800)
Patents	1,000	900
	1,00,000	1,15,200
Current Liabilities	30,000	32,000
Bonds Payable	22,000	22,000
Bonds Payable Discount	(2,000)	(1,800)
Capital Stock	35,000	43,500
Retained Earnings	15,000	19,500
	1,00,000	1,15,000

Additional Information:

(*a*) Income for the period Rs. 10,000.

(*b*) A building that cost Rs. 4,000 and which had a book value of Rs. 1,000 was sold for Rs. 1,400.

(*c*) The depreciation charge for the period was Rs. 800.

(*d*) There was Rs. 5,000 issue of common stock.

(*e*) Cash dividends Rs. 2,000 and a Rs. 3,500 stock dividend were declared.

(**Ans:** Increase in Working Capital Rs. 13,100; Sources Rs. 17,100, Applications Rs. 4,000).

3. From the following balance sheets of X Ltd. on 31st December 2001 and 2002, you are required to prepare:

(*a*) A schedule of changes in working capital and

(*b*) A funds flow statement.

Liabilities	*2001* Rs.	*2002* Rs.	*Assets*	*2001* Rs.	*2002* Rs.
Share Capital	1,00,000	1,00,000	Goodwill	12,000	12,000
General Reserve	14,000	18,000	Building	40,000	36,000
Profit & Loss A/c	16,000	13,000	Plant	37,000	36,000
Sundry Creditors	8,000	5,400	Investments	10,000	11,000
Bill payable	1,200	800	Stock	30,000	23,400
Provision for Taxation	16,000	18,000	Bills Receivable	2,000	3,200
Provision for doubtful debts	400	600	Debtors	18,000	19,000
			Cash at Bank	6,600	15,200
	1,55,600	1,55,800		1,55,600	1,55,800

The following additional information has also been given:

(a) Depreciation Charge on Plant was Rs. 4,000 and on building Rs. 4,000.

(b) Provision for taxation of Rs. 19,000 was made during the year.

(c) Interim dividend of Rs. 8,000 was paid during the year 2002.

Ans: Increase in working capital Rs. 7,000, Funds from operations Rs. 36,000.

4. Find out cash from operations from the following profit and loss account.

Profit and Loss Account for the year ending December, 2001

	Rs.		*Rs.*
To Rent	50,000	By Gross Profit	12,50,000
To Salaries	2,50,000	By Gain on sale of plant	2,50,000
To Depreciation	1,00,000	By Income tax refund	1,50,000
To Loss on sale of Plant	50,000		
To Goodwill written off	2,00,000		
To Proposed dividends	2,50,000		
To Provision for taxation	2,50,000		
To Net profit	5,00,000		
	16,50,000		16,50,000

Ans: Cash from operations Rs. 9,50,000.

5. The details about the current assets of a company are as follows:

	2001 (Rs.)	*2002 (Rs.)*
Debtors	20,000	24,000
Provision for bad debts	2,000	2,400
Bills receivable	8,000	6,000
Bills payable	10,000	12,000
Creditors	16,000	18,000
Inventories	10,000	16,000
Short-term investments	20,000	24,000
Outstanding expenses	2,000	3,000
Prepaid expenses	4,000	2,000
Accrued Income	6,000	8,000

Find out cash from operations

Ans: Rs. 15,400.

6. Tiny Tot Limited furnishes you the following Balance Sheets for the years ending on 31 December 2001 and 2002. You are required to prepare a Cash Flow Statement for the year ended 31 December 2002.

Liabilities	*2001*	*2002*	*Assets*	*2002*	*2003*
Equity Share Capital	10,00,000	10,00,000	Goodwill	1,20,000	1,20,000
General Reserve	1,40,000	1,80,000	Land	4,00,000	3,60,000
Profit and Loss A/c	1,60,000	1,30,000	Building	3,70,000	3,60,000
Sundry Creditors	80,000	54,000	Investments	1,00,000	1[illegible],000
Outstanding Expenses	12,000	8,000	Inventories	3,00,000	2[illegible],000
Provision for taxation	1,60,000	1,80,000	Account Receivable	2,00,000	[illegible]22,000
Provision for bad debts	4,000	6,000	Bank Balance	66,000	1,52,000
	15,55,000	15,58,000		15,56,000	15,58,000

Following additional information has also been supplied to you:

(*i*) A piece of land has also been sold for Rs. 40,000.

(*ii*) Depreciation amounting to Rs. 70,000 has been charged on building.

(*iii*) Provision for taxation has been made for Rs. 1,90,000 during the year

(**Ans.** Cash from operations Rs. 2,86,000, Sources Rs. 3,26,000, Application Rs. 2,40,000).

7. A Ltd. supplies you the following Balance Sheet on 31st December:

(Rs. '000)

Liabilities	*2001 Rs.*	*2002 Rs.*	*Assets*	*2001 Rs.*	*2002 Rs.*
Share capital	1,40,000	1,48,000	Cash	18,000	15,600
Bonds	24,000	12,000	Debtors	29,800	35,400
Sundry Creditors	20,720	23,680	Stock	98,400	85,000
Provision for bad debt	1,400	1,600	Land	40,000	55,000
Reserves & Surplus	22,080	21,120	Goodwill	20,000	15,000
	2,06,200	2,06,400		2,06,200	2,06,400

Following additional information has also been supplied to you.

(*i*) Dividends amounting Rs. 70,00,000 were paid during the year 2002.

(*ii*) Depreciation on land was provided at the rate of 5% p.a. You are required to prepare a Cash Flow Statement.

8. The Balance sheets of T Ltd. as at 31 December 2001 and 31 December 2002 are as follows:

(Rs. in lakhs)

Liabilities	*2001*	*2002*	*Assets*	*2001*	*2002*
Share Capital	300.00	300.00	Freehold Property	225.000	240.00
Reserves	225.00	240.00	Plant and Machinery at cost less depreciation	135.00	165.00
6 percent Debentures	75.00	75.00			
Mortgage on freehold property	27.00	14.25	Investment in share of companies under the same management	150.50	150.00
Creditors	45.00	45.00			
Proposed dividend (subject to deduction of tax)	22.50	23.25	Investments in shares of other companies	112.00	112.50
Provision for taxation	21.00	37.50	Market value 2002, 120 lakhs		
Secured overdraft (by a floating charge on assets)	15.00	82.50	2001, 150 lakhs)		
			Stock	52.50	75.00
			Debtors	45.00	75.00
			Bank	10.50	
	730.50	817.50		730.50	817.50

The following additional information for the year 2002 is relevant:

(1) Credit Sales 675 lakhs

(2) Credit Purchases Rs. 520 lakhs

(3) Overheads Rs. 83.751 lakhs

(4) Depreciation on plant and machinery Rs. 17.50 lakhs

(5) Dividend for 2002 was paid in full

(6) Amount paid towards taxation for the year 2001 Rs. 21.50 lakhs

In view of credit squeeze, the company has been asked by the Bank to reduce the overdraft substantially within six months, if possible by 50 per cent.

You are required to prepare a cash flow statement and briefly comment on the financial position of the company and suggest remedial measures to overcome the financial crisis.

Ans: Cash from operations is Rs. 41.25 lakh. Applications at Rs. 119.25 lakh. Operations is the only source. Company has a safe financial position as far as long-term financial solvency is concerned, it is rather unduly conservative. Current ratio is extremely poor. ROI before interest and tax is 22.62 per cent which is quite satisfactory. The company can improve its current ratio by disposing of a part of quoted shares in other companies or converting a part of the bank overdraft in a term loan).

9. Wearwell Ltd. supplies you the following Balance Sheets on 31 December:

(Rs. '000)

Liabilities	*2001* Rs.	*2002* Rs.	*Assets*	*2001* Rs.	*2002* Rs.
Share Capital	70,000	74,000	Bank Balance	9,000	7,800
Bonds	12,000	6,000	Accounts Receivable	14,900	17,700
Accounts payable	10,360	11,840	Inventories	49,200	42,700
Provision for doubtful debts	700	800	Land	20,000	30,000
Reserves and Surplus	10,040	10,560	Goodwill	10,000	5,000
	1,03,100	1,03,200		1,03,100	1,03,200

Following additional information has also been supplied to you:

(*i*) Dividends amounting to Rs. 35,00,000 were paid during the year 2002.

(*ii*) Land was purchased for Rs. 1,00,00,000.

(*iii*) Rs. 50,00,000 were written off on goodwill during the year.

(*iv*) Bonds of Rs. 60,00,000 were paid during the course of the year. You are required to prepare a cash flow statement.

(Ans: Cash from operations Rs. 1,43,00,000, Sources Rs. 1,83,00,000 and Applications 1,95,00,000).

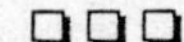

Chapter 3

FINANCIAL STATEMENT ANALYSIS

MEANING OF FINANCIAL STATEMENT ANALYSIS

Financial Statement Analysis is an analysis which highlights important relationships in the financial statements. It focusses on the evaluation of past operations as revealed by the analysis of basic statements. Financial Statement analysis embraces the methods used in assessing and interpreting the results of past performance and current financial position as they relate to particular factors of interest in investment decisions. It is an important means of assessing past performance and in forecasting and planning future performance.

OBJECTIVES OF FINANCIAL STATEMENT ANALYSIS

The major objectives of financial statement analysis is to provide decision makers information about a business enterprise for use in decision-making. Users of financial statement information are the decision makers concerned with evaluating the economic situation of the firm and predicting its future course. The major groups of users are the management for evaluating the operational and financial efficiency of the enterprise as a whole or of subunits (e.g. departments), investors for making investment decisions and portfolio decisions, lenders and creditors for determining the creditworthiness and solvency position, employees and labour unions for deciding economic status of the enterprise and making sound decisions in wage and salary negotiations; regulatory authorities for controlling the activities of the firm and making overall corporate policy, economists, researchers and planners for studying firm and specific data behaviour.

FOCUS OF FINANCIAL STATEMENT ANALYSIS

Financial Statement Analysis involves evaluating different aspects of a business enterprise which are of great importance to different users such as management, investors, creditors, bankers, analysts, investment advisors etc. Generally, the following analyses are made while making financial statement analysis:

I. Liquidity or Short-Term Solvency Analysis

II. Profitability Analysis,

III. Capital Structure or Gearing Analysis,

IV. Market Strength or Investor Analysis and

V. Growth and Stability Analysis.

I. LIQUIDITY OR SHORT-TERM SOLVENCY ANALYSIS (OR RATIOS)

Liquidity or short-term solvency analysis aims to determine the ability of a business to meet its financial obligations during the short-term and to maintain its short-term debt-paying ability. The aim of liquidity analysis is for a company to have adequate funds on hand to pay bills when they are due and to meet unexpected needs for cash. If a business enterprise cannot maintain its short-term debt paying ability, obviously it cannot maintain a long-term debt-paying ability or long-term solvency. Shareholders also will not be satisfied with such a state of affairs of the company. Even a business enterprise on a very profitable course will find itself bankrupt if it fails to meet its obligations to short-term creditors.

Liquidity analysis mainly focusses on balance sheet relationships that indicate the ability of a business to liquidate current and non-current liabilities. The ratios that evaluate liquidity relate to working capital or some part of it, because it is out of working capital that debts are paid as they mature. The comparisons and ratios related to evaluating liquidity or short term solvency are as follows:

(i) Working Capital Position:

The working capital of a business is the excess of current assets over current liabilities; this is computed by subtracting current liabilities from the current assets. The resulting working capital figure is taken as one of the primary indications of the short-term solvency of the business. The working capital formula is as follows:

Working Capital = Current assets – Current liabilities

The current working capital amount should be compared with past amounts to determine if working capital is reasonable. Caution must be exercised, because the relative size of the firm may be expanding or contracting. Further, the absolute amounts of working capital are difficult to use in comparing companies of different sizes or in comparing such amounts with industry figures.

(ii) Current Ratio:

Current ratio is sometimes referred to as working capital ratio or banker's ratio. Current ratio expresses the relationship of current assets to current liabilities. It is widely used as a broad indicator of a company's liquidity and short-term debt-paying ability. The current ratio is computed by dividing the total current assets by the total current liabilities. The current ratio formula is as follows:

$$\text{Current ratio} = \frac{\text{Current assets}}{\text{Current liabilites}}$$

Current ratio is a more dependable indication of solvency than is working capital. For many years, the guideline for the minimum current ratio has been 2:1. The assumption is even if the value of current assets declines by 50%, the firm can still pay its current liabilities. But nowadays there has been a decline in the liquidity of many firms. It can be said that in some industries, a current ratio substantially below 2 is adequate, while some other industries may require a ratio much larger than 2. In general, the shorter the operating cycle, the lower the normal current ratio. The longer the operating cycle, the higher the normal current ratio. A higher current ratio enables a firm to pay off current obligations and thus provides adequate margin of safety to the creditors.

A company's current ratio can be compared with the company's past current ratios and with industry averages as well. Such comparisons can help in determining if the current ratio is high or low at this period in time. However, these comparisons do not indicate why the current ratio is high or low. Possible reasons for unsatisfactory current ratio can be found from an analysis of the individual accounts and items which make up the current asset and current liability.

Examples: The following are the current assets and current liabilities in respect of two companies, Company A and Company B.

	Company A	*Company B*
Current assets	Rs. 4,50,000	Rs. 1,60,000
Current liabilities	Rs. 1,50,000	Rs. 80,000

The current ratio will be as follows:

$$\text{Current ratio} = \frac{\text{Current assets}}{\text{Current liabilites}}$$

$$\text{Company A} = \frac{\text{Rs. } 4,50,000}{\text{Rs. } 1,50,000}$$

$$= 3.1$$

$$\text{Company B} = \frac{\text{Rs. } 1,60,000}{\text{Rs. } 80,000}$$

$$= 2:1$$

3. Acid Test Ratio or Quick Ratio

The current ratio is generally used to evaluate an enterprise's overall short-term solvency or liquidity position. At many times, it is desirable to know more immediate position or instant-debt-paying ability of a firm than that indicated by the current ratio. Further, the current ratio does not take into account the make-up or composition of current assets. For example, a rupee of cash or debtor is considered more readily available to meet obligations than a rupee of inventory. The quick ratio is designed to overcome this problem by relating the most liquid assets to current liabilities. Cash, marketable securities or short-term investments, receivables and prepaids are included within the meaning of most liquid assets; inventory is excluded. The acid test ratio is as follows:

$$\text{Acid Test} = \frac{\text{Current Assets} - \text{Inventory}}{\text{Current Liabilities}}$$

It may be preferable to have a better view of liquidity by excluding some other items in current assets that may not represent relatively current cash flow. Examples of items to be excluded are prepaids and miscellaneous items such as assets held for sale. This is considered a more conservative manner of computing the acid test ratio and the formula of acid test ratio in this situation will be as follows:

$$\text{Acid Test} = \frac{\text{Cashn} + \text{Marketable Securities} + \text{Net Receivables and Debtors}}{\text{Current Liabilities}}$$

Inventory should be removed from current assets when computing the acid test ratio. Some of the reasons for this are that inventory may be slow moving or possibly obsolete and parts of the inventory may have been pledged to specific creditors.

The usual guideline for the acid test ratio is 1.00. However, some industries may find that a ratio less than 1.00 is adequate, while others need a ratio greater than 1.00. For example, a typical grocery store sells only for cash and therefore does not have receivables. This type of business can have an acid test substantially below the 1.00 guideline and still have adequate liquidity.

Example: A firm has the following current assets and current liabilities:

Debtors	Rs. 5,000
Inventory	Rs. 20,000

Cash	Rs. 5,000
Total current assets	Rs. 30,000

Total current liabilities Rs. 20,000

The acid test or quick ratio is as follows:

$$\text{Quick ratio} = \frac{\text{Quick assets}}{\text{Current liabilities}}$$

$$= \frac{\text{Rs. } 10,000}{\text{Rs. } 20,000}$$

$$= 0.5:1$$

4. Cash Ratio

Liquidity of a firm can be viewed from an extremely conservative point of view. This may be the case when severe liquidity problems with inventory and receivables are likely to happen or when the company has pledged its receivables and inventory. In this situation, the short-term liquidity of a company may be measured through cash ratio. The cash ratio relates cash and marketable securities to current liabilities. The cash ratio is computed as follows:

$$\text{Cash Ratio} = \frac{\text{Cash + Marketable Securities}}{\text{Current liabilities}}$$

Cash ratio is not given much importance unless a firm is in deep financial trouble. It is not considered pragmatic to expect a business enterprise to have enough cash and marketable securities to cover current liabilities. However, in the case of very slow-moving inventories and receivables and highly speculative companies, cash ratio is of great importance. A high cash ratio indicates that a business enterprise is not using its resource cash to best advantage. A low cash ratio reflects an immediate problem with paying bills.

5. Receivables Turnover

The ability of a company to collect for credit sales in a timely way affects the company's liquidity. The relationship between credit sales and accounts receivables may be stated as the receivable turnover. Receivables or debtors' turnover determines the liquidity of one item of current assets and finds out how faster debts are being collected. It is computed by dividing net credit sales by the average net accounts receivable. The formula for computing receivables turnover is as follows:

$$\text{Receivables Turnover} = \frac{\text{Net Credit Sales}}{\text{Average accounts receivables or debtors}}$$

Receivables turnover shows how many times, on an average, the receivables were turned into cash during the period. A high debtors' turnover ratio indicates shorter time span between credit sales and cash collection. This ratio requires one balance sheet account and one profit and loss account item. In case, credit sales figure is not given, total sales figure can be used to compute receivables turnover.

Example: A firm has opening and closing debtors of Rs. 40,000 and Rs. 75,000 respectively and credit sales of Rs. 3,45,000. The debtors' turnover ratio is as follows:

$$\text{Debtors' turnover ratio} = \frac{\text{Credit Sales}}{\text{Average Debtors}}$$

$$= \frac{\text{Rs. } 3,42,000}{\text{Rs. } 57,000}$$

$$= 6 \text{ times per year}$$

$$\text{Debt Collection period} = \frac{12 \text{ months}}{\text{Debtors' Turnover}}$$

$$= \frac{12 \text{ months}}{6 \text{ times}}$$

$$= 2 \text{ months}$$

6. Inventory Turnover

Inventory turnover measures the relative size of inventory and influences the amount of cash available to pay liabilities. A smaller, faster-moving inventory means that the company has less cash tied up in inventory. On the contrary, a build up in inventory means that a recession or some other factor is preventing sales from keeping pace with purchasing and production. Ideally, inventory should be maintained at an optimum level to support production and sales. Inventory turnover ratio is calculated by using the following formula:

$$\text{Inventory turnover} = \frac{\text{Cost of goods sold}}{\text{Average inventory}}$$

Average inventory is obtained using a simple average process by dividing the opening and closing inventory by the two. Cost of goods sold is obtained by deducting gross profit from sales.

Example: A firm has opening and closing inventory of Rs. 56,000 and Rs. 44,000 respectively. The firm has sold goods for Rs. 5,00,000 at gross profit margin of 20%. The inventory turnover ratio is as follows:

$$\text{Inventory Turnover} = \frac{\text{Cost of goods sold}}{\text{Average inventory}}$$

$$= \frac{\text{Rs. } 5,00,000 - \text{Rs. } 1,00,000}{1/2\,(\text{Rs. } 56,000 + \text{Rs. } 44,000)}$$

$$= \frac{\text{Rs. } 4,00,000}{\text{Rs. } 50,000}$$

$$= 8 \text{ times per year}$$

II. PROFITABILITY ANALYSIS (OR RATIOS)

The long-term survival of a business enterprise depends on satisfactory income earned by it. An evaluation of a company's past profits may give the investors, creditors and others a better understanding for decision-making. The profitability position also affects the liquidity position which is vital to creditors as well. Profitability ratios try to establish relationship among profit, turnover, capital employed etc. These ratios are:

1. Earnings Margin

It is the ratio of net income to turnover, expressed as a percentage.

$$\text{Earnings Margin} = \frac{\text{Net Income}}{\text{Turnover}} \times 100\%$$

Earnings margin is not the same as margin of profits. Margin of profits refers to the direct operating results only and is the amount before income tax and before non-operating income and charges. In earnings margin, only the final net profit is used.

2. Return on Capital Employed

This ratio measures profitability in relation to the total capital employed in a business enterprise. The terms invested capital, capital funds and total capital may be used interchangeably. It is a useful ratio when comparing the overall performances of companies, particularly where they have different proportions of debt in their capital structure.

$$\text{Return of Capital} = \frac{\text{Profit before interest and tax}}{\text{Total capital employed}}$$

According to some analysts, short-term borrowings, such as bank loans, commercial paper and deferred tax liability should be included under capital. Current accrued payables which are not interest bearing should be excluded because their interest component is not observable.

3. Return on Equity

Return on equity is derived by taking net income and dividing it by the shareholders' equity. This indicates the returns which the management is realising from the shareholders' equity and shows how effectively ordinary shareholder funds are being utilised by the management. As long as it is above the current interest rates, a company is doing fairly well.

$$\text{Return on Equity} = \frac{\text{Profit after preference taxation} - \text{Dividends}}{\text{Ordinary shareholders' funds}} \times 100\%$$

It is obvious that both the ratios — return on capital and return on equity - will be influenced when a company has raised new capital during the course of the year. That is, in other words, the ratios will be artificially low. Also, the ratios do not take into account the effect of financial leverage which undesirably tends to increase the variability of earnings for the ordinary shares. In fact, ordinary shareholders of a company having higher dose of borrowings expect large returns to compensate for the high levels of risk. Financial analysis, sometimes in such cases, find out the trade-off between higher earnings and increased variability of earnings to determine whether the management has chosen the optimum amount of financial leverage.

4. Asset Turnover Ratio

This ratio reveals the number of times the net tangible assets (i.e. total assets less current liabilities less intangibles) are turned over during the year. Strictly speaking, average net tangible assets should be used in calculating this ratio. But invariably net tangible assets at the end of the year is used.

$$\text{Asset Turnover} = \frac{\text{Turnover}}{\text{Net Tangible Assets}}$$

An improvement in asset turnover ratio as compared to the previous year indicates that the turnover of the company has improved. In cases where assets are not revalued or replaced, its magnitude will be decreasing over the years due to depreciation. Then, obviously, the ratio will be higher as the turnover figures for the future will reflect an increasing trend.

III. CAPITAL STRUCTURE OR GEARING ANALYSIS (RATIOS)

Gearing ratio, i.e. the relationship of long-term debt to total capital is considered the most important by many investors and financial analysts. Popularly known as debt-equity ratio, this ratio has utility to many including shareholders, creditors, business managers, suppliers and other user groups. Gearing ratios are used to indicate:

(*i*) The cushion of assets/profits available to holders of fixed income capital should assets/profits decline.

(*ii*) The gearing advantage of potentially higher assets/profits attributable to ordinary shareholders and the correspondingly higher risk which is incurred and (*iii*) The scope for raising additional fixed-income capital at reasonable costs, from the point of view of the company. The debt-equity ratio is computed as follows:

$$\text{Debt equity ratio} = \frac{\text{Loan capital + Preference share capital}}{\text{Net tangible assets}} \times 100$$

Net tangible assets (or total capital) is obtained by subtracting the intangible assets and the current assets from total assets. Loan capital plus preference capital constitutes the amount of long-term debt. Alternatively, long-term debt can be derived by subtracting current liabilities from total liabilities.

Sometimes capital gearing is calculated in terms of debt to equity ratio and not total capital. Capital gearing ratios, calculated in these two manners, provide essentially the same information. It is desirable that the investors select a standard method and follow it consistently throughout. It is said that as a rule of thumb, one should not opt for a company whose long-term debt exceeds two-thirds of its total capitalisation. Debt equity ratio is very helpful in assessing a company — whether the company is marching steadily into or out of debt. In younger and aggressive companies, comparatively speaking, the long-term debts may at times exceed the shareholders' equity which means that a company will not be able to get out of the difficult situation easily. A company depending on large amounts of debt should manage and perform well to avoid any worse contingencies. Debt equity ratios should be analysed not for one but for many years to determine a trend. If it is found that equity component is continuously increasing than the long-term debt, there may not be any cause for concern.

Interest Coverage Ratio

Interest coverage ratio determines the debt servicing capacity of a business enterprise keeping in view fixed interest on long-term debt. The formula for this ratio is:

$$\text{Interest Coverage ratio} = \frac{\text{Earnings before Interest and taxes (EBIT)}}{\text{Interest}}$$

If a business enterprise is able to earn a return on the assets higher than the rate of interest on long-term debt, the enterprise makes an overall profit. However, if the enterprise runs the risk of not earning a return on assets equal to the interest cost of the long-term loan, the enterprise makes an overall loss. The interest coverage ratio measures the degree of protection creditors have from default on the payment of interest by the company.

IV. MARKET STRENGTH ANALYSIS OR INVESTOR ANALYSIS

The market strength analysis or investor analysis are especially important for investors while analysing information about a company. This analysis helps the investors to decide about a company as an investment opportunity at a point of time. These ratios are also known as stock market ratios, investment ratios or market test ratios. The ratios under this category are as follows:

1. Earnings Per Share

Earnings per share is derived by dividing the profit of a company by the total number of shares outstanding. Earnings here means the net profit, net income or the net earnings. This is the amount by which the total revenues exceed the total expenses for the year.

$$\text{Earnings After Tax} = \frac{\text{Earnings after tax - Preference dividends}}{\text{Number of Ordinary shares}}$$

The net earnings figure is the amount which is completely free from any obligations and the company can plough it back into the company, pay to the ordinary shareholders as dividends or a combination of both. This amount is also known as the earnings available for ordinary shareholders.

Earnings per share can either be primary or diluted. Primary earnings per share is the earnings per share for the number of ordinary shares outstanding as on the beginning of the report period. Diluted earnings per share, on the other hand, is calculated after taking into account convertible debentures, bonds etc. (which have been converted into ordinary shares) during the year. It is computed in the same manner as primary earnings per share except that it assumes that all investments with the convertibility clause were converted at the beginning of the year. In case a company has bonds and debentures which are convertible into ordinary shares, it is always useful to compute fully diluted earnings per share (assuming full conversion) as well as earnings per share on a normal basis. This implies adding back the interest paid on the convertibles, recalculating the numerator and then dividing by the total number of ordinary shares on the assumption that conversion has taken place.

2. Dividend Per Share

The dividend per share can be net or gross. Net dividend per share is the dividend declared on a single ordinary share for the year, the net of basic rate tax.

$$\text{Net Dividend Per Share} = \frac{\text{Ordinary dividends paid to ordinary shareholders}}{\text{Number of ordinary shares}}$$

Gross dividend per share is net dividend per share together with the associated tax credit.

$$\text{Gross Dividend Per Share} = \frac{\text{Net dividend per share}}{\text{1 - Basic rate of tax}}$$

Alternatively,

Gross Dividend Per Share = Net Dividend Per Share + Associated Tax Credit

3. Gross Dividend Yield

The gross dividend yield is the gross dividend per share dividend by the ordinary share price, expressed as a percentage.

$$\text{Gross Dividend Yield} = \frac{\text{Gross dividend per share}}{\text{Ordinary share price}} \times 100\%$$

The gross dividend yield indicates the current level of income from a share. Dividend yields are normally calculated using gross dividends rather than net dividends because it helps in better analysis and comparison with other types of investments. Also, investors pay income tax at rates other than the basic rate. If the dividend yield is calculated on a net basis, the level of tax rate which has been deducted should be made clear.

Besides indicating the general level of the market, dividend yield reflects the market estimates of future dividend growth and risk. The higher the dividend growth expectations for a given share, the lower the current yield; the higher the market's estimate of risk, the higher the current yield.

4. Dividend Cover

Dividend cover denotes the number of times the dividend per share is covered by earnings per share

$$\text{Dividend Cover} = \frac{\text{Earnings per share}}{\text{Dividend per share}}$$

Dividend cover helps in assessing the prospects for dividend increases, or alternatively, the possibility of a dividend cut, should profits decline. For the purpose of dividend cover, full distribution earnings per share is normally taken into account. In other words, it is assumed that all profits are distributed as dividends. The gross dividend per share should be taken to ensure consistency in the resulting figure of dividend cover.

5. Payout Ratio

Payout ratio measures the proportion of earnings per share which are paid out as dividends:

$$\text{Payout Ratio} = \frac{\text{Net dividend per share}}{\text{Net earnings per share}} \times 100\%$$

The percentage of available earnings paid out as ordinary dividends has a vital influence on the market's behaviour towards those issues which are not in the growth category. For those companies which have paid dividends in the form of stock dividends and cash, only the cash dividend should be included in calculating the payout ratio. In the case of dividends paid out as stock dividends, the investor receives nothing that was not already owned and the company gives up nothing of value.

6. Dividends to Cashflow

'Dividends to cash flow' is a more useful ratio than the payout ratio. It helps in understanding the past trend in this regard and is greatly helpful in estimating future dividends than the conventional payout ratio.

$$\text{Dividend to Cash Flow} = \frac{\text{Dividend paid on ordinary shares}}{\text{Net earnings available for ordinary share}}$$

7. Price/Earnings (P/E) Ratio

It is the market price of shares expressed as a multiple of earnings per share.

$$\text{Price Earnings (P/E) Ratio} = \frac{\text{Price per ordinary share}}{\text{Earnings per share}}$$

Many investors consider P/E ratio as the best indicator of the ongoing performance of a company. This ratio along with the payout ratio indicates the market estimates of future dividend growth and risk. High growth shares have high P/E ratios as investors are willing to pay a greater multiple of current earnings to achieve a higher future growth. If high risk is found in a share, it reduces its market price and hence automatically reduces its P/E ratio. Payout ratios can have a positive influence on P/E ratio. High P/Es are not always bad. If investors are willing to pay a high price for a share in relation to its earnings, then they are doing so in the belief that the company has a bright future and that it will continue to strengthen and grow in future. Buying a share with a high P/E is described as buying a security with a high multiple. It should be understood here that the common share dividends come out of the earnings per share. A drop in earnings could mean that a dividend is in trouble.

The elements which govern the P/E ratio are:

(*i*) Those factors that are fully reflected in the financial data (tangible factors) — growth of earnings and sales in the past profitability or rate of returns on invested capital, stability of past earnings, dividend rate and record and financial strength or credit standing.

(*ii*) Those factors that are reflected to an indefinite extent in the data (intangible factors) — quality of management, nature and prospects of the industry and competitive position and individual prospects of the company.

8. Net Asset Value Per Share

This ratio is also known as the book value per share. Net asset value per share is the value of net tangible assets attributable to one ordinary share. Net asset value is, simply put, the shareholders' equity. Net asset value or book value has nothing to do with the market value as shares usually sell in the stock market at several times its net asset or book value.

$$\text{Net Asset Value Per Share} = \frac{\text{Ordinary share capital + Reserves - Intangibles}}{\text{Number of ordinary shares outstanding at balance sheet date}}$$

Net asset value applies to ordinary shares only. However, it does not mean that investors can get that amount if the company is liquidated. The amounts attributed to the assets are only attempts at fair and systematic evaluation, not at guessing what these assets would bring if sold in the market place. Net asset or book value can be considered only as the theoretical value of ordinary shares if the assets of the company were liquidated at the amounts attributed to them on the balance sheet. It is not unusual for a share price to be very different from the net asset value per share, even where assets in the balance sheet have recently been revalued. In general, the market price of a share will be influenced by earnings and the dividend-paying potential. Share prices will not be significantly influenced by the net asset value per share except where:

(*a*) The company is an investment vehicle for specific types of assets (e.g. investment trusts, property companies).

(*b*) It seems probable that the company will be liquidated and

(*c*) A takeover bid of the company seems likely.

The net asset value per share figure is useful while comparing shares of one company with shares of other companies operating in the same industry. If it is found that a company is selling shares at a much lower ratio of the market price to book value than other companies in the same industry, it indicates a good investment opportunity. When a share can be bought for less than its net asset value, it is an indication that share will have good value in the future. In case of mutual funds, net asset value ratio is important as it is determined at or near the price at which the mutual fund will buy and sell its shares. In the stock market, it is often found that a share is selling five times, seven times (and more) its book value. The lower the multiple, the greater will be the probable value of the share.

9. Cash Flow Per Share

Cash flow per share is a useful indicator of a company's general ability to leverage itself, to pay dividends, to convert accounting earnings into cash and to enjoy financial flexibility.

$$\text{Cash Flow Per Share} = \frac{\text{Cash flow from operations after taxes}}{\text{Ordinary shares outstanding at balance sheet date}}$$

The amount of cash flow does not totally belong to ordinary shareholders, as the earnings belong; it is also meant to pay the expenses and claims prior to the payment of dividend.

V. GROWTH AND STABILITY ANALYSIS OR RATIOS

Growth and stability ratios measure the performance and financial strength of a company apart from market valuation. Stability ratios are useful in evaluating the quality of bonds, debentures, preference shares, etc. These ratios are calculated over time and relate to sales, total returns, and earnings per share. Such ratios are:

(*i*) $\text{Growth in Sales} = \frac{\text{Sales in final period}}{\text{Sales in base period}}$

(*ii*) $\text{Growth in Total Returns} = \frac{\text{Net earned for total capital in final period}}{\text{Net earned for total capital in base period}}$

(*iii*) $\text{Growth in earnings} = \frac{\text{Earnings per share in final period}}{\text{Earnings per share in base period}}$

(*iv*) Maximum decline in coverage of interest charges = $\dfrac{\text{Worst year (or lowest year)}}{\text{Average of previous three years}}$

Normally interest charges may include any of the following combinations:

- Interest on short and long-term debts, including capital leases
- Interest on expenses plus an interest component for operating leases
- Interest on expenses on short and long-term debts plus rentals on both capital and operating bases
- Total fixed charges, rentals and preferred dividends.

(*v*) Per cent Decline in Return on Total Capital = $\dfrac{\text{Worst year (or lowest year)}}{\text{Average of previous three years}}$

(*vi*) Per cent Decline in Return on Ordinary Capital = $\dfrac{\text{Worst year (or lowest year)}}{\text{Average of previous three years}}$

(*vii*) Per cent Decline in Earnings Per Share = $\dfrac{\text{Worst year (or lowest year)}}{\text{Average of previous three years}}$

Limitations of Financial Ratios

Financial statement analysis through ratios is useful because they highlight relationships between items in the financial statements. However, they have a number of limitations which should be kept in mind while preparing or using them:

(1) Ratios are based on accounting figures given in the financial statements. However, accounting figures are themselves subject to deficiencies, approximations, diversity in practice or even manipulation to some extent. Therefore, ratios are not very helpful in drawing reliable conclusions.

(2) Ratios have inherent problem of comparability. Companies otherwise similar may employ different accounting methods, which can cause problems in comparing certain key relationships. For example, inventory turnover can be different for a company using FIFO than for the other company using the LIFO method of inventory valuation. Similarly the differences in accounting methods relating to depreciation, estimates of the life of assets, amortisation of intangibles and preliminary expenses, treatment of extraordinary items etc. can create the problem of comparability among the companies even in the same industry.

(3) Inflation may limit the utility of accounting ratios. Due to inflation, historical cost-based financial statements and accounting figures do not reflect current value figures, especially in the case of assets purchased at different dates by the different enterprises. Since financial statements are not adjusted in terms of inflation effect, accounting ratios calculated (using varying cost or prices) have distortions and become deceptive. Sometimes, gains (reflected through ratios), overtime in sales, net income and other key figures disappear when the accounting data are adjusted for changes in price levels.

(4) Accounting ratios are not totally dependable and they must be used after giving due weightage to general economic conditions, industry situation, position of firms within the industry, mode of operations, size of firm, diversity of products which can make the business enterprises completely dissimilar and thus affect the computation of accounting ratios.

(5) The different methods of computation also influence the utility of accounting ratios. The different concepts used for determining numerator and denominator in a particular accounting ratio will not help in drawing reliable conclusions even in identical situations.

Therefore, it can be said that accounting ratios should be used with utmost care. Infact, accounting ratios pinpoint areas which require further investigation and analysis. Also it should be understood that the ratios are only one among many inputs needed for making sound decisions about the solvency, profitability, financial position, risk, growth prospects, earning potential and investment opportunities of business enterprises.

Example 1

The working capital of ABC Ltd. has deteriorated in recent years and now stands as under:

Current Assets		*Current Liabilities*	
Inventory	5,60,000	Creditors	4,90,000
Debtors	3,50,000	Bank loan	2,10,000
Cash	70,000		
	9,80,000		7,00,000

(*a*) Compute the current and quick ratios.

(*b*) A further bank loan of Rs. 50,000 against debtors is under negotiation. Assuming that the loan is received, calculate the revised current and quick ratios.

(*c*) There is also a negotiation going on for discounting the debtors of Rs. 3,50,000 for Rs. 3,15,000 to a collection agency for immediate cash. Also obsolete stocks worth Rs. 1,25,000 are being sold for Rs. 80,000. Of the cash to be realised by the two transactions, the bank loan is proposed to be reduced to Rs. 1,00,000. Calculate the current ratio after the transactions are put through.

Solution:

(*a*) $$\text{Current Ratio} = \frac{\text{Current assets}}{\text{Current liabilities}} = \frac{9,80,000}{7,00,000} = 1.4$$

$$\text{Quick Ratio} = \frac{\text{Liquid assets}}{\text{Current liabilities}} = \frac{4,20,000}{7,00,000} = 0.6$$

(*b*) $$\text{Revised current ratio} = \frac{10,30,000}{7,50,000} = 1.37$$

$$\text{Revised quick ratio} = \frac{4,70,000}{7,50,000} = 0.63$$

(*c*) Financial position after the transactions:

	Rs.
Current Assets:	
Inventory	4,35,000
Debtors	—
Cash	3,55,000
	7,90,000
Current Liabilities:	
Creditors	4,90,000
Bank Loan	1,00,000
	5,90,000

$$\text{New current ratio} = \frac{7,90,000}{5,90,000} = 1.34$$

$$\text{New quick ratio} = \frac{3,55,000}{5,90,000} = 0.6$$

Cash balance = Rs. 70,000 + Rs. 3,15,000 + Rs. 80,000 – Rs. 1,10,000

= Rs. 3,55,000

Example 2

Following is the Balance Sheet of M/s Bintex Co. Ltd. Banglore, as on 31st December, 2002.

Liabilities	*Rs.*	*Assets*	*Rs.*
Share Capital:		Land	4,00,000
Authorised, issued and fully paid up:		Building	21,00,000
50,000 preference		Plant and machinery	1,19,00,000
shares of Rs. 100 each	50,00,000	Furniture and Fittings	1,50,000
5,00,000 equity shares of Rs. 10 each	50,00,000	Office cars, trucks	1,50,000
	1,00,00,000	Stock	1,50,00,000
Capital reserves	5,00,000	Accounts receivable	6,00,000
General reserves	10,00,000	Cash and bank	2,00,000
Sinking fund reserves	15,00,000		
7% Debentures	50,00,000		
Bank Overdraft	85,00,000		
Notes payable	15,00,000		
Account payable	25,00,000		
	3,05,00,000		3,05,00,000

Compute the following from the above balance sheet:

(1) Net worth
(2) Total value of equity
(3) Shareholders' reserves
(4) Total fixed assets
(5) Total current assets
(6) Working capital and
(7) Long-term liabilities.

(Show the workings, where necessary)

Solution:

(1) Net Worth

This represents the net assets of the company. It is also equivalent to proprietors' fund, viz. paid up capital plus reserves. This can be obtained by calculating both ways Assets Approach and Liabilities Approach as given below:

(*a*) Gross assets as per balance sheet		Rs. 3,05,00,000
Less: Liabilities		
7% Debentures	Rs. 50,00,000	
Bank overdraft	85,00,000	
Notes payable	15,00,000	
Accounts payable	25,00,000	
		1,75,00,000
Net worth		1,30,00,000

Alternatively

(a) Paid up capital

Preference share capital	50,00,000	
Equity share capital	50,00,000	
		1,00,00,000
Reserves:		
Capital reserve	5,00,000	
General reserve	10,00,000	
Sinking fund reserve	15,00,000	
		30,00,000
Net worth		1,30,00,000

(2) Total value of equity

This can be obtained by adding up Equity Paid up Capital with reserves and surpluses belonging to equity shareholders. Alternatively the same can be obtained by subtracting from the net worth of the company what is due to preferences shareholders:

	Net worth as calculated under (1)	Rs. 1,30,00,000
Less:	Preference share capital	50,00,000
	Total value of equity	80,00,000

(3) Shareholders reserves

Capital reserve	5,00,000
General reserve	10,00,000
Sinking fund reserve	15,00,000
Total	30,00,000

(4) Total fixed assets

Land	Rs. 4,00,000
Building	21,00,000
Plant and machinery	1,19,00,000
Furniture and fittings	1,50,000
Office cars and trucks	1,50,000
Total	1,47,00,000

(5) Total current assets

Stock	1,50,00,000
Account receivable	6,00,000
Cash at bank	2,00,000
Total	1,58,00,000

(6) Working capital

This represents excess of current assets over current liabilities:

	Current assets as calculated under (5)		Rs. 1,58,00,000
Less:	Current liabilities		
	Bank overdraft	Rs. 85,00,000	
	Notes payable	15,00,000	
	Accounts payable	25,00,000	1,25,00,000
	Working capital		33,00,000

(7) Long-term liabilities
7% debentures Rs. 50,00,000

Rs. 50,00,000

Example 3

Calculate and comment on the rate of return on total assets from the following data of two companies:

	Go Slow Co.	Go Fast Co.
Sales		2,52,75,000
Total assets	42,50,000	
Net profit in sales	6%	4%
Turnover of assets	6 times	6 times
Gross margin	20,68,000	12%

Solution:

	Rs.	Rs.
Sales	42,50,000 × 6 = 2,55,00,000	2,52,75,000
Total assets	42,50,000	2,52,75,000 ÷ 6 = 42,12,500
Net profit in sales	6% of 2,55,00,000 = 15,30,000	4% of 25 = 2,52,75,000 = 10,11,000
Rate of return on total assets	$\frac{15,30,000}{42,50,000} \times 100$ = 36%	$\frac{10,11,000}{42,12,500}$ = 24%

The rate of return on total assets in respect of Go Fast Co. is less than that of Go Slow Co. as the total assets are same (approx.) in both the companies. Net profit in sales in Go Fast Co. is 2/3rd of the net profit of Go Slow Co. and similar is the case of rate of return on total assets.

Example 4

The following figures relate to trading activities of Hind Traders Limited for the year ended 30th June...

Sales	Rs. 5,20,000	Closing stock	Rs. 98,500
Purchases	3,22,350	Sales returns	Rs. 20,000
Opening stock	76,250		
Selling and distribution expenses:			
Salaries Rs. 15,300, Advertising Rs. 4,700;		Travelling	Rs. 2,000.
Salaries	27,000	Depreciation	Rs. 9,300
Rent	2,700	Other charges	Rs. 16,500
Stationery, postage etc.	2,500	Provision for taxation	40,000

Non-operating income: Dividend on shares Rs. 9,000; Profit on sales of shares Rs. 3,000; Non-operating expenses: Loss on sale of assets Rs. 4,000.

You are required to:

(*i*) Arrange the above figures in a form suitable for analysis.

(*ii*) Show separately the following ratios: (*i*) Gross profit ratios; (*ii*) Operating ratio and (*iii*) Stock turnover ratio.

(*iii*) State what an increase in gross profit ratio as compared with that for the previous year would indicate.

Solution:

Hind Traders Limited

(1) Income Statement for the year ended 30th June...

	Sales		Rs. 5,20,000
Less:	Returns		20,000
	Net Sales (1)		5,00,000
	Opening stock	76,250	
	Purchases	3,22,250	
		3,98,500	
Less:	Closing Stock	98,500	
	Cost of sales (2)		3,00,000
	Gross Margin (1 – 2) = (3)		2,00,000
	Salaries	27,000	
	Rent	2,700	
	Stationery, postage etc.	2,500	
	Depreciation	9,300	
	Other charges	16,500	
	Administrative expenses (4)	58,000	
	Salaries	15,300	
	Advertising	4,700	
	Travelling	2,000	
	Selling and distribution expenses (5)	22,000	
	Operating expenses (4+5) = (6)		80,000
	Net margin (3 – 6) = (7)		1,20,000
	Dividend on shares	9,000	
	Profit on sale of shares	3,000	
	Non-operating income (8)	12,000	
	Less on sale of asset (9)	4,000	
	Net non-operating income (8 – 9) = (10)		8,000
	Income before taxation (7 + 10) = (11)		1,28,000
	Provision for taxation = (12)		40,000
	Income after taxation (11 – 12) = (13)		88,000

(2) (*i*) Gross profit ratio = $\frac{\text{Gross Profit}}{\text{Sales}} \times 100 = \frac{2,00,000}{5,00,000} \times 100 = 40\%$

(*ii*) Operating ratio = $\frac{\text{Cost of sales + Operating Expenses}}{\text{Sales}} \times 100$

$$\frac{3,00,000 + 80,000 \times 100}{5,00,000} = 76\%$$

(*iii*) Stock turnover ratio = $\frac{\text{Cost of goods sold}}{\text{Average stock}} = \frac{3,00,000}{1,72,750 \div 2} = 3.44$ times

(3) An increase in the gross profit ratio as compared to the previous period (provided the valuation is uniform) would indicate that the business is earning a bigger margin on its sales. This in turn means that the selling price has moved up or the costs have been reduced or partially both. This can be checked up by comparing unit selling prices and unit costs.

Example 5

The capital of E. Co. Ltd. is as follows:	*(Rs.)*
9% Preference shares of Rs. 10 each	3,00,000
Equity shares of Rs. 10 each	8,00,000
	11,00,000

The accountant has ascertained the following information:

Profit (after tax at 60%) Rs. 2,70,000, Depreciation Rs. 60,000; Equity dividend paid 20%, market price of equity shares Rs. 40. You are required to state the following, showing the necessary workings:

(*a*) Dividend yield on the equity shares.

(*b*) Cover for the preference and equity dividends.

(*c*) Earnings for equity shares and

(*d*) Price-earnings ratio.

Solution:

(*a*) Dividend yield on the equity shares:

$$= \frac{\text{Dividend per share}}{\text{Market price per share}} \times 100$$

$$= \frac{\text{Rs. } 2(20\% \text{ of Rs. } 10) \times 100}{\text{Rs. } 40} \times 100 = 5\%$$

(*b*) Dividend coverage ratio:

(*i*) Preference $= \dfrac{\text{Profits after taxes}}{\text{Dividend payable to preference shareholders}}$

$$= \frac{\text{Rs. } 2,70,000}{\text{Rs. } 27,000 \ (9\% \text{ of Rs. } 3,00,000)}$$

$= 10$ times

(*ii*) Equity $= \dfrac{\text{Profits after taxes - Preference share dividends}}{\text{Dividend payable to equity shareholders at current rate of Rs. 2 per share}}$

$$= \frac{\text{Rs. } 2,70,000 - \text{Rs. } 27,000}{\text{Rs. } 1,60,000 \ (80,000 \text{ shares} \times \text{Rs. } 2)}$$

$$= \frac{\text{Rs. } 2,43,000}{\text{Rs. } 1,60,000} = 1.52 \text{ times}$$

(*c*) Earnings for equity shares:

$$= \frac{\text{Earnings available to equity shareholders}}{\text{Number of the equity share outstanding}}$$

$$= \frac{\text{Rs. } 2,43,000}{\text{Rs. } 80,000} = \text{Rs. } 3.04 \text{ per share}$$

(*d*) Price-earning (P/E) ratio:

$$\text{P/E ratio} = \frac{\text{Market price per share}}{\text{Earnings per share}}$$

$$= \frac{\text{Rs. } 40.00}{\text{Rs. } 3.04} = 13.2 \text{ times}$$

Example 6

Below are given summarised accounts of Alok Ltd. for the year ended 31st December, 2001 and 31 st December, 2002:

Balance Sheet

(Rupees in lakhs)

			31.12.2001	31.12.2002
Liabilities:				
Share Capital			250	250
General Reserve			100	172
Debentures			180	150
Term Loan from IFCI			30	30
Creditors			70	56
			630	658
Assets:				
Fixed Assets (at cost)	500	500		
Less accumulated depreciation	80	115		
Net fixed assets			420	385
Cash			55	85
Debtors			65	75
Inventories			90	113
			530	658

Income Statement

	Year 2001	Year 2002
Net sales	350	450
Less cost of material	90	113
Wages	70	70
Cost of goods sold	160	183
Gross profit	190	267
Less selling, general and administrative costs	50	60
Earnings before depreciation, interest and tax	140	207
Less depreciation	30	35

Earnings before interest and tax	110	172
Less interest	25	27
Earnings before tax	85	145
Less Tax	15	97
Earnings after tax	70	48
Less Dividend	25	25
Retained earnings	45	72

Compute liquidity, leverage, activity and profitability ratios and comment.

Solution:

Alok Limited

Computation of Ratios for the year 2001 and 2002:

(*a*) Liquidity Ratios — *2001* — *2002*

(*i*) Current ratio: $\frac{\text{Current assets}}{\text{Current liabilities}}$ — $\frac{210}{70} = 3.1$ — $\frac{273}{56} = 4.9:1$

(*ii*) Quick ratio: $\frac{\text{Current assets less inventory}}{\text{Current liabilities}}$ — $\frac{120}{70} = 1.7:0$ — $\frac{160}{56} = 2.9:1$

(*b*) Leverage Ratios

(*i*) Debt-equity ratio:

$\frac{\text{(Long - term debt)}}{\text{Equity}}$ — $\frac{210}{350} = 0.6:1$ — $\frac{180}{422} = 0.4:1$

(*ii*) Interest coverage ratio:
(or Fixed Charges Cover)

$\frac{\text{Earnings before interest and tax}}{\text{Interest}}$ — $\frac{110}{25} = 4.4$ times — $\frac{172}{27} = 6.4$ times

(*iii*) Operating Leverage:
(Profit before interest and tax)

$\frac{\text{Contribution}}{\text{Operating profit}}$ — $\frac{190}{110} = 1.73$ — $\frac{183}{172} = 1.06$

(*iv*) Financial Leverage:

$\frac{\text{Operating profit}}{\text{Profit after interest}}$ — $\frac{110}{85} = 1.29$ — $\frac{172}{145} = 1.19$

(*c*) Activity Ratios

(*i*) Capital turnover ratio:

$\frac{\text{Sales}}{\text{Capital employed}}$ — $\frac{130}{560} = 0.625$ — $\frac{450}{602} = 0.748$

(*ii*) Fixed assets turnover ratio:

$$\frac{\text{Sales}}{\text{Net fixed assets}} \qquad \frac{350}{420} = 0.833 \qquad \frac{450}{305} = 1.169$$

(*iii*) Working Capital turnover ratio:

$$\frac{\text{Sales}}{\text{Net working capital}} \qquad \frac{350}{420} = 2.5 \qquad \frac{450}{305} = 2.074$$

(*iv*) Inventory turnover:

$$\frac{\text{Cost of goods sold}}{\text{Inventories}} \qquad \frac{160}{90} = 1.8 \qquad \frac{183}{113} = 1.6$$

(*v*) Debt collection period:

$$\frac{\text{Accounts receivable}}{\text{Average daily sales}} \qquad \frac{65}{350} \times 365 \qquad \frac{75}{450} \times 365$$

$$= 68 \text{ days} \qquad = 61 \text{ days}$$

(*d*) Profitability Ratios

(*i*) Gross profit ratio:

$$\frac{\text{Gross profit}}{\text{Sales}} \times 100 \qquad \frac{190}{350} \times 100 = 54.29\% \qquad \frac{267}{450} \times 100 = 59.33\%$$

(*ii*) Net profit ratio: $\frac{\text{Net Profit (EBIT)}}{\text{Sales}} \times 100 \qquad \frac{110}{350} \times 100 = 31.43\% \qquad \frac{172}{450} \times 38.22\%$

(*iii*) Return on investment: $\frac{\text{EBIT}}{\text{Capital employed}} \times 100 \qquad \frac{110}{560} \times 100 = 19.64\% \qquad \frac{172}{602} \times 100 = 28.57\%$

Findings:

(i) Liquidity ratios: Traditionally, if current ratio is 2:1 and quick ratio is 1:1, the liquidity position of the firm is considered to be satisfactory. In the present case, these ratios are much above the standard norms. In 2002, these ratios further went up indicating that the firm has undesirable liquidity and is not able to utilise current assets profitably. Sales have gone up. There is an increase in various current assets but the amount due to creditors has declined.

(ii) Leverage ratios: The generally acceptable debt-equity ratio is 2:1, i.e. debt can be twice the shareholders' funds. In Alok Ltd., the debt-equity ratio is quite low indicating that the company is not making good use of the financial leverage to enhance the return to equity shareholders. In 2002, the debt-equity ratio has further improved, indicating that the firm is in a sound condition; it has the capacity to raise additional resources by way of loans. The company's financial and operating leverages are also quite low. The company should be advised to look for fresh investment opportunities, to raise funds by way of loans and by release of working capital.

(iii) Activity ratios: The overall activity ratio has shown an increase, from 0.625 to 0.748; there is also an increase in the turnover of fixed assets. However, the working capital and inventory turnover ratios have shown a decline in 2002 over 2001, indicating that the firm has excessive investment in these current assets.

(iv) Profitability ratios: All the profitability ratios have shown improvement in 2002 over 2001 indicating that the operations of the firm are quite profitable. There is 50% rise in the rate of return on investment in 2002 over 2001, indicating that the company has been conducting its operations most efficiently. However, from the point of financial management, the firm's profitability can be further improved greatly by making effective use of the company's present and potential resources.

Example 7

An analytical statement of AB Company is shown below. It is based on an output (sales) level of 80,000 units:

	Rs.
Sales	9,60,000
Variable cost	5,60,000
Revenue before fixed costs	4,00,000
Fixed costs	2,40,000
	1,60,000
Interest	60,000
Earning before tax	1,00,000
Tax	50,000
Net Income	50,000

Calculate the degree of (*i*) operating leverage (*ii*) financial leverage and (*iii*) the combined leverage from the above data.

Solution:

Calculation of the various leverages:

(*a*) (*i*) Degrees of operating leverage:

$$\frac{\text{Contribution}}{\text{Earnings before interest and tax}} = \frac{4,60,000}{1,60,000} = 2.5$$

(*ii*) Degree of financial leverage:

$$\frac{\text{Earnings before interest and tax}}{\text{Earnings before tax}} = \frac{1,60,000}{1,00,000} = 1.6$$

(*iii*) Degree of combined leverage:

$$\frac{\text{Contribution}}{\text{Earnings before tax}} = \frac{4,00,000}{1,00,000} = 4$$

or

Operating leverage × Financial leverage = 2.5 × 1.6 = 4

THEORY QUESTIONS

1. What do you mean by financial statement analysis. What are its purposes.
2. Discuss the importance of financial ratios.
3. Explain the financial ratios:
   (*a*) Liquidity ratios
   (*b*) Profitability ratio and
   (*c*) Capital structure ratio.

4. In what way are market strength ratios useful to investors.
5. Discuss the computation and significance of the following financial ratios:
   (*a*) Current ratio
   (*b*) Quick ratio
   (*c*) Inventory turnover ratio
   (*d*) Debt-equity ratio
   (*e*) Accounts receivables ratio
   (*f*) Earnings margin and
   (*g*) Earning per share.
6. What are the limitations of accounting ratios.
7. What is asset turnover. What influence does a higher asset turnover tend to have on the rate of return on assets.
8. What is the key question in assessing liquidity. What ratios are used in this regard.
9. Discuss the significance of equity ratio and explain how it is computed.

PROBLEMS

1. From the following annual statement of Pioneer Ltd., calculate the following ratios:
   (*a*) Gross Profit Ratio, (*b*) Current Ratio; (*c*) Liquid Ratio: (*d*) Debt-Equity Ratio, and (*e*) Return on Equity Ratio.

Trading and Profit and Loss Account for the Year ended 31st Dec. 2002

	Rs.		*Rs.*
Materials Consumed:		Sales	85,000
Opening Stock	9,050	Profit on Sale of Investments	600
Purchases	54,525	Interest on Invetements	300
	63,575		
Closing Stock	14,000		
	49,575		
Carriage Inwards	1,425		
Office Expenses	15,000		
Sales Expenses	3,000		
Financial Expenses	1,500		
Loss on Sale of Assets	400		
Net Profit	15,000		
	85,900		85,900

Balance Sheet as on 31st December 2002

		Rs.			*Rs.*
Share Capital:			Fixed Assets		
2,000 Equity Shares of Rs. 10 each		20,000	Buildings	15,000	
Reserves		9,000	Plant	8,000	23,000
Profit and Loss account		6,000	Current assets:		
Bank overdraft		3,000	Stock in trade	14,000	
Sundry creditors:			Debtors	7,000	
for expenses	2,000		Bills Recev.	1,000	
for others	8,000	10,000	Bank	3,000	25,000
		48,000			48,000

Ans: (*a*) Gross Profit Ratio. 40%; (*b*) Current Ratio – 1.92: 1;
(*c*) Liquid Ratio – 1.1:1 Bank overdraft has not been taken as a current liability (*d*) Debt-Equity Ratio:

(*i*) $\frac{\text{All Debts}}{\text{Equity}} = 0.371:1$

(*ii*) $\frac{\text{All Debts}}{\text{All Debts + Equity}} = 0.271:1$

(*c*) Return on Investment Ratio: $\frac{\text{Net Profit}}{\text{Capital Employed}}$

$\frac{\text{Rs. 15,000}}{\text{Rs. 35,000}} = 42.85$

2. Following is the Profit and Loss Account and balance sheet of A Limited for the year ended 31st December, 2001 and balance sheet as on that date. Calculate the different ratios and comment on the financial position of the company.

Profit and Loss Account
for the year ended 31 December, 2001

		Rs.
Net sales		3,00,000
Less: Cost of Goods sold		2,58,000
Gross profit		42,000
Operating Expenses		
Selling	2,200	
General and administration	4,000	
Rent of Office	2,800	
		9,000
Gross Operating Profit		33,000
Depreciation		10,000
		23,000
Other Income:		
Interest on Government Securities		1,500
Gross Income		24,500
Other expenses:		
Interest on bank overdraft	300	
Interest on debentures	4,200	
		4,500
Net Income before Tax		20,000
Tax @ 50 per cent on Net Income		10,000
Net Income after Tax		10,000

Balance Sheet as on 31st December 2001

Liabilities	*Rs.*	*Assets*	*Rs.*
Sundry Creditors	6,000	Cash	5,000
Bills Payable	10,000	Investments (Govet. Securities)	15,000
Outstanding Expenses	1,000	Sundry Debtors	20,000
Provision for Taxation	13,000	Stock	30,000
Total current liabilities	30,000	Total current Assets.	70,000

6 per cent Mortgage Debentures	70,000	Fixed Assets	1,80,000	
7 per cent preference shares	10,000	*Less:* Provision for depr.	50,000	
Equity Shares	50,000			1,30,000
Reserve and surplus	40,000			
Total Claim on Assets	2,00,000			2,00,000

Ans: Gross Profit Ratio 14 per cent, Net Profit Ratio (after considering interest on bank overdraft): 7.56 per cent, ROI 13.53 per cent, Stock Turnover Ratio 8.6, Debt Collection Period 24 days, Fixed Assets Turnover 2.3, Fixed Assets Ratio 76, Debt-equity ratio 70/100 = .7, Current ratio 2.3)

3. Following is the balance sheet of C Ltd. as on 31st December, 2002.

Liabilities		*Rs.*	*Assets*	*Rs.*
Equity share capital		20,000	Goodwill	12,000
Capital reserves		4,000	Fixed Assets	28,000
8% Loan on mortgage		16,000	Stocks	6,000
Trade creditors		8,000	Debtors	6,000
Bank overdraft		2,000	Investments	2,000
Taxation: Current		2,000	Bank	6,000
Future		2,000		
Profit and Loss A/c:				
Profit 2002 after taxation and interest on fixed deposits	Rs. 12,000			
Less Transfer to Reserve	4,000			
Dividend	2,000	6,000		
		60,000		60,000

Sales amounted to Rs. 1,20,000

Calculate ratio for:

(*i*) Testing liquidity

(*ii*) Testing solvency

(*iii*) Testing profitability

(*iv*) Testing capital gearing and

(*v*) Comment on the significance thereof.

4. The following financial statement is summarised from the books of Armstrong Ltd; as at 31st March 2002:

Capital and Liabilities	*As at 31.3.2002 Rs.*	*Property and Assets*	*As at 31.3.2002 Rs.*
Paid-up-capital	15,00,000	Fixed Assets	16,50,000
Reserves and Surplus	6,00,000	Stock in trade	9,10,000
Debentures (long-term)	5,00,000	Book debts	12,40,000
Bank overdraft	2,00,000	Investment	
Sundry Creditors	12,00,000	(Short term)	1,60,000
		Cash	40,000
	40,00,000		40,00,000

Annual Sales	Rs. 74,40,000
Gross Profit	Rs. 7,44,000

You are required to calculate the following ratios for the year and comment on the financial position as revealed by these ratios:

(*a*) Debt Equity Ratio

(*b*) Current Ratio

(*c*) Proprietary Ratio

(*d*) G.P. Ratio

(*e*) Debtors' Turnover Ratio

(*f*) Stock Turnover Ratio

Bank overdraft is payable on demand.

5. From the following particulars extracted from the financial statements of Sun and Co. Ltd. compute: (*a*) Current Ratio, (*b*) Acid Test Ratio, (*c*) Stock Turnover Ratio, (*d*) Debtors Turnover Ratio and (*e*) Creditors Turnover Ratio for the two years 2001 and 2002 independently and comment on the liquidity position of the company:

	2001 (Rs.)	*2002 (Rs.)*
Opening stock	47,000	53,000
Closing stock	53,000	67,000
Sales less returns	2,52,000	3,65,000
Provision for bad debts	2,000	3,000
Sundry creditors	32,000	35,000
Purchases	1,80,000	1,90,000
Sundry debtors	42,000	63,000
Cash	10,000	15,000
Bank	8,000	10,000
Bills Receivable	15,000	20,000
Bills Payable	29,000	30,000
Marketable Securities	8,000	8,000

6. A Ltd. and B. Ltd. produce and sell the same product but under different brand names. Their profit and loss statements and balance sheets are given below for the year ending 2002.

Profit and Loss Statements

(Figures in Rs. lakhs)

			A. Ltd.	*B. Ltd.*
	Sales		25.00	30.00
Less:	Costs:	Materials	4.00	2.00
		Labour	2.00	7.00
	Overheads:	Fixed	9.00	2.00
		Variable	2.00	9.00
	Total cost		17.00	20.00
	Gross margin		8.00	10.00
	Interest		2.00	4.00
	Profit before taxes		6.00	6.00
	Taxes		3.00	3.00
	Profit after taxes		3.00	3.00
	Dividends declared		2.00	2.00
	Retained earnings		1.00	1.00

Balance Sheet

(Fig. in Rs. Lakhs)

	A Ltd.	*B Ltd.*
A. Capital Liabilities:		
1. Equity Capital	10.00	20.00
2. Debenture Capital	8.00	20.00
3. Creditors	5.00	15.00
4. Reserves	17.00	5.00
	40.00	60.00
B. Assets:		
1. Plant and machinery	8.00	34.00
2. Buildings	6.00	16.00
3. Inventories	18.00	2.00
4. Debtors	7.00	1.00
5. Cash	1.00	7.00
	40.00	60.00

Required: Evaluate the performance of two organisations for the current year and assess the expected problem by using the relevant ratios.

Chapter 4

COST CLASSIFICATIONS

CONCEPT OF COST

Cost is the amount of expenditure actual (incurred) or notional (attributable) relating to a specific thing or activity. The specific thing or activity may be a product, job, service, process or any other activity.

Cost is the cash or cash equivalent value sacrificed to obtain some goods or services. Cash equivalent means that non-cash assets can be exchanged for the desired goods or services. For example, it may be possible to exchange land for some needed equipment.

Basically, when a cost is incurred, it could be in the form of deferred cost (asset) or expired cost (expense). Deferred costs are unexpired costs which provide benefits in the future periods. They are capitalised costs and known as assets and hence appear on the balance sheet. Example of deferred or unexpired costs are plant, equipment, building, inventory, prepaid rent and insurance. When these deferred costs (assets) are used up or give up their usefulness, they are written off or expensed and to that extent they become expenses and appear on the income statement and deducted from revenues.

Expired costs are those costs which have been used in generating revenue and benefits have been received immediately. They are not capitalised but deducted from revenues to calculate net income.

Expenses

Expenses are expired costs. When a cost or expenditure is incurred and totally used up in generation of revenue, the total expenditure will become expense and shown in the income statement. Examples of expired costs are cost of goods sold expense, selling and administrative expense. Expenses need not necessarily have to be paid in cash immediately, even a promise to pay could be made for the benefits obtained. The manufacturing costs are capitalised in the form of finished goods inventory, and when a sale is made, they expire (becoming expenses). The cost of unsold inventory which was an asset earlier now becomes expenses (cost of goods sold) as it has contributed to the generation of revenue.

Types of Costs

There are many objectives of cost classifications, depending on the requirements of management. However, the following cost objectives are considered very useful and significant in classifying costs:

(*i*) Determining product costs for stock valuation and profit measurement

(*ii*) Planning

(*iii*) Decision Making and

(*iv*) Control

1. Traditional Classification of Costs:

   (*i*) Direct material

   (*ii*) Direct labour

   (*iii*) Direct expenses

   (*iv*) Factory overheads and

   (*v*) Selling and distribution and administrative overheads.

The above cost classification is also used for the purpose of stock valuation and profit measurement.

2. Cost Behaviour (In Relation to Changes in Output, Activity or Volume):

   (*i*) Fixed cost

   (*ii*) Variable cost and

   (*iii*) Mixed cost (semi-variable and semi-fixed cost)

3. Degree of Traceability to the product:

   (*i*) Direct cost and

   (*ii*) Indirect cost

4. Degree of Association with the product:

   (*i*) Product Cost and

   (*ii*) Period Cost

This cost classification is also used for the purpose of stock valuation and profit measurement.

5. Functional Classification of Costs:

   (*i*) Manufacturing Cost

   (*ii*) Selling and Distribution Cost and

   (*iii*) Administrative Cost

6. Relationship with the Accounting Period:

   (*i*) Capital Cost and

   (*ii*) Revenue Cost

7. Costs for Decision making and Planning:

   (*i*) Opportunity Cost

   (*ii*) Sunk Cost

   (*iii*) Relevant Cost

   (*iv*) Differential Cost

   (*v*) Imputed Cost

   (*vi*) Out-of-pocket Cost

   (*vii*) Fixed, Variable and Mixed Cost

   (*viii*) Direct Cost and Indirect Cost

   (*ix*) Shut down Cost

8. Costs for Control:
   (*i*) Controllable and Uncontrollable Cost
   (*ii*) Standard Cost and
   (*iii*) Fixed, Variable and Mixed Cost
9. Other Costs:
   (*i*) Joint Cost and
   (*ii*) Common Cost

Traditional Classification of Costs

The term 'traditional classification' refers to the basic physical characteristics of the cost. The natural process of classifying costs means that all costs of a product should be grouped. In a manufacturing concern, the total cost of a product includes the following four elements:

Direct material:

Direct materials refers to the cost of materials which become a major part of the finished product. They are the raw mateirals that become an integral part of the finished product and are conveniently and economically traceable to specific units of output. The following group of materials fall within this definition:

(*a*) All materials specially purchased for a particular job, order, process or product.

(*b*) All material (including primary materials and raw materials) acquired and subsequently requisitioned from the stores for production.

(*c*) Components or parts purchased or produced and requisitioned from the storeroom.

(*d*) Material passing from one process to another process and

(*e*) Primary packing materials, e.g. wrappings, cardboard boxes etc.

Items such as import duties, dock charges, transport cost of materials, storing of materials, cost of purchasing and receiving materials are properly added to their invoiced price and thus the materials are charged out at this increased cost.

Direct Labour: Direct labour is defined as the labour of those workers who are engaged in the production process. It is the labour costs for specific work performed on products that is conveniently and economically traceable to end products. Direct labour is expended directly upon the materials comprising the finished product.

Direct expenses: These include any expenditure other than direct material and direct labour directly incurred on a specific cost unit (product or job). Such special necessary expenses can be identified with cost units and are charged directly to the product as part of the prime cost. These expenses are sometimes known as chargeable expenses. Examples of direct expenses are:

(*i*) Cost of hiring special machinery or plant.

(*ii*) Cost of special moulds, designs and patterns.

(*iii*) Experimental costs and expenditure on model and pilot schemes.

(*iv*) Fees paid to architects, surveyors and other consultants.

(*v*) Cost of transport and conveyance to the site of job or operations.

(*vi*) Inward carriage and freight charges on special materials.

(*vii*) Cost of patents and royalties.

(*viii*) Cost of defective work, e.g. where several trials are necessary before an appropriate one is obtained. The cost of such trials is taken as direct expense.

(*ix*) Licence fees and

(*x*) Hire charges for plants and equipments for a specific product or job.

(*xi*) Components and parts processed for a special job and

(*xii*) Insurance charges on special materials chargeable to a job.

The total of the above three elements of costs (*i*) direct materials, (*ii*) direct labour and (*iii*) direct expenses are prime cost.

Factory overheads: Factory overheads also called manufacturing expenses or factory burden, may be defined as the cost of indirect materials, indirect labour and indirect expenses. The term 'indirect materials' refers to materials that are needed for the completion of the product but whose consumption with regard to the product is either so small or so complex that it would not be appropriate to treat it as a direct materials item. They are production supplies and other materials that cannot conveniently or economically be charged to a specific unit of output. Examples of such items are lubricants, cotton waste, handtools, works and stationery.

The term 'indirect labour' may be defined as that labour which does not affect the construction or the composition of the finished products. In other words, it is the labour cost of production-related activities that can be associated with or conveniently and economically traced to end products. Some examples of indirect labour are: foremen, shop clerks, general helpers, cleaners, material handlers, plant guards and employees engaged in maintenance work or other service work.

The term 'indirect expenses' covers all indirect expenditure incurred by the manufacturing enterprise from the time production has started to its completion and transfer to the finished goods store. Any expenses not classified as direct expenses are known as indirect expenses. Expenses of this type include items such as heat, light maintenance, factory manager's salary etc. Because these expenses cannot be assigned (allocated) directly, they are recorded in total and then apportioned to the various activities.

The total of (*i*) prime cost and (*ii*) factory overhead is known as 'Factory Cost.' Direct labour and factory overheads together are known as conversion costs because they are the costs of converting raw materials into finished products.

Selling and Distribution and Administrative Overheads: Selling and distribution overheads usually begin when the factory costs end. Such expenses are generally incurred when the product is in saleable condition. It covers the cost of making sales and delivering/dispatching products. These costs include advertising, salesmen salaries and commissions, packing, storage, transportation and sales administrative costs.

Administrative overhead includes costs of planning and controlling the general policies and operations of a business enterprise. Usually, all costs which cannot be charged either to the production or sales division are considered as administrative costs. Typical of such items are fees of the board of directors, the Chairman's salary, the rent for general offices and costs of the general accounting department. Sometimes, some of such expenses as manager's salary are often allocated to manufacturing and included in factory overheads.

The sum of (*i*) Prime Cost, (*ii*) Factory Overhead and (*iii*) Selling and Distribution and Administrative Overhead is the Total Cost i.e., the cost 'to make and sell.'

Figure 4.1 presents the traditional classification of costs as discussed above.

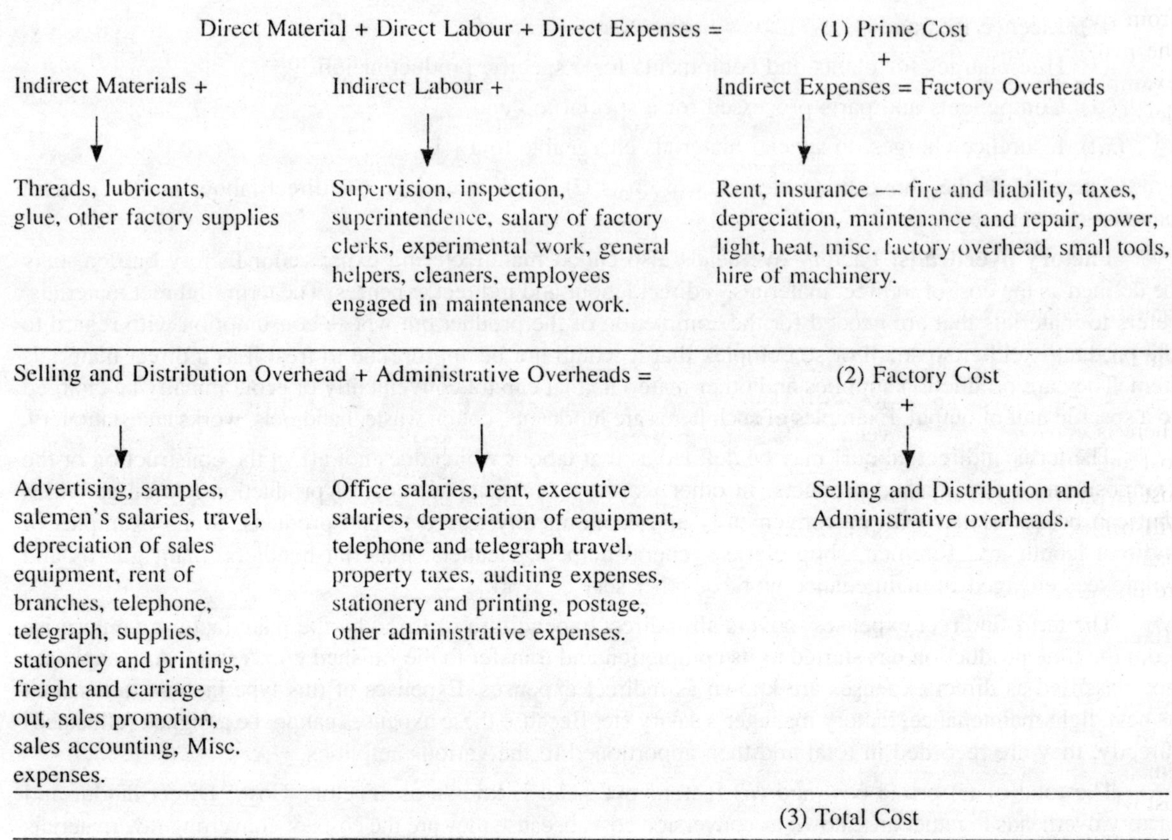

Fig. 4.1 Traditional Classification of Costs in a Manufacturing Concern

Cost Behaviour (In Relation to Changes In Output or Activity or Volume)

Costs can be classified into (i) fixed, (ii) variable and (iii) mixed costs, in terms of their variability or changes in cost behaviour in relation to changes in output, in activity or volume.

Fixed Cost

Fixed cost is a cost which does not change in total for a given time period despite wide fluctuations in output or volume of activity. This includes expenses which must be incurred irrespective of the changes in use of direct materials and in production. Fixed costs enable a business firm to do a business, but they are not purely incurred for manufacturing. Examples of fixed costs are rent, property taxes, supervising salaries, deprecation on office facilities, advertising, insurance etc.

Fixed costs can be classified in the following categories for the purpose of analysis:

1. Committed costs: Such costs are primarily incurred to maintain the company's facilities and physical existence and over which management has little or no discretion. They cannot be easily or quickly eliminated. Plant and equipment depreciation, taxes, insurance premium rate and rent charges are examples of committed costs.

2. Managed Costs: Managed costs are related to current operations which must continue to be paid to ensure the continued operating existence of the company, e.g. management and staff salaries.

3. Discretionary Costs: They are also known as programmed costs. Discretionary costs are not related to current operations or activities and are subject to management discretion and control. These costs result from special policy decisions, management programmes, new researches etc. Such costs can be avoided at the management's discretion in a relatively short period of time as compared to committed costs. Some examples of such costs are research and development costs, marketing programmes and new system development costs.

4. Step Costs: A step cost is constant for a given amount of output and then increases in a fixed amount at a higher output level. For example, in a manufacturing company, one supervisor is required at a salary of Rs. 10,000 p.m. for every 50 workers. So long as 50 workers or less than that are woking, the supervision costs will be Rs. 10,000 p.m. But as soon as the 51st worker is employed the cost of supervision increases by Rs. 10,000 p.m. to Rs. 20,000. The cost of supervision remains fixed at Rs. 20,000 if not more than 100 workers are working. But it will go up if more than 100 workers have been employed.

Variable Cost

Variable costs are those costs that vary in total amount directly and proportionately with the output. There is constant ratio between the change in the cost and change in the level of output. Direct materials cost and direct labour cost are the costs which are generally variable costs. For example, if direct material cost is Rs. 100 per unit, then for producing each additional unit, a direct material cost of Rs. 100 per unit will be incurred. That is, the total direct material cost increases in direct proportion to increase in units manufactured. However, it should be noted that it is only the total variable costs that change as more units are produced; and the per unit variable cost remains constant.

Mixed Costs

Mixed costs are costs made up of fixed and variable elements. They are a combination of semi-variable costs and semi-fixed costs. Because of the variable component, they fluctuate with volume; because of the fixed component, they do not change in direct proportion to output. Semi-fixed costs are those costs which remain constant upto a certain level of output after which they become variable. Semi-variable cost is the cost which is basically variable but whose slope may change abruptly when a certain output level is reached.

DEGREE OF TRACEABILITY TO THE PRODUCT

Cost is divided into direct and indirect cost in terms of degree of traceability to the product.

Direct Cost

An important problem in cost accounting is to determine the costs that are clearly identifiable and traceable to a costing object, such as units of product, company segments or some other specific activity. Costs which are easily traceable or identifiable with a product are called *direct costs*. If output units are the objects of costing, then direct costs represent costs and resources that can be traced to or identified with the finished product. Direct materials, direct labour and direct expenses are examples of direct costs. The term 'direct' indicates that the related direct material, direct labour and direct expenses used/incurred in producing a product are easily traceable to and identifiable with that product.

Indirect Cost

Indirect costs are those costs which cannot be identified with or traced to a single product because they are common to several products. The examples of indirect costs are indirect materials (lubricants and scrap material), salary of factory supervisors (indirect labour), rent, rates and depreciation (indirect expenses) Indirect costs are often referred to as *overheads*. Overhead costs are indirect costs with respect to a specific product since they are incurred for all products manufactured in a company.

Costs also may be direct or indirect with respect to particular company segments or divisions. That is, some costs which are indirect for a product, may be traced to a segment or department and thus, will be direct costs for that department. A segment may mean any one of a number of things, viz. department, division, specific activity, sales territory and the like. For example, the salary of the plant manager of Plant A is a direct cost of Plant A. But if multiple products are produced in plant A, the manager's salary is indirect to the specific products. Thus, what is a direct cost for one purpose may be an indirect cost for another purpose.

ASSOCIATION WITH THE PRODUCT

Cost is classified into product costs and period costs in terms of association with the product.

Product Cost

Product costs are those costs which are identified with the product and included in stock valuation. In other words, the costs that are included in the cost of manufacturing a product are called *product costs*. In a manufacturing concern, it is composed of four elements: (*i*) direct materials, (*ii*) direct labour (*iii*) direct expenses and (*iv*) manufacturing overheads. That is, product cost is a full factory cost. Prior to sale, product costs are deferred as inventories and until the goods are sold, are shown on the balance sheet as assets. As finished inventory goods are sold, product costs are transferred from the inventory accounts to the cost of goods sold account, thus becoming part of the period costs at the time revenue is realised.

Period Costs

Period costs are those costs which are not included in stock-valuation and are treated as expenses during the period in which they are incurred. They are not carried forward as a part of value of stock to the next accounting period. In a manufacturing organisation, period costs include many selling and administrative costs needed to keep the business operating. These costs are necessary to generate revenues but they cannot be directly associated with the units of product. Rather they can be assigned with periods of time in which they are consumed (expired). They are treated as expenses in the same period in which the costs are incurred.

Difference of opinion exists regarding whether certain costs should be considered as product or period costs. It is generally accepted that non-manufacturing costs such as selling and administrative costs should not be included in stock valuation and be treated as period costs. The reasons for such treatment are as follows:

(*i*) It is difficult to select equitable bases to apportion these costs to products. On the other hand, products costs can be assigned to specific products through objective and direct measurements and some by allocation.

(*ii*) The majority of these expenses are fixed regardless of the change in production or activity.

(*iii*) It is difficult, if not impossible, to determine the relationship between the incurrence of these costs and the production of individual units of output.

(*iv*) It is difficult to get evidence as to any future benefits that would be obtained from these expenses at the end of the accounting period. Such is the case with clerical salaries, used postage, office supplies, rent and the like. Even if it is argued that there will be future benefits, it is difficult to make accurate measurements of such benefits. Therefore objectivity and conservatism demand that such costs be treated as period costs and expensed. For example, costs like advertising, sales promotion and consulting fees may be expected to provide future benefits, but they are usually expensed when incurred.

Effect of Product Costs and Period Costs

The net income of a business enterprise is influenced by the amount of product costs and period costs. Therefore, the manner in which some costs are divided as product or period will surely have a bearing on the reported net income of a business firm. Product costs, because of their association with the actual production process, are added to the cost of product and period costs are treated only as expenses in the period in which they have occurred. Product costs, therefore, in the first instance, influence the value of inventory as such costs by nature should be included in the cost of product. Product costs affect net income in the period in which products representing the product costs have been sold. Apparently this may be a subsequent accounting period and not necessarily the period in which the product has been manufactured and product costs have been incurred. In other words, products costs do not reach the income statement and will not influence net income of a business enterprise until the product is sold. This event of influencing net income may take place in the current accounting period or subsequent accounting period. However, period costs appear directly on the income statement in the month or the period in which they expire.

FUNCTIONAL CLASSIFICATION OF COSTS

Functional classification of costs refers to how the cost was used (manufacturing, administration or selling). A functional classification implies that the business performs many functions for which costs are incurred. In measuring net income, expenses are usually classified by function and grouped under the headings of manufacturing, selling and administrative costs. Manufacturing costs are all production costs incurred to manufacturing the products and to bring them to a saleable condition, including direct materials, direct labour and indirect manufacturing (or factory overhead) costs. Selling and administrative charges may be treated as expenses when incurred or charged to prepaid expense accounts such as prepaid insurance. Functional classification is also important because it provides an opportunity to the management to evaluate the efficiency of departments performing different functions in the organisations. In cost accounts, there is a need for both traditional and function classification of costs to serve the interests of management in planning, control and decision-making.

RELATIONSHIP WITH ACCOUNTING PERIOD

Capital Cost and Revenue Cost

Costs can also be divided into two broad classes on the basis of the accounting period to which they relate: (*i*) capital expenditure and (*ii*) revenue expenditure. A capital expenditure provides benefits to future periods and is classified as an asset; a revenue expenditure is assumed to benefit the current period and is classified as an expense. A capital expenditure will flow into the cost stream as an expense when the asset is used up or written off.

The distinction between capital and revenue expenditures is vital to the proper matching of costs and revenue and to the accurate measurement of periodic net income.

Although the management aims at classifying costs into capital and revenue as correctly as possible, it is not possible to have a precise and accurate division under all circumstances. The ease and accuracy with which costs may be divided are the major considerations in classifying costs as capital or revenue. The amount of expenditure often determines whether the cost should be capital or revenue. Whatever classification is decided upon, it can and does affect the computed unit cost and reported net income of an accounting period.

COSTS FOR DECISION-MAKING AND PLANNING

Opportunity Cost

Opportunity cost is the cost of opportunity lost. An opportunity cost is the benefit given up or scarified when one alternative is chosen over another. Opportunity cost is the income foregone by selecting another alternative. It is generally thought of as the value of the best alternative not taken.

Opportunity costs are often market values. Alternatively, they are measured by the profit that would have been earned had the resources been used for the other purpose. For example, choosing to attend college instead of working has an opportunity cost equal to the salary foregone. Further, assume that a manufacturer can sell a semi-finished product to a customer for Rs. 50,000. He decides, however, to keep it and finish it. The opportunity cost of the semi-finished product is Rs. 50,000 because this is the amount of economic resources foregone by the manufacturer to complete the product. Similarly, capital which is invested in plant and inventories cannot now be invested in shares and debentures that will earn interest and dividends, the loss of interest and dividend that would be earned is the opportunity cost. Other examples of opportunity cost are when the owner of a business foregoes the opportunity to employ himself elsewhere; or a machine used to make product. A is said to have an opportunity cost if the machine can be sold or if it can also make product B. Similarly, suppose a person has three job offers – one for Rs. 40,000 p.m., another Rs. 35,000 p.m. and a third for Rs. 28,000 p.m. By selecting the best offer of Rs. 40,000, the opportunity cost will be Rs. 35,000, the next best alternative Rs. 35,000 was given up to get Rs. 40,000. The general rule is that the opportunity cost should not exceed the value of option selected.

Opportunity costs are important in decision-making and evaluating alternatives. Decision-making is selecting the best alternative which is facilitated by the help of opportunity costs. But opportunity costs are not recorded in an accounting system as they are not based on past payments or commitments to pay in future. Such costs do not require cash outlays and are only imputed costs.

Sunk Cost

A sunk cost is the cost that has already been incurred. It is a past or commited cost, cost gone forever. Sunk costs (past costs) cannot be changed once they have been incurred and cannot be avoided by any decision that is made in the future. Any asset obtained from the incurred cost can be used or sold, but its value is its present or future value – not the cost paid. Thus, any historical cost is a sunk cost. Examples of sunk costs are book values of existing assets such as plant and equipment, inventory, investment in securities etc. For example, if a plant was purchased five years ago for Rs. 5,00,000 with the expected life of 10 years and nil scrap value, then the written down value will be Rs. 2,50,000 if the straight line method of depreciation has been used. This written down value (Rs. 2,50,000) will have to be written off, no matter what alternative future action is chosen. For instance, if the plant is to be used in the future, Rs. 2,50,000 will be written off and if the plant is decided to be scrapped, again Rs. 2,50,000 will be written off. This historical cost cannot be changed by any future decision and it therefore becomes sunk cost.

Relevant Cost

Relevant costs are those future costs which differ between alternatives. Relevant costs may also be defined as the costs which are affected and changed by a decision. If a cost increases, decreases, appears or disappears as different alternatives are compared, it is a relevant cost. On the contrary, irrelevant costs are those costs which remain the same and are not affected by the decision whatever alternative is chosen. Irrelevant costs do not mean that such costs are forgotten or that such costs need not be evaluated. It simply means that irrelevant cost is not one of the factors that will quantitatively affect the decision. Relevant costs have the following two features:

(*i*) Relevant costs are only future costs i.e., those costs which are expected to be incurred in future. They are, therefore, not historic (sunk) costs which have already been incurred and cannot be changed by a decision.

(*ii*) They are only incremental (additional) or avoidable costs. Incremental costs refer to an increase in cost between two alternatives. Avoidable costs are those which are not incurred from one alternative to another.

To take an example, assume that a business firm purchased a plant for Rs. 1,00,000 and has now a book value of Rs. 10,000. The plant has become obsolete and cannot be sold in its present condition. However, the plant can be sold for Rs. 15,000 if some modification is done on it which will cost Rs. 6,000.

In this example, Rs. 6,000 (modification cost) and Rs. 15,000 (sales value) both are relevant as they reflect future incremental costs and future revenues respectively. The firm will have incremental benefit of Rs. 9,000 (Rs. 15,000 – Rs. 6,000) on sale of the plant.

Rs. 1,00,000 has already been incurred and being a sunk cost, it is not relevant to the decision i.e. whether modification should be done. Similarly, the book value of Rs. 10,000 which has to be written off whatever alternative future action is chosen, is also not relevant because it cannot be changed by any future decision.

Differential Cost

Decision-making is basically a selection process. Different alternatives are evaluated and the most profitable alternative is chosen. Selection criteria may be 'increased profits' or 'the least costly alternative.' Differential cost is the difference in total costs between any two alternatives. This cost is equal to the additional variable expenses incurred in respect of the additional output, plus the increase in fixed costs, if any. This means that differential cost is only the difference in the amount of the two costs. This cost may be calculated by taking the total cost of production without the additional contemplated output and comparing it with the total costs incurred if the extra output is undertaken.

Differential costs are also known as incremental costs, although technically an incremental cost should refer only to an increase in cost from one alternative to another; decrease in cost should be referred to as decremental cost. Differential cost is a broader term, encompassing both cost increase (incremental costs) and cost decrease (decremental costs) between alternatives.

Imputed cost

Imputed costs are costs not actually incurred in some transaction but which are relevant to the decision as they pertain to a particular situation. These costs do not enter into traditional accounting systems. But they being related with economic reality, help in making better decisions. Interest on internally generated funds, rental value of company-owned property and salaries of owners of a single proprietorship or partnership are some examples of imputed costs. Costs paid or incurred are not imputed costs. For example, if Rs. 50,000 is paid for purchase of raw materials, it is an outlay cost but not an imputed cost, because it would enter into ordinary accounting systems. By itself, Rs. 50,000 measures the monetary impact of this particular event. When a company uses internally generated funds, no actual interest payment is required. But if the internally generated funds are invested in some projects, interest would have been earned. The revenue foregone (loss of interest) represents an opportunity cost, and thus imputed costs are opportunity costs. Similarly, the owner or manager should deduct from the profits of the business an amount equivalent to the salary the owner would have earned by working in some other profession and the interest which the owner's capital would have earned in an alternative business.

Out-of-Pocket Cost

While imputed costs do not involve cash outlays, out-of-pocket costs signify the cash cost associated with an activity. Non-cash costs such as depreciation are not included in out-of-pocket costs. This cost concept is significant for the management in deciding whether or not a particular project will atleast return the cash expenditure associated with the project selected by the management. Similarly, acceptance of a special order for production may necessitate the consideration of out-of-pocket costs that need not be incurred if the special order proposal is not accepted. Depreciation on plant and equipment is not relevant in decision-making because no cash goes outside the business.

Fixed, Variable and Mixed Costs

Fixed, variable and mixed costs have been explained in the preceding sections.

Direct Cost and Indirect Cost

Direct cost and indirect cost have been explained in the preceding sections.

Shut Down Cost

Shut Down costs are those costs which have to be incurred under all situations in the case of stopping manufacture of a product or closing down a department or a division. These costs are always fixed costs. If the manufacture of a product is stopped, variable costs like direct materials, direct labour, direct expenses and variable factory overheads will not be incurred. However, a part of fixed costs (if not total fixed costs) associated with the product will be incurred such as rent, watchman's salary, property taxes etc. Such fixed costs are unavoidable. Some fixed costs associated with the product become avoidable and need not be incurred in case production is stopped such as supervisor's salary, factory manager's salary, lighting etc. Shut down costs, thus, refer to minimum fixed costs which are incurred in the event of closure of a department or division.

COSTS FOR CONTROL

Controllable and Uncontrollable Cost

The concept of controllable cost is very important in cost accounting and contributes effectively to the achievement of the objectives of cost control and responsibility accounting. The ICMA (UK) defines controllable cost as "a cost which can be influenced by the action of a specified member of an undertaking" and non-controllable cost as "a cost which cannot be influenced by the action of a specified member of an undertaking." Basically, a controllable cost is the cost over which a manager has direct and complete decision authority, i.e. controllable costs can be controlled or reduced by a manager at a given organisational level. Some examples of controllable costs are indirect labour, lubricants, cutting tools and power costs incurred in the machine department. The manager of a production department controls indirect labour and factory supplies used in the department. However, such a manager cannot control his own salary or the salary of other managers working in the factory. The salary of such managers are apportioned (charged) to all departments on some equitable basis.

Controllable costs do not imply that they are 100% controllable. Some costs are only partly controllable by a responsibility centre manager. Maintenance cost is such an example which can be influenced (controlled), on the one hand, by the production manager through minimising misuse of plant and machinery, and on the other hand, by the maintenance manager by proving skilled repairmen. Such joint controllable costs are found in business firms, both manufacturing and non-manufacturing. For example, the cost of raw materials is controlled by the production managers as well as purchase managers. The production manager controls at the quantity level, and the purchase manager at the price level. Such costs are reported to both of them, but one responsible manager should be held accountable for those costs which he can control.

The term 'controllable cost' should not be confused with the terms *variable cost* and *direct cost*. These terms are not synonymous. Variable costs vary with the output but are not necessarily controllable. For example, factory supplies used for servicing plant and equipment may vary with the output in the production department, but the production manager cannot control them.

Similarly, controllable costs and direct costs are not necessarily the same. A cost may be a direct cost of a given department but may not be controlled by the department supervisor. For example, the salary of a departmental supervisor, which is a direct cost of the department, is controlled at a higher level of management rather than by the supervisor.

Further, it should not be assumed that all fixed costs are uncontrollable. While a fixed cost, such as property insurance may be uncontrollable at certain managerial levels, it is nevertheless subject to control by a manager who has the authority to obtain insurance coverage. Controllable and uncontrollable costs, infact, should not be viewed as variable costs or fixed costs and as direct costs or indirect costs as well.

Standard Costs

Standard costs are those costs which are planned or predetermined cost estimates for a unit of output in order to provide a basis for comparison with actual costs. Standard costs are used to prepare budgets. Standard cost is a unit concept and indicates standard cost per unit of output, per labour hour etc. On the contrary, the term *budgeted cost* is a total concept and indicates total budgeted cost of an item, activity level or output level — such as budgeted cost of material is Rs. 8,00,000 if 8000 units are manufactured.

Fixed, Variable and Mixed Cost

Fixed, variable and mixed costs have been discussed earlier in the chapter.

OTHER COSTS

Joint Cost

Joint costs arise where the processing of a single raw material or production resources results in two or more different products simultaneously. Sometimes, joint costs and common costs are used having identical meaning. However, both the terms have different meanings. Joint costs relate to a situation in which the factors of production by their basic nature result in two or more products. The jointness results from there being more than one product, and these multi-products are the result of the method of production or the nature of raw material and not of a decision by the management to produce both. In other words, joint costs relate to two or more products produced from a common production process or element — material, labour or overhead or any combination thereof, or so locked together that one cannot be produced without producing the other(s).

Thus, joint cost is the cost of two or more products that are produced simultaneously by a single process and are not identifiable as individual types of products until a certain stage of production known as the *split-off* point (point of separation) is reached. For example, kerosene, fuel oil, gasolene and other oil products are derived from crude oil. These costs are total costs incurred upto the point of separation. Sometimes it is found that one product is of major importance and the others are of minor importance. In such situations products of lesser importance are known as *by-products.*

Joint costs can be apportioned to different products only by means of some suitable bases of apportionment. Total costs of production of multiple products combine both joint costs and equitable individual product costs. The latter are easily identified and traced to the individual products, and no problem of apportionment is involved in such costs.

Common Cost

Common costs are those costs which are incurred for more than one product, job, territory or any other specific costing object. These costs are not easily identifiable with individual products, and therefore, are generally apportioned. The National Association of Accountants (USA) defines the term 'common cost' as "the cost of services employed in the creation of two or more outputs which is not allocatable to those outputs on a clearly justified basis." According to this definition, common costs are not allocatable. However, in practice, cost accountants allocate these costs. The important distinguishing characteristic of a common costs is that there is no clearly definable association between the incurrence of the cost and the cost objectives that benefit from the use of these facilities.

Common costs are not only common to products, but they may be common to processes, functions, responsibilities, customers, sales territories, periods of time and similar costing units. For example, the salary of a manager of the production department which is manufacturing three products is an example of common cost with respect to the products. But his salary is direct cost to the production department. Similarly, the rent of the factory is common to all departments located in the factory. The basic point is that a particular (common) cost may be direct to one object and common as far as other objects are concerned.

Although both the terms, 'common costs' 'joint costs' are sometimes used interchangeably, they differ from each other. Joint costs emerge when multiple products are manufactured in a common process and when common inputs are used. The multiple products have a definite quantitative relationship to each other and the production of one product influences the output of the other product, though in a lesser proportion. Common costs are not the result of any manufacturing compulsion or the use of any single raw material. Besides common costs can be apportioned to costing objects like products, jobs, departments etc. without much difficulty. But the apportionment of joint costs involves many complexities and difficulties in cost accounting. The incurrence of common costs are influenced by management decisions and on the contrary, joint costs are influenced by common production process and the use of common raw materials.

Example 1

A company manufactures and retails clothing. You are required to group the costs which are listed below and numbered 1 to 20 into the following classification: (Each cost is intended to belong to only one classification).

(*a*) Direct Materials

(*b*) Direct Labour

(*c*) Direct Expenses

(*d*) Indirect Production Overheads

(*e*) Selling and Distribution Costs

(*f*) Research and Development Costs

(*g*) Finance Cost

(*h*) Administration Costs

1. Telephone rental plus metered calls.
2. Wages of security guards for factory.
3. Parcels sent to customers.
4. Wages of operatives in the cutting department.
5. Developing a new product in the laboratory.
6. Wage of fork lift truck drivers who handle raw materials.
7. Wages of storekeepers in materials store.
8. Chief accountant's salary.
9. Cost of painting advertising slogans in delivery vans.
10. Auditor's fee.
11. Cost of advertising on television.
12. Lubricants for sewing machines.
13. Floppy disks for general office computer.
14. Maintenance contract of office photocopying machine.
15. Interest on bank overdraft.
16. Market Research undertaken prior to new product launch.
17. Carriage on purchase of raw materials.
18. Royalty paid on number of units of a particular product produced.
19. Road licenses for delivery vehicles and
20. Amount payable to a company for broadcasting music throughout the factory.

Solution:

Cost Element	*Numbers*
Direct Materials	17
Direct Labour	4
Direct Expenses	18
Finance Cost	15
Research and Development Expenses	5
Selling and Distribution Cost	16, 19, 3, 11, 9
Administration Cost	13, 14, 1, 10, 8
Indirect Production Costs	12, 20, 2, 7, 6

THEORY QUESTIONS

1. Define the term 'Cost.' How is it different from expense.
2. Define the terms 'fixed costs,' 'variable costs,' 'semivariable costs' and give examples of each one.
3. Define and illustrate the following concepts of cost:
   (*a*) Direct and indirect cost
   (*b*) Product and period cost
   (*c*) Controllable and non-controllable cost and
   (*d*) Joint cost and common cost.
4. "Cost may be classified in a variety of ways according to their nature and the information needs of management." Explain and discuss this statement, illustrating with examples the classifications required for different purposes.
5. What is the meaning of the term 'incremental cost.' Does incremental cost mean the same thing as variable cost.
6. Bring out clearly the significance of the following costs for management:
   (*a*) Opportunity cost
   (*b*) Sunk cost
   (*c*) Imputed costs and
   (*d*) Out-of-pocket costs.
7. Why is classification of costs into controllable and uncontrollable heads vital in the institution of responsibility accounting.
8. Which costs are included in product costs.
9. Why are sunk costs not relevant in decision-making.
10. "All controllable costs are direct costs. Not all direct costs are controllable, however." Do you agree. Explain with the help of suitable examples.
11. Distinguish between the variable costs and differential costs and highlight the importance of differential costs in non-routine decisions.
12. What are the differences between controllable cost and a non-controllable cost.
13. Discuss the various costs used in decision-making and explain their characteristics.
14. Distinguish between period costs and product costs. Why is this distinction considered important.
15. (*a*) Distinguish between out of pocket cost and opportunity cost.
   (*b*) Explain and illustrate the distinction between 'direct cost' and 'indirect cost' specially from the point of view of decision-making.

16. Why should the term 'cost' have an objective attached to it to have meaning for a manager.
17. Define an opportunity cost and explain its relevance to decision-making. When would a decision maker look at the opportunity cost of a decision.
18. Explain whether the following statements are true:
    (*a*) All future costs are relevant costs.
    (*b*) All sunk costs are irrelevant.
    (*c*) A cost can be relevant for one decision and irrelevant for another decision.
    (*d*) All relevant costs are present or future amounts and
    (*e*) All irrelevant costs are past costs.
19. Explain how time has an effect upon the controllability of cost.
20. Expenses and costs are often used interchangeably, yet they do not always mean the same thing. Distinguish between the two terms.
21. Identify and describe the three elements that make up manufacturing costs.
22. "All differential costs are variable costs." Comment.
23. Why is the idea of controllability important when accounting data are used for performance evaluation and decision-making.
24. What effect does an increase in output have on:
    (*i*) Unit fixed costs
    (*ii*) Unit variable costs
    (*iii*) Total fixed costs and
    (*iv*) Total variable costs.
25. Explain why knowledge of cost behaviour is useful information for a manager to have.
26. On a per unit basis, fixed costs are variable and variable costs are fixed. Do you agree. Explain your reasoning.

❑❑❑

Chapter 5

MARGINAL (VARIABLE) COSTING

CONCEPT OF MARGINAL COST, MARGINAL COSTING

Marginal cost, in cost accounting, means variable production costs, i.e. the costs which tend to vary in direct proportion to changes in the production level. If an extra unit of output is produced, the costs which could be incurred for producing this extra unit, will only be marginal (variable) costs since fixed costs remain constant.

Marginal costing is a costing technique in which only variable manufacturing costs are considered and used while valuing inventories and determining the cost of goods sold. That is, only variable manufacturing costs are considered product costs and are allocated to products manufactured. These costs include direct materials, direct labour and variable factory overheads. Fixed factory (manufacturing) overheads are not considered product costs and are not used to value inventories and determine the cost of goods sold and are excluded from the cost of product. Fixed manufacturing costs are treated as period costs in marginal costing, i.e. costs which are a function of a time rather than of production. In marginal costing, fixed manufacturing overheads are written off to the profit and loss account in the period in which they are incurred.

ABSORPTION COSTING

Absorption costing, also known as full costing, is a costing technique in which all manufacturing costs, variable and fixed, are considered as costs of production and are used in determining the cost of goods manufactured and inventories. All manufacturing costs are fully absorbed into finished goods.

Difference between Marginal Costing and Absorption Costing

Marginal costing and absorption costing differ from each other in the following respects:

(*i*) *Cost element in product cost:* Marginal costing and absorption costing differ only in the treatment of fixed factory (manufacturing) overheads in the accounting records and financial statements. In both the costing techniques, it is agreed that selling and administrative expenses, whether variable or fixed, are period costs and these costs are not treated as product costs with the result that selling and administrative expenses are not included in the costs of inventories and costs of goods sold. Similarly it is also agreed that variable manufacturing costs are product costs, i.e. costs to be charged to the product. The disagreement between the two is only in regard to the treatment of fixed manufacturing costs.

(*ii*) *Inventory values:* Marginal costing and absorption costing do influence inventory values differently. The value of inventories under marginal costing is relatively at a lower figure as inventories are determined in terms of only variable production costs. In absorption costing, the value of inventories is comparatively at a higher figure because it considers fixed factory overhead also besides the variable production costs.

(*iii*) *Difference in net income:* The treatment of fixed factory overhead brings differences in the net income figures in the two costing techniques. The magnitude of any difference in net income is the function of fixed manufacturing costs per unit and the change in inventory levels.

The question of difference in net income has been further explained in the following pages while discussing income statement under absorption costing and marginal costing.

INCOME STATEMENTS UNDER ABSORPTION COSTING

Under absorption costing, all costs are divided into three categories: manufacturing, selling and administrative costs. In the income statement, all manufacturing costs (variable and fixed) are subtracted from the sales revenue to get a gross margin/gross profit on sales: and selling and administrative expenses (fixed and variable) are deducted from the gross margin to arrive at the net income.

It should be clearly understood that fixed manufacturing overheads are charged to units produced on the basis of per unit fixed manufacturing overhead rate obtained by dividing the standard fixed manufacturing overhead by normal output level as follows:

$$\frac{\text{Standard fixed manufacturing overhead}}{\text{Normal output (Capacity)}}$$

Income Statement (Absorption Costing)

	Amount Rs.
Sales	....
Less: Manufacturing costs:	
(1) Variable production costs:	
Direct material cost	....
Direct labour cost	....
Variable manufacturing overheads	....
(2) Fixed factory (manufacturing) overheads	....
Cost of goods manufactured	....
Add: Beginning inventory	....
Cost of goods available for sale	....
Less: Closing inventory	....
Cost of goods sold	....
Over-or under-applied factory (manufacturing) Overhead	....
(Over-absorption to be deducted and under-absorption to be added)	....
Cost of goods sold at actual	....
Gross profit on sales	....
Less: Fixed selling and administrative expenses	....
Variable selling and administrative expenses	....
Net Income	....

Fig. 5.1: Income Statement Proforma (Absorption Costing)

If production is above or below the normal or standard output, adjustments are made for volume (capacity) variances. If the volume (capacity) variance is favourable, i.e. over-absorption (actual production being higher than normal capacity production), the amount of over-absorption is deducted from the total cost of goods manufactured and sold. If the volume (capacity) variance is unfavourable, i.e. under-absorption (actual production being lesser than normal capacity production), the amount of under-absorption is added to the cost of goods manufactured and sold. A proforma of the income statement prepared under absorption costing is given in Fig. 5.1.

INCOME STATEMENT UNDER MARGINAL COSTING

Under marginal costing, only variable costs of production (direct material, direct labour and variable manufacturing) are subtracted from sales revenue to determine a balance which is known by different names, such as marginal contribution, marginal income (profit), marginal revenue, marginal balance, profit pick-up etc. All fixed costs, variable selling and distribution and administrative costs are deducted from this balance to arrive at the net income. Since fixed manufacturing costs are not charged to products under marginal costing, there can be no volume (capacity) variance. Marginal contribution and marginal income under marginal costing is greater than the gross profit/gross margin under absorption costing. Fig. 5.2 depicts a Proforma of income statement prepared under marginal costing.

Income Statement (Marginal Costing)

	Amount (Rs.)
Sales	....
Less: Variable production costs:	
Direct material costs	....
Direct labour cost	....
Variable manufacturing (factory) overheads	....
Cost of goods manufactured	....
Add: Beginning inventory	....
Cost of goods available for sale	....
Less: Closing inventory	....
Cost of goods sold	....
Marginal contribution	....
Less: Fixed manufacturing overheads	....
Variable selling and administrative expenses	....
Fixed selling and administrative expenses	....
Net Income	....

Fig. 5.2: Income Statement Proforma (Marginal Costing)

Under marginal costing, fixed manufacturing overheads are excluded and therefore inventory values are lower than inventory value computed under absorption costing. Income may be higher or lower, depending upon whether inventories are built up or liquidated. That is the income statement under absorption costing may reflect higher profit if the production is more than the normal capacity production and also lower sales has been made. This happens because above normal capacity production has over-absorbed its actual fixed manufacturing overhead.

Absorption full costing and marginal costing influence differently gross profit, net profit and inventory values of different months/periods. The following data and income statement prepared under both costing techniques explain this situation.

Data:

Normal capacity of 20,000 units per month

Variable costs (direct materials, direct labour, variable factory overhead) per unit at Rs. 6.

Fixed factory overhead of Rs. 25,000 per month or Rs. 1.25 per unit at normal capacity.

Fixed selling and administrative expenses are Rs. 5,000 p.m.

Variable selling and administrative expenses are Re. 1.00 per unit sold.

Sales prices per unit is Rs. 10.

Actual production, sales and inventories in units are:

	First month	*Second month*	*Third month*	*Fourth month*
Unit in beginning inventory	—	—	3,000	1,000
Units produced	17,500	21,000	19,000	20,000
Units sold	17,500	18,000	21,000	16,500
Units in closing inventory	—	3,000	1,000	4,500

Solution

Income Statement (Absorption Costing)

(Rs.)

	First month	*Second month*	*Third month*	*Fourth month*
Sales Rs.	1,75,000	1,80,000	2,10,000	1,65,000
Variable cost per unit Rs. 6	1,05,000	1,26,000	1,14,000	1,20,000
Fixed factory overhead @ Rs. 1.25	21,875	26,250	23,750	25,000
Cost of goods manufactured	1,26,875	1,52,250	1,37,750	1,45,000
Add: Beginning inventory	—	—	21,750	7,250
Cost of goods available for sales	1,26,875	1,52,520	1,59,500	1,52,250
Less: Ending inventory	—	21,750	7,250	32,625
Cost of goods sold	1,26,875	1,30,500	1,52,250	1,19,625
Over-or under-applied factory overhead	3,125	(1,250)	1,250	
Cost of goods sold at actual	1,30,000	1,29,250	1,53,500	1,19,625
Gross profit on sales	45,000	50,750	56,500	45,375
Selling and administrative Expenses (fixed and variable)	22,500	23,000	26,000	21,500
Net income for the month	22,500	27,750	30,500	23,875

Note: In the absorption costing income statement, fixed factory expenses are included in the unit cost and also in the inventory values.

(*i*) Ending inventory: Second month $\frac{3,000}{21,000} \times$ Rs. 1,52,250 = Rs. 21,750

Third month $\frac{1,000}{22,000} \times$ Rs. 1,50,500 = Rs. 7,250

Fourth month $\frac{4,500}{21,000} \times$ Rs. 1,52,250 = Rs. 32,625 (*ii*) In first month, Rs. 3,125 is under-absorbed factory overhead due to production less than normal capacity and should be added to the cost of goods sold.

(*iii*) In the second month, Rs. 1,250 is over-absorbed due to higher production and has therefore been subtracted.

(*iv*) In the third month, Rs. 1,250 is under-absorbed and has been added back to cost of goods sold.

(*v*) In the fourth month, production is at normal capacity and there is no under-or over-absorption.

Income Statement (Marginal Costing)

(*Rs.*)

	First Month	*Second Month*	*Third Month*	*Fourth Month*
Sales (Rs.)	1,75,000	1,80,000	2,10,000	1,65,000
Variable production cost: Variable manufacturing Costs Rs. 6 per unit	1,05,000	1,26,000	1,14,000	1,20,000
Cost of goods manufactured	1,05,000	1,26,000	1,14,000	1,20,000
Add: Beginning inventory	—	—	18,000	6,000
Cost of goods available for sale	1,05,000	1,26,000	1,32,000	1,26,000
Less: Closing inventory	—	18,000	6,000	27,000
Cost of goods sold	1,05,000	1,08,000	1,26,000	99,000
Contribution	70,000	72,000	84,000	66,000
Less: Fixed factory overhead	25,000	25,000	25,000	25,000
Fixed selling and Administrative expenses	5,000	5,000	5,000	5,000
Variable selling and Administrative expenses	17,500	18,000	21,000	16,500
Total fixed costs and non-manufacturing variable costs	47,500	48,000	51,000	46,500
Net income for the month	22,500	24,000	33,000	19,500

Note: Under marginal costing, fixed factory (manufacturing) overhead costs are not included in the product unit costs and costs of inventories.

(*i*) Valuation of closing inventory

Second month = 3,000 × Rs. 6 = Rs. 18,000

Third month = 1,000 × Rs. 6 = Rs. 6,000

Fourth month = 4,500 × Rs. 6 = Rs. 27,000

(*ii*) The question of under- or over-absorption of factory overheads does not arise under marginal costing.

A comparison of the income statements leads to the following conclusions:

1. Under variable costing, the closing inventory is costed at a smaller figure because only variable costs are charged to the product.
2. Both costing methods report the same amount of profit in periods in which production and sales are equal and there is no inventory change (first month). This is because the amount of fixed factory overhead costs charged to the period was the same in each case. Under marginal costing Rs. 25,000 was deducted from sales as period costs. Under marginal costing, Rs. 25,000 was charged to the sales in two parts: (*a*) Rs. 21,875 as part of the cost of sales (17,500 units × Rs. 1.25) and (*b*) Rs. 3, 125 as unfavourable volume (capacity) variance.
3. When inventory of manufactured goods fluctuates from period to period, net income will differ somewhat under the two methods because absorption costing requires that part of the period costs be included in inventory, whereas marginal costing excludes period costs. Therefore:

(*i*) When production exceeds sales (the inventory is increased), the net income reported under absorption costing is higher than reported under variable costing. This follows because under absorption costing, a portion of the fixed costs budgeted for the period is shifted to the following period in the closing inventories whereas under marginal costing, the total fixed costs are charged against income. This is clear from comparing the net income of the second and fourth month.

(*ii*) When sale exceeds production (the inventories are decreased), marginal costing shows a higher profit because only current period costs are being charged against current revenues, whereas under absorption costing, the period costs previously included in inventory are now being charged against current revenues. This situation is illustrated by the income of the third month.

4. Under marginal costing, profits always move in the same direction as sales volume. They cannot, of course, increase or decrease in direct proportion because unit fixed costs do not remain constant. Profit reported under absorption costing behave irregularly and sometimes in the opposite direction from sales. For example, sales of the fourth month are lower than the sales of the first month, yet the net income reported for the fourth month is higher than the net income for the first month.
5. The above income statements are prepared on the assumption that selling prices remained constant and that there were no changes in either the manufacturing costs or the selling and administrative expenses. Further, it has been assumed that overheads costs are absorbed at predetermined rates based on normal capacity.
6. The aggregate net income (of different months or periods taken together) will be the same under both costing methods provided production and sales, in total, are equal. In the above example, total production are 77,500 units and total sales are 73,000 units. Since production and sales are unequal, the combined net income is not the same.

Reconciliation of Net Income

The differences in the net income between absorption costing and marginal costing are due to: (*i*) amount of fixed factory overhead charged to inventory, (*ii*) over or under-absorbed fixed factory overhead having been deferred in absorption costing. The entire difference in net income can be explained by the amount of fixed factory overhead that is included in both the beginning and closing inventories.

Reconciliation of Differences between Absorption and Marginal Costing Income

	Second month (Rs.)	*Third month (Rs.)*	*Fourth month (Rs.)*
Marginal costing income	24,000	33,000	19,500
Absorption costing income	27,750	30,500	23,875
Difference to be explained	(3,750)	2,500	(4,375)
1. Differences in the value of opening and closing inventories:			
(*a*) Second month:			
Opening	0	—	—
Closing 18,000 – 21,750	(3,750)		
(*b*) Third month:			
Opening 18,000 – 21,750	—	3,750	
Closing 6,000 – 7,250	—	(1,250)	—
(*c*) Fourth month:			
Opening 6,000 – 7,250	—	—	(1,250)
Closing 27,000 – 32,625	—	—	(5,625)
	(3,750)	2,500	(4,375)

Inventory Values

Differences between the net incomes reported under absorption costing and marginal costing are also reflected in inventory values. As stated earlier, inventories under absorption costing absorb a part of the fixed manufacturing costs of a period, whereas inventories under marginal costing include only the variable manufacturing costs. Closing inventories calculated from the data given above would be as follows:

Closing Inventories

	First month	*Second month*	*Third month*	*Fourth month*
Absorption costing @ Rs. 7.25 per unit	—	21,750	7,250	32,625
Marginal costing @ Rs. 6.00 per unit	—	18,000	6,000	27,000

The following summarises the differences between marginal costing and absorption costing with regard to effect on net income:

(*i*) If production = sales; absorption profit = marginal costing profit.

(*ii*) If production > sales; absorption profit > marginal costing profit.

(*iii*) If production < sales; absorption profit < marginal costing profit.

(*iv*) If production fluctuates and sales are constant; absorption profit fluctuates and marginal costing profit is constant and

(*v*) If production is constant and sales fluctuate; both profits vary in the direction of sales.

APPLICATIONS (ADVANTAGES) OF MARGINAL COSTING

Marginal costing has great potentialities for management in different managerial tasks and decision-making processes. Marginal costing is particularly useful to management in (*i*) profit planning, (*ii*) product pricing decisions, (*iii*) cost control, (*iv*) managerial decision-making and (*v*) the impact of fixed costs.

Profit Planning

Profit planning, generally known as budget or plan of operations, may be defined as the planning of future operations to attain a defined profit goal. Under marginal costing, the cost data needed for profit planning and decision-making are readily available from the accounting records and statements. It facilitates the analysis of cost-volume-profit relationships by separating fixed and variable costs on the income statement. Marginal costing helps management in planning and evaluating the profit resulting from a change in volume, in the sales-mix, in make or buy situations, in the selection of the most profitable products, customers, territories and other segments of the entire business.

Product Pricing Decisions

Marginal costing provides more useful information to the management for pricing than absorption costing. It serves as the basis of product pricing in many cases. Under marginal costing, management has the data to determine when it is advisable to accept orders if other than normal conditions exist. In some cases, a sales order can be accepted even if it contributes partly to fixed costs. However, the full cost and not only the variable cost should be the basis of product pricing in the long-run. The full cost is the cost which includes variable manufacturing cost and fixed manufacturing cost incurred in the production process.

Cost Control

Marginal costing provides continuing opportunities to review period costs in relation to the level of sales and net income. Separation of variable and period costs supports the use of standards, budgets and responsibility reporting to aid the management in controlling costs. Marginal costing helps in preparing reports for all departments or responsibility centres based on standard costs, flexible budgets and a division of all costs into their fixed and variable components. All managers can examine and interpret their reports with respect to the cost variances originating in their respective areas of responsibility. Reports prepared on the marginal costing basis and accompanied by additional information become valuable planning and control tools.

Impact of Fixed Costs

Marginal costing evaluates the impact of fixed costs on profits because the total amount of fixed costs for the period appears in the income statement. It is argued that managerial decisions can be easily made if fixed expenses are separated and are not mixed in controlling operating costs.

Managerial Decision Making

The identification and classification of costs as either fixed or variable provide a framework for the accumulation and analysis of costs. This also provides a basis for the study of contemplated changes in production levels or proposed actions concerning new markets, plant expansion or contraction or special promotional activities. The marginal income figure is useful to the management because it can be readily projected to measure increments in net income which accompany increment in sales.

LIMITATIONS OF MARGINAL COSTING

The limitations of marginal costing are listed below:

1. The marginal costing method requires that all costs should be divided into fixed and variable components. It cannot be true under all circumstances. Examples of factors that might affect this assumption include quantity discounts on materials and labour efficiency variances.
2. Complete product cost does not depend only on variable costs. Fixed costs should be considered in determining the product cost and long-range pricing and other long-run policy decisions.
3. Income figures obtained under marginal costing have to be used carefully if the management decides to expand business or drop a product line. Management has to consider other factors also before deciding to drop a product line such as customer goodwill.

COST BEHAVIOUR

Cost behaviour can be defined as the manner in which costs changes due to changes in volume or activity. In relation to cost behaviour analysis, fixed and variable cost classifications are basically found. A proper analysis of cost behaviour patterns is the basis of all profit planning and cost control. The separation of costs into fixed, variable and semi-variable is necessary in order to determine, analyse, control, measure or evaluate the following:

(*i*) Departmental expenses allowed at various levels of production.

(*ii*) Operating efficiency of a department.

(*iii*) Use of variable costing method.

(*iv*) Utilisation of facilities.

(*v*) Break-even point.

(*vi*) Relative profitability of territories, departments and customers.

(*vii*) Company profit position.

(*viii*) Cost-profit-volume analysis.

(*ix*) Marginal or differential cost for various decision-making purposes.

(*x*) Effect of proposed capital expenditures and

(*xi*) Effect of alternative courses of action.

Methods of Determining Cost behaviour

Several methods are used for segregating semi-variable costs into fixed and variable. There are four major techniques that are found in practice and they may be listed as follows:

(*i*) High and low points method

(*ii*) Scattergraph method.

(*iii*) Least squares regression method and

(*iv*) Accounting or analytical approach.

High and Low Points Method

This approach considers the difference in total cost between two different volumes, and divides the incremental cost by the volume. As the words 'high' and 'low' imply, the two levels of volume chosen are the highest and the lowest for the period under review. The result of this division is the estimated variable cost per unit. Then, the average activity level is computed together with the average cost for the periods in the database. The fixed cost is estimated by taking the total average cost and subtracting the variable cost for the average activity level. The variable cost is computed by multiplying the average activity level by the variable cost per unit as determined above.

As a simple illustration, assume that a company incurred the following costs in two periods (high and low) in which 5,000 units and 10,000 units were produced:

	Cost incurred	
	5,000 units	10,000 units
Insurance on factory building	Rs. 30,000	30,000
Indirect material	45,000	70,000

Since insurance remained constant at the two volumes, there is no variable component. Indirect materials contain both fixed and variable components.

Separation is made as follows:

Variable components:		
Indirect material cost of 10,000 units		Rs. 70,000
Indirect material cost of 5,000 units		Rs. 45,000
Cost of production of additional 5,000 units		Rs. 25,000
Variable cost per unit Rs. 25000 ¸ 5,000 units		Rs. 5
Fixed components:	5,000 units	10,000 units
Total indirect material cost	Rs. 45,000	Rs. 70,000
Variable components @ Rs. 5 per unit	25,000	50,000
Fixed costs for period	Rs. 20,000	Rs. 20,000

Scattergraph Method

In this method, various costs are plotted on a vertical line, the y-axis, and measurement figures (activity levels such as direct labours, units of output, percentage of capacity or direct labour cost) are plotted along a horizontal line, the *x*-axis. A straight line is fitted to this scatter of points by visual approximation. The slope of the line is used to estimate the variable costs and the intercept of the line with the vertical axis is considered as the estimated fixed cost.

Least Squares Regression Method

The method of least squares uses the equation for a straight line:

$Y = a + bx$, with a as the fixed element, and b the degree of variability. For many accounting applications, regression provides an accurate estimate of fixed and variable costs.

Accounting or Analytical Approach

This approach to cost behaviour analysis is a close scrutiny of the chart of accounts and a classification of costs into their fixed and variable components according to their basic characteristics determined by the accountant using good judgement, knowledge and experience. This approach is simple and inexpensive but in its simplicity lies its inherent weakness. The results obtained are not accurate and may happen to be mere guesses.

Example 5.1

The following are the maintenance costs incurred in a machine shop for six months with corresponding machine hours:

Month	*Machine hours*	*Maintenance costs (Rs.)*
January	2,000	30,000
February	2,200	32,000
March	1,700	27,000
April	2,400	34,000
May	1,800	28,000
June	1,900	29,000
Total	12,000	1,80,000

Analyse the Maintenance Cost which is semi-variable into fixed and variable element.

Solution:

Computation of Variable Cost and Fixed Cost has been done according to Rang Method.

	Machine hours	*Maintenance costs (Rs.)*
Highest point, April	2,400	34,000
Lowest point, March	1,700	17,000
	700	7,000

$$\text{Variable cost per machine hour} = \frac{\text{Change in maintenance costs}}{\text{Change in hours}}$$

$$= \frac{7,000}{700} = \text{Rs. } 10$$

Total variable cost for 2,400 machine hours will be 2,400 × Rs. 10 = Rs. 24,000

Hence, fixed cost is (Rs. 34,000 – Rs. 24,000) = Rs. 10,000

Analysis of Maintenance Cost into Fixed and Variable Element

	Machine hours	*Maintenance cost (Rs.)*	*Fixed cost (Rs.)*	*Variable cost (Rs.)*
January	2,000	30,000	10,000	20,000
February	2,200	32,000	10,000	22,000
March	1,700	27,000	10,000	17,000
April	2,400	34,000	10,000	24,000
May	1,800	28000	10000	18000
June	1,900	29000	10000	19000

COST-VOLUME PROFIT (CVP) ANALYSIS

Profit of business firms are the result of many factors such as: (*i*) selling prices, (*ii*) volumes of sales (*iii*) unit variable costs (*iv*) combinations in which the various product lines are sold etc. To do an affective job in planning, the management must have analyses which allow reasonably correct predictions of how profits will be affected by a change in any one of these factors. A cost volume profit (CVP) analysis is useful to management in knowing how profit is influenced by sales volume, sales price, variable expenses and fixed expenses.

Broadly, CVP analysis uses the techniques of (*i*) Break-even analysis and (*ii*) Profit-volume (P/V) analysis.

Break-even Analysis

A break-even analysis indicates at what level cost and revenue are in equilibrium. It is a simple and easily understandable method of presenting to the management the effect of changes in volume on profits. Detailed analysis of break-even data will also reveal to the management the effect of alternative decisions which reduce or increase costs and which increase sales volume and income. It is a device which portrays the effect of any type of future planning by evaluating alternative courses of action.

Break-even Point

The break-even point can be defined as the point of sales level at which profits are zero and there is no loss. That is, break-even point is that point at which total costs are equal to total sales revenue. At the break-even point profit being zero, contribution (sales-variable cost) is equal to the fixed cost. If the actual volume of sales is higher than the break-even volume, there will be a profit. Beyond the break-even point, all the marginal contributions represent income.

Assume that a company manufactures and sells a single product as follows:

Selling price per unit = Rs. 20

Variable cost per unit = Rs. 10

Total fixed cost = Rs. 1,00,000

The break-even sales to cover fixed costs will be 10,000 units,

Selling price per unit = Rs. 20

Variable cost per unit = Rs. 10

Contribution = Rs. 10

$$\text{Break-even volume} = \frac{\text{Rs.1,00,000 fixed cost}}{\text{Rs.10 contribution margin}}$$

$$= 10{,}000 \text{ units}$$

If the company can sell more than 10,000 units, it will earn profits because fixed costs remain constant. If less than 10,000 units are sold, a loss will be incurred. The profits will be equal to the number of units sold in excess of 10,000 units multiplied by the unit contribution margin. For example, if 25,000 units are sold, the company will be operating at 15,000 units above its break-even point and will earn a profit of Rs. 1,50,000 (15,000 units × Rs. 10 contribution margin).

Break-even Formula

The break-even point can be obtained directly by a mathematical formula. The basic formula to find out the break-even point is:

$$\text{Break-even sales (units)} = \frac{\text{Fixed cost}}{\text{Contribution margin per unit}}$$

$$\text{Break-even sales (volume)} = \frac{\text{Fixed cost}}{\text{C/S ratio (also known as P/V ratio*)}}$$

$$\text{Break-even sales volume} = \frac{\text{Total fixed expenses}}{1 - \text{Total variable expenses/Total sales volume}}$$

$$\text{Cash break-even point (units)} = \frac{\text{Cash fixed cost}}{\text{Cash contribution per unit}}$$

*C/S ratio is popularly known as P/V ratio because after fixed costs are fully recovered, i.e. after break-even point, all contributions (sales-variable costs) become profit. However, before break-even point all contributions will not become profit since fixed costs are yet to be recovered.

Break-even Chart

Total revenues and total costs at different sales volume can be estimated and plotted on a break-even chart. This chart is constructed as follows:

1. A horizontal base line, the *x*-axis, is drawn and spaced into equal distances representing either plant capacity, sales volume or number of units.
2. A vertical line, the *y*-axis is drawn on the left side of the chart and also spaced into equal parts. This line indicates sales revenue and also costs.
3. A line parallel to the horizontal line (*x*-axis) is drawn for fixed costs.
4. A total cost line is drawn starting at the y-axis fixed cost point and moving to the right. This total cost line represents the total of all items of cost, fixed and variable.
5. The sales line is drawn starting at the zero point on the vertical axis and ending at the top on the right side.
6. The total cost line intersects the sales line at a point which is known as the break-even point.
7. The are to the left of the break-even point between the total cost line and the sales line is the loss area; the profit area lies to the right of the break-even point above the total cost line.

The data from the previous example are presented on the break-even chart (see Fig. 5.3).

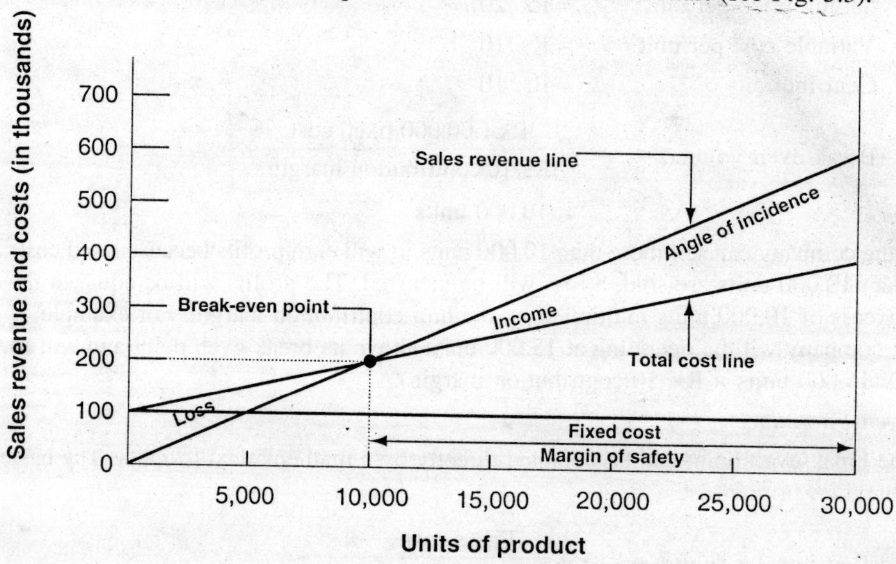

Fig. 5.3 Break-even Chart

From this figure, it can be observed that the break-even point occurs when sales are 10,000 units at Rs. 2,00,000.

Cash Break-Even Point

If a firm has a minimum of available cash or the opportunity cost of holding excess cash is high, management may want to know the volume of sales that will cover all cash expenses, during a period. This is known as the cash break-even point.

Not all fixed operating costs involve cash payments. For example, depreciation expense is a non-cash charge. To find the cash break-even point, the non-cash charges must be subtracted from total fixed operating costs. Therefore, the cash break-even point is lower than the usual break-even point. The formula is:

$$BEP = \frac{FC - d}{P - V}$$

Where P = selling price per unit

V = unit variable cost

FC = Fixed operating costs and

d = depreciation expenses

Thus, cash break-even point indicates break-even sales to cover only the fixed costs involving cash payments and to break even.

This is illustrated below:

Let Sales 20,000 units at Rs. 10 per unit

Variable costs, Rs. 4 per unit

Fixed cost Rs. 5,000 including depreciation, Rs. 10,000

Preference divided to be paid Rs. 20,000

Taxed to be paid Rs. 25,000

Assume that there are no lags in payment.

Break-even point (in units) will be 6667 units as displayed in Fig. 5.4 below.

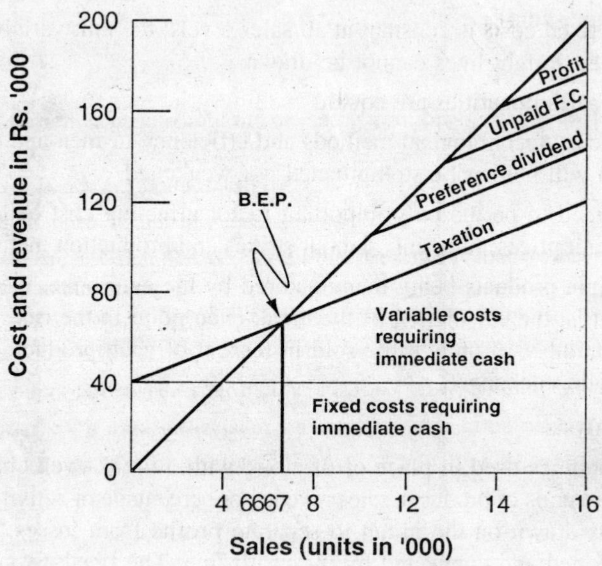

Fig. 5.4: Break-even Chart

Margin of Safety

This is the difference between sales and break-even point. If the distance is relatively short, it indicates that a small drop in production or sales will reduce profits considerably. If the distance is long, it means that the business can still make profits even after a serious drop in production. It is important that there should be a reasonable margin of safety, otherwise a reduced level of production may prove dangerous. The margin of safety can be found by using the following formula:

Margin of safety = Profit ÷ P/V ratio

$$\text{or Margin of safety} = \frac{\text{Profit} \times \text{Sales}}{\text{Sales} - \text{Variable cost}}$$

Angle of Incidence

This is the angle at which the sales line cuts the total cost line. Management's aim will be to have as large an angle of incidence as possible because a large angle of incidence shows a high rate of profit. A narrow angle would show that even fixed overheads are absorbed and profit accrues at a relatively low rate of return, indicating that variable costs form a large part of cost of sales.

Sales Formula

Often it is necessary to know what level of sales is required to achieve a desired level of profit. The desired sales can be expressed in various ways:

Sales = Fixed cost + Variable cost + Profit

Or

Sales = (Profit + Fixed cost)/P/V/ ratio

Basic Assumptions in Break-even Analysis

Break-even analysis is based on several assumptions, listed as follows:

(*i*) Selling prices and pricing policy will remain constant at all sales levels. If this is not true, sales revenue cannot be plotted as a straight line.

(*ii*) All costs and expenses can be separated into fixed and variable components.

(*iii*) The total of the fixed costs is constant at all sales levels; the unit variable costs remain the same. If this is not true, straight lines cannot be drawn.

(*iv*) Production and sales quantities are equal.

(*v*) Managerial policies, technological methods and efficiency of men and machines will not change and cost control will neither be strengthened nor weakened.

(*vi*) Volume is assumed to be the only important factor affecting cost behaviour. Other influencing factors such as unit prices, sales-mix, labour strikes and production methodology remain constant.

(*vii*) In case of multiple products being manufactured by the enterprise, the sales-mix should remain unchanged. That is, the calculation of the break-even point in the case of multiple products pre-determines the number of units to be sold in respect of each product. This multi-product sales-mix should remain unchanged.

Profit/Volume (P/V) Analysis

A P/V graph is sometimes used in place of or along with a break-even chart. Profits and losses are given on a vertical scale; and units of products, sales revenue or percentage of activity are given on a horizontal line. The horizontal line is drawn on the graph to separate profits from losses. The profits and losses at various sales levels are plotted and connected by the profit line. The break-even point is measured at the point where the profit line intersects the horizontal line. The P/V graph may be preferred to the break-even chart because profit and losses at any point can be read directly from the vertical scale; but the P/V graph does not clearly show how costs vary with activity.

Data used earlier to prepare the break-even chart are also used in preparing the P/V graph (see Fig. 5.5).

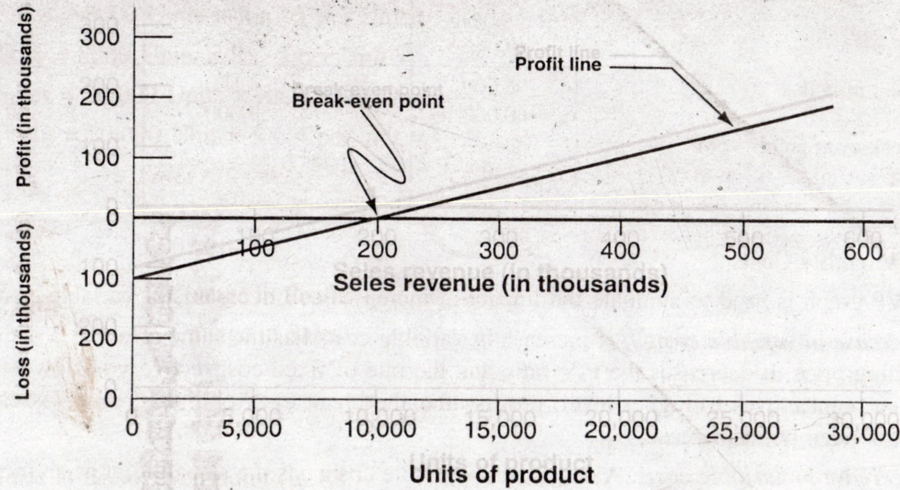

Fig. 5.5 Profit Volume (P/V) Graph

Role of CVP analysis

A cost-volume profit analysis can be used to measure the effect of factor changes and management decision alternatives on profits. These factors include possible changes in selling prices, changes in variable or fixed cost, expansion or contraction of sales volume or other changes in operating methods or policies. Cost-volume profit analysis is also useful for problems of product pricing, sales mix, adding or deleting product lines and accepting special orders.

Changes in Selling Prices

The CVP graph is frequently used to illustrate the potential profit effects of contemplated price changes. Effects on the profit pattern are as follows:

1. *Increase in selling price:* If the selling price is increased, it increases the P/V ratio and the rate of fixed costs recovery is increased. The break-even point (break-even volume) declines, profit beyond the break-even point increases and losses below the break-even point decreases.
2. *Decrease in selling price:* If the selling price decreases, it decreases the P/V ratio and the rate of fixed cost recovery declines. The break-even point increases.

Assume, for example, that a company produces a product with a selling price of Rs. 10 per unit and a variable cost of Rs. 4 per unit. Fixed costs are Rs. 36,000 per year. The effect of a 20% increase and 20% decrease in the present selling price is given below:

	Present	Selling price 20% Increase	20% Decrease
Selling price per unit	Rs. 10.00	Rs. 12.00	Rs. 8.00
Variable cost per unit	4.00	4.00	4.00
Marginal contribution per unit	6.00	8.00	4.00
P/V ratio	60%	$66^2/_3$%	50%
Fixed costs	36,000	36,000	36,000
Break-even point in units	6,000	4,500	9,000
In volume	60,000	54,000	72,000
Changes in break-even point	—	—	—
In units	0%	– 25%	+ 50%
In sales volume	0%	– 10%	+ 20%

Changes in Variable Costs

The CVP graph is used to evaluate the impact of increases and decreases in variable costs per unit.

1. *Increase in variable costs.* An increase in variable costs has the same effect as a decrease in the selling price. It decreases the P/V ratio and the rate of fixed cost recovery is slower. The break-even point moves to higher level; profits after the break even point decrease; losses before the break even point increase.
2. *Decrease in variable costs.* A decrease in variable costs has the same effect as an increase in the selling price. A higher P/V ratio is achieved and the rate of fixed costs recovery is increased. The break-even point declines, profits beyond the break-even point are higher and losses before the break-even point are lower.

To illustrate the effect of change in variable costs, assume that a company is selling a product for Rs. 40 a unit and has a variable cost of Rs. 20 per unit. Fixed costs total Rs. 48,000 per year. The effects of a 20% increase and a 20% decrease in variable cost are given in the following table:

	Present variable cost	20% Increase	20% Decrease
	(Rs.)	(Rs.)	(Rs.)
Unit selling price	40.00	40.00	40.00
Variable cost per unit	20.00	24.00	16.00
Marginal contribution	20	16.00	24.00
P/V ratio	50%	40%	60%
Fixed costs	48,000	48,000	48,000
Break even point:			
Sales Volume	96,000	1,20,000	80,000
Units	2,400	3,000	2,000

Changes in Fixed Cost

Increase and decrease in the fixed cost do not have any impact on the P/V ratio but they change the break-even point. With the same P/V ratio, the rate of the fixed costs recovery remains the same.

1. *Increase in fixed costs:* If fixed costs are increased, the break-even point (break-even-volume) is higher. Profits above the break-even point are lower by the amount of the increase in fixed costs; below the break-even point, losses increase by the amount of increase.

2. *Decrease in fixed costs:* If fixed costs are decreased, it lowers the break-even point. The profits are greater by the amount of the decrease, and losses are smaller by the amount of the decrease in fixed costs

Assume that a company has a P/V ratio of 40% and present fixed costs of Rs. 50,000. The effects of change in the fixed costs by Rs. 10,000 are as follows:

	Present fixed cost	*Increase by*	*Decrease by*
		Rs. 10,000	Rs. 10,000
Fixed costs	Rs. 50,000	Rs. 60,000	Rs. 40,000
P/V ratio	40%	40%	40%
Break-even point	1,25,000	1,50,000	1,00,000
Decrease	0	+ 25,000	– 25,000

From the above example, it is clear that the P/V ratio is the same in each situation and break-even point can be determined by dividing the amount of the change by the P/V ratio:

$$\frac{\text{Change in fixed costs}}{\text{P/V ratio}}$$

$$= \frac{\text{Rs.}10{,}000}{40\%} = \text{Rs. } 25{,}000$$

Desired or Target Profit

Sometimes, management faces two decisions: (*i*) to increase sales volume through reduction in selling prices and (*ii*) to increase selling prices in case the P/V ratio is low, with the expectation that a higher profit will be earned. These decisions should be taken carefully after studying the profit pattern and other factors, otherwise the results can be harmful particularly for those companies whose P/V ratios are already low. Also, if reduction in selling prices does not increase the sales volume, the price reduction will result only in lower profits.

The increase in sales volume required to overcome the effect of a price reduction is relatively greater when the rate of the contribution margin per unit is relatively greater as compared to when the rate of the contribution margin per unit is relatively low. If a product makes only a small contribution, then a reduction in selling price makes it all the more difficult to recover the fixed costs and to earn profits.

Similarly, a business firm may think of increasing the selling price if the P/V ratio is low. However, increase in selling price may reduce the sales volume.

Multi-product Situations

When there are multiple products with different contribution margins, the mix of the product has a direct effect on the fixed costs recovery and total profits of the firm. Different products have different P/V ratios because of different selling prices and variable costs. The total profits depend to some extent upon the promotions in which the products are sold.

For example, assume that a company with fixed costs of Rs. 25,00,000 per year manufactures two products A and B with P/V ratio as follows:

	Product A	*Product B*
Unit selling price	Rs. 100	Rs. 200
Variable costs	40	160
Marginal contribution	60	40
P/V ratio	60%	20%

With comparatively low variable costs, product A has a relatively high P/V ratio; each unit of product A sold contributes Rs. 60 to fixed costs recovery and profit. Product B, with comparatively high variable costs, has a low P/V ratio; each unit sold contributes only Rs. 40 to fixed costs recovery and profit. Other things being equal, the sale of product A is more profitable than that of product B, despite the fact that the selling price of product B is twice that of product A. It is correct to say that profits will decline as the sales mix shifts from product A to product B. This also implies, however, that new analysis of profit volume relationship must be made as the product-mix changes.

Limitations of CVP Analysis

CVP analysis is a useful planning and control device, usually in the form of a chart, showing how revenue, costs and profit fluctuate with volume. The CPV technique is useful to the management in areas of budgeting, cost control and decision making. Inspite of CVP being a useful technique, it suffers from some limitations. Firstly, because of the many assumptions, CVP is only an approximation at best. If prices, unit costs, sales-mix, operating efficiency or other relevant factors change, then the overall CVP analysis and relationships also must be modified. Because of these assumptions, cost data are of limited significance.

In a multi-product situation, different products typically yield different contribution margins and are produced in various volumes with differing costs. As a result, neither the revenue cover nor the cost curve is necessarily straight and the break-even point is difficult to find.

Therefore, while preparing or interpreting cost-volume profit analysis, all assumptions and limitations should be carefully considered. A series of CVP analysis based on different sets of assumptions and circumstances may be prepared to reflect situations prevailing in different business enterprises. When circumstances change, CVP analysis should also be revised to reflect the changing situations. It is also necessary to have up-to-date analysis so that it can act as a useful device in profit forecast, budgeting, cost control and managerial decision-making.

Example 5.2

Prepare Income Statements under Absorption costing and under Marginal costing from the following information for the year 2002-2003:

Opening Stock	= 1,000 units valued at Rs. 70,000 including variable cost of Rs. 50 per unit.
Fixed Cost	= Rs. 1,20,000
Variable Cost	= Rs. 60 per unit
Production	= 10,000 units
Sales	= 7,000 units @ Rs. 100 per unit.

Stock is valued on the basis of FIFO.

Solution:

Income Statement
(Absorption Costing)

		(Rs.)	(Rs.)
	Sales		7,00,000
Less:	Cost of good sold:		
	Opening stock (1,000 units × Rs. 70)	70,000	
	Variable cost (10,000 units × Rs. 60)	6,00,000	
	Fixed cost	1,20,000	
	Cost of goods available for sales	7,90,000	
Less:	Closing stock (4000 units Rs. 72)	2,88,000	
			5,02,000
	Net Income		1,98,000

Income Statement (Marginal Costing)

		(Rs.)	(Rs.)
	Sales		7,00,000
Less:	Cost of goods sold:		
	Opening stock (1,000 units × Rs. 50)	50,000	
	Variable cost (10,000 units × Rs. 60)	6,00,000	
		6,50,000	
Less:	Closing stock (4000 units × Rs. 60)	2,40,000	4,10,000
	Contribution margin		2,90,000
Less:	Fixed Cost		1,20,000
	Net Income		1,70,000

Difference in Net Income = Rs. 198000 – 1,70,000

= Rs. 28,000

This difference in net income is due to difference in inventory values

	Absorption Costing (Rs.)	*Marginal Costing* (Rs.)
Opening stock	70,000	50,000
Closing stock	2,88,000	2,40,000
Difference	2,18,000	1,90,000

Net difference = 2,18,000 – 1,90,000

= Rs. 28,000

Notes:

1. It has been assumed that fixed cost is fixed production cost.
2. It has been assumed that variable cost (Rs. 60 per unit) is variable production cost.

Example 5.3

Your company has a production capacity of 12,500 units and normal capacity utilisation is 80%. Opening inventory of finished goods on 1-1-1999 was 1,000 units. During the year ending 31-12-1999, it produced 11,000 units while it sold only 10,000 units.

Standard variable cost per unit is Rs. 6.50 and standard fixed factory cost per unit Rs. 1.50. Total fixed selling and administration overheads amounted to Rs. 10,000. The company sells its product at Rs. 10 per unit.

Prepare Income Statements under Absorption Costing and Marginal Costing. Explain the reasons for difference in profit, if any.

Solution:

Income Statement for the year ended 31st Dec. 1999 (Under Absorption Costing Method)

	Rs.	Rs.
Sales: 10,000 Units @ Rs. 10 per unit		1,00,000
Less: Cost of goods sold:		
Variable Production Costs:		
11,000 units @ Rs. 6.50 per unit	71,500	
Fixed Factory cost @ Rs. 1.50 per unit 11,000 × 1.50 =	16,500	
	88,000	
Add: Opening stock: 1000 units @ Rs. 8 per unit (i.e., Rs. 6.50 + Rs. 1.50)	8,000	
Costs of goods available for sales	96,000	
Less: Closing stock 2000 units valued at current cost.	16,000	80,000
Gross Profit		20,000
Less: Fixed selling and administrative overhead.		10,000
Net profit		10,000

Income Statement for the year ended 31st Dec. 1999 (Under Marginal Costing Method)

	Rs.	Rs.
Sales: 10,000 Units @ Rs. 10 unit		1,00,000
Less: Marginal Cost:		
Variable production cost:		
11,000 units @ Rs. 6.50 per unit	71,500	
Variable cost of opening stock of finished stock (1000 units @ Rs. 6.50 per unit)	6,500	
Cost of goods available for sales	78,000	
Less: Closing stock of finished stock: 2000 units @ Rs. 6.50 per unit	13,000	
	65,000	65,000
Contribution		35,000
Less: Fixed selling and administrative overhead	10,000	
Fixed factory cost @ Rs. 1.50 per unit	16,500	26,500
Net Profit		8,500

Reason for difference: The difference in profits, Rs. 1,500 (i.e., Rs. 10,000 – Rs. 8,500), as arrived at under absorption and marginal costing methods is due to the element of fixed costs included in the valuation of opening and closing stock under the absorption costing method.

Example 5.4

'LMN' Ltd., sells its product at Rs. 3 per unit. The company uses a First-in, First-out (FIFO) actual costing system. A new fixed manufacturing overhead allocation rate is computed each year by dividing the actual fixed manufacturing overhead cost by the actual production costs. The following simplified data are related to its first two years of operation:

	Year I	*Year II*
Unit Data		
Sales	1,000	1,200
Production	1,400	1,000
Cost in Rupees		
Variable manufacturing	700	500
Fixed manufacturing	700	700
Variable marketing and administration	1,000	1,200
Fixed marketing and administration	400	400

Required:

(*i*) Prepare income statements based on:

(*a*) absorption costing and (*b*) variable costing for each year.

Give reasons for differences in the answer.

Solution:

Income Statement
(Absorption Costing)

	Year I (*Rs.*)	*Year II* (*Rs.*)
Sales	3,000	3,600
Less: Cost of goods sold:		
Opening stock	Nil	400
Variable manufacturing	700	500
Fixed manufacturing	700	700
Cost of goods available for sales	1,400	1,600
Less: Closing inventory $\frac{400}{1,400}$ × Rs. 1,400	400	240*
Cost of goods sold	1,000	1,360
Gross Profit	2,000	2,240
Less: Variable marketing & Administration	(1,000)	(1,200)
Fixed marketing and Administration	(400)	(400)
Net Income	600	64

Note: In Year II, FIFO method of inventory valuation is used. That is, closing inventory of 200 units belong to current production lot. Therefore, value of 200 units will be:

$\frac{200}{1,000}$ × Rs. 1,200 = Rs. 240

Income Statement
(Marginal Costing)

	Year I (Rs.)	*Year II (Rs.)*
Sales	3,000	3,600
Less: Cost of goods sold:		
Opening stock	Nil	200
Variable manufacturing	700	500
Cost of goods available for sales	700	700
Less: Closing stock @ Re. 0.50 (400 units, 200 units)	200	100
Cost of goods sold	500	600
Contribution margin	2,500	3,000
Less: Fixed manufacturing	(700)	(700)
Variable marketing & Administration	(1,000)	(1,200)
Fixed marketing & Administration	(400)	(400)
Net Income	400	700

(*ii*) The difference in profit figures between absorption costing and variable costing is due to the factory cost attached to inventory. Difference in Net Income is due to difference in inventory values. This is explained as below:

	Year I (Rs.)	*Year II (Rs.)*
Absorption costing net income	600	640
Marginal costing net income	400	700
	200	60
Absorption costing inventory: Opening	Nil	400
Closing	400	240
Difference	400	160
Marginal costing inventory: Opening	Nil	200
Closing	200	100
Difference	200	100
Net difference	200	60

Example 5.5

Hind Central Corporation produces only one product which had the following costs:

Variable manufacturing costs	Rs. 4 per unit
Fixed manufacturing costs	Rs. 2,00,000 per year

The normal capacity is set at 2,00,000 units. There are no work-in-progress inventories.

In 2001, the company produced 2,00,000 units and sold 90 per cent of them at a price of Rs. 7 per unit. In 2002, the company produced 2,10,000 units and sold 2,15,000 units at the same price.

You are required to prepare income statements for 2001 and 2002 based on absorption costing and marginal costing.

Solution:

Hind General Corporation
Income Statement (Marginal costing basis)

Particulars	*2001* *Rs.*	*2002* *Rs.*
Sales at Rs. 7	12,60,000	15,05,000
Inventory-opening at Rs. 4	Nil	80,000
Variable manufacturing costs at Rs. 4	8,00,000	8,40,000
Standard variable cost of goods available for sales	8,00,000	9,20,000
Inventory-closing at Rs. 4	80,000	60,000
Standard variable cost of sales	7,20,000	8,60,000
Contribution margin	5,40,000	6,45,000
Fixed manufacturing costs	2,00,000	2,00,000
Net Income	3,40,000	4,45,000

Income Statement
(Absorption Costing Basis)

Particulars	*2001* *Rs.*	*2002* *Rs.*
Sales at Rs. 7	12,60,000	15,05,000
Inventory opening at Rs. 5	Nil	1,00,000
Variable manufacturing costs at Rs. 4	8,00,000	8,40,000
Fixed manufacturing cost at Rs. 1	2,00,000	2,10,000
Total goods at standard cost	10,00,000	11,500,000
Inventory closing at Rs. 5	1,00,000	75,000
Standard cost of sales	9,00,000	10,75,000
Under (over) absorbed fixed costs	Nil	(10,000)
Actual cost of sales	9,00,000	10,65,000
Net Income	3,60,000	4,40,000

Example 5.6

The following cost information relates to factory X for two years:

	2001	*2002*
Installed capacity (units)	10,000	10,000
Opening stock (units)	Nil	1,000
Closing stock (units)	1,000	Nil
Output (units)	10,000	9,000
Selling price per unit (Rs.)	14	14
Fixed costs for the year (Rs.)	85,000	85,000
Variable cost per unit (Rs.)	2.90	2.90

Work out the profit under absorption costing and marginal costing for the two years. Also state any abnormality in the results disclosed by absorption costing. Assume FIFO basis.

Solution:

Income Statement
(Absorption Costing)

	2001 (Rs.)	2002 (Rs.)
Sales	1,26,000	1,40,000
Less: Cost of goods sold:		
Opening stock	Nil	11,400
Variable production cost	29,000	26,100
Fixed cost	85,000	85,000
Costs of goods available for sales	1,14,000	1,22,500
Less: Closing stock	11,400	Nil
Cost of sales	1,02,600	1,22,500
Net profit	23,400	17,500
Net profit as percentage of sales	18.6%	12.5%

Note: It has been assumed that variable cost and fixed cost are production cost.

Income Statement
(Marginal Costing)

	2001 (Rs.)	2002 (Rs.)
Sales	1,26,000	1,40,000
Less: Cost of goods sold:		
Opening stock	Nil	2,900
Variable production cost	29,000	26,100
Cost of goods available for sales	29,000	29,000
Less: Closing stock	2,900	Nil
Cost of goods sold	26,100	29,000
Contribution margin	99,900	1,11,000
Less: Fixed Cost	85,000	85,000
Net Profit	14,900	20,000
Net profit as percentage of sales	11.8%	18.6%

Example 5.7

Using the information below prepare profit statements for the months of June and July using (*i*) marginal costing and (*ii*) full absorption costing. Also, explain why the two methods disclose different amounts of profit for June and July.

Data per unit:

	Rs.
Selling price	50
Direct material cost	18
Direct labour cost	4
Variable production overheads	3
Monthly costs:	
Fixed production overheads	99000
Fixed selling expenses	15000
Fixed administration expenses	25000

Variable selling costs are 10% of sales revenue and normal production capacity is 11,000 units per month.

	Sales (units)	Production (units)
June	10,000	12,000
July	12,000	10,000

Profit Statement – Marginal Costing

	June	July
Sales units	10,000	12,000
Production units	12,000	10,000
Sales at Rs. 50	5,00,000	6,00,000
Less: Cost of goods sold:		
Variable production costs at Rs. 25	3,00,000	2,50,000
Add: Opening stock		50,000
Cost of goods available for sales	3,00,000	3,00,000
Less: Closing stock	50,000	
Cost of goods sold	2,50,000	3,00,000
Contribution	2,50,000	3,00,000
Less: Fixed costs:		
Production overheads	(99,000)	(99,000)
Selling expenses	(15,000)	(15,000)
Variable selling expenses	(50,000)	(60,000)
Administration expenses	(25,000)	(25,000)
Net profit	61,000	1,01,000

Working Note:

Variable production costs:	
Direct material cost	18
Direct wages	4
Variable production overheads	3
	Rs. 25

Profit Statement — Absorption Costing

	June	July
Sales units	10,000	12,000
Production units	12,000	10,000
Sales at Rs. 50	5,00,000	6,00,000
Less: Cost of goods sold:		
Production costs absorbed at Rs. 34	4,08,000	3,40,000
Add: Opening stock	—	68,000
Cost of goods available for sales	4,08,000	4,08,000
Less: Closing stock	68,000	—
Cost of goods sold	3,40,000	4,08,000
(over) under-absorbed fixed		

Production overheads at Rs. 9	(9,000)	9,000
Adjusted cost of goods sold	3,31,000	4,17,000
Gross profit	1,69,000	1,83,000
Less: Variable selling expenses	(50,000)	(60,000)
Fixed selling expenses	(15,000)	(15,000)
Fixed administration expenses	(25,000)	(25,000)
Net profit	Rs. 79,000	Rs. 83,000

Working Note:

Production costs:	Rs.	
Direct material cost	18	
Direct wages	4	
Variable production overheads	3	
Fixed production overheads	9	(Rs. 99,000 ÷ 11,000 units)
	Rs. 34	

Taken together, the two costing techniques disclose the same total profit for the two months. In June marginal costing disclosed Rs. 18000 less profit than full absorption costing. This difference is caused by 20000 units being in stock. Under absorption costing, the fixed production overheads absorbed by these units cost Rs. 18000 (2,000 × Rs. 9), and this amount is carried forward in the cost of stock rather than being written off against profit in June as with the marginal costing.

In July, sales exceed production by 2000 units, and Rs. 18,000 of fixed production overheads is charged against revenues, as the stocks created in June have been sold.

Example 5.8

ABC Motors assembles and sell motor vehicles. It uses an actual costing system, in which unit costs are calculated on a monthly basis. Data relating to March and April 2000 are:

	March	*April*
Unit data:		
Beginning Inventory	0	150
Production	500	400
Sales	350	520
Variable-cost data:		
Manufacturing Costs per unit produced	Rs. 10,000	Rs. 10,000
Distribution costs per unit sold	3,000	3,000
Fixed-cost data:		
Manufacturing Costs	Rs. 20,00,000	Rs. 20,00,000
Marketing Costs	6,00,000	6,00,000

The selling price per motor vehicle is Rs. 24,000

Required:

(*i*) Present income statements for ABC Motors in March and April of 2000 under (*a*) variable costing, and (*b*) absorption costing.

(*ii*) Explain the differences between (*a*) and (*b*) for March and April.

Solution:

(i) Income Statement (Variable Costing)

	March (Rs.)	April (Rs.)
Sales	84,00,000	1,24,80,000
Less: Variable cost of goods sold:		
Opening stock	Nil	15,00,000
Variable manufacturing cost	50,00,000	40,00,000
Cost of goods available for sales	50,00,000	55,00,000
Less: Closing stock	15,00,000	3,00,000
Cost of goods sold	35,00,000	52,00,000
Contribution Margin	49,00,000	72,80,000
Less: Other costs:		
Fixed manufacturing	(20,00,000)	(20,00,000)
Fixed marketing	(6,00,000)	(6,00,000)
Variable distribution	(10,50,000)	(15,60,000)
Net Income	12,50,000	31,20,000

Income Statement
(Absorption Costing)

	March (Rs.)	April (Rs.)
Sales	84,00,000	1,24,80,000
Less: Cost of goods sold:		
Opening stock	Nil	21,00,000
Variable manufacturing cost	50,00,000	40,00,000
Fixed manufacturing cost	20,00,000	20,00,000
Cost of goods available for sales	70,00,000	81,00,000
Less: Closing stock	21,00,000	4,50,000
Cost of goods sold	49,00,000	76,50,000
Gross profit	35,00,000	48,30,000
Less: Distribution Cost	(10,50,000)	(15,60,000)
Fixed marketing	(6,00,000)	(6,00,000)
Net Income	18,50,000	26,70,000

Note: The company follows actual costing system and calculates unit costs on monthly basis. Therefore, for the month of April, inventory of 30 units has been valued as follows:

Variable manufacturing cost 30 × Rs. 10,000 = 30,00,000
Fixed manufacturing cost @ Rs. 5000 × 30 = 15,00,000
(Rs. 20,00,000 ÷ Current Production 400 units)
That is, inventory at Rs. 15,000 per unit = 45,00,000

For the month of March, inventory of 150 units has been calculated as follows:

Variable manufacturing Rs. 10,000 × 150 = Rs. 15,00,000
Fixed manufacturing Rs. 4000 × 150 = Rs. 6,00,000
That is, inventory at Rs. 14,000 per unit = Rs. 21,00,000

(ii) Difference in Profit

	March	April
Absorption Costing profit	Rs. 18,50,000	Rs. 26,70,000
Variable costing profit	12,50,000	31,20,000
	6,00,000	4,50,000

Difference in profit is due to difference in inventory values in the two costing techniques.

	March (Rs.)	April (Rs.)
Absorption costing:		
Opening stock	Nil	21,00,000
Closing stock	21,00,000	4,50,000
Difference	21,00,000	16,50,000
Variable costing:		
Opening stock	Nil	15,00,000
Closing stock	15,00,000	3,00,000
Difference	15,00,000	12,00,000
Net difference (effect)	6,00,000	4,50,000

Example 5.9

The ratio of variable cost to sales is 70%. The break-even point occurs at 60% of the capacity sales. Find the capacity sales when fixed costs are Rs. 90,000. Also compute profit at 75% of the capacity sales.

Solution:

Basic Calculations

$$\frac{\text{Variable Cost}}{\text{Sales}} = 70\%$$

$$\text{Hence } \frac{\text{Contribution}}{\text{Sales}} = 30\% \text{ or P/V Ratio} = 30\%$$

Computation of Capacity Sales

$$\text{Break-even Point} = \frac{\text{Fixed cost}}{\text{P/V ratio}} = \frac{\text{Rs. } 90{,}000}{30\%} = \text{Rs. } 3{,}00{,}000 \quad \text{(i)}$$

Break-even Point (as given) = 60% of capacity sales

$$\text{Hence Capacity Sales} = \frac{\text{Rs. } 3{,}00{,}000}{60\%} = \text{Rs. } 5{,}00{,}000$$

Computation of Profit at 75% of the Capacity Sales

	Rs.
75% of Capacity sales (75% × Rs. 5,00,000)	3,75,000
Less: Variable Cost (70% × Rs. 3,75,000)	2,62,500
Contribution	1,12,500
Less: Fixed Cost	90,000
Profit	22,500

Example 5.10

A company sells its product at Rs. 15 per unit. In a period, if it produces and sells 8,000 units, it incurs a loss of Rs. 5 per unit. If the volume is raised to 20,000 units, it earns a profit of Rs. 4 per unit.

Calculate break-even point in terms of rupees as well as in units.

Solution:

I.	Sales = 8000 Units × Rs. 15 per Unit =	1,20,000
	Loss = 8000 Units × Rs. 5 per Unit =	40,000
II.	Sales = 20,000 Units × Rs. 15 per Unit =	3,00,000
	Profit = 20,000 Unit × Rs. 4 per unit =	80,000

	Sales	*Profit/Loss*
I.	1,20,000	(–) 40,000
II.	3,00,000	(+) 80,000

$$\text{P/V Ratio} = \frac{\text{Change in Profit}}{\text{Change in Sales}}$$

$$= \frac{1,20,000}{1,80,000} = \frac{2}{3} \text{ or } 66\tfrac{2}{3}\%$$

Sales at Break even point (in Rs.)

Fixed Cost = S × PV Ratio – Profit

(On the basis raised volume II)

$$\text{Fixed Cost} = \text{Rs. } 3,00,000 \times \frac{2}{3} - 80,000$$

Fixed Cost = Rs. 2,00,000 – Rs. 80,000 = Rs. 1,20,000

$$\text{B.E.P.} = \frac{F}{P/V \text{ Ratio}} = \frac{1,20,000 \times 3}{2} = \text{Rs. } 1,80,000$$

$$\text{Sales at break-even point (in units)} = \frac{\text{Sales in Rs.}}{\text{Selling price per unit}}$$

$$= \frac{\text{Rs. } 1,80,000}{15} = 12,000 \text{ units.}$$

Notes:

(1) Rs. 5 per unit loss is given is the question, in the indirect way it is a variable cost per unit.

(2) Change in Profit is computed by adding loss of Rs. 40,000 in the profit of Rs. 80,000 because loss of Rs. 40,000 has also been covered in the second period of time or in the second option if the volume is raised to 20,000 units.

Example 5.11

B & Co. has recorded the following data in the two most recent periods:

Total Cost of Production (Rs.)	*Volume of Production (units)*
14,600	800
19,400	1,200

What is the best estimate of the firm's fixed costs per period?

Solution:

	Period 1	*Period 2*	*Difference*
Total Cost of Production (Rs.)	14,600	19,400	4,800
Volume of Production (Units)	800	1,200	400

$$\text{Variable Cost per unit} = \frac{\text{Difference in Total Cost of Production}}{\text{Difference in Volume of Production}}$$

$$= \frac{\text{Rs. } 4{,}800}{400 \text{ units}} = \text{Rs. } 12$$

Fixed Cost = Total Cost of Production of a period – Total Variable Cost

= Rs. 14,600 – 800 units × Rs. 12

= Rs. 14,600 – Rs. 9,600 = Rs. 5,000

Example 5.12

A. Ltd. maintains a margin of safety of 37.5% with an overall contribution to sales ratio of 40%. Its fixed costs amount to Rs. 5 lakh. Calculate the following:

(*i*) Break-even Sales,

(*ii*) Total Sales,

(*iii*) Total Variable Costs,

(*iv*) Current Profit,

(*v*) New 'Margin of Safety' if the sales volume is increased by 7½%.

Solution:

$$(i)\ \text{Break-even Sales} = \frac{\text{Fixed Cost}}{\text{P/V Ratio}}$$

$$= \frac{5 \text{ lakhs}}{40\%} = \text{Rs. } 12.50 \text{ lakh}$$

(*ii*) Total Sales = Break-even sales + Margin of Safety

Margin of Safety = Actual sales – Break-even Sales

Let Actual Sales be Rs. 100

Margin of Safety is Rs. 37.5

Hence, Break-even Sales will be Rs. 62.5

In case Beak-even Sales is 62.5; Actual Sales stands at Rs. 100

Hence, if Break-even Sales is Rs. 12.5 lakh

Actual sales will be $= \frac{100}{62.5} \times 12.5$

= Rs. 20 lakh

(*iii*) Contribution = Sales – Variable Costs

Hence, Total Variable Costs = 60% of Rs. 20 lakh

= Rs. 12 lakh

(*iv*) Current Profit = Sales – (Variable Costs + Fixed Costs)

= Rs. 20 lakh – (Rs. 12 lakh + Rs. 5 lakh)

= Rs. 20 lakh – Rs. 17 lakh

= Rs. 3 lakh

(*v*) New Margin of Safety if sales volume is increased by 7.5%

New Sales Value = Rs. 20 lakh + 7.5% of 20 lakh = Rs. 21.50 lakh

Hence, New Margin of Safety = 21.50 lakhs – B.E. Sales of Rs. 12.50 lakh = Rs. 9 lakh.

Example 5.13

A company has annual fixed costs of Rs. 14,00,000. In 1996 sales amounted to Rs. 60,00,000 as compared with Rs. 45,00,000 in 1995 and profit in 1996 was Rs. 4,20,000 higher than in 1995.

(*i*) At what level of sales does the company break-even?

(*ii*) Determine profit or loss on a forecast sales volume of Rs. 80,00,000.

(*iii*) If there is a reduction in selling price in 1997 by 10% and the company desires to earn the same profit as in 1996, what would be the required sales volume?

Solution:

$$\text{P/V Ratio} = \frac{\text{Increase in Profit}}{\text{Increase in Sales}} \times 100$$

$$= \frac{4{,}20{,}000}{15{,}00{,}000} \times 100 = 28\%$$

(*i*) Break-even Sales $= \frac{\text{Fixed Cost}}{PV \text{ Ratio}}$

$$= \frac{14{,}00{,}000}{28\%}$$

= Rs. 50,00,000

(*ii*) Profit on sales of Rs. 80,00,000

Total Contribution 80,00,000 × 28/100	22,40,000
Less: Fixed Cost	14,00,000
Profit	8,40,000

(*iii*) If Present Selling Price is		Rs. 100
Variable Cost is (100 – 28)		Rs. 72
New Selling Price (100 – 10)		Rs. 90
New Contribution		Rs. 18
New P/V Ratio	$\frac{18}{90} \times 100 =$	20%

Profit in 1996:

Contribution 60,00,000 × 28/100 =	16,80,000
Less: Fixed Cost	14,00,000
Profit	2,80,000

$$\text{Sales for Desired Profit of Rs. 2,80,000} = \frac{\text{Fixed Cost + Desired Profit}}{\text{New P/V Ratio}}$$

$$= \frac{14,00,000 + 2,80,000}{20\%}$$

$$= \frac{16,80,000}{20\%} = \text{Rs. } 84,00,000$$

Example 5.14

A Company manufactures radios which are sold at Rs. 1,600 per unit. The total cost is composed of 30% for direct materials, 40% for direct wages and 30% for overheads. An increase in material price by 30% and in wage rates by 10% is expected in the forthcoming year, as a result of which the profit at current selling price may decrease by 40% of the present profit per unit. You are required to prepare a statement showing current and future profit at present selling price.

How much Selling Price should be increased to maintain the present rate of profit?

Solution

Let X be the cost, *Y* be the profit and Rs. 1,600 selling price per unit of radio manufactured by a company.

Hence,

$X + Y = \text{Rs. } 1,600$ (*i*)

Statement of present and future cost of a radio

Particulars	*Present cost (Rs.)*	*Increase in cost (Rs.)*	*Anticipated future cost (Rs.)*
	(*a*)	(*b*)	(*c*) = (*a*) + (*b*)
Direct material	0.3 X	0.09 X	0.39 X
Direct labour	0.4 X	0.04 X	0.44 X
Overheads	0.3 X	—	0.30 X
Total	X	0.13 X	1.13 X

An increase in material price and wage rates resulted into a decrease in current profit by 40 per cent at the present selling price; therefore we have:

$1.13 X + 0.6 Y = 1,600$ (ii)

On solving (i) and (ii), we get:

X = Rs. 1,207.55

Y = Rs. 392.45

Current profit Rs. 392.45 or 32.5% of cost

Future profit Rs. 235.47

Statement of revised selling price to maintain the present rate of profit

	Rs.
Direct material cost 0.39 × Rs. 1,207.55	470.94
Direct labour cost (0.44 × Rs. 1,207.55)	531.32
Overheads 0.30 × Rs. 1,207.55)	362.27
Total cost	1,364.53
Profit (32.5% of total cost)	443.47
Revised selling price	1,808.00

Example 5.15

XYZ Ltd. furnishes you the following income information:

Particulars	*Year 1994*	
	First-half (Rs.)	*Second-half (Rs.)*
Sales	8,10,000	10,26,000
Profit earned	21,600	64,800

From the above, you are required to compute the following assuming that the fixed cost remains the same in both the periods:

(*i*) P/V Ratio

(*ii*) Fixed Costs

(*iii*) The amount of profit or loss where sales are Rs. 6,48,000 and

(*iv*) The amount of sales required to earn a profit of Rs. 1,08,000.

Solution

(*i*) Computation of P/V Ratio

$$\text{P/V Ratio} = \frac{\text{Change in Profit}}{\text{Change in Sales}} \times 100$$

$$= \frac{43,200}{2,16,000} \times 100 = 20\%$$

(*ii*) Computation of Fixed Cost

Fixed Cost = Contribution – Profit

(For 1st half) = 8,10,000 × 20% - 21,600

= 1,62,000 – 21,600

= Rs. 1,40,400

(*iii*) Contribution = 20% × Rs. 6,48,000 = Rs. 1,29,600

Loss = Rs. 1,29,600 – 1,40,400 = Rs. 10,800

(*iv*) Computation of sales to earn a profit of Rs. 1,08,000.

$$\frac{\text{Fixed Cost + Desired Profit}}{\text{P / V Ratio}}$$

$$= \frac{1,40,400 + \text{Rs.}\,1,08,000}{20\%} = \text{Rs. } 12,42,000$$

Example 5.16

The following costs and sales of a manufacturing company for the first half and second half of 1998-99 are given:

	First-half Rs.	*Second-half* Rs.
Sales	24,00,000	30,00,000
Total Costs	21,80,000	26,00,000

You are asked to determine:

(*i*) Contribution/Sales Ratio of the firm.

(*ii*) Annual Fixed Costs.

(*iii*) Break-even Point and

(*iv*) Margin of Safety as Percentage of Sales:

Solution:

(a) Computation of Contributions/Sales Ratio

Particulars	*First Half Rs.*	*Second Half Rs.*	*Change Rs.*
Sales	24,00,000	30,00,000	6,00,000
Total Cost	21,80,000	26,00,000	4,20,000
Profit	2,20,000	4,00,000	1,80,000

$$\text{Contribution/Sales Ratio} = \frac{\text{Change in Profit}}{\text{Change in Sales}}$$

$$= \frac{1,80,000}{6,00,000}$$

$$= 0.3 \text{ or } 30\%$$

(*b*) Computation of Fixed Cost for 1998-99

Total Sales for the year = Rs. 54,00,000

Total Costs = Rs. 47,80,000

P/V Ratio is = 30%

Total Variable Costs = 70% of Rs. 54,00,000

= Rs. 37,80,000

Fixed Costs = Total Costs – Variable Costs

= Rs. 47,80,000 – Rs. 37,80,000

= Rs. 10,00,000

(*c*) Break-even Point $= \dfrac{\text{Fixed Costs}}{\text{P/V Ratio}}$

$= \dfrac{\text{Rs.}10{,}000}{30\%}$

= Rs. 33,33,333

(*d*) Margin of Safety as a percentage of Sales

Margin of Safety (MS) = Sales – Break-even Sales

= Rs. 54,00,000 – Rs. 33,33,333

= Rs. 20,66,667

Margin of Safety as % of Sales $= \dfrac{20{,}66{,}667}{54{,}00{,}000} \times 100 = 38.3\%$

Example 5.17

Raj Ltd. manufactures three products X, Y and Z. The unit selling prices of these products are Rs. 100, Rs. 160 and Rs. 75 respectively. The corresponding unit variable costs are Rs. 50, Rs. 80 and Rs. 30. The proportions (quantity-wise) in which these products are manufactured and sold are 20%, 30% and 50% respectively. The total fixed costs are Rs. 14,80,000.

Calculate overall break-even quantity and the product-wise break up of such quantity.

Solution:

Overall Break-Even Quantity

Products	*X*	*Y*	*Z*
Selling Price per unit (Rs.)	100	160	75
Less: Variable Cost per unit (Rs.)	50	80	30
Contribution per unit (Rs.)	50	80	45
Share in Total Sales	20%	30%	50%
Proportionate Contribution per unit	10	24	22.50

Composite Contribution per unit = 56.5

Composite Break-even Point $= \dfrac{\text{Total Fixed Cost}}{\text{Composite contribution per unit}}$

$$= \frac{\text{Rs. }14{,}80{,}000}{\text{Rs. }56.5} = 26{,}195 \text{ units}$$

Product-wise break-up of overall break-even quantity:

Product X: 26,195 units × 20/100 = 5,239 units

Product Y: 26, 195 units × 30/100 = 7,858 units

Product Z: 26,195 units × 50/100 = 13,098 units

Example 5.18

A single product company sells its products at Rs. 60 per unit. In 1996, the company operated at a margin of safety of 40%. The fixed costs amounted to Rs. 3,60,000 and the variable cost ratio to sales was 80%.

In 1997, it is estimated that the variable cost will go up by 10% and the fixed costs will increase by 5%.

Find the selling price required to be fixed in 1997 to earn the same P/V ratio as in 1996.

Assuming the same selling price of Rs. 60 per unit in 1997, find the number of units required to be produced and sold to earn the same profit as in 1996.

Solution:

Basic Calculations

1. P/V Ratio in 1996

$$P/V = \frac{\text{Selling Price per unit} - \text{Variable Cost per unit}}{\text{Selling Price per unit}} \times 100$$

$$= \frac{\text{Rs. }60 - \text{Rs. }48}{\text{Rs. }60} \times 100 = \frac{\text{Rs. }12}{\text{Rs. }60} \times 100 = 20\%$$

2. Number of units sold (in 1996)

$$\text{Break-even Point} = \frac{\text{Fixed cost}}{\text{Contribution per unit}} = \frac{\text{Rs. }3{,}60{,}000}{\text{Rs. }12} = 30{,}000 \text{ units}$$

The margin of safety is 40%. Hence break-even point is at 60% of units sold.

$$\text{or No. of units sold} = \frac{\text{Break-even point}}{60\%} = \frac{30{,}000 \text{ units}}{60} \times 100 = 50{,}000 \text{ units}$$

3. Profit earned in 1996

Profit = Units sold in 1996 × Contribution per unit – Fixed costs

= 50,000 units × Rs. 12 – Rs. 3,60,000

= Rs. 6,00,000 – Rs. 3,60,000 = Rs. 2,40,000

Fixation of Selling Price in 1997

Variable Cost per unit in 1997 = Rs. 48 + Rs. 4.80 = Rs. 52.80

Fixed cost in 1997 = Rs. 3,60,000 + Rs. 18,000 = Rs. 3,78,000

P/V Ratio in 1996 = 20%

Since P/V ratio is 20%, Variable cost is 80%

Hence the required selling price = $\frac{\text{Rs. } 52.80}{80\%}$ = Rs. 66

Number of units to be produced and sold in 1997 to earn the same profit as in 1996

Profit in 1996 = Rs. 2,40,000

Fixed cost in 1997 = Rs. 3,78,000

Desired contribution in 1997

(Rs. 2,40,000 + Rs. 3,78,000) = Rs. 6,18,000

Contribution per unit in 1997 = Selling price per unit – Variable cost per unit

= Rs. 60 – Rs. 52.80 = Rs. 7.20

Number of units to be produced and sold in 1997 =

= $\frac{\text{Fixed cost in 1997}}{\text{Contribution per unit in 1997}}$ = 85, 833 units

= $\frac{\text{Rs. } 6,18,000}{\text{Rs. } 7.20}$ = 85.833units

Example 5.19

A company producing a single product sells it at Rs. 50 per unit. Unit variable cost is Rs. 35 and fixed cost amounts to Rs. 12 lakh per annum. With this data, you are required to calculate the following, treating each independent of the other:

(*a*) P/V Ratio and Break-even Sales

(*b*) New Break-even Sales if variable cost increases by Rs. 3 per unit, without increase in selling price.

(*c*) Increase in sales required if profits are to be increased by Rs. 24 lakh.

(*d*) Percentage increase/decrease in sales volume units to off-set

(*i*) an increase of Rs. 3 in the variable cost per unit.

(*ii*) a 10% increase in selling price without affecting existing profits quantum.

(*e*) Quantum of advertisement expenditure permissible to increase sales by Rs. 1.2 lakh, without affecting existing profits quantum.

Solution:

(*a*) P/V Ratio = $\frac{\text{Contribution per unit}}{\text{Selling Price per unit}}$

= $\frac{50-35}{50}$ = 30%

Break-even Sales = $\frac{\text{Fixed Cost}}{\text{P/V Ratio}}$

= $\frac{12.00}{30\%}$ = Rs. 40 lakh

(*b*) Revised P/V Ratio $= \dfrac{\text{Existing Contribution per unit}}{\text{Selling price per unit}}$

$= \dfrac{15-3}{50} = \dfrac{12}{50} = 24\%$

Revised Break-even Sales $= \dfrac{12}{24\%} =$ Rs. 50 lakhs

(*c*) Increase in Sales Required $= \dfrac{\text{Increase in Contribution}}{\text{New Contribution per unit}}$

$= \dfrac{24}{30\%} =$ Rs. 8 lakh

(*d*) (*i*) Percentage in Sales Volume (units) $= \dfrac{\text{Reduction in Contribution}}{\text{New Contribution per unit}}$

$= \dfrac{3}{12} \times 100$

$= 25\%$

(*ii*) Percentage Decrease in Sales Volume (units)

$= \dfrac{\text{Increase in Contribution}}{\text{New Contribution per unit}}$

$= \dfrac{5 \text{ (i.e., 10\% of Rs. 50)}}{20 \text{ i.e., } (55-35)}$

$= 25\%$

(*e*) The contribution by sales arising out of advertisement expenses should be equal to the amount of Rs. 1.2 lakhs, i.e. the sale increase to avoid profit or loss. Hence, 30% of 1.2 lakhs or Rs. 36,000 should be the maximum permissible advertisement expenditure for being incurred to get an increase of sale of Rs. 1.2 lakh without affecting existing profits.

Example 5.20

A company has three factories situated in North, East and South with its Head Office in Mumbai. The management has received the following summary report on the operations of each factory for a period:

(Rs. in '000)

Particulars	*Sales*		*Profit*	
	Actual	*Over/(Under) Budget*	*Actual*	*Over/(Under) Budget*
North	1,100	(400)	135	(180)
East	1,450	150	210	90
South	1,200	(200)	330	(110)

Calculates for each factory and for the company as a whole for the period:

(*i*) Fixed costs and

(*ii*) Break-even sales

Solution

Computation of Profit Volume Ratio

(Rs. in '000)

	Sales			Profit			P/V Ratio
	Actual	*Over/ (Under) Budget*	*Budgeted Sales*	*Actual*	*Over/ (Under) Budget*	*Budgeted Profit*	*(Diff. Between Profit) / (Diff. Between Sales)*
North	1,100	(400)	1,500	135	(180)	315	45% (180/400 × 100)
East	1,450	150	1,300	210	90	120	(60%) (90/150 × 100)
South	1,200	(200)	1,400	330	(110)	440	55% (110/200 × 100)

(i) Computation of Fixed Costs

(Rs.'000)

Particulars	*Actual Sales (1)*	*P/V Ratio (2)*	*Contribution (3) = (1) × (2)*	*Actual Profit (4)*	*Fixed Cost (5) = (3) – (4)*
North	1,100	45	495	135	360
East	1,450	60	870	210	660
South	1,200	55	660	330	330
Total	3,750	54	2,025	675	1,350

(ii) Computation of Break-even Sales

(Rs. '000)

Particulars	*Fixed Cost*	*P/V Ratio*	*Break-even Sales*
	(a)	*(b)*	*(a)/(b)*
North	360	45	800
East	660	60	1,100
South	330	55	600
			2,500

Break-even Sales (company as whole): $\frac{\text{Fixed Cost}}{\text{Composite P/V Ratio}} = \frac{1350}{54} = 2{,}500$ (in Rs. '000).

Example 5.21

A company wants to buy a new machine to replace one which is having frequent breakdowns. It received offers for two models M1 and M2. Further details regarding these models are given below:

	M1	*M2*
Installed capacity (units)	10,000	10,000
Fixed overhead per annum (Rs.)	2,40,000	1,00,000
Estimated profit at the above capacity (Rs.)	1,60,000	1,00,000

The product manufactured using this type of machine (M1 and M2) is sold at Rs. 100 per unit. You are required to determine:

(*a*) Break-even level of sales for each model.

(*b*) The level of sales at which both the models will earn the same profit.

(*c*) The model suitable for different levels of demand for the product.

Solution:

(*a*) *Basic Calculations*

Statement showing Comparative Parameters of two Machines

	Type of Machines	*Model M1*	*Model M2*
1.	Installed capacity (units)	10,000	10,000
2.	Fixed Overhead per annum (Rs.)	2,40,000	1,00,000
3.	Selling Price of the Product (Rs.)	100	100
4.	Estimated Profit at the above Capacity (Rs.)	1,60,000	1,00,000
5.	Total Sales Value (Rs.)	10,00,000	10,00,000
6.	Total Contribution (Rs.) (2) + (4)	4,00,000	2,00,000
7.	Variable Cost	6,00,000	8,00,000
8.	Variable Cost per unit	Rs. 60	Rs. 80
9.	P/V Ratio = Contribution/Sales	0.40	0.20

Computation of Break-even Sales

	Model M1	*Model M2*
Break-even Sales	$= \frac{\text{Fixed Cost}}{\text{PV Ratio}}$	$= \frac{\text{Fixed Cost}}{\text{PV Ratio}}$
	$\frac{\text{Rs. } 2,40,000}{.40}$	$= \frac{\text{Rs. } 1,00,000}{.20}$
	= Rs. 6,00,000	Rs. 5,00,000
BEP in units	= 6,000 units	5,000 units

(*b*) Sales at which both models will earn the same profit.

Let the units sold be taken as x

Total Cost for Model 1 = $60x$ = 2,40,000

Total Cost for Model 2 = $80x$ = 1,00,000

On putting these figures in the form of a simultaneous equation:

$60x + 2,40,000 = 80x + 1,00,000$

or $20x = 1,40,000$

or x = 7,000 units

Thus, at 7,000 units of output, the total costs under both the machines will be the same and hence earn the same profit.

(c) *Model Suitable for different levels of Demand.* In view of the above stated comparative parameters Model M2 is suitable for low demand since it has a lower Break-even Point and Lower Fixed Cost and makes higher profit between 5,000 units and 7,000 units than Model M1. In case the level of demand for the product exceeds 7,000 units, Model M1 is better since it makes higher profit.

This can be substantiated by profitability of the two models of the machines at different levels (6,000 units and 8,000 units) as being depicted below:

Levels of Demand	*6,000 units*		*8,000 units*	
Types of Machines	*M1*	*M2*	*M1*	*M2*
Total Contribution (Rs.)	2,40,000	1,20,000	3,20,000	1,60,000
Less: Fixed Cost (Rs.)	2,40,000	1,00,000	2,40,000	1,00,000
	—	20,000	80,000	60,000

Example 5.22

The variable cost structure of a product manufactured by a company during the current year is as under:

	Rs. per unit
Material	120
Labour	30
Overheads	12

The selling price per unit is Rs. 270 and the fixed cost and sales during the current year are Rs. 14 lakh and Rs. 40.5 lakh respectively.

During the forthcoming year, the direct workers will be entitled to a wage increase of 10% form the beginning of the year and the material cost, variable overhead and fixed overhead are expected to increase by 7.5%, 5% and 3% respectively.

The following are required to be computed:

(*i*) New sale price in the forthcoming year if the current P/V ratio is to be maintained and

(*ii*) Number of units that would require to be sold during the forthcoming year so as to yield the same amount of profit in the current year, assuming that selling price per unit will not be increased.

Solution

Current Year's Statement of Profitability

(Units sold 15,000)

Particulars		*Rs.*	*Total*
Selling Price per unit (Rs.)		270	
Less: Variable Cost per unit (Rs.):			
Material	120		
Labour	30		
Overheads	12		
		162	
		108	
Total Contribution (15,000 units × Rs. 108)			16,20,000
Less: Fixed Cost			14,00,000
Profit			2,20,000
P/V Ratio (108/270)			40%

(a) Statement Showing New Selling Price for the Forthcoming Year (Retaining Current Year's P/V Ratio)

Particulars		*Rs*
(1) Variable Cost per unit:		
Material	129.00	
Labour	33.00	
Overheads	12.60	
		174.60
(2) Selling Price 174.60 × 100/60)		291.00
(3) Contribution (2) – (1)		116.40
(4) P/V Ratio		40%

(b) Computation of Number of Units to be Sold during Forthcoming Year (Maintaining the Current year's Profit)

Particulars	*Rs*	*Rs*
(*i*) Current Year Profit	2,220,000	
(*ii*) Revised Fixed Cost	14,42,000	16,62,000
(*iii*) Required Contribution (Rs 270 – Rs 174.60)		95.40
(*iv*) Number of Units to be sold (16,62,000/95.40)		17,422 units

Working Note:

Computation of Variable Cost per Unit

	Current Year	*Forthcoming Year*	
	Rs.	*Increase %*	*Total (Rs.)*
Material	120.00	7.5% (120 × 1.075)	129.00
Labour	30.00	10% (30 × 1.10)	33.00
Overhead	12.00	5% (12 × 1.05)	12.60
	162.00		174.60
Fixed Cost	Rs. 14,00,000	3% (14,00,000 × 1.03)	14,42,000

Example 5.23

The comparative profit statement of two quarters of a firm is as under:

	Quarter I	*Quarter II*
Units sold	2,500	3,750
	Rs.	Rs.
Direct materials	87,500	?
Direct wages	62,500	?
Fixed and variable Factory overheads	75,000	95,000
Sales	2,75,000	?
Profit	50,000	66,250

In the second quarter, the direct material price has increased by 20%. There was a saving of Rs. 5,000 in fixed overheads in the second quarter. The other costs and selling price remained the same. Determine the quantity that should have been sold in the second quarter to maintain the same amount of profit per unit as in the first quarter.

Solution:

Working Notes:

1. Direct material, Direct wages, Selling price and Profit per unit

$$\text{Direct material (p.u.)} = \frac{\text{Rs. } 87,500}{2,500 \text{ units}} = \text{Rs. } 35$$

$$\text{Direct wages (p.u)} = \frac{\text{Rs. } 62,500}{2,500 \text{ units}} = \text{Rs. } 25$$

$$\text{Selling price (p.u.)} = \frac{\text{Rs. } 2,75,000}{2,500 \text{ units}} = \text{Rs. } 110$$

$$\text{Profit (p.u.)} = \frac{\text{Rs. } 50,000}{2,500 \text{ units}} = \text{Rs. } 20$$

2. Variable factory overheads per unit and Fixed factory overheads for the II Quarter

$$\text{Variable factory overhead (p.u.)} = \frac{\text{Changes in semi-variable overheads}}{\text{Changes in production volume}}$$

$$= \frac{\text{Rs. } 1,00,000^{**} - \text{Rs. } 75,000}{3,750 \text{ units} - 2,500 \text{ units}}$$

$$= \frac{\text{Rs. } 25,000}{1,250 \text{ units}} = \text{Rs. } 20$$

** Infact the fixed and variable factory overheads during the quarter (II) were Rs. 1,00,000 but due to saving of Rs. 5,000, the balance amount of Rs. 95,000 was paid.

Fixed factory overheads for II Quarter

	Rs.
Total factory overheads of II quarter	1,00,000
Less: Variable factory overheads (3,750 units × Rs. 20)	75,000
Total fixed factory overheads for II quarter	25000
Less: Saving of fixed factory overheads	5,000
Net fixed factory overheads for II quarter	20,000

Statement of quantity of units to be sold in second quarter to maintain same amount of profit per unit as in the first Quarter

	Rs.	*Rs.*
Selling price per unit: (A) *(Refer to working note 1)*		110
Variable costs: (per unit):		
Direct materials $\left(\text{Rs. } 35 \times \frac{120}{100}\right)$	42	
Direct wages	25	
Variable factory overheads *(Refer to working note 2)*	20	
Total variable cost: (B)		87
Contribution per unit: {(A – D)}		23
Less: Profit per unit (Refer to working note 1)		20
Balance for fixed cost per unit		3
Total fixed cost		20,000

Hence the number of units to be sold in the second quarter to maintain the same amount of profit p.u.

as in the first quarter $= \frac{\text{Total fixed cost}}{\text{Balance for fixed cost p.u.}}$

$$= \frac{\text{Rs. } 20{,}000}{\text{Rs. 3 per unit}} = 6{,}667 \text{ units (approx.)}$$

Example 5.24

A Company manufactures a product, currently utilising 80% capacity with a turnover of Rs. 8,00,000 at Rs. 25 per unit. The cost data are as under:

Material cost Rs. 7.50 per unit, Labour cost Rs. 6.25 per unit.

Semi-variable cost (Including variable cost of Rs. 3.75 per unit) Rs. 1,80,000.

Fixed cost Rs. 90,000 upto 80% level of output, beyond this an additional Rs. 20,000 will be incurred.

Calculate:

(*i*) Activity level at Break-Even-Point

(*ii*) Number of units to be sold to earn a net income of 8% of sales

(*iii*) Activity level needed to earn a profit of Rs. 95,000

(*iv*) What should be the selling price per unit, if break-even-point is to be brought down to 40% activity level.

Solution:

Working Notes:

1. (*i*) *Number of units sold at 80% capacity*

$$= \frac{\text{Turnover}}{\text{Selling price p.u.}} = \frac{\text{Rs. } 80{,}000}{\text{Rs. } 25} = \text{Rs. } 32{,}000 \text{ units}$$

(*ii*) *Number of units sold at 100% capacity*

$$= \frac{32{,}000 \text{ units}}{80} \times 100 = 40{,}000 \text{ units}$$

2. *Component of fixed cost included in semi-variable cost of 32,000 units*

Fixed cost = {Total semi-variable cost – Total variable cost}

= Rs. 1,80,000 – 32,000 units × Rs. 3.75

= Rs. 1,80,000 – Rs. 1,20,000

= Rs. 60,000

3. (*i*) *Total fixed cost beyond 80% capacity*

= Fixed cost + Component of fixed cost included in semi-variable cost

(Refer to working note 2)

= Rs. 90,000 + Rs. 60,000 = Rs. 1,50,000

(*ii*) *Total fixed cost beyond 80% capacity*

= Total fixed cost at 80% capacity + Additional fixed cost to be incurred

= Rs. 1,50,000 + Rs. 20,000 = Rs. 1,70,000

4. *Variable cost and contribution per unit*

Variable cost per unit = Material cost + Labour cost + Variable cost component in semi-variable cost

= Rs. 7.50 + Rs. 6.25 + Rs. 3.75 = Rs. 17.50

Contribution per unit = Selling price per unit – Variable cost per unit

= Rs. 25 – Rs. 17.50 = Rs. 7.50

5. *Profit at 80% capacity level*

= Sales revenue – Variable cost – Fixed cost

= Rs. 8,00,000 – Rs. 5,60,000 (32,000 units × Rs. 17.50) – Rs. 1,50,000

= Rs. 90,000

(*i*) Activity level at Break-Even-Point

$$\text{Break-even point (units)} = \frac{\text{Fixed cost}}{\text{Contribution per unit}} = \frac{\text{Rs. } 1{,}50{,}000}{\text{Rs. } 7.50} = 20{,}000 \text{ units}$$

(Refer to working notes 3 & 4)

$$\text{Activity level at Break-Even-Point} = \frac{\text{Break-Even point (units)}}{\text{No. of units at 100\% capacity level}} \times 100$$

(Refer to working note 1(*ii*)

$$= \frac{20{,}000 \text{ units}}{40{,}000 \text{ units}} \times 100 = 50\%$$

(*ii*) Number of units to be sold to earn a net income of 8% of sales

Let x be the number of units sold to earn a net income of 8% of sales.

Mathematically, it means that:

(Sales revenue of x units) = Variable cost of x units + Fixed cost + Net income

or Rs. $25x$ = Rs. $17.5x$ + Rs. 1,50,000 + $\frac{8}{100}$ × (Rs. $25x$)

or Rs. 25x = Rs. $17.5x$ + Rs. 1,50,000 + Rs. $2x$

or x = (Rs. 1,50,000/Rs.5.5) units

or x = 27,273 units.

(*iii*) *Activity level needed to earn a profit of Rs. 95,000*

The profit at 80% capacity level is Rs. 90,000 which is less than the desired profit of Rs. 95,000, therefore the needed activity level would be more than 80%. Thus, the fixed cost to be taken to determine the activity level needed should be Rs. 1,70,000 [*Refer to Working Note 3(ii)*]

$$\text{Units to be sold to earn profit of Rs. 95,000} = \frac{\text{Fixed cost + Desired profit}}{\text{Contribution per unit}}$$

$$= \frac{\text{Rs.}\,1{,}70{,}000 + \text{Rs.}\,95{,}000}{\text{Rs.}\,7.5}$$

$$= 35{,}333.33 \text{ units}$$

$$\text{Activity level needed to earn a profit of Rs. 95,000} = \frac{35{,}333.33}{40{,}000 \text{ units}} \times 100$$

$$= 88.33\%$$

(*iv*) *Selling price per unit, if break-even-point is to be brought down to 40% (16,000 units) activity level*

Let x be the selling price per unit

Units at Break-even-point = 16,000 units

$$\text{Break-even-point} = \frac{\text{Fixed cost}}{\text{Contribution per unit}}$$

$$\text{At 16,000 units} = \frac{\text{Rs.}\,1{,}50{,}000}{(x - \text{Rs.}\,17.50)}$$

$$\text{or } (x - \text{Rs. } 17.50) = \frac{\text{Rs.}\,1{,}50{,}000}{16{,}000 \text{ units}}$$

$$\text{or } (x - \text{Rs. } 17.50) = \frac{\text{Rs. } 75}{8 \text{ units}}$$

or $8x - 8 \times$ Rs. 17.50 = Rs. 75

or $8x$ – Rs. 140 = Rs. 75

or $8x$ = Rs. 215

or x = Rs. 26.875

Hence, S.P. (per unit)= Rs. 26.875

Example 5.25

Fill in the blanks for each of the following independent situations:

	A	*B*	*C*	*D*	*E*
Selling Price per unit	—	Rs. 50	Rs. 20	—	Rs. 30
Variable Cost as % of Selling Price	60	—	75	75	—
No. of units sold	10,000	4,000	—	6,000	5,000
Marginal Contribution	Rs. 20,000	Rs. 80,000	—	Rs. 25,000	Rs. 50,000
Fixed Costs	Rs. 12,000		Rs. 1,20,000	Rs. 10,000	—
Profit/Loss	—	Rs. 20,000	Rs. 30,000	—	Rs. 15,000

Solution

Independent Situation	*Blank space to be filled*	*Figure of blank*
A	Profit/(Loss) *[Refer to working note 1 (i)]*	Rs. 8,000
	Selling price per unit [Refer to working note 1 (ii)]	Rs. 5
B	Fixed costs *[Refer to working note 2(i)]*	Rs. 60,000
	Variable cost as % of selling price *[Refer to working note 2(ii)]*	60%
C	No. of units sold *[Refer to working 3 (ii)]*	30,000 units
	Marginal contribution	Rs. 1,50,000
D	*[Refer to working note 3 (i)]*	
	Selling price per unit *[Refer to working note 4 (ii)]*	Rs. 16.66
	Profit/(Loss) *[Refer to working note 4 (i)]*	Rs. 15,000
E	Variable cost as % of selling price *[Refer to working note 5(ii)]*	66.66%
	Fixed costs *[Refer to working note 5 (i)]*	Rs. 35,000

Working Notes:

1. (*i*) Profit/(Loss) = Contribution – Fixed costs

= Rs. 20,000 – Rs. 12,000 = Rs. 8,000

(*ii*) Let selling price per unit be (x)

(Selling price per unit – Variable cost per unit) No. of units sold = Marginal contribution

or $\left(x - \frac{3}{5}x\right) \times 10{,}000$ units = Rs. 20,000

Variable Cost as %

or $x\frac{2}{5}$ = Rs. 2

or x = Rs. 5

2. (*i*) Fixed costs= Marginal contribution – Profit

= Rs. 80,000 - Rs. 20,000 = Rs. 60,000

(*ii*) Variable Cost as % of selling price

$$= \frac{\text{Selling price per unit} - \text{Marginal contribution per unit}}{\text{Selling price per unit}} \times 100$$

$$= \frac{\text{Rs. } 50 - \text{Rs. } 20}{\text{Rs. } 50} \times 100 = 60\%$$

3. (*i*) Marginal contribution = Fixed costs + Profit

= Rs. 1,20,000 + Rs. 30,000 = Rs. 1,50,000

(*ii*) No. of units sold $= \frac{\text{Marginal Contribution}}{\text{Contribution per unit}}$

$$= \frac{\text{Rs. } 1{,}50{,}000}{(\text{Rs. } 20 - \text{Rs. } 15)} = \frac{\text{Rs. } 1{,}50{,}000}{\text{Rs. } 5}$$

= 30,000 units

4. (*i*) Profit/(Loss) = Marginal contribution – Fixed costs

= Rs. 25,000 – Rs. 10,000 = Rs. 15,000

(*ii*) Selling price per unit (x)

(Selling price per unit – Variable cost per unit) No. of units sold = Marginal contribution

or $\left(x - \frac{3}{4}x\right)$ 6,000 units = Rs. 25,000

or $\frac{x}{4} \times 6{,}000$ = Rs. 25,000

or x = Rs. 16.66 per unit

5. (*i*) Fixed costs = Marginal contribution – Profit

= Rs. 50,000 – Rs. 15,000 = Rs. 35,000

(*ii*) Variable cost per unit = Selling price – Marginal contribution per unit

= (Rs. 30 – Rs. 50,000/5,000)

= Rs. 20

$$\text{Variable costs as \% of selling price} = \frac{\text{Variable cost per unit}}{\text{Selling price per unit}} \times 100$$

$$= \frac{\text{Rs. } 20}{\text{Rs. } 30} \times 100 = 66.66$$

Example 5.26

ABC Ltd. which produces three products furnishes the following data for the year 1998.

	Products		
	Alfa	*Beta*	*Gama*
Selling Prices per unit	Rs. 100	75	50
Profit/Volume Ratio	10%	20%	40%
Maximum Sales Potential (units)	40,000	25,000	10,000
Raw Material as % of Variable Cost	50%	50%	50%

The company uses the same raw material for all the three products. Raw material is in short supply and the company has a quota for supply of raw material of the value of Rs. 18,00,000 for the year 1998 for manufacture of its products to meet its sales. Total fixed costs is Rs. 6,80,000.

You are required to:

(*a*) Determine a sales mix which will give the maximum overall profit keeping in view the short supply of raw materials and

(*b*) Compute the maximum profit. *(B.Com., Hons. Delhi 1999)*

Solution:

Particulars	*Products*		
	Alfa	*Beta*	*Gama*
Selling Price per unit	100	75	50
Profit Volume Ratio	10%	20%	40%
Contribution per unit	10	15	20
Variable Cost per unit	90	60	30
Raw Material per unit	45	30	15
Contribution per rupee of raw material	10/45	15/30	20/15
	2/9	½	4/3
Ranking	3	2	1

(a) Computation of Sales Mix

Product	*Units* *Rs.*	*Sales* *Rs.*	*Raw Material used*
Gama	10,000	5,00,000	1,50,000
Beta	25,000	18,75,000	7,50,000
Alfa	20,000	20,00,000	9,00,000
Balance	55,000	43,75,000	18,00,000

(b) Computation of Profit

Product	*Sales* *Rs.*	*P/V Ratio*	*Contribution*
Gama	5,00,000	40	2,00,000
Beta	18,75,000	20	3,75,000
Alfa	20,00,000	10	2,00,000
			7,75,000
	Less: Fixed Cost		6,80,000
	Net Profit		95,000

Example 5.27

A company has two Plants at Locations I and II, operating at 100% and 75% of their capacities respectively. The company is considering a proposal to merge the two plants at one location to optimise available capacity. The following details are available in respect of the two plants, regarding their present performance/operations:

Particulars	*Location I*	*Location II*
Sales (Rs. in lakhs)	200	75
Variable Cost (Rs. in lakhs)	140	54
Fixed Cost (Rs. in lakhs)	30	14

For decision-making purposes, you are required to work out the following information:

(*a*) The capacity at which the merged plant will breakeven.

(*b*) The profit of the merged plant working at 80% capacity and

(*c*) Sales required if the merged plant is required to earn an overall profit of Rs. 22 lakh.

Solution:

Comparative Performance of Plant at 100% Capacity

(Rs. in lakhs)

Plants	*Plant Location-I*	*Plant Location-II*	*Merged Plant*
Capacity Levels	100%	100%	100%
Sales	200	100	300
Less: Variable Cost	140	72	212
Contribution	60	28	88
Less: Fixed Cost	30	14	44
Profit/(Loss)	30	14	44
P/V Ratio (%): (Contribution/Sales)	30%	28%	29.33
Break-even Sales (Fixed Cost/P/V Ratio)	44/29.33%		150

(*a*) Capacity at BEP(%): $\frac{150}{300} \times 100 = 50\%$

(*b*) Computation of Profitability of the Merged Plant at 80% Capacity

(Rs. in lakhs)

Particulars	*Rs.*
Sales (80% of 300)	240.00
Less: Variable Cost	169.60
Contribution	70.40
Less: Fixed Cost	44.00
Profit	26.40

(*c*) Computation of sales required to earn Desired Profit of Rs. 22 lakh:

Contribution required (Rs. in lakhs):		
Fixed Cost	44.00	
Desired Profit	22.00	66.00
P/V Ratio (%)		29.33%
Desired Sales Level (Rs. in lakhs)	$\frac{66 \times 100}{2933}$	= 225.00

Example 5.28

An automobile manufacturing company produces different models of cars. The budget in respect of model 118 for the month of September, 1996 is as under:

Budgeted Output		*40,000 units*
		(Rs. in lakhs)
Net Realisation	*Rs. in lakhs*	700
Variable Costs:		
Materials	264	
Labour	52	
Direct Expenses	124	440
Specific Fixed Costs	90	
Allocated Fixed Costs	112.50	202.50
Total Costs		642.50
Profit		57.50
Sales		700.00

Calculate:

(*i*) Profit with 10 per cent increase in selling price with a 10 per cent reduction in sales volume.

(*ii*) Volume to be achieved to maintain the original profit after a 10 per cent rise in material costs, at the originally budgeted selling price per unit.

Solution:

(i) Statement of Profit
(With 10 per cent increase in selling price with a 10 per cent reduction in sales-volume)

	(Rs. in Lakh)
Sale Revenue: (A) *(See WN 1)*	693
Less: Variable Costs: (B) *(See WN 2)*	396
Contribution {(A) – (B)}	297
Less: Total Fixed Costs	202.5
Profit	94.5

Working Notes:

1. Selling Price (per unit) $= \dfrac{\text{Rs. } 7,00,00,000}{40,000 \text{ units}}$ = Rs. 1,750

   New Selling Price (per unit) = Rs. 1,750 + Rs. 175 = Rs. 1,925

   Reduced Sales Volume = 36,000 units

   Total Sales Revenue = Rs. 1,925 × 36,000 = Rs. 693 lakh

2. (*i*) *Variable Costs per unit*

		Rs.
Materials Cost	=	660
Labour Cost	=	130
Direct Expenses	=	310
Total Variable Cost	=	1,100

(ii) Volume to be achieved to maintain original profit

	Rs.	Rs.
Selling Price (per unit) (as per Working Note)		1,750
Less: Variable Costs		
Material Cost (Rs. 660 + Rs. 66)	726	
Labour Cost	130	
Direct Expenses	310	1,166
Contribution per unit		584

Desired Contribution = Fixed Cost + Original Profit
= Rs. 202.50 + Rs. 57.50
= Rs. 260 lakh

No. of cars to be sold to maintain original profit at original sales price = $\frac{\text{Rs. 260 lakh}}{\text{Rs. 584}}$

= 44,520.547 or say 44,521 cars.

Example 5.29

(*a*) A Company had incurred fixed expenses of Rs. 4,50,000, with sales of Rs. 15,00,000 and earned a profit of Rs. 3,00,000 during the first half year. In the second half, it suffered a loss of Rs. 1,50,0000.

Calculate:

(*i*) The profit-volume ratio, break-even point and margin of safety for the first half year.

(*ii*) Expected sales volume for the second half year assuming that selling price and fixed expenses remained unchanged during the second half year.

(*iii*) The break-even point and margin of safety for the whole year.

(*b*) A company manufactures and markets three products X, Y and Z. All the three products are made from the same set of machines. Production is limited by machine capacity. From the data given below, indicate priorities for products, X, Y and Z with a view to maximising profits.

Particulars		*Products*		
		X	*Y*	*Z*
Raw Material Cost per unit	(Rs.)	11.25	16.25	21.25
Direct Labour Cost per unit	(Rs.)	2.50	2.50	2.50
Other Variable Cost per unit	(Rs.)	1.50	2.25	3.55
Selling Price per unit	(Rs.)	25.00	30.00	35.00
Standard Machine time required Per unit in minutes		39	20	28

Solution

(*a*) (*i*) *Computation of Profit-Volume Ratio, Break-even Point and Margin of Safety: (for the first half year)*

$$\text{Profit-volume Ratio} = \frac{\text{Contribution}}{\text{Sales}} \times 100$$

$$= \frac{\text{Fixed Expenses + Profit}}{\text{Sales}} \times 100$$

$$= \frac{\text{Rs. } 4,50,000 + \text{Rs.} 3,00,000}{\text{Rs.} 15,00,000} \times 100$$

$$= 50\%$$

$$\text{Break-even Point} = \frac{\text{Fixed Expenses}}{P/V \text{ Ratio}}$$

$$= \frac{\text{Rs.} 4,50,000}{50\%}$$

$$= \text{Rs. } 9,00,000$$

Margin of Safety = Actual Sales – Break-even Sales

= Rs. 15,00,000 – Rs. 9,00,000

= Rs. 6,00,000

(ii) *Computation of Expected Sales Volume*

$$\text{Expected Sales Volume} = \frac{\text{Fixed Expenses} - \text{Loss}}{\text{P/V ratio}}$$

$$= \frac{\text{Rs. } 4,50,000 - \text{Rs.} 1,50,000}{50\%}$$

$$= 6,00,000$$

(iii) *Computation of Break-even Point and Margin of Safety (for the whole year)*

$$\text{Beak-even Point} = \frac{\text{Fixed Expenses for the whole year}}{P/V \text{ Ratio}}$$

$$= \frac{\text{Rs. } 9,00,000}{50\%} = \text{Rs. } 18,00,000$$

$$\text{Margin of Safety} = \frac{\text{Profit for the year}}{P/V \text{ Ratio}}$$

$$= \frac{\text{Rs. } 3,00,000 - \text{Rs.} 1,50,000}{50\%}$$

$$= \text{Rs. } 3,00,000$$

(b) Statement showing Priorities for Products X, Y and Z to Maximise Profits

Products			*X*	*Y*	*Z*
Selling Price per unit	(Rs.)		25.00	30.00	35.00
Less: Variable Cost per unit *(see working note)*	(Rs.)		15.25	21	27.30
Contribution per unit	(Rs.)	(A)	9.75	9	7.70
Std. Machine time required in Minutes per unit		(B)	30	20	28
Contribution per minute	(Rs.)	(A)/(B)	0.25	0.45	0.275
Priorities for Products			III	I	II

Working Note:

Computation of Variable Cost per Unit

Particulars	*Products*		
	X	*Y*	*Z*
	Rs.	*Rs.*	*Rs.*
Raw Material Cost	11.25	16.25	21.25
Direct Labour Cost	2.50	2.50	2.50
Other Variable Cost	1.50	2.25	3.55
Total Variable Cost per unit	15.25	21.00	27.30

Example 5.30

Two firms A & Co. and B & Co. sell the same type of product in the same market. Their budgeted Profit & Loss Account for the year ending 31st March, 1996 are as follows:

Particulars	*A & Co.*		*B & Co.*	
	Rs.	*Rs.*	*Rs.*	*Rs.*
Sales		5,00,000		6,00,000
Variable Costs	4,00,000		4,00,000	
Fixed Costs	30,000	4,30,0000	70,000	4,70,000
Net Profit		70,000		1,30,000

Required:

1. Calculate at which sales volume both the firms will earn equal profit.
2. State which firm is likely to earn greater profits in condition of:
   (*i*) heavy demand for the product and
   (*ii*) low demand for the product.

Give reasons.

Solution:

Computation of Sales Volume for Equal Profits

Particulars	*A & Co.*	*B & Co.*
Sales (Rs.)	5,00,000	6,00,000
Less: Variable Costs (Rs.)	4,00,000	4,00,000
Contribution (Rs.)	1,00,000	2,00,000
P/V Ratio (C/S × 100)	20%	33.33%

$$\text{Sales Volume} = \frac{\text{Difference in Fixed Cost}}{\text{Difference in P/V ratio}}$$

$$\text{(for both the firms to earn equal profit)} = \frac{\text{Rs. } 40{,}000}{13.33\%}$$

$$= \text{Rs. } 3{,}00{,}000$$

2. The P/V ratio of B & Co. at 33.33% is higher than that of A & Co. at 20% and therefore B & Co. will earn higher profit if the sales volume exceeds the level of Rs. 3,00,000.

As a matter of fact, for each additional unit of product's sales above Rs. 3,00,000, the profit of B & Co. will rise by Rs. 33.33 which exceeds by Rs. 13.33, the profit of A & Co. under similar circumstances. However, below that level, profit for A & Co. will be greater. Hence, it can generally be concluded that B & Co. is likely to earn higher profits under conditions of heavy demand for the product above Rs. 3,00,000. On the other hand A & Co. is expected to make higher profits under conditions of low demand for the product below sales volume of Rs. 3,00,000.

Example 5.31

A manufacturing company has an installed capacity of 1,20,000 units per annum. The cost structure of the product manufactured is as under:

	Rs.
(*i*) Variable cost per unit —	
Materials	8
Labour (Subject to a minimum of Rs. 56,000 per month)	8
Overheads	3

(*ii*) Fixed overheads – Rs. 1,68,750 per annum.

(*iii*) Semi-variable overheads Rs. 48,000 per annum at 60% capacity, which increase by Rs. 6,000 per annum for increase of every 10% of the capacity utilisation or any part thereof for the year as a whole.

The capacity utilisation for the next year is estimated at 60% for two months, 75% for six months and 80% for the remaining part of the year. If the company is planning to have a profit of 25% on the selling price, calculate the selling price per unit. Assume that there are no opening and closing stocks.

Solution:

Statement of Selling Price and Profit

	Rs.
Materials 89,000 units × Rs. 8 per unit (WN 1)	7,12,000
Labour Cost (WN 2)	7,28,000
Variable Overheads (89,0000 units × Rs. 3)	2,67,000
Semi-variable overheads (WN 3)	60,000
Fixed Overheads	1,68,750
Total Cost	19,35,750
Add: Profit 25% of selling price or 33 1/3% on cost	6,45,250
Total Sales Value	25,81,000
Selling Price per unit (Rs. 25,81,000/89,000 units)	29.00

Working Notes:

1. Computation of Capacity Utilisation (for the next year):

60% of capacity for first two months	= 2 months × 6,000 units	= 12,000 units
75% of capacity for next six months	= 6 months × 7,500 units	= 45,000 units
80% of capacity for the remaining four months	= 4 months × 8,000 units	= 32,000 units
Total capacity utilisation		= 89,000 units

$$\text{Capacity utilisation} = \frac{89{,}000 \text{ units}}{1{,}20{,}000 \text{ units}} \times 100 = 74\frac{1}{6}\ \%$$

2. Computation of labour cost (subject to a minimum of Rs. 56,000 p.m.)

	Rs.
Labour Cost of first two months 12,000 units × Rs. 8 = Rs. 96,000 However Minimum is 56,000 × 2	1,12,000
Labour cost of next six months 45,000 units × Rs. 8	3,60,000
Labour cost of last four months 32,000 units × Rs. 8	2,56,000
Total Labour Cost	7,28,000

3. *Computation of semi-variable overheads (per annum):*

	Rs.
Semi-variable Overheads (at 60% capacity)	48,000
Semi-variable Overheads for additional (14-16% capacity are the same as that for 20% of the capacity utilisation for the entire year)	12,000
	60,000

Example 5.32

Indian Plastics makes plastic buckets. An analysis of their accounting reveals:

Variable cost per bucket	Rs. 20
Fixed cost	Rs. 50,000 for the year
Capacity	Rs. 2,000 buckets per year
Selling price per bucket	Rs. 70

Required:

(*i*) Find the break-even point.

(*ii*) Find the number of buckets to be sold to get a profit of Rs. 30,000.

(*iii*) If the company can manufacture 600 buckets more per year with an additional fixed cost of Rs. 2,000, what should be the selling price to maintain the profit per bucket as at (ii) above?

Solution:

(*i*) BEP = Fixed cost/contribution per unit
= 50,000/50 = 1,000 buckets.

(*ii*) Buckets to be sold for desired profit of Rs. 30,000

$$\text{Sales for Desired Profit} = \frac{\text{Fixed cost + Desired profit}}{\text{Contribution per unit}}$$

$$= \frac{50{,}000 + 30{,}000}{50}$$

= 80,000/50

= 1,600 buckets

		Rs.
(*iii*)	Computation of new selling price:	
	Profit per bucket at sales of 16000 buckets:	
	Sales (1,600 × 70)	1,12,000
Less:	Variable cost 1,600 × 20	32,000
	Contribution	80,000
Less:	Fixed costs	50,000
	Profit	30,000
	Profit per bucket 30,000/1,600	18.75
	Total sales 1,600 + 600 = 2,200 buckets	
	Total profit desired = 2,200 × 18.75 =	Rs. 41,250
	Let selling price be '*x*'	

The following equation can be made:

Total sales	= Total cost + Profit
2,200x	= 20 (2,200) + 52,000 + 41,250
2,200x	= 1,37,250
or x	= Rs. 62,39 per bucket

Note: It has been assumed that 600 more buckets to be manufactured are in addition to 1,600 buckets as computed under (ii) above.

Example 5.33

A retail dealer in garments is currently selling 24,000 shirts annually. He supplies the following details for the year ended 31st December, 2001.

	Rs.
Selling price per shirt	40
Variable cost per shirt	25
Fixed Cost: Staff salaries for the year	1,20,000
General office costs for the year	80,000
Advertising costs for the year	40,000

As a cost accountant of the firm, you are required to answer the following each part independently:

(*i*) Calculate the break-even point and margin of safety in sales revenue and number of shirts sold.

(*ii*) Assume that 20,000 shirts were sold in a year. Find out the net profit of the firm.

(*iii*) If it is decided to introduce selling commission of Rs. 3 per shirt, how many shirts would require to be sold in a year to earn a net income of Rs. 15,000.

(*iv*) Assuming that for the year 2002 an additional staff salary of Rs. 33,000 is anticipated, and price of a shirt is likely to be increased by 15%, what should be the break-even point in the number of shirts and sales revenue?

Solution:

(*i*) BEP = Fixed cost/Contribution per unit

= 2,40,000/15 = 16,000 units or

= 16,000 × 40 = Rs. 6,40,000

Margin of Safety (MS) = Actual sales – Break-even sales

= 24,000 × 40 – 6,40,000

= 9,60,000 – 6,40,000

Rs. 3,20,000

(*ii*) Net profit when 20,000 shifts are sold:

Contribution: 20,000 × 15	Rs. 3,00,000
Less: Fixed costs	Rs. 2,40,000
Profit	Rs. 60,000

(*iii*) Sales for desired profit:

$$= \frac{\text{Fixed cost + Desired profit}}{\text{New contribution per unit}}$$

$$= \frac{2,40,000 + 15,000}{15 - 3}$$

$$= \frac{2,55,000}{12} = 21,250 \text{ shifts}$$

(*iv*) New break-even point:

In units: New fixed cost/New contribution unit

$$= \frac{2,40,000 + 33,000}{46 - 25}$$

= 2,73,000/21 = 13,000 shirts

In Rs. = 13,000 × 46 = Rs. 5,98,000

Example 5.34

An enthusiastic marketing manager suggests to his managing director that only if he is permitted to reduce the selling price of a product by 20%, he would be able to achieve a 30% increase in sales volume. The managing director finding that the sales volume increase exceeds in percentage, the extent of requested reduction in price gives the clearance.

You are given the following information:

Present selling price per unit	Rs. 7.50
Present volume of sales	2,00,000 Nos.
Total variable costs	Rs. 10,50,000
Total fixed costs	Rs. 3,60,000

Assuming no changes in the costs pattern in the coming period:

(*i*) Examine the consequences of the managing director's decision assuming that 30% increase in sales is realised and

(*ii*) At what volume of sales can the present quantum of profits be sustained, after affecting the price reduction.

Solution:

Statement Showing the Present Result and Result after Price Reduction

	Present result *Rs.*	*Proposed result* *Rs.*
Selling price per unit	7.50	6.00
Sales volume	2,00,000 units	2,60,000 units
Variable cost per unit	5.25	5.25
Contribution per unit	2.25	0.75
Total contribution	4,50,000	1,95,000
Total fixed costs	3,60,000	3,60,000
Profit (loss)	90,000	(1,65,000)

(*i*) The above statement shows that on account of reduction in the selling price, there will be loss of Rs. 1,65,000 as compared to the present profit of Rs. 90,000, inspite of increase in the sales volume. Thus, there will be an effective drop of profit of Rs. 2,55,000 on account of the decision taken by the managing director on the suggestion made by the marketing manager.

(*ii*) Statement showing the volume of sales at which the present profit can be retained after price reduction.

$$\text{Volume of sales for the profit} = \frac{\text{Fixed cost + Desired profit}}{\text{Contribution per unit}}$$

$$= \frac{3,60,000+90,000}{0.75^*} = 6,00,000 \text{ units}$$

*Rs. 6 – Rs. 5.25

The above statement shows that 200 per cent increase is required to justify a reduction of selling price by 20% without in any way affecting the present profit.

Example 5.35

Cadbury Schweppes Limited, a British chocolate and soft drink company, is planning to establish a subsidiary company in India to produce Schweppes Mineral Water.

Based on the estimated annual sales of 40,000 bottles of the mineral water, cost studies produced the following estimates for the Indian subsidiary:

	Total annual costs	*Per cent of total annual Cost that is variable*
Material	Rs. 193,600	100%
Labour	90,000	70%
Overheads	80,000	64%
Administration	30,000	30%

The Indian production will be sold by manufacturer's representatives who will receive a commission of 8 per cent of the sale price. No portion of the British office expenses is to be allocated to the Indian subsidiary.

It is required to:

(*i*) compute the sale price per bottle to enable management to realise an estimated 10 per cent profit on sales proceeds in India and (*ii*) calculate the break-even point in rupee sales for the Indian subsidiary on the assumption that the sale price is Rs. 11 per bottle.

Solution:

(i) Computation of Selling Price per Unit

Let the selling price per unit be x

Total sales	$40{,}000\ x$
Total Commission	$3{,}200\ x$
Total Profit	$4{,}000\ x$

Total sales = Total cost + Profit

$40{,}000\ x = 1{,}93{,}600 + 90{,}000 + 80{,}000 + 30{,}000 + 3{,}200\ x + 4{,}000\ x$

or $40{,}000\ x = 3{,}93{,}600 + 7{,}200\ x$

or $32{,}800\ x = 3{,}93{,}600$

$x =$ Rs. 12

(ii) Computation of Break-even Point

	Sales (40,000 × 11)		Rs. 4,40,000
Less:	Marginal cost		
	Material	Rs. 1,93,600	
	Labour 90,000 × 70/100	63,000	
	Overhead 80,000 × 64/100	51,200	
	Administration $30{,}000 \times \frac{30}{100}$	9,000	
	Sales Commission 4,40,000 × 8/100	35,200	3,52,000
	Total contribution		88,000

$$\text{Break-even sales} = \frac{\text{Fixed cost} \times \text{Total sales}}{\text{Total contribution}}$$

$$= \frac{27{,}000 + 28{,}800 + 21{,}000 \times 4{,}40{,}000}{88{,}000}$$

$$= \frac{76{,}800}{88{,}000} \times 4{,}40{,}000 = \text{Rs. } 3{,}84{,}000$$

Example 5.36

A factory engaged in manufacturing plastic buckets is working to 40% capacity and produces 10,000 buckets per annum.

The present cost break-up for one bucket is as under:

Material	Rs. 10
Labour cost	3
Overheads	5 (60% fixed)

The selling price Rs. 20 per bucket.

If it is decided to work the factory at 50% capacity, the selling price falls by 3%. At 90% capacity, the selling price falls by 5% accompanied by a similar fall in the prices of material.

You are required to calculate the profit at 50% and 90% capacities and also calculate break-even points for the same capacity productions.

Solution:

Statement Showing Profit and Break-even Point at Different Capacity Levels

Capacity levels *Production (units)*	*50%* *12.500*		*90%* *22.500*	
	Per unit	*Total*	*Per unit*	*Total*
(*i*) Sales	Rs. 19.40	Rs. 2,42,500	Rs. 19.00	Rs. 4,27,500
Variable cost:				
Materials	10.00	1,25,000	9.50	2,13,750
Wages	3.00	37,500	3.00	67,500
Variable overheads	2.00	25.000	2.00	45.000
(*ii*) Total variable cost	15.00	1,87,500	14.50	3,26,250
(*iii*) Contribution (*i* - *ii*)	4.40	55,000	4.50	1,01,250
(*iv*) Fixed costs		30,000		30,000
(*v*) Net Profit (*iii* – *iv*)		25,000		71,250

Break-even point at 50% capacity

$$\frac{\text{Fixed cost}}{\text{Contribution per unit}}$$

at 90% capacity

$$\frac{\text{Fixed cost}}{\text{Contribution per unit}}$$

Units $\frac{30{,}000}{4.40} = 6{,}818$ units $\qquad \frac{30{,}000}{4.50} = 6{,}667$ units

Sales value Rs. 132,270 Rs. 1,26,673

Example 5.37

Triple X company produces these products with the following characteristics:

	Product I	*Product II*	*Product III*
Price per unit	Rs. 5	Rs. 6	Rs. 7
	3	2	4
Expected sales (units)	1,00,000	1,50,000	2,50,000

Total fixed costs for the company are Rs. 12,40,000.

Assuming that the product mix would be the same at the break-even point, compute the break-even point in:

(*a*) Unit (total and by product line) and

(*b*) Sales Rupees (total and by product line).

Solution:

(*a*) Compute weighted-average contribution margin:

	Product I	*Product II*	*Product III*
Product mix	$\frac{1{,}00{,}000 \text{ units}}{5{,}00{,}000 \text{ units}}$	$\frac{1{,}50{,}000 \text{ units}}{5{,}00{,}000 \text{ units}}$	$\frac{2{,}50{,}000 \text{ units}}{5{,}00{,}000 \text{ units}}$
	= .20	= .30	= .50

Weighted-average Contribution margin = .20 (Rs. 2) + .30 (Rs. 4) + .50 (Rs. 3) = Rs. 3.10

or

$$\frac{(1,00,000 \text{ units})(\text{Rs. }2) + (1,50,000)(\text{Rs.}4) + (2,50,000)(\text{Rs. }3)}{5,00,000 \text{ units}}$$

$$= \text{Rs. } 3.10$$

$$x = \frac{\text{Rs. }12,40,000}{\text{Rs. }3.10}$$

$$x = 4,00,000 \text{ units}$$

(*b*) To compute break-even sales rupees, find the weighted-average price and variable costs:

$$P = (.20)(\text{Rs. }5) + (.30)(\text{Rs. }6) + .50(\text{Rs. }7)$$
$$= \text{Rs. } 6.30$$
$$V = (.2)(\text{Rs. }3) + (.30)(\text{Rs. }2) + (.50)(\text{Rs. }4)$$
$$= \text{Rs. } 3.20$$

$$\text{Break-even point} = \frac{F}{\frac{P-V}{P}} = \frac{\text{Rs. }12,40,000}{\text{Rs. }3.10/\text{Rs. }6.30} = \text{Rs. } 12,40,000$$

$$= \frac{\text{Rs. }12,40,000}{.492}$$

$$= \text{Rs. } 25,20,000 \text{ approx.}$$

(Check 4,00,000 units × Rs. 6.30 = 25,20,000)

Product line amounts:

	Total	*Product I*	*Product II*	*Product III*
	(100%)	(20%)	(30%)	(40%)
Units	4,00,000	80,000	1,20,000	2,00,000
Units price (Rs.)	6.30	5	6	7
Sales Rupees	25,20,000	4,00,000	7,20,000	14,00,000

Example 5.38

The Chief Cost Accountant of Vikas Limited found to his surprise that the actual profit for the period ending 30th June 1997 was the same as budgeted inspite of realising 10% more than the budgeted selling prices. The following were the results:

Particulars	*Budget* Rs.	*Actuals* Rs.
Sales	5,00,000	8,25,000
Variable costs of sales	3,00,000	5,75,000
Fixed costs	1,00,000	1,50,000
Profit	1,00,000	1,00,000

You are required to assist the Chief Cost Accountant in preparing the necessary explanations as to why the profit remained the same despite an increase in sales.

Solution:

In order to assist the Chief Accountant of Vikas Ltd. in preparing the necessary explanations for the profit remaining the same inspite of an increase in sale revenue, the following factors may be considered:

Factors contributing to the increase in profit:

	Rs.
(*i*) Increase in sales revenue due to increased selling price (Working Note 1)	75,000
(*ii*) Increase in contribution on account of increased sales volume (Working Note 4)	1,00,000
	1,75,000

Factors contributing to the increase in cost:

(*i*) Increase in variable costs: (Working Note 5)	1,25,000
(*ii*) Increase in fixed cost	50,000
	1,75,000

Working Notes:

1. Increase in sales revenue due to price increase (10% more than the budgeted)

$$= \frac{\text{Rs.}8,25,000 \times 100}{110} = \text{Rs. } 75,000$$

2. Increase in sales volume = (Actual sales – Sales revenue due to increased selling price – Budgeted sales)

= Rs. 8,25,000 – Rs. 75,000 – 5,00,000

= Rs. 2,50,000

(2) Statement of Contribution

Products (*i*)	*Units* (*ii*)	*Selling price per unit* (*iii*)	*Variable cost per unit* (*iv*)	*Sales revenue* (*v*)	*Variable cost* (*vi*)	*Contribution* (*vii*)
A	2,000	200	120	4,00,000	2,40,000	1,60,000
B	1,600	160	120	2,56,000	1,92,000	64,000
C	2,400	100	40	2,40,000	96,000	1,44,000
	Total			8,96,000	5,28,000	3,68,000

Example 5.39

The budgeted income statement by product lines of Multiproducts Ltd. for 2001 is as follows:

	Product A Rs.	*Product B* Rs.	*Product C* Rs.
Sales	2,00,000	5,00,000	3,00,000
Variable Expenses:			
Cost of goods sold	90,000	2,70,000	1,50,000
Selling	30,000	90,000	45,000
Fixed Expenses:			
Overhead	36,000	90,000	54,000
Administrative	16,000	40,000	24,000
Income before tax	28,000	10,000	27,000
Income tax @ 40%	11,200	4,000	10,800
Net Income	16,800	6,000	16,200

All products are manufactured in the same facilities under common administrative control. Fixed expenses are allocated among the products in proportion of their budgeted sales volume:

(*a*) Compute the budgeted break-even point of the company as a whole from the data provided.

(*b*) What would be the effect on Budgeted Income, if half of the budgeted sales volume of product B were shifted to product A and C in equal rupee amounts, so that the total budgeted sales in rupees remain the same.

(*c*) What would be the effect of the shift in the product mix suggested in (b) above on the budgeted break-even point of the whole company?

Solution:

(*a*) Budgeted BEP for the company as a whole

$$\text{Composite P/V ratio} = \frac{\text{Total contribution}}{\text{Total sales}} \times 100$$

$$= \frac{80,000 + 1,40,000 + 1,05,000}{10,00,000} \times 100$$

$$= \frac{3,25,000}{10,00,000} \times 100 = 32.5\%$$

$$\text{BEP for the company} = \frac{\text{Total fixed costs}}{\text{Composite P/V ratio}}$$

$$= \frac{52,000 + 1,30,000 + 78,000}{32.5\%}$$

$$= \frac{2,60,000}{32.5} \times 100 = \text{Rs. } 8,00,000$$

(*b*) Effect on Budgeted Income if half the sales of Product B are shifted equally to Products A and C.

	Product A	*Product B*	*Product C*
Sales (*i*)	3,25,000	2,50,000	4,25,000
Variable Expenses			
Cost of goods sold	1,46,250	1,35,000	2,12,500
Selling	48,750	45,000	63,750
Fixed Expenses (Apportioned according to sales):			
Overheads	58,500	45,000	76,500
Administrative	26,000	20,000	34,000
Total Cost (*ii*)	2,79,500	2,45,000	3,86,750
Income before tax (i) – (ii)	45,500	5,000	32,250
Income tax @ 40%	18,200	2,000	15,300
Net Income	27,300	3,000	22,950
Total Net Income			Rs. 53,250

The original budgeted income is Rs. 39,000. Hence, the income would increase by Rs. 14,250 as a result of the proposed change.

(*c*) Break-even after shift in the product mix

$$\text{Composite P/V Ratio} = \frac{\text{Total contribution}}{\text{Total sales}} \times 100$$

$$= \frac{1,30,000 + 70,000 + 1,48,750}{10,00,000} \times 100$$

$$= \frac{3,48,750}{10,00,000} \times 100 = 34.875\%$$

Break-even point of the company as a whole:

$$= \frac{\text{Total fixed expenses}}{\text{Composite P/V ratio}}$$

$$= \frac{2,60,000}{34.475\%}$$

$$= \text{Rs. } 7,45,520$$

Thus, the break-even point will stand reduced to sales of Rs. 7,45,520 from Rs. 8,00,000 as a result of shift in the total production-mix.

Example 5.40

A company manufactures a single product with a capacity of 1,50,000 units per annum. The summarised profitability statement for the year is as under:

	Rs.	*Rs.*
Sales: 1,00,000 units @ Rs. 15 per unit		15,00,000
Cost of sales:		
Direct Materials	3,00,000	
Direct Labour	2,00,000	
Production Overhead: Variable	60,000	
Fixed	3,00,000	
Administration Overheads (Fixed)	1,50,000	
Selling and Distribution Overheads: Variable	90,000	
Fixed	1,50,000	12,50,000
Profit		2,50,000

You are required to evaluate the following options:

(*i*) What will be the amount of sales required to earn a target profit of 25% on Sales, if the packing is improved at a cost of Re. 1 per unit?

(*ii*) There is an offer from a large retailer for purchasing 30,000 units per annum, subject to providing a packing with a different brand name at a cost of Rs. 2 per unit. However, in this case, there will be no selling and distribution expenses. Also this will not, in any way, affect the company's existing business. What will be the break-even price for this additional offer?

(*iii*) If an expenditure of Rs. 3,00,000 is made on advertising, the sales would increase from the present level of 1,00,000 units to 1,20,000 units at a price of Rs. 18 per unit. Will that expenditure be justified?

(*iv*) If the selling price is reduced by Rs. 2 per unit, there will be 100% capacity utilization. Will the reduction in selling price be justified?

Solution:

Working Notes:

	Rs.
(1) Contribution per unit:	
Selling price per unit: (A)	15.00
Variable cost per unit:	
Direct materials	3.00
(Rs. 3,00,000/1,00,000 units)	
Direct labour	2.00
(Rs. 2,00,000/1,00,00 units)	
Variable production overheads)	0.60
(Rs. 60,000/1,00,000 units)	
Variable selling and distribution overheads	0.90
(Rs. 90,000/1,00,000 units)	
Total variable cost per unit: (B)	6.50
Contribution per unit: {(A) – (B)}	8.50
(Rs. 15 – Rs. 6.50)	

	Rs.
(2) *Total fixed cost:*	
Production overheads	3,00,000
Administration overheads	1,50,000
Selling and distribution overheads	1,50,000
Total fixed cost	6,00,000

(i) Amount of sales required to earn a target profit of 25% on sales after improving the packing

	Rs.
Present variable cost per unit	6.50
(Refer to working note 1)	
Improved packing cost per unit	1.00
Revised variable cost per unit	7.50

$$\text{P/V ratio} = \frac{\text{Contribution}}{\text{Sales}} \times 100 = \left\{\frac{\text{Rs.}15 - \text{Rs.}7.50}{\text{Rs.}15} \times 100\right\} = 50\%$$

Let x be the desired sales revenue to earn a target profit of 25% on sales; then the desired contribution would be: Total fixed cost + 25% × x

$$\text{Since P/V ratio} \quad = \frac{C}{S} \times 100 = \frac{\text{Fixed Cost + Profit}}{x} \times 100$$

$$\therefore x = \frac{\text{Rs. } 6,00,000 + 25\% x}{50\%} \quad \textit{(Refer to working note 2)}$$

$$\text{or } x \times 50\% = \text{Rs. } 6,00,000 + 25\% x$$

$$\text{or } \left[\frac{x}{2} - \frac{x}{4}\right] = \text{Rs. } 6,00,000$$

$$\text{or } x = \text{Rs. } 24,00,000$$

Hence, the desired amount of sales required to earn a target profit of 25% on sales is Rs. 24,00,000. On the sale of Rs. 24,00,000, the desired contribution is 50% of sales i.e., Rs. 12,00,000 and profit is 25% of sales i.e., Rs. 6,00,000.

(ii) Evaluation of an offer of purchasing 30,000 units per annum (subject to providing a packing with a different brand name at a cost of Rs. 2 per unit) from a large retailer. Determine also the break-even price for this additional offer.

	Rs.
Present variable cost per unit	6.50
Less: Variable selling and distribution overheads per unit	0.90
	5.60
Add: Special packing cost per unit	2.00
Revised variable cost per unit	7.60

The break-even price per unit for this additional offer of 30,000 units would be Rs. 7.60 per unit. In other words, the break-even price for this additional offer here means the price per unit at which 30,000 units offer can be accepted without earning any profit on it.

Note: The existing business will bear the impact of fixed costs. Fixed costs will not affect this additional offer of 30,000 units.

(iii) Justification of incurring advertisement expenses of Rs. 3,00,000 for increasing the sale from 1,00,000 units to 1,20,000 units.

	Rs.
New selling price per unit	18.00
Less: Variable cost per unit *(Refer to working note 1)*	6.50
Contribution per unit	11.50
Total contribution *(1,20,000 units × Rs. 11.50)*	13,80,000
Less: Present fixed cost	(6,00,000)
Less: Additional expenditure on advertising	(3,00,000)
Profit	4,80,000

Justification: The amount of profit on the sale of 1,00,000 units was Rs. 2,50,000 *(Refer to the statement of the question)*. On increasing the sale of product units from 1,00,000 to 1,20,000, the profit of the concern increased from Rs. 2,50,000 to Rs. 4,80,000, therefore, the expenditure on advertisement is justifiable and the proposal under consideration is viable.

(iv) Justification of reduction in selling price to increase capacity utilisation to 100%

		Rs.
	Revised selling price per unit	13.00
Less:	Variable cost per unit *(Refer to working note 1)*	6.50
	Contribution per unit	6.50
	Total contribution at 100% capacity utilization (1,50,000 units × Rs. 6.50)	9,75,000
Less:	Fixed cost	6,00,000
	Profit	3,75,000

Justification: A reduction in selling price by Rs. 2/- per unit for 100% capacity utilisation, increases the present profit of Rs. 2,50,000, to Rs. 3,75,000. Hence the reduction in selling price is justified.

THEORY QUESTIONS

1. What do you mean by marginal costing. Discuss its usefulness and limitations.
2. Write a lucid note on marginal costing indicating its effect on profit computations.
3. What are the most important areas of management decisions opened up by the application of the marginal (direct) costing method. Answer breifly and to the point.
4. Marginal costs reveal the lowest price at which a product can be sold during a trade depression, but they also reveal to the management the most profitable line during the period of intense trade activity. Explain with examples, the second part of this statement.
5. Discuss the following terms in relation to marginal costing:
   (*a*) Key factor, (*b*) P/V Ratio and (*c*) Margin of Safety.
6. (*a*) What do you understand by the term "margin of safety" with reference to volume of production.
   (*b*) How do the following reflect on a break-even volume and on a P/V ratio: (*i*) increase in total fixed cost; (*ii*) increase in total physical sales and (*iii*) decrease in variable costs per unit.
7. What do you understand by the term "break-even analysis." Enumerate its uses.
8. How do income statements prepared under the absorption costing and marginal costing concepts differ.
9. Compared with absorption costing, when will variable costing report lower profits, higher profits, the same profits.
10. In what ways is variable costing better adapted to managerial use in profit planning, decision-making and control.
11. Why do the supporters of marginal costing state that fixed costs are not to be included in inventories.
12. Discuss the uses of CVP analysis and its significance to management.
13. "In classifying a particular cost as fixed or variable, the volume or activity level is extremely important." Discuss and illustrate this statement.
14. "The contribution approach is the foundation of CVP logic and related techniques." Discuss.
15. Discuss the role of contribution in marginal costing in decision relating to fixation of the selling price.
16. State with reasons whether following propositions are correct:
    (*a*) In an undertaking with a high fixed cost, break-even point can be attained at a lower level of activity.
    (*b*) Profit is represented by the product of the margin of safety and the P/V ratio.
    (*c*) In relation to normal sales, a low margin of safety along with a high P/V ratio is generally an indication of high fixed costs.
17. Distinguish between "marginal costing" and "absorption costing."
18. "The effect of a price reduction is always to reduce the P/V ratio, to raise the break-even point and to shorten the margin of safety." Explain with a suitable illustration.

19. Define break-even point. How can the break-even point be computed.
20. How is a break-even chart prepared. What information does the break-even chart give.
21. What are the basic assumptions in cost-volume-profit analysis under (*a*) absorption costing and (*b*) variable costing.
22. Describe how a P/V chart is drawn. How does the P/V chart differ from a break-even chart.
23. For product-mix decisions, what criteria can be used to select products that will maximise net income?
24. Break-even analysis assumes that variable costs and revenues are linear and that fixed costs are fixed. Briefly explain why these assumptions may not be realistic.
25. Can there be two break-even points. Show with the help of a graph.
26. Distinguish between contribution and profit.

PROBLEMS

1. The following data has been taken from the records of a company. You are required to find out net profit using the technique of marginal costing.

		Rs.
Sales		75,000
Variable costs:		
Direct materials	22,500	
Direct wages	12,500	
Factory overheads	5,250	
Administration, selling and distribution overheads	8,000	
	48,250	
Fixed costs:		
Factory overheads	2,000	
Administrative and other overheads	3,350	
	5,350	
Total cost		53,600
Profit		21,400

2. Using the information given below, calculate the net income for the months of October, November and December and the value of finished goods on hand at the end of period using absorption costing and marginal costing. Also, comment on the differences in profits under these two methods.

	October	*November*	*December*
Production	45,000	36,000	45,000
Sales	36,000	42,000	48,000
Opening stock	—	9,000	3,000
Closing stock	9,000	3,000	—
Additional information:			
Selling price per unit	Rs. 50		
Variable cost per unit	Rs. 30		
Fixed cost per unit	Rs. 10		
Total fixed costs per month	Rs. 3,90,000		
Normal output per month	39,000 units		

Ans: Profit under absorption costing, October Rs. 4,20,000, November Rs. 3,90,000, December Rs. 5,40,000. Profit under marginal costing. October Rs. 3,30,000 November Rs. 4,50,000, December Rs. 5,70,000. Difference in profits of different months is due to differences in values of closing stocks which are determined differently under both the methods.

3. The following data were taken from the cost and production records of a company at the end of an accounting period:

		Rs.
Sales revenue		1,28,000
Cost of goods manufactured:		
Fixed	32,000	
Variable	48,000	80,000
Selling and administrative expenses:		
Fixed	20,000	
Variable	0	20,000
Opening inventory of finished goods		Nil
Normal and actual production		10,000 units
Closing inventory of finished goods		2,000 units

Calculate the net income for the period and the value of the finished goods on hand at the end of the period using (*a*) absorption costing and (*b*) marginal costing.

Ans: Net profit, Absorption costing Rs. 44,000, Variable costing Rs. 37,600. Closing stock absorption costing Rs. 16,000. Variable costing Rs. 9,600.

4. A company produces a single product that sells for Rs. 150 per unit. Standard capacity is 1,00,000 units per year. On Jan. 1, 2002 there was no inventory of finished goods, production and sales for the year were as follows:

	Number of units	
Quarter	*Produced*	*Sold*
First	2,00,000	1,00,000
Second	3,00,000	2,50,000
Third	2,00,000	2,50,000
Fourth	3,00,000	4,00,000
	10,00,000	10,00,000

Manufacturing costs and selling and administrative expenses were as follows:

	Fixed	*Variable (per unit)*
Raw material	—	27
Direct labour	—	25
Indirect manufacturing cost	Rs. 2,00,00,000	25
Selling and administrative expenses	80,00,000	20
	Rs. 2,80,00,000	Rs. 90

Prepare: (a) Quarterly income statements under absorption costing and variable costing; (b) account for the difference between the net incomes reported under each concept.

5. The directors of a company have been studying the following condensed profit reports for the years 2001 and 2002:

Sales (Rs.)	3,00,000	4,50,000
Profit (or loss) (Rs.)	55,000	35,000

The directors are perturbed over the trend, for a 50% increase in sales resulted in a decrease in profit in 2002. The chief cost accountant explains that unabsorbed overheads was charged to 2002 operations. His statement was based on the following data:

Data	*2001*	*2002*
Sales (units)	20,000	30,000
Production (units)	30,000	20,000
Sales price per unit (Rs.)	15	15
Variable cost per unit (Rs.)	5	5
Fixed factory overhead (Rs.)	1,80,000	1,80,000
Fixed factory overhead per unit (standard) (Rs.)	6	6
Fixed selling and administrative expenses (Rs.)	25,000	25,000

Prepare: (*a*) income statement by the conventional method to which the chief cost accountant referred; (*b*) income statements by variable costing method.

Ans: Net profit, Absorption costing 2001, Rs. 55,000; 2002, Rs. 35,000. Variable costing 2001, Rs. 5000 loss; 2002 Rs. 95,000.

6. From the following data calculate:

(*i*) P/V ratio
(*ii*) Profit when sales are Rs. 20,000
(*iii*) New break-even point if selling price is reduced by 20%

Fixed expenses	Rs. 4,000
Break-even point	Rs. 10,000

Ans: P/V ratio 40%; Profit Rs. 4,000; BEP Rs. 16,000.

7. Calculate from the following data (i) the value of output at which the business breaks-even and (ii) the percentage capacity at which it breaks-even:

	Budget for year 2003 Based on 100% Capacity (Rs.)	*Estimated shut-down expenditure (Rs.)*
Direct wages	2,09,964	
Direct materials	2,44,552	
Works expenses	1,81,820	93,528
Selling and distribution expenses	61,188	40,188
Administration expenses	30,000	20,508
Net sales	8,40,000	

Ans: (*i*) BEP sales Rs. 485746
(*ii*) 57.83%

shutdown expenditures should be treated as fixed costs.

8. The following figures are available from the records of Venus Enterprises as on 31st March:

	2001 *Rs. lakhs*	*2002* *Rs. lakhs*
Sales	150	200
Profit	30	50

Calculate:

(*a*) The P/V ratio and total fixed expenses,
(*b*) The break-even level of sales;
(*c*) Sales required to earn a profit of Rs. 90 lakh and
(*d*) Profit or loss that would arise if the sales were Rs. 280 lakh.

Ans: (*a*) 40% 130 lakh (*b*) Rs. 75 lakh
(*c*) Rs. 300 lakh (*d*) Rs. 82 lakh

9. Two manufacturing companies which have the following operating details decide to merge.

	Company No.1	*Company No.2.*
Capacity utilization %	90	60
Sales (Rs. lakhs)	540	300
Variable cost (Rs. lakhs)	396	225
Fixed costs (Rs. lakhs)	80	50

Assuming that the proposal is implemented, calculate:

(*i*) Break-even sales of the merged plant and capacity utilization at that stage.

(*ii*) Profitability of the merged plant at 80% capacity utilization.

(*iii*) Sales turnover of the merged plant to earn a profit of Rs. 75 lakh.

(*iv*) When the merged plant is working at a capacity to earn a profit of Rs. 75 lakh, what percentage increase in selling price is required to sustain an increase of 5% of fixed overheads.

Ans: (*i*) 25.90% P/V ratio, Rs. 501.67 lakh, 45.6% (*ii*) Rs. 98 lakh (*iii*) Rs. 791.23 lakh (*iv*) 0.8215%

10. Company A and Company B, both under the same management, make and sell the same type of product. Their budgeted profit and loss accounts for January – June 2002 are as under:

	Company A		*Company B*	
	Rs.	*Rs.*	*Rs.*	*Rs.*
Sales		3,00,000		3,00,000
Less: Variable cost	2,40,000		2,00,000	
Fixed costs	30,000	2,70,000	70,000	2,70,000
		30,000		30,000

You are required to:

(*i*) Calculate the break-even point for each company.

(*ii*) Calculate the sales volume at which each of two companies will make a profit of Rs. 10,000 and

(*iii*) Assess how their profitability will change with decrease or increase in volume.

Ans: (*i*) A Rs. 1,50,000, B Rs. 2,10,000 (*ii*) A Rs. 2,00,000 B Rs. 2,40,000

11. The following figures relate to a company manufacturing a varied range of products:

	Total cost	*Total sales*
Year ending 31st Dec., 2001	19,83,600	22,23,000
Year ending 31st Dec., 2002	21,43,200	24,51,000

Assuming stability in prices, with variable costs carefully controlled to reflect predetermined relationships, and an unvarying figure for fixed costs, calculate:

(*a*) The profit/volume ratio, to reflect the rates of growth for profit and sales

(*b*) Fixed cost

(*c*) Fixed cost % to sales

(*d*) Break-even point

(*e*) Margin of safety for the year 2001 and the year 2002.

Ans: (*a*) 30% (*b*) Rs. 4,27,500

(*c*) 2001, 19.23%, 2002, 17.44% (*d*) Rs. 14,25,000

(*e*) 2001, Rs. 7,98,000,2002, Rs. 10,26,000

12. A company has a P/V ratio of 40 per cent. By what percentage must sales be increased to offset –

(*i*) 10 per cent reduction in selling price and

(*ii*) 20 per cent reduction in selling price.

Ans: Hint

Let the present units sold be 100@ Re 1/- per unit	*Rs.*
Present total sales	100
Present variable cost	60
Present contribution	40
(P/V ratio 40%)	

(*i*) If selling price is reduced by 10%

Selling price per unit	0.90
Variable cost per unit	0.60
Contribution per unit	0.30

In order to maintain the same contribution, viz. Rs. 40, the volume of sales should be:

$$\frac{\text{Present total contribution}}{\text{New contribution per unit}} \times \text{New selling price per unit}$$

$$\frac{40}{30} \times 90 = 120 \text{ or } \frac{1200}{.90} \text{ units or } 133\tfrac{1}{3} \text{ units}$$

Thus, the volume of sales will have to be increased by 33% from the existing level if the selling price is reduced by 10%.

(*ii*) If the selling price is reduced by 20%

	Re
Selling price unit	0.80
Variable cost per unit	0.60
Contribution per unit	0.20

For maintaining the same contribution the volume of sales should be:

$$\frac{40}{0.20} \times 0.80 = \text{Rs. } 160 \text{ or } \frac{160}{.80} = 200 \text{ units}$$

Thus, the volume of sales will have to be increased by 100% over the existing, if the selling price is reduced by 20%.

13. Two competing companies ABC Ltd. and XYZ Ltd. produce and sell in the same type of product in the same market. For the year ending March 2003, their forecasted profit and loss accounts are as follows:

		ABC Ltd.		XYZ Ltd.
Sales		Rs. 2,50,000		Rs. 2,50,000
Less: Variable costs				
of sales	Rs. 2,00,000		1,50,000	
Fixed costs	25,000	2,25,000	75,000	2,25,000
Forecasted net				
Profit before tax		25,000		25,000

You are required to compute:

1. P/V ratio
2. Break-even sales volume

You are also required to state which company is likely to earn greater profits in conditions of:

(*a*) low demand and

(*b*) high demand.

Ans: P/V Ratio ABC Ltd., 20%, XYZ Ltd. 40% Break-even sales volume ABC Ltd., Rs. 125000, XYZ Ltd., Rs. 1,87,500. In case of low demand, profit situation for ABC Ltd. will be better as it has a larger safety margin and lower amount of fixed costs. In case of high demand, XYZ will do better since additional sales will give profit at 40% (P/V ratio) whereas in case of ABC Ltd. additional sales will give profit at 20% (P/V ratio).

14. The budgeted sales of three products of a company are as follows:

	Product		
	X	*Y*	*Z*
Budgeted sales in units	10,000	15,000	20,000
Budgeted selling price per unit	4	4	4
Budgeted variable cost per unit	2.5	3	3.5
Budgeted fixed expenses total	12,000	9,000	7,500

From the information, you are required to compute the following for each product:

(*a*) The budgeted profit

(*b*) The budgeted break-even sales and

(*c*) The budgeted margin of safety in terms of sales value.

Ans:

	X	*Y*	*Z*
Profit	Rs. 3,000	6,000	2,500
Break-even sales	Rs. 32,000	36,000	60,000
Margin of safety	Rs. 8,000	24,000	20,000

15. Tractors Ltd. have an installed capacity of 5000 tractors per annum. They are presently operating at about 35% of installed capacity. For the coming year, they have budgeted as follows:

Production/Sales	*4,000 units*
Costs	*Rs. (Crores)*
Direct materials	8.00
Direct wages	0.60
Factory expenses	0.80
Administrative expenses	0.20
Selling expenses	0.20
Profit	1.00

Factory expenses as well as selling expenses are variable to the extent of 20%.

Calculate the break-even capacity utilisation percentage.

Ans: 40%

16. From the following data, calculate break-even point expressed in terms of units and also the new B.E.P. if selling price is reduced by 10%

Fixed expenses:	
Depreciation	Rs. 1,00,000
Salaries	Rs. 1,00,000
Variable expenses:	
Materials	Rs. 3 per unit
Labour	Rs. 2 per unit
Selling price	Rs. 10 per unit

Ans: (*i*) 40,000 units (*ii*) 50,000 units

17. From the following information relating to Quick Standards Ltd., you are required to find out: (*a*) Contribution, (*b*) Break-even point in units, (*c*) Margin of safety, and (*d*) Profit.

Total fixed costs	Rs. 4,500
Total variable costs	7,500
Total sales	15,000
Units sold	5,000 (Units)

Also calculate the volume of sales to earn profit of Rs. 6,000.

Ans: (*a*) Rs. 75,000 (*b*) 3,000 units

(*c*) Rs. 6,000, 40% (*d*) Rs. 30,000

18. S. Ltd. furnishes you the following information related to the half year ended 30th June, 2001.

Fixed expenses	Rs. 45,000
Sales value	1,50,000
Profit	30,000

During the second half of the year, the company has projected a loss of Rs. 10,000.

Calculate:

(*i*) The break-even point and margin of safety for six months ending 30th June, 2001

(*ii*) Expected sales volume for second half of the year assuming that the P/V ratio and fixed expenses remain constant in the second half year also.

(*iii*) The break-even point and margin of safety for the whole year 2001.

Ans: (*i*) BEP Rs. 90,000, Margin of safety Rs. 60,000.

(*ii*) Sales Rs. 70,000

(*iii*) BEP Rs. 1,80,000

Margin of safety Rs. 40,000

19. S.M. Ltd. produces two products and the Budget for 60% level of activity for the year 2001-2002 gives the following information:

	Product A Rs.	*Product B* Rs.
Raw material cost per unit	75	35
Direct labour cost per unit	40	30
Variable overheads per unit	20	15
Fixed overheads per unit	60	45
Selling price per unit	200	150
Production and sales	4,000 units	6,000 units

The Managing Director, not being satisfied with the projected results as stated above, referred the budget to the marketing director for improvement of the performance. The marketing director proposed that the sale quantities of Product A and B could each be increased by 50% provided the selling prices were reduced by 5% in the case of Product A and 10% in the case of Product B. The price reduction should be made applicable to the entire quantity of sales of each of the two products.

Required: (*i*) Present the overall profitability under the original budget and the revised budget after taking the increased sales into consideration and

(*ii*) Find the overall break-even sales under the original budget and the revised budget.

20. Mansarovar Auto Products produces and sells two small components P and Q used in automobiles. The details regarding unit income and costs of these components are as under:

	Products P	Q
Selling price	Rs. 1,200	Rs. 2,000
Direct materials	200	400
Direct labour	200	100
Variable factory overheads	200	400
Fixed factory overheads	200	400
Total cost of goods sold	800	1,300
Gross profit per unit	400	700

Factory overheads, both fixed and variable, have been accounted for on a machine hour basis. As far as it can be determined, the sales outlook is such that the plant could operate at full capacity on either or both products. Both P and Q are processed through the same cost centres. Selling costs are all fixed. Which product should be preferred? Give a brief explanation in support of your answer.

21. Delhi Equipments Ltd., manufactures four components, the cost particulars of which are given below:

	Components			
	A	*B*	*C*	*D*
Elements of cost:				
Direct material	Rs. 80	100	100	120
Direct labour	20	25	25	30
Variable overhead	10	12	15	10
Fixed overhead	15	23	20	20
	125	160	160	180
Output per machine hour (units)	4	2	3	3

The key factor is shortage of machine capacity.

You are required to advise the management as to whether they should continue to produce all or some of these components (which are used in its main product) or they should buy them from a supplier who has quoted the following prices:

A = Rs. 115; B = Rs. 175; C = 135; D = Rs. 185.

Ans: Hint:

Statement of Profitability

	Components			
	A	*B*	*C*	*D*
Direct material	Rs. 80	Rs. 100	Rs. 100	Rs. 120
Direct labour	20	25	25	30
Variable overhead	10	12	15	10
Marginal cost per unit	110	137	140	160
Purchase price per unit	115	175	135	185
Excess of purchase price Over marginal cost	5	38	—	25
Excess of marginal cost over purchase price	—	—	5	—
Decline in profitability Per machine hour if purchase is made from outside	5 × 4	38 × 2	—	25 × 3
Increase in profitability per machine hour if purchase is made from outside			– 5 × 3 = 15	

The above analysis shows:

(*i*) Component C should be purchased from outside whether there is a key factor or not since its marginal cost is more than its purchase price. Purchasing from outside will push up the profitability by Rs. 15 per machine hour.

(*ii*) Continue the production of components A, B and D is case shortage of machine capacity is not the key factor.

(*iii*) In case shortage of machine capacity is the key factor as given in the question, the management must decide about the ranking of the three components. The above analysis shows that ranking should be in the order of A, D and B.

This is because in case of A, if it is purchased from outside, the loss of profitability will be only Rs. 20 per machine hour, while in case of D and B it will be Rs. 75 and Rs. 76 per machine hour respectively.

22. (*a*) From, the following data, which product would you recommend for manufacture in the factory?

Per unit of	*Product A*	*Product B*
Standard manufacturing time	2 hours	3 hours
Direct materials	50	30
Direct labour @ Rs. 10 per hour	20	30
Direct labour @ Rs. 6 per hour	12	18
Selling price	200	240

Total machine hours available in the factory are 60,000.

(*b*) Calculate the effects on profit of a proposed change in "Sales Mix" from the following data:

Existing sales mix	*M*	*N*	*O*	*P*	*Total*
Sales (in Rs.)	80,000	1,00,000	40,000	20,000	2,40,000
Variable cost (in Rs.)	48,000	68,000	32,000	8,000	1,56,000
Fixed cost (in Rs.)	—	—	—	—	58,800
Proposed sales					
Mix	Rs. 60,000	88,000	80,000	12,000	2,40,000

Ans: Hint:

(a) Machine capacity seems to be the limiting factor and since Product A uses minimum machine time, it is more profitable to produce Product A than Product B.

Comparative Profitability Statement

	Product A	*Product B*
Selling price	200	240
Total variable costs	82	78
Contribution margin	118	162
Contribution per machine hour	59	54
Total output possible (units)	30,000	20,000
Total contribution possible (Rs.)	35,40,000	32,40,000

Product A may, therefore, be recommended for manufacture provided its selling is not a problem.

(b) Computation of Estimated Profit on the Proposed Change

Products	*M*	*N*	*O*	*P*	*Total*
Proposed	60,000	88,000	80,000	12,000	2,40,000
Variable cost	36,000	59,840	64,000	4,800	1,64,640
Proposed contribution	24,000	28,160	16,000	7,200	75,360
Fixed costs					58,800
Proposed profit					16,560
Present contributions	32,000	32,000	8,000	12,000	84,000
Fixed costs					58,800
present profit					25,200
Profit/Volume ratio	40%	32%	20%	60%	

The sales-mix proposed is less profitable since the sale of Product D, which is the least profitable, is proposed to be doubled while that of Product P which is most profitable, is proposed to be reduced. Similarly, sale of products M and N which are relatively more profitable than Product D is proposed to be reduced while that of Product D is being doubled. The overall effect has been a decline in profit by Rs. 8,640.

23. (*a*) The following particulars are extracted from the records of a company:

	Product A	*Product B*
Sales (per unit)	Rs. 100	Rs. 120
Consumption of material	2 kg	3 kg
Material cost	Rs. 10	Rs. 15
Direct wages cost	15	10
Direct expenses	5	6
Machine hours used	3	2

Overhead expenses:		
Fixed	5	10
Variable	15	20

Direct wage per hour is Rs. 5. Comment on the profitability of each product (both use the same raw material) when (*i*) Total sales potential in units is limited; (*ii*) Total sales potential in value is limited; (*iii*) Raw material is in short supply; and (*iv*) Production capacity (in terms of machine hours) is the limiting factor.

(*b*) Assuming raw material as the key factor, availability of which is 10,000 kg and maximum sales potential of each product being 3,500 units, find out the product mix which will yield the maximum profit.

Ans: Hint:

	Per unit of	
	A	*B*
Sales	Rs. 100	Rs. 120
Direct material	10	15
Direct wages	15	10
Direct expenses	5	6
Variable overhead	15	20
Marginal cost	45	51
Contribution per unit	55	69
P/V ratio	55%	57.5%
Contribution per kg of material	27.5	23
Contribution per machine hour	18.3	34.5

(*i*) In case total sales potential in units is a limiting factor, B is more profitable as it is making a larger contribution per unit as compared to A.

(*ii*) In case total sales potential in value is a limiting factor, still B is more profitable since its P/V ratio is higher than that of A.

(*iii*) In case raw material is in short supply, A is more profitable as its contribution per kg of material is higher than that of Product B.

(*iv*) In case production capacity is limited, B is more profitable since it gives higher contribution per machine hour than A.

Note: Best situation is obtained when contribution per unit of the key factor is the maximum.

(*b*) In case raw material is the key factor, A is more profitable to produce as its contribution per kg of material is higher than that of B. If 3,500 units of A are manufactured, total material consumption will be 7,000 kg (i.e., 3,500 × 2 kg). The balance of 3,000 kg of material can be used to manufacture 1,000 units (3,000 ÷ 3) of B. The total profit by this product mix will be as follows:

Contribution:

Product A 3,500 units @ Rs. 55 each	Rs. 1,92,500	
Product B 1,000 units @ Rs. 69 each	69,000	
		2,61,500
Total Contribution:		
Total fixed costs:		
Product A 5 × 3,500	= Rs. 17,500	
Product B 10 × 3,500	= 35,000	52,500
		2,09,000

24. A, B and C are three similar plants under the same management who want them to merge for better operation. The details are as under:

Plant	A	B	C
Capacity operated	100%	70%	50%
	Rs. (in lakhs)	Rs. (in lakhs)	Rs. (in lakhs)
Turnover	300	280	150
Variable cost	200	210	75
Fixed cost	70	50	62

Find out:

(*i*) The capacity of the merged plant for break-even.

(*ii*) The profit at 75% capacity of the merged plant.

(*iii*) The turnover from the merged plant to give a profit of Rs. 28 lakh.

Ans: (*i*) 52% (*ii*) Profit Rs. 80.5 (lakh) (*iii*) Rs. 600 lakh

25. Sunita Manufacturing Company produces chairs. An analysis of their accounting reveals:

Fixed cost	Rs. 50,00,000 for the year
Variable cost	Rs. 200 per chair
Capacity	2,000 chairs per year
Selling price	Rs. 700 per chair

(*i*) Find the break-even point.

(*ii*) Find the number of chairs to be sold to get a profit of Rs. 3,00,000.

(*iii*) What will be the answer for (*i*) and (*ii*) if selling price changes to Rs. 600 per chair.

(*iv*) If the company can manufacture 600 chairs more per year with an additional fixed cost of Rs. 20,000, what should be the selling price to maintain the profit per chair as at (*ii*) above?

26. S. V. Ltd., a multi-product company furnishes you the following data relating to the year 2002:

	First half of the year Rs.	*Second half of the year* Rs.
Sales	45,00,000	50,00,000
Total Cost	40,00,000	43,00,000

Assuming that there is no change in prices and variable cost and that the fixed expenses are incurred equally in the two half year periods, calculate for the year 2002:

(*i*) The P/V ratio

(*ii*) Fixed expenses

(*iii*) Break-even sales

(*iv*) Percentage of margin of safety

(*i*) 40% (*ii*) Rs. 26,00,000

(*iii*) Rs. 65,00,000 (*iv*) 31.58%.

❑❑❑

Chapter 6

DIFFERENTIAL ANALYSIS AND DECISION MAKING

DECISION-MAKING

Decision-making is the process of evaluating two or more alternatives leading to a final choice, sometimes known as Alternative Choice Decisions. Decision making is closely associated with planning for the future and is directed towards a specific objective or goal. The case put into each decision often determines the level of outcome. The overall decision process (also referred to as decision model) contains the following decision-making steps or elements:

(*i*) Identify and define the problem.

(*ii*) Identify alternatives as possible solutions to the problem.

(*iii*) Eliminate alternatives that are clearly not feasible.

(*iv*) Collect relevant data (costs and benefits) associated with each feasible alternative.

(*v*) Identify costs and benefits (revenues) as relevant or irrelevant and eliminate irrelevant costs and benefits (revenues) from consideration.

(*vi*) Identify, to the extent possible, non-financial advantages and disadvantages (also known as qualitative factors) about each feasible alternative.

(*vii*) Total the relevant costs and benefits (revenues) for each alternative.

(*viii*) Select the alternative with the greatest overall benefit i.e. make the decision.

(*ix*) Implement or execute the decision and

(*x*) Evaluate the results of the decision made.

Differential Analysis

Managerial decision-making is the process of making choices. If a choice is to be made among alternatives, there must be differences among the alternatives.

Relevant costs and benefits are very important in evaluating alternatives, in ascertaining the effect of various alternatives of profit and selecting the alternative with the greatest benefit. *Differential analysis may be defined as the use of relevant costs and revenues in making decisions. The relevant costs and revenues are the differences between the alternatives under consideration. The amount of such differences are called differentials and the (accounting) analysis concerned with the effect of alternatives on revenues and costs is called **differential analysis.***

Relevant revenues and relevant costs are defined as the current and future values that differ among the alternatives under consideration. They are also known as differential revenues and differential costs. Differential revenue is the amount of increase or decrease in revenue and differential costs. Differential revenue is the amount of increase or decrease in revenue expected from a particular course of action as compared with an alternative. For instance, assume that a plant is being used to manufacture product A, which gives a revenue of Rs. 3,00,000. If the plant could be used to make product B, which will provide revenue of Rs. 3,50,000, the differential revenue from making and selling product B will be Rs. 50,000. Differential cost is the amount of increase or decrease in cost that is expected from a particular course of action as compared with an alternative.

Differential analysis provides a decision rule to managers in decision-making which is 'the alternative that gives the greatest incremental profit should be selected'. Incremental profit is the difference between the relevant revenues and relevant costs of each alternative. Differential analysis has the objective of focussing on the relevant revenues and costs related to different alternatives. Differential analysis thus emphasises the significant factors bearing on the decision, help to clarify the issues and save the time of the decision-maker. Differential analysis helps the management in making decisions in different short-run managerial decision making situations. (some short-run decisions have been discussed below).

In case decision affects both revenue and costs, management must estimate the changes in each to estimate the change in profit. In many decisions, only costs will change. In this case, the most beneficial (profitable) decision will be the one with the lowest cost because the lowest cost alternative will give the highest profit for the business enterprise, provided all other factors and situations remain constant.

Relevant Costs

Whatever alternatives are evaluated, the decision-maker has to decide which costs are relevant. Relevant costs are those that are pertinent, and bear upon the decision to be made. They pertain to various levels of information that will affect the accomplishment of the objectives of the decision-maker and will change as a result of the decision:

(*i*) Relevant costs are expected future costs and

(*ii*) They differ between different decision alternatives.

Expected future costs imply that the costs are expected to occur during the time period covered by the decision. For example, new products will need the incurrence of direct material, direct labour and other costs. Relevant costs also differ between decision alternatives. For example, a graduate may choose between advanced education and immediate employment. The costs that are relevant in this decision and which differ between the two decisions are the costs of books, fees etc., because these costs will not be incurred if the graduate takes up employment. However, irrelevant costs are costs of accommodation, clothes etc. which will have to be incurred under both the decisions.

Qualitative factors

Differential analysis or relevant cost analysis should be considered as only one input for the final decision to be made by the managers. Infact, a number of qualitative factors may have vital impact on managerial decisions. Qualitative factors are those elements relating to a decision which cannot be expressed in monetary terms or can be expressed similarly with great difficulty or inaccuracy. Managers should consider qualitative factors also while making decisions otherwise it is likely that a wrong decision decisions will be made.

For example, in make or buy decisions, decision makers should consider many qualitative factors also such as quality of items being purchased from outside, reliability of supply sources, expected stability of prices over the next several years, service quality, labour relations in the supplier's company etc. It may also be found that the decision to purchase from outside could result in closing down of the company's facilities for manufacturing the component. Such a decisions will influence adversely the morale of company's employees which may, in turn, affect future production and plans of the company. Dependence on an outside supplier is also risky as the suppliers sometimes may not supply the components on time. In such a case, the buyer-company will not be in a position to fulfil customers' orders and thus the company may lose its goodwill in the market, resulting further in poor future sales. These qualitative factors are difficult to quantify in monetary terms. However, the decision maker should try to have as much quantifiable information as possible in these situations. For instance, the effect on customer goodwill due to delay on the part of the supplier in meeting orders can be estimated. If there are many suppliers available in the market components, this qualitative factor can be ignored as components can be purchased from any supplier in case of delay. However, if the components can be purchased from a single supplier, these qualitative factors will be of great importance. In this situation, the decision-maker should compare the cost savings due to purchasing the component form outside (rather than manufacturing within the company) with the risk associated with suppliers delaying the fulfilment of orders. If cost savings are more the (quantifiable) risk, the company may continue to purchase form outside; if cost savings are more (quantifiable) than the risk, the company may continue to purchase from outside; if cost savings are insufficient to cover the risks related with this quantitative aspect, probably it may not be advisable to purchase the component from outside.

Limitations of Differential Analysis

Differential analysis helps in evaluating decision alternatives. The primary objective is to select the least costly alternative. However, cost computations and profit estimates are strategic means of tackling such problems. Many projects and proposals are rejected simply because the costs involved are too high or relative income potential was lower than that of an alternative. Yet the project may have been beneficial to the company in that it would have allowed the company to balance its risk, or to offer a complete product line which would have attracted new customers to all the company's products. Perhaps this is the very reason why the cost accountant needs to be extremely careful in the translation of the data with which he works.

Managers must study carefully data to be used in decision-making. Other quantitative factors besides cost should also be given proper attention. The pressure of competition, the maintenance of sources of supply and of certain marketing outlets, and the maintenance of the existing personnel in an organisation and their morale may often be the real determinants of business decisions. The quantitative information alone dos not provide a solution to all business problems. Sometimes, other factors are mote important than cost factors. If the qualitative factors are essentially equal across alternatives, however, relevant costs become the deciding factor instead of being just one input among several factors to be considered for managerial decisions. The cost of developing information for decision-making should not exceed the potential benefits to be obtained. It should be ensured that accurate and timely information is available to managers for decision-making and planning at the least possible expense.

TYPES OF DIFFERENTIAL ANALYSIS DECISIONS

Most differential analysis decisions are referred to as alternative choice decisions.

These types of decisions cover situations with two or more alternative courses of action from which the manager (decision-maker) must select the best alternative. For instance, should a company enter a foreign market or depend on domestic sales? This decision involves choosing between two alternatives. A decision involving more than two alternatives is called a *multiple-alternative choice decision*. Some examples of alternative choice decisions are: make or buy, own or lease, retain or replace, repair or renovate, now or later, change versus status quo, slower or faster, export versus local sales, shut down or continue, expand or contract, change the produce-mix, take or refuse orders, place special orders, select sales territories, replace present equipment with new machinery, sell at split-up point or process further etc.

Some of the above alternative decisions and the information relevant to the decisions are discussed below:

Make-or-Buy

Make-or-buy decisions arise when a company with unused production capacity considers the following alternatives:

(*a*) To buy certain raw materials or sub-assemblies from outside suppliers and

(*b*) To use available capacity to produce the items within the company.

A make-or-buy decision is basically one of determining which alternative is economically most desirable and most effectively utilises the firm's resources, Individually, these decisions may or may not produce a significant impact of the firm's operations; however, taken in aggregate, they can have a critical long-range effect on the firm's operating characteristics. These decisions can affect the firm's production methods and capacities, available working capital, cost of borrowing funds and competitive position. Therefore, before a make-or-buy decision can be made, the firm must establish goals with respect to the nature and extent of its production facilities. The firm must also define the manufacturing processes that are congruent with its overall company goals and strategies. Costs that will be incurred under both alternatives are not relevant to the analysis.

For example, assume that a company can make a part that it has been purchasing at a unit cost of Rs. 3. The company has been operating at 75% of normal capacities and in the foreseeable future, no use for excess capacity is contemplated except for the possible production of the part. Fixed manufacturing cost amounts Rs. 1,70,000 a year whether the plant operates at 45% or 100% of capacity. The cost to manufacture 50,000 units of the part that will be needed has been estimated as follows:

	Unit cost	*Total cost*
	Rs.	*Rs.*
Direct materials	1.25	62.500
Direct labour	0.80	40,000
Variable manufacturing overheads	0.50	25,000
Total incremental cost	2.55	1,27,500
Cost to purchase part	3.00	1,50,000
Net advantage in parts production	0.45	22,500

In the above analysis, the fixed manufacturing overhead has not been considered because it has to be incurred under both alternatives.

Add or Drop Products

The decision to eliminate an unprofitable product is a special case of segment or product profitability evaluation. To evaluate the financial consequences of eliminating a product, it is necessary to concentrate on the differential or incremental profit effect of the decision. An important factor in the decision to add or drop a product is whether it will increase or decrease the future income of the business. Appropriate costs and profit measures must be developed for each alternative.

Assume a company is considering dropping product B from its line because accounting statements show that product B is being sold at a loss.

Income Statement

	Product A Rs.	Product B Rs.	Product C Rs.	Portal Rs.
Sales revenue	50,000	7,500	12,500	70,000
Cost of sales:				
Direct material	7,500	1,000	1500	10000
Direct labour	15,000	3,000	2,500	10,500
Indirect manufacturing cost (50% of direct labour)	7,500	1,000	1,350	9,750
	30,000	4,000	5,250	39,250
Gross margin on Sales	20,000	3,500	7,250	30,750
Administrative expenses (allocation on arbitrary basis)	12,500	4,500	4,000	21,000
Net income (loss)	7,500	(1,000)	3,250	9,750

Additional Information:

(*i*) Factory overhead costs are made up of fixed costs of Rs. 5,850 and variable costs of Rs. 3,900. Variable costs by products are: product A Rs. 3,000, product B. Rs. 400 and product C Rs. 500.

(*ii*) Fixed costs and expenses will not be changed if product B is eliminated.

(*iii*) Variable selling and administrative expenses to the extent of Rs. 11,000 can be traced to the product as follows: A, Rs. 7,500; B, Rs. 1,500: C. Rs. 2,000.

(*iv*) Fixed selling and administrative expenses are Rs. 10,000.

The decision to drop product B cannot be reasonably made from the above data prepared under a conventional income statement. This information together with the following statement may be helpful to the management.

	Product A Rs.	Product B Rs.	Product C Rs.	Total; Rs.
Sales revenue	50,000	7,500	12,500	70,000
Less: Variable product cost				
Direct material	7,500	1,000	1,500	10,000
Direct labour	15,000	2,000	2,500	19,500
Factory overheads	3,000	400	500	3,900
Selling and administrative expenses	7,500	1,500	2,000	11,000
	33,000	4,900	6,500	44,400
Contribution margin	17,000	2,600	6,000	25.600
Less: Fixed costs:				
Factory overhead				5,850
Selling and administrative expenses				10,000
Total fixed cost				15,850
Net income				9,750

This statement shows that product B exceeds its variable costs by Rs. 2,600. If the sale of product B was discontinued, this marginal contribution would be lost and the net income of the firm would be reduced by Rs. 2,600. That is, net income will be Rs. 7,150 (Rs. 9,750 – Rs. 2,600). In this illustration, it has been assumed that sales of products A and C will not be increased after product B is dropped. Further, it has been assumed that dropping product B will not change the fixed costs and expenses. If these assumptions are not true, new analysis must be made. Assume, for example, that after dropping product B, the sales of product A increase by 10%. The total profit of the firm will not increase by this sales increase. Product A makes only a marginal contribution of 34%.

Sales revenue	Rs. 50,000	100%
Variable costs	33,000	66%
Margin contribution	17,000	34%

On additional sales of Rs. 5,000, the marginal contribution would be Rs. 1,700:

Sales revenue	Rs. 5,000
Variable costs (66%)	3,300
Marginal contribution (34%)	1,700

This contribution is less than Rs. 2,600 now being realised on the sales of product B. It would take additional sales of product A of approximately Rs. 7,647 to equal the marginal contribution of Rs. 2,600 now being made by product B:

$$\frac{\text{Marginal contribution of product B}}{\text{Marginal contribution of Product A}} = \frac{2{,}600}{34\%}$$

It is possible that dropping product B may result in reduction in some of the fixed costs. Product B now contributes Rs. 2,600 towards recovery of fixed costs and expenses. Only if the fixed costs and expenses can be reduced by more than this amount, it will be advisable to drop product B.

Sell or Process Further

The decision whether a product should be sold at the split-off point or processed further is faced by many manufacturers. The choice between selling under a product at split-off or processing it further is a short-run operating decision. Additional processing adds value to a product and increases its selling price above the amount for which it could be sold at split-off. The decision to process further depends upon whether the increase in total revenues exceeds the additional costs incurred for processing beyond split-off. Generally speaking, there are two general conditions under which a sell or process further decision could occur:

(*i*) The company is evaluating the possibility of processing beyond split-off and must incur certain equipment costs and other fixed costs if additional processing is to occur and

(*ii*) The company already processes a product beyond split-off and has invested in the equipment and required personnel.

The first situation is, really a capital budgeting problem and here it is not sufficient to determine whether incremental revenues exceed incremental costs. Since new investments in machinery and building are involved, the rate of return on this investment must also be considered.

In the second situation, the relevant costs are only those costs which relate to the additional processing of each product beyond the spit-off point. The joint costs are relevant to the further processing decisions. Certain fixed costs such as supervisory salaries are related to additional processing. If these costs are eliminated by selling products at split-off, they are incremental and should be included in the decision analysis. If salaried personnel are assigned other duties in the company when additional processing is discontinued, the salary costs are not incremental since they are incurred under either decision alternative. If the equipment used for additional processing sits idle or can be used in other processes, it should be ignored in the decision analysis. Depreciation expense is never relevant in short-run operating decisions, since depreciation is an allocation of costs incurred in a past time period.

In deciding upon which course of action to follow, the company compares the contribution margin from sale of the partially processed product with the contribution margin form the sale of the completely processed product. The revenue to be derived from the sale of the partially processed product is the opportunity cost attached to the decision of further processing. Assume for example, a partially processed product can be sold for Rs. 9 per unit which is manufactured at a cost of Rs. 6. Further processing can be done at an additional cost of Rs. 3 per unit and the final product can be sold at Rs. 15 per unit. The firm can produce 10,000 units. The analysis is shown below:

	Sell	*Process & Sell*
Sales revenue (10, 000 units)	Rs. 90.000	Rs. 1,50,000
Less: Manufacturing costs	60,000	90,000
	30,000	60,000

Net advantage in further processing 60,000 – 30,000 = Rs. 30,000.

Thus, there is a net advantage of Rs. 30,000 in processing the product further. The market value of the partially processed product (Rs. 90,000) is considered to be the opportunity cost of further processing. The figure of net advantage of Rs. 30,000 can be arrived at in the following manner also:

Revenue from sale of final product (10,000 × 15)		Rs. 1,50,000
Revenue from sale of intermediate product	90,000	1,20,000
Net advantage in further processing		Rs. 30,000

Operate or Shutdown

Differential cost analysis is also used when a business is confronted with the possibility of a temporary shutdown. This type of analysis has to determine whether in the shortrun, a firm is better off operating than not operating. As long as the products sold recover their variable costs and make a contribution towards the recovery of fixed costs, it may be preferable to operate and not to shut down. Also the management should consider the investment in the training of its employees which would be lost in the event of a temporary shutdown. Recruiting and training new workers would add to present costs. Another factor is the loss of established markets. Also, a temporary shutdown does not eliminate all costs. Depreciation, taxes, interest and insurance costs are incurred during shutdown also. The other points (benefits) which should be considered are the following: avoiding operating losses, savings in maintenance and repair costs, savings in indirect labour costs and savings in fixed costs.

A company operating below 50% of its capacity expects that the volume of sales will drop below the present level of 10,000 units per month. Management is concerned that a further drop in sales volume will create a loss and has under consideration a recommendation that operations be suspended, until better market conditions prevail and also a better selling price. The present operating income statement is as follows:

Sales revenue (10,000 units @ Rs. 3.00		Rs. 30,000
Less: Variable costs @ Rs. 2.00 per unit	20,000	
Fixed costs	10,000	Rs. 30,000
Net income		0

The following income statements have been prepared for sales at different capacities:

	Units produced					
	Shutdown	2,000	4,000	6,000	8,000	10,000
Sales revenue @ Rs. 3	0	6,000	12,000	18,000	24,000	30,000
Variable costs @ Rs. 2	0	4,000	8,000	12,000	16,000	20,000
Contribution	0	2,000	4,000	6,000	8,000	10,000
Fixed costs	4,000	10,000	10,000	10,000	10,000	10,000
Loss	4,000	(8,000)	(6,000)	(4,000)	(2,000)	0

It would appear that shutdown is desirable when the sales volume drops below 6,000 units per month, the point at which operating losses exceed the shutdown cost. The volume of 6,000 units could be arrived at without an income statement as follows:

Fixed costs if plant operates	Rs. 10,000
Fixed costs if plant shuts down	Rs. 4,000
Additional costs to be recovered when operating	Rs. 6,000

Each unit of product sold contributes Re. 1,00 to fixed costs recovery:

Selling price per unit	Rs. 3.00
Variable cost per unit	Rs. 2.20
Contribution	Rs. 1.00

Sale of 6,000 units is necessary to recover Rs. 6,000 of fixed costs.

$$\frac{\text{Rs. } 6,000}{\text{Rs. } 1.00} = 6,000 \text{ units}$$

If the selling price is cut to Rs. 2.80, the contribution margin will be Re. 0.80 per unit.

Required sale to recover an additional Rs. 6,000 of fixed costs

$$\frac{\text{Rs. } 6,000}{\text{Rs. } 0.80} = 7,500 \text{ units}$$

That is, sales of 7,500 units would be necessary to recover an additional Rs. 6,000 of fixed costs.

Special Orders

All business decisions should not be evaluated in the same way. Sometimes special orders or one time orders often have different characteristics from recurring orders. Therefore, each order should be evaluated based on costs relevant to the situation and the goals of the business firm. The question of special orders arises when a company has excess or idle production capacity and management considers the possibility of selling additional products at less than normal selling prices, provided that such a special order will not affect the regular sales of the same product.

The basic problem is to determine an acceptable price for the special order units. Cost analysis using the contribution approach is a useful technique to determine the short-run profit effects of special order transactions. In deciding the pricing of special orders where normal operations are not disturbed and where unused production capacity exists, it is not advisable to attach fixed costs to products. Price determination should take into account the recovery of incremental (variable) costs caused by accepting the special order. If the normal fixed costs are included in the price of the special order, the price may be too high and the business firm could lose the entire order and the contribution margin to be earned on the special order. Only the relevant (variable) costs should be used in the decision analysis to arrive at an appropriate price. Fixed costs are relevant only if incurred to facilitate the special order.

The following example illustrates the special order decisions.

A manufacturing company produces 20,000 units by operating at 60% of the capacity and sell at a price of Rs. 30 per unit. The budgeted figures for the year 1994 are as follows:

	Production (20,000 units)
Raw materials @ Rs. 4.25	Rs. 85,000
Direct labour @ Rs. 5.75	Rs. 1,15,000
Variable factory overhead @ Rs. 7.75	Rs. 55,000
Fixed factory overhead	Rs. 1,25,000
Variable selling costs 2.75% of selling price	
Fixed selling and administrative cost	Rs. 72,500

The company receives a special order for 10,000 units from a firm. The company desires to earn a profit of Re. 1.00 per unit and no selling expenses are to be incurred for the special order. The minimum price on the special order and income statements are as follows:

Pricing of Special Order

	(10,000 units) Rs.
Variable costs to be incurred:	
Raw materials	4.25
Direct labour	5.75
Variable overhead	7.75
Variable cost per unit (no selling expenses)	17.75
Desired profit	1.00
Minimum price	18.75

Increase in sales =10,000 units x Rs. 18.75 = Rs. 1,87, 500

Income Statement

	Without special order (Rs.)	*Special order (Rs.)*	*With special order (Rs.)*
Sales	6,00,000	1,87,500	7,87,500
Less: Variable costs:			
Raw materials	85,000	42, 500	1,27,500
Direct labour	1,15,000	57,500	1,72,500
Variable factory overhead	1,55,000	77,500	2,321,500
Variable selling costs (2.75% of selling price)	16,500	—	16,500
Total variable costs	3,71,500	1,77,50	5,49,000
Less: Fixed costs:			
Fixed factory overhead	1,25,000	—	1,25,000
Fixed selling & administrative costs	72,500	—	72,500
Total fixed costs	1,97,500	—	1,97,500
Total costs	5,69,000	1,77,500	7,46,500
Net income before taxes	31,000	10,000	41,000

From the above analysis, it is clear that the acceptance of the special order will increase the profit by Rs. 10,000. Also the bid price (Rs. 18.75) is significantly less than the normal price of Rs. 30. However, before arriving at a proper decision, management should consider factors other than just the immediate impact on income. An important point is the effect on regular customers. If regular customers are paying more for the products, they may demand price reduction or quit buying from the firm and seek another source of supply. Another consideration is the possibility of special order customers being the regular customers.

Replace or Retain

The decision to replace or retain plant and equipment is a capital investment or long-term decision and should be taken very carefully. The differential costs which are important in retaining or replacing decisions are the following: change in fixed overhead costs, loss on sale of old equipment, capital investment and related costs such as rate of return and interest. Management should also consider differential benefits likely to be derived such as higher production and increased sales, realisable value of old machines, saving in operating cost, tax advantages, if any. Suppose a company has purchased a plant for Rs. 1,00,000 five years ago which has a life of 10 years with no salvage value. The present book value is Rs. 50,000. Management is considering the replacement of this plant with a new plant costing Rs. 80,000 having a life of five years with no scrap value at the end of its life. The costs of operating both present and the proposed plant are as follows:

	Present Plant Rs.	*Proposed plant* Rs.
Variable costs:		
Labour, supplies, power, etc.	80,000	48,000
Fixed costs 10,000	12,000	
Insurance, taxes, etc.	10,000	16,000
Deprecation	1,00,000	76,000

It appears that the proposed plant would result into cost savings of Rs. 24,000 (1,00,000-76,000). However, the book value of the present equipment is a sunk cost and not relevant in the decision. The following analysis helps in making a better use of the data:

	Rs.	Rs.
Variable costs:		
Labour, supplies, power, etc.	80,000	48,000
Fixed costs:		
Insurance, taxes, etc.	10,000	12,000
Deprecation		16,000
	90,000	76,000

The purchase of the new plant results in a saving of Rs. 14,000 (Rs. 90,000 – 76,000). Management has to consider whether its benefit is enough to justify the investment of Rs. 80,000 in new machinery.

Example 1

A company is at present working at 90 per cent of its capacity and producing 13,000 units per annum. It operates a Flexible Budgetary Control System. The following figures are obtained from its budget:

	90% Rs.	*100%* Rs.
Sales	15,00,000	16,00,000
Fixed Expenses	3,00,500	3,00,600
Semi-Fixed Expenses	97,300	1,00,500
Variable Overhead Expenses	1,45,000	1,49,500
Units made	13,500	15,000

Labour and material cost per unit are constant under present conditions. Profit margin is 10 per cent.

(*a*) You are required to determine the differential cost of producing 1,500 units by increasing capacity to 100 per cent and

(*b*) What would you recommend for an export price for these 1,500 units taking into account that overseas prices are much lower than indigenous prices?

Solution:

	Rs.
Basic calculation:	
Sales at 90% capacity	15,00,000
Less: Profit 10%	1,50,000
Cost of Goods sold	13,50,000
Less: Expenses (Fixed, Semi-variable and variable)	5,43,000
Cost of Material and Labour	8,07,000
Labour and Material at 100% capacity=	Rs. 8,07,000 × 100/90
= 8,96,667	

Differential Cost Analysis can now be done as follows:

Capacity levels	*90%*	*100%*	*Differential Cost*
Production (Units)	13,500	15,000	1,500
Material and Labour	8,07,000	8,96,667	89,667
Variable overhead expenses	1,45,000	1,49,500	4,500
Semi-variable Expenses	97,500	1,00,000	3,000
Fixed Expenses	3,00,500	3,00,600	100
	13,50,000	14,47,267	97,267

(*a*) Differential Cost = Rs. 97, 267 (Rs. 14, 47, 267 – 13.50,000)

(*b*) Minimum price for export = $\frac{\text{Rs. } 97,267}{1,500}$

At this price there is no addition to revenue; any price above Rs. 64.84 per unit may be acceptable.

Note: It has been presumed that:

(*i*) no capital investment is necessary,

(*ii*) no export charges are incurred and

(*iii*) the export price will have no effect on the home market where the product will continue to be sold at the old price. It has also been assumed that necessary precautions have been taken to ensure that the product is not 'dumped back.'

Example 2

The Hi-Tech Manufacturing Company is presently evaluating two possible processes for the manufacture of a toy, and makes available to you the following information:

	Process A (*Rs.*)	*Process B* (*Rs.*)
Variable cost per unit	12	14
Sales price per unit	20	20
Total fixed costs per year	30,00,000	21,00,000
Capacity (in units)	4,30,000	5,00,000
Anticipated sales (next two years, in units)	4,00,000	4,00,000

You are required to suggest:

(*i*) Which process should be chosen? Substantiate your answer.

(*ii*) Would you change your answer as given above if you were informed that the capacities of the two processes are as follows: A., 6,00,000 units; B, 5,00,000 units? Why? Substantiate your answer.

Solution:

Comparative Profitability Statement

		Process A *Rs.*	*Process B* *Rs.*
(*i*)	Selling price per unit	20	20
	Variable cost per unit	12	14
	Contribution per unit	8	6
	Total annual contribution (as per anticipated sales)	32,00,000	24,00,000
	Total fixed costs per year	30,00,000	21,00,000
	Total Income	2,00,000	3,00,000
	Process B may be chosen		
	Total contribution (if utilized to present capacity and sold)	34,40,000	30,00,000
	Total Income	4,40,000	9,00,000
	Process B may be chosen		
(*ii*)	Total contribution (if capacity of A of 6,00,000 units and of B 5,00,000 units)	48,00,000	30,00,000
	Total Income	18,00,000	9,00,000
	Process A may be chosen		

Example 3

A company is considering expansion. Fixed costs amount to Rs. 4,20,000 and are expected to increase by Rs. 1,25,000 when plant expansion is completed. The present plant capacity is 80,000 units a year. Capacity will increase by 50 per cent with the expansion. Variable costs are currently Rs. 6.80 per unit and are expected to go down by Rs. 0.40 per unit with the expansion. Variable costs are currently Rs. 6.80 per unit and are expected to go down by Rs. 0.40 per unit with the expansion. The current selling price is Rs. 16 per unit and is expected to remain same under either alternative. What are the break-even points under either alternative? Which alternative is better and why?

Solution

Statement Of Comparative Profitability

Particulars	*Present*		*After expansion*	
Production & Sales – Units 80,000				1,20,000
	Per unit	Amount	Per unit	Amount
Sales	16.00	12,80,000	16.00	19,20,000
Variable costs	6.80	5,44,000	6.450	7,68,000
Contribution	9.20	7,36,000	9.60	11,52,000
Fixed cost		4,20,000		5,45,000
Profit		3,16,000		6,07,000

$$\text{BEP (units)} = \frac{\text{Fixed costs}}{\text{Contribution per unit}}$$

$$= \frac{4,20,000}{9.20} \qquad \frac{5,45,000}{9.60}$$

= 45,652 units (before expansion) and 56771 units (After expansion).

The profitability after expansion is very good and hence it is better to expand.

Example 4

A company annually manufactures 10,000 units of a product at a cost of Rs. 4 per unit and there is home market for consuming the entire volume of production at the sale price of Rs. 4.25 per unit. In the year 1987, there was a fall in the demand for home market which can consume 10,000 units only at a sale price of Rs. 3.72 per unit. The analysis of the cost per 10,000 units is:

Materials	Rs. 15,000
Wages	11,000
Fixed overheads	8,000
Variable overheads	6,000

The foreign market is explored and it is found that this market can consume 20,000 units of the product if offered at a sale price of Rs. 3.55 per unit. It is also discovered that for additional 10,000 units of the product (over initial 10,000 units), the fixed overheads will increase by 10 per cent. Is it worthwhile to try to capture the foreign market?

Solution:

Statement Showing the Advisability of Selling Goods in Foreign Market

	Year 1986		*1987*	
	Home market	*Home market*	*Foreign market*	*Total*
	10,000	*10,000*	*20,000*	*30,000*
	(1)	*(2)*	*(3)*	*(4)*
Materials	15,000	15,000	30,000	45,000
Wages	11,000	11,000	22,000	33,000
Overheads:				
Fixed	8,000	8,000	1,600	9,600
Variable	6,000	6,000	12,000	18,000
Total cost	40,000	40,000	65,600	1,05,600
Profit (Loss)	2,500	(2,800)	5,400	2,600
Sales	42,500	37,200	71,000	1,08,200

From the above, it is clear that it is advisable to sell goods in the foreign market. It will compensate not only of the loss on account of sale in the domestic market but will also result in an overall profit of Rs. 2,600.

Example 5

Due to industrial depression, a plant is running, at present, at 50% of its capacity. The following details are available.

	Cost of Production per unit
Direct material	Rs. 2
Direct labour	1
Variable overhead	3
Fixed overhead	2
	8
Production per month	20,000 units
Total cost of production	Rs. 1,60,000
Sale price	1,40,000
Loss:	20,000

An exporter offers to buy 5,000 units per month at the rate of Rs. 6.50 per unit and the company hesitates to accept the offer for fear of increasing its already large operating losses.

Solution:

Statement of Profit

	Existing situation	*Proposed situation*		
	20,000 Units	20,000 Units	5,000 Units	25,000 Units
A. Sales	1,40,000	1,40,000	32,500	1,72,500
B. Variable costs:				
Direct materials	40,000	40,000	10,000	50,000
Direct labour	20,000	20,000	5,000	25,000
Variable overhead	60,000	60,000	15,000	75,000
Total variable costs	1,20,000	1,20,000	30,000	1,50,000
C. Contribution (A) – (B)	20,000	20,000	2,500	22,500
D. Fixed costs	40,000	40,000	—	40,000
Profit (loss)	(20,000)	(20,000)	2,500	(17,500)

The company should accept the offer since the amount of loss will stand reduced from Rs. 20,000 to Rs. 17,500.

Moreover, acceptance of such an order will result in earning of foreign exchange for the country which may entitle the company to get some subsidy from the Government. The domestic market will also not be affected.

Example 6

A toy manufacturer earns an average net profit of 3 per piece in a selling price of Rs. 15 by producing and selling 60,000 pieces at 60% of the potential capacity. Composition of his cost of sales is:

Direct material	Rs. 4
Direct wages	Rs. 1
Works overhead	Rs. 6 (50% fixed)
Sales	Re. 1 (25% variable)

During the current year, he intends to produce the same number but anticipates that:

(*a*) his fixed charges will go up by 10%
(*b*) rates of direct labour will increase by 20%
(*c*) rates of direct material will increase by 5%
(*d*) selling price cannot be increased.

Under these circumstances, he obtains an order for a further 20% of his capacity. What minimum price will you recommend for accepting the order to ensure the manufacturer an overall profit of Rs. 1,80,500.

Solution

Marginal Cost For The Current Year

Direct material	4.20
Direct wages	1.20
Variable overheads:	
Works overhead	3.00
Sales overhead	0.25
Total marginal cost	8.65
Contribution per unit	6.35
Selling price	15.00

Statement of Profit on Sales of 60,000 Units

			Rs.
	Sales		9,00,000
Less:	Variable cost (60,000 × 8.65)		5,19,000
	Contribution		3,81,000
Less:	Fixed costs:		
	Works overheads (1,80, 000 + 18,000)	1,98,000	
	Sales overheads (45, 000 + 4, 500)	49,500	2,47,500
	Profit		1,33,500
	Profit required	1,80,500	
	Profit on 60,000 units	1,33,600	
	Profit to be earned on 20,000 units	Rs. 47,000	

Statement of Minimum Selling Price Per Unit- For an Order Of 20,000

	Rs.
Variable costs (20,000 × 8.65)	1,73,000
Desired profit	47,000
Total sales	2,20,000

Selling price per unit = $\frac{2,20,000}{20,000}$ Rs. 11

The above can be verified as under:

	Sales 60,000 units × 15 =	9,00,000	
	20,000 units × 11 =	2,20,000	
Less:	Variable costs:	11,20,000	
	80000 × 8.65 =	6,92,000	
	Fixed costs =	2,47,500	9,39,500
	Profit		1,80,500

Example 7

Auto Parts Ltd. has an annual production of 90,000 units for a motor component. The component's cost structure is as below:

	Rs.
Materials	270 per unit
Labour (25% fixed)	180 per unit
Expenses:	
Variable	190 per unit
Fixed	135 per unit
Total:	675 per unit

(*a*) The Purchase Manager has an offer from a supplier who is willing to supply the component at Rs. 540. Should the component be purchased and production stopped?

(*b*) Assume the resources now used for this component's manufacture are to be used to produce another new product for which the selling price is Rs. 485.

In the latter case, the material price will be Rs. 200 per unit. 90,000 units of this product can be produced on the same cost basis as above for labour and expenses. Discuss whether it would be advisable to divert the resources to manufacture the new products, on the footing that the component presently being produced would, instead of being produced, be purchased from the market.

Solution:

(*a*)

Statement Showing the Variable Cost and Purchase Cost of Component ... Used by Auto Parts Ltd.

Variable cost	*Per unit* (*Rs.*)	*Total for 90,000 units* (*Rs.*)
Materials	270	2,43,00,000
Labour	135	1,21,50,000
Expenses	90	81,00,000
Total variable cost (when component is produced)	495	4,45,50,000
Cost of purchase (when component is purchased)	540	4,86,00,000
Difference, excess of purchase price over variable cost	45	40,50,000

Fixed expenses not being affected, it is evident from the above statement that if the component is purchased from the outside supplier, the company will have to spend Rs. 45 per unit more and on 90,000 units, the company will have to spend Rs. 40,50,000 more. Therefore, the company should not stop the production of the component.

(*b*) The following statement shows the cost implications of the proposal to divert the available facilities for a new product.

Statement showing the contribution per unit if the existing resources are used for the production of another new product:

	(*Rs.*)	(*Rs.*)
Selling price of the new product per unit		485
Less: Materials cost	200	
Labour (variable)	135	
Expenses (variable)	90	425
Contribution per unit		60

Loss per unit if the present component is purchased:	
Purchase price of the existing product	540
Less: Total variable cost of producing the existing component	495
Excess cost	45

Thus, if the company diverts its resources for the production of another new product, it will benefit by Rs. 15, i.e. Rs. 60 – 45 per unit. On 90,000 units, the company will save Rs. 13,50,000. Therefore, it is advisable to divert the resources to manufacture the new product and the component presently being produced should be purchased from the market. This is also brought out by the following figures:

		Rs.
Total cost producing the component (90,000 × 674) (A)		6,07,50,000
Cost of purchasing the component (90, 000 × 540)		4,86,00,0000
Fixed expenses, not having been saved (90,000 × 180, i.e. 675-495)		1,62,00,000
		6,48,00,000
Less: Contribution from the new product (90,000 × 60)	54,00,000	
Total cost if component is purchased and new product is purchased and new product is made (B)	5,94,00,000	
Savings (A – B)	13,50,000	

Example 8

Part No. X-293 used in the assembly of a product manufactured by your company has, during the past three years, been a bought-out item. The current price of this part is Rs. 120. Transportation and other delivery costs account for Rs. 15 per piece. Sales tax at 10% is added to the invoice price.

Your company had been manufacturing this part earlier but decided subsequently to discontinue its own manufacture. There is sufficient unutilised capacity which can be used, if it is decided to manufacture this part again in its own plant. Annual requirements of this part are 6,000 units.

Prepare a study to enable the management to come to a decision on a proposal to manufacture the part within its own plant. The following estimates are available:

	Part No. X-293 estimated cost (Rest. per unit)
Raw materials	96
Direct wages	8
Overhead at 800% of direct wages	64
Total cost	168
Mark up for return on investment 12%	12
	180

In addition, special tools, jigs and fixtures required to manufacture this part are needed to be acquired at a cost of Rs. 1,50,000. These are to be amortised over five years.

The overhead rate is the budgeted recovery rate for products manufactured by the company. The variable portion of this amounts to 100% of direct wages.

Make your recommendations.

Solution:

Cost incurred to buy the requirements of Part X-293

	Per unit *Rs.*	*Total* *Rs.*
Purchase price	120.00	7,20,000
Transportation and delivery charges	15.00	90,000
Sales tax	12.00	72,000
	147.0	8.82,000
Cost incurred to manufacture 6,000 units of Part X-293:		
Raw materials	96.00	5,76,000
Direct wages	8.00	48,000
Special tools, jigs, etc. (1/5 of the total investment)	5,00	30,000
Interest, say @ 12% on the investment in special tools	3.00	18,000
	120.00	7,20,000

The manufacture of the part by the company itself results in a saving of Rs. 1,62,000 before tax. It will stand at Rs. 81,000 after tax if the taxation rate is presumed at 50%. The company, before taking the decision, should consider the following points:

(i) Whether a saving of Rs. 81,000 is adequate for purchasing and installing a new plant and increased fixed overheads on account of interest etc.

(ii) Another question that needs to be considered is whether the spare capacity which can now be utilised for manufacturing Part X-293 on account of which fixed overheads have not been considered, can be utilised for some other purpose, now or later? If, after some time, manufacture of something else has to be undertaken, additional facilities will then be required and the new project will have to bear the total cost which does not appear to be equitable.

The company should, therefore, consider whether the spare capacity with the company can be put to some other use. If not, manufacture of Part X-293 may be undertaken.

Example 9

An industrial concern which had no costing system appointed a cost accountant. After installation of a system of cost data, the cost accountant observed that out of the three products were being produced independent of each other, loss was being incurred on product B. He immediately decided to advise management to discontinue manufacture of this product supported by the following tabulation:

	Product A	*Product B*	*Product C*
Sales	1,00,000	65,000	4,90,000
Variable manufacturing cost	52,000	26,000	140000
Fixed manufacturing overheads (apportioned)	6,500	19,000	1,05,000
Variable selling and administration costs	18,000	17,000	18.000
Fixed selling and administration costs	4,600	4,600	4,000
Total cost	81,100	66,600	2,67,000
Net profit	18,900		2,23,000
Net loss		1,600	

Do you agree with the cost accountant's conclusions? Argue your own views on the basis of data.

Solution:

In order to ascertain true profitability of the different products, it will be appropriate to rearrange the entire information in the following manner:

		Products		
		A	*B*	*C*
1.	Sales	1,00,000	65,000	4,90,000
	Variable cost:			
	Manufacturing	52,000	26,000	1,40,000
	Selling and distribution	18,000	17,000	18,000
2.	Total variable cost	70,000	43,000	1,58,000
3.	Contribution (1) – (2)	30,000	22,000	3,32,000
	Fixed costs:			
	Manufacturing	6,500	19,000	1,05,000
	Selling and distribution	4,600	4,600	4,000
4.	Total fixed cost	11,100	23,600	1,09,000
5.	Profit/loss (3)-(4)	18,900	– 1,600	2,23,000
6.	Profit/Volume ratio	30.00	34.0	6.78
7.	Percentage of profit on sales	18.9	– 2.5	45.5
8.	Percentage of fixed cost to variable cost:			
	(*a*) Manufacturing	12.5	73.1	75.0
	(*b*) Selling and distribution	25.5	27.1	22.0
9.	Total selling and distribution cost as a percentage of sales	22.6	33.2	4.5

Comments:

1. Product B has a higher P/V ratio (34%) as compared to product A (30%).
2. Product B is showing a loss because of the arbitrary manner in which the fixed manufacturing costs have been charged to it. They are 73% of the variable costs while in case of product A, they are only 12.5%.
3. The percentage of fixed selling and distribution costs charged to product B is the highest though it has the lowest volume of sales.
4. In case product B is discontinued, the contribution of Rest. 22,000 will not be available to meet the fixed costs. Thus, the burden of Rs. 23,600. (fixed costs charged to product B) will fall on the remaining two products A and C.

Thus, it is not advisable to discontinue the production of product B unless the surplus capacity reodered by its discontinuance can be put to a more profitable use, i.e. manufacturing another product which will give a P/V ratio of more than 34%.

Example 10

Vinak Ltd. operating at 75% level of activity produces and sells two products A and B. The cost sheets of the two products are as under:

	Product A	*Product B*
United produced and sold	600	400
Direct materials	Rs. 2.00	Rs. 4.00
Direct labour	4.00	4.00
Factory overheads (40% fixed)	5,00	3,00
Selling and administration overheads (60% fixed)	8.00	5.00
Total cost per unit	19.00	16.00
Selling price per unit	23.00	19.00

Factory overheads are observed on the basis of machine hours which is the limiting (key) factor. The machine hour rate is Rs. 2 per hour.

The company receives an offer from the purchase of product A at a price of Rs. 17.50 per unit.

Alternatively, the company has another offer from the Middle East for the purchase of product B at a price of Rs. 15.50 per unit.

In both the cases, a special packing charge of 50 p. per unit has to be borne by the company.

The company can accept either of the two export orders and in either case, the company can supply such quantities as may be possible to be produced by utilising the balance of 25% of its capacity.

You are required to prepare:

(*i*) A statement showing the economies of the two export proposals giving your recommendations as to which proposals should be accepted and

(*ii*) A statement showing the overall profitability of the company after incorporating the export proposal recommended by you.

Solution:

(i) Economics of the Two Export Proposals

	Order from Canada for Product A	*Order from the Middle East for Product B*
Marginal cost per unit:		
Materials	2.00	4.00
Labour	4.00	4.00
Variable factory overheads	3.00	1.80
Overheads		
Variable selling and administration	3.20	2.00
Special packing charges	0.50	0.50
Total variable cost	12.70	12.30
Export price per unit	17.50	15.50
Contribution per unit	4.80	3.20

Since machine hour is the limiting (key) factor, the contribution should be linked with the machine hours. This has been worked out as follows:

Machine hour per unit	2.5 hours	1.5 hours
Contribution per machine hour	Rs. 1.92	Rs. 2.13

Product B yields a better contribution per machine hour.

To order from the Middle East should therefore be accepted as compared to the Canadian offer.

Working notes

	A	*B*	Total
Factory overheads per units	Rs. 5	Rs. 3	
Machine hour rate per hour	Rs. 2	Rs. 2	
Units produced	600	400	
Machine hours utilised	1,500	600	2,100
Level of activity			75%

Maxim hours at 100% activity: $\frac{2,100}{75} \times 100 = 2,800$ hr.

Capacity hours available for export 2,800 –2,100 = 700 hr.

(ii) Statement of Overall Profitability

Units	*Product A* 600 *(Rs.)*	*Product B* 867 *(Rs.)*	*Total* *(Rs.)*
Materials	1,200	3,468	4,668
Labour	2,400	1,561	3,361
Factory overhead:			
Variable	1,800		
Fixed	1,200	3,468	1,680
Selling & Admn. Overheads:		480	
Variable	1,920	1,734	3,654
Fixed	2,880	1,200	4,080
Special packing	—	234	234
Total costs	11,400	12,145	23,545
Sales	13,800	14,839	28,639
Profit	2,400	2,694	5,094

Working notes

1. Number of units of B:

Sales in the home market	400
Export market 700 hr/1.5	467
Total	867

2. Sales values of B:

400 units in the home market @ Rs. 19	Rs. 7,600
467 units for export @ Rs. 15.50	Rs. 7,839
Total:	Rs. 14,839

Example 11

A company is facing a short term problem of insufficient raw materials to meet next month's budgeted production of its three products A, B and C. The original budgets for next month were:

	A (Rs.'000)	B (Rs.'000)	C (Rs.'000)	Total (Rs. '000)
Variable Costs:				
Raw materials	34	18	26	78
Direct labour	40	34	58	129
Variable overheads	16	11	12	39
Fixed cost apportionment	60	44	56	160
Total costs	150	104	152	406
Profit	44	28	36	108
Sales	195	132	188	514

The amount of raw materials available for next month's total production of all three products is unlikely to exceed Rs. 50,000. You are required:

(*a*) to calculate the most profitable sales mix possible in this case, assuming that the company wants to produce a minimum of 50% of the budget for all three products.

(*b*) to state your conclusions and the reasoning behind your approach.

Solution:

Raw materials to be used = 50% of budgeted levels
= 50% of Rs. 78,000
= Rs. 39,000

Remaining raw materials = Rs. 50,000 – 39,000
= Rs 11,000

Remaining Rs. 11,000 should be allocated to product(s) having highest contribution margin per Re 1 of raw material used on that product. This requires calculating contribution on individual product lines in terms of Re 1 of raw material used.

Product Contribution Statement

	A (Rs '000)	B (Rs '000)	C (Rs '000)	Total (Rs '000)
Sales	194	132	188	514
Less: Variable costs	90	60	96	247
Contribution	104	72	92	268
Raw material used	34	18	26	78
Contribution per Re 1 of raw material	3.06	4.00	3.54	

Product B is having the highest contribution margin in terms of raw materials used. Therefore, more raw material should be allocated to this product. This will use up Rs. 9000 of Rs. 11,000 available.The remaining Rs. 2,000 of raw material should then be allocated to product C. The revised budget will be as follows:

	A (Rs '000)	B (Rs '000)	C (Rs '000)	Total (Rs '000)
Sales	97	132	108.5	337.5
Less: Variable Costs:				
Raw materials	17	18	15	50.0
Direct labour	20	31	33.5	84.5
Variable overheads	8	11	6.9	25.9
Total variable costs	45	60	55.4	160.4
Contribution	52	72	53.1	177.1
Less: Fixed Costs				160.0
Profit				17.1

Example 12

When Alps Ltd. operates at normal capacity, it manufacturers 2,00,000 units of its product per year. The unit cost of manufacturing at normal capacity is as follows:

	(Rs.)
Direct materials	7.80
Direct labour	2.10
Variable overheads	2.50
Fixed overheads	4.00
Product cost (unit)	16.40
Selling price	21.00

During the next three months, only 10,000 units can be produced and sold. Management plans to shut down the plant, estimating that the fixed manufacturing overheads can be reduced to Rs. 74,000 for the quarter when the plant is not operating; the fixed overhead costs are incurred at a uniform rate throughout the year. Additional costs of plant shutdown for the three months are estimated at Rs. 14,000.

You are required to answer:

(*a*) Should the plant be shut down for three months? Show computations.

(*b*) What is the shutdown point for the three months in units of product?

Solution:

(a) Decision Analysis (shut down plant)

Particulars		*Operating plant (Rs.)*	*Shutdown plant (Rs.)*
(*i*) Estimated revenue (10,000 × Rs. 21)		2,10,000	
(*ii*) Estimated costs:	(Rs.)		
Direct materials	7.80		
Direct labour	2.10		
Variable overheads	2.50		
	12.40		
Total variable costs		(1,24,000)	—

(*iii*) Estimated contribution	86,000	—
Less: Fixed costs	(2,00,000)	(74,000)
Shut-down costs	—	(14,000)
Net profit (loss)	(1,14,000)	(88,000)

The plant should shut down for three months as the loss is Rs. 88,000 only, while operating the plant would entail a greater loss (Rs. 1,14,000).

(*b*) The shut down point is the point at which losses from continued operation are equal to the shut-down costs. That is,

$$\frac{\text{Fixed cost when plant is operating – shut down costs when plant is non-operating}}{\text{Contribution margin per unit}}$$

$$= \frac{\text{Rs. } 2,00,000 - \text{Rs. } 88,000}{\text{Rs. } 8.60} = 13.023 \text{ units}$$

Example 13

Mahan Co. manufactures special automobile mirrors. It frequently subcontracts work to other manufacturers, depending upon whether Mahan's facilities are fully occupied. The company is about to make some final decisions regarding the use of its manufacturing facilities for the coming year.

The following is the cost of making clips for the mirror, a key component in his line:

	Total cost for 60,000 units	*Cost per unit*
	Rs.	*Rs.*
Direct material	3,00,000	5
Direct labour	4,80,000	8
Variable factory overhead	3,60,000	6
Fixed factory overhead	3,00,000	5
Total manufacturing costs	14,40,000	24

Another manufacturer has offered to sell the clip to Mahan for Rs. 22 each. The fixed overhead consists of depreciation, property taxes, insurance and supervisory salaries. All of the fixed overheads would continue if Mahan bought the clip except that the costs of Rs. 1,20,000 pertaining to some supervisory and custodial personnel could be avoided.

(*i*) Assume that the capacity now used to make parts will become idle if the clips are purchased. Should the clips be made or bought? Show computations. (*ii*) Assume that the capacity now used to make clips will either (*a*) be rented to a nearby manufacturer for Rs. 50,000 a year or (*b*) used to make a new item that will yield a profit contribution of Rs. 80,000. Should the clip be made or bought? Show computations.

Solution:

(*i*) Since the existing capacity and facilities cannot be used for any other work, it is advisable to continue making the clips. In case of purchase from outside, the present business has to be closed down and therefore all implications associated with closure of business should be carefully assessed and considered. The fact that Rs. 2 $\left(\frac{\text{Rs.}1,20,000}{60,000}\right)$ will be saved as cost if the clips are purchased from outside will not influence the decision to continue manufacturing the clips.

(*a*) If the clips are purchased from outside for Rs. 22 each, the existing capacity will be rented for Rs. 50,000 p.a. In such a case, there will still be a loss of Rs. 1,30,000 (Rs. 1,80,000 – 50,000) per year. Therefore it will not be advisable to buy the clips from outside (Note: Rs. 1,80,000 (Rs.3,00,000 – 1,20,000) are unavoidable fixed costs).

(*ii*) (*b*) Assuming Rs. 80,000 as net profit from manufacturing a new item (in place of manufacturing the clips and incurring the related costs) it may be advisable to buy the clips from outside @ Rs. 22 per clip. This part is vague as it does not say as to whether Mahan Co. is currently operating at profit or loss. In case it is operating at a loss, it may be preferable to make the new item and earn a profit of Rs. 80,000. In case it is operating at profit, it will be better to give up the manufacture of the clip, to buy clips from outside and to use the existing capacity for manufacturing the new items.

Example 14

Barrera Equipment Manufacturing built a new facility in 1984 but has only been able to use 60% of its capacity in manufacturing its major machine products. Management would like to use the excess capacity and has three possibilities. Only one of the three may be selected:

(*i*) The company could produce an additional 6,000 units per year of its most popular machine and develop a foreign market. Management estimates that additional freight cost would amount to Rs. 200 per machine and fixed factory overheads would increase by Rs. 60,000. To cover the additional cost, the selling price per machine would be increased by Rs. 300 per machine,

(*ii*) The company could produce and market a new laser lathe. The capacity could be used to produce 2,000 units per year that would sell for Rs. 1,800 each. Management has estimated the following unit variable costs:

	Rs.
Direct materials	600
Direct labour	300
Variable overhead	450
Variable selling	50
	Rs. 1,400

The new lathe would require additional fixed costs at Rs. 2,00,000 in fixed overhead and Rs. 80,000 in fixed selling.

(*iii*) The Paco-Pole Company has offered to lease the facilities at Rs. 30,000 per month plus 10% of the net revenues generated by the facilities. Net revenues are estimated at Rs. 1,500,000 per year.

Required:

1. Which of the alternatives should management select?
2. What is the opportunity cost of the decision?

Solution:

Books of Barrera Equipment Manufacturing Company

(*i*) The Company could produce an additional 6000 units per year of its most popular machine and develop foreign markets.

Additional freight cost Rs. 200/- machine

Total freight costs 6000 × Rest. 200 =	Rs. 12,00,000
Fixed factory overheads would increase =	Rs. 60,000
Total costs	Rs. 12,60,000

To cover the additional costs, the selling price per machine would be increased by Rs. 300/- per machine:

Increased sales revenue of 6000 units = 6,000 × Rs. 300 = Rs. 18,00,000

Net advantage in producing 6000 additional units of its most popular machine = Rs. 5,40,000 (Rs. 10,00,000 – 12,60,000)

(*ii*) New Laser Lathe – The company could produce and market a new laser lathe. The capacity could be used to produce 2000 units per year that would sell for Rs. 1600 each.

Thus, estimated rates revenue = 2000 units × Rs. 1,800 = Rs. 36,00,000. Management has estimated the following variable costs @ Rs. 1,400 per lathe.

Total variable costs of 2000 units = 2000 × Rs. 1,400	= Rs. 28,00,000
Estimated contribution margin of 2000 laser lathes = 36,00,000- 28,00,000 = Rs. 8,00,000	
Additional fixed costs:	
Fixed overhead	Rs. 2,00,000
Fixed selling	80,000
	2,80,000

Estimated increase in net income = Rs. 8,00,00-2,80,000 = Rs. 5,20,000

(*iii*) Estimated Lease Rental of the Facility

Rs. 30,000 p.m. × 12 months =	Rs. 360,000
Add: 10% of Rs. 15,00,000 =	Rs. 1,50,000
Total Estimated Revenue to be realised from Paco-Pole Company =	Rs. 5,10,000

Decision: Thus, out of three alternatives, the management should select the first alternative of producing an additional 6,000 units per year of its most popular machine. This alternative is likely to result in the maximum increase in the net income of the company, i.e. by Rs. 5,40,000. Besides, it will also be able to develop a foreign market.

Opportunity cost of the Decision

The opportunity cost of decision will be as follows:

(*i*) It would forgo, the alternative of producing and marketing a new laser lathe which would have brought income to the extent of Rs. 5,20,000.

(*ii*) It would also forgo the alternative of leasing the facilities which would have brought in the additional note revenue of Rs. 5,10,000 per year.

Thus, the net advantage of selecting the first alternative, in comparison to the second alternative is of Rs. 20,000 and Rs. 30,000 compared with the third alternative.

Example 15

Calculate the effect of sales-mix form the following data by comparing the P/V ratio and break-even point.

		P *Rs.*	*Q* *Rs.*	*R* *Rs.*	*S* *Rs.*
Sales		40,000	50,000	20,000	10,000
Variable Cost		24,000	34,000	16,000	6,000
New Sales Mix		30,000	44,000	40,000	6,000
Fixed cost	Rs. 29,400				

Solution:

Existing Sales Mix

Products	*P* Rs.	*Q* Rs.	*R* Rs.	*S* Rs.	*Total* Rs.
Sales	40,000	50,000	20,000	10,000	1,20,000
Variable cost	24,000	34,000	16,000	4,000	78,000
Contribution	16,00	16,000	4,000	6,000	42,000
P/V ratio	0.40	0.32	0.20	0.60	0.35

$$\text{Break-even Point} = \frac{\text{Fixed cost}}{\text{P/V}} = \frac{\text{Rs. } 29,400}{0.35} = \text{Rs. } 84,000$$

New Sales Mix

Products	*P*	*Q*	*R*	*S*	*Total*
Sales	30,000	44,000	40,000	6,000	1,20,000
Variable cost	18,000	29,920	32,000	2,400	82,320
Contribution	12,000	14,080	8,000	3,600	37,680
P/V ratio	0.40	0.32	0.20	0.60	0.314

$$\text{Break-even Point} = \frac{\text{Rs. } 29,400}{0.314} = \text{Rs. } 93,630 \text{ (rounded off)}$$

It will thus be seen from the above analysis that the new Sales Mix is not favourable because this reduces the P/V ratio from 0.35 to 0.314 and pushes up the break-even point from Rs. 84,000 of sales to Rs. 93,630.

Example 16

Mikado Engineering Company has received an export order for its sole product that would require the use of half of the factory's total capacity which is estimated at 400,000 units per annum. The factory is currently operating at 60% level to meet the demand of its domestic customers only. As against the current price of Rs. 6.00 per unit, the export offer is Rs. 4.50 per unit which is less than the total cost of production, the breakdown of which is given below:

Variable cost	Rs. 4.00 per unit
Fixed overhead	Rs. 1.00 per unit
Total cost	Rs. 5.00 per unit

The condition of the export order is that it has either to be accepted in full or totally rejected. The following alternatives are available for decision making:

(a) Accept the order and keep domestic sales unfulfilled to the extent of excess demand for the same.

(b) Increase factory capacity by installing a few balancing machines and equipment and also by working overtime to meet the balance of the required capacity. This will increase fixed overheads by Rs. 15,000 annual and the additional cost for overtime work will Rs. 40,000 per annum and

(c) Reject the order and remain with the domestic market only.

Prepare statements indicating the alternative and suggesting the proposal which would be most convenient to the company.

Solution:

The position under the three alternatives will be as follows:

Alternative	*A*		*B*		*C*
	Domestic	*Export*	*Domestic*	*Export*	*Domestic*
Units (in lakh)	2.00	2.00	2.40	2.00	2.40
	Rs.	*Rs.*	*Rs.*	*Rs.*	*Rs. (in lakh)*
Sales	12.00	9.00	14.40	9.00	14.40
Variable cost	8.00	8.00	0.60	8.00	9.60
Overtime			.40		
Contribution	4.00	+ 1.00	4.40	+ 1.00	4.80
Total contribution	5.00		5.40		
Fixed cost	2.40		2.40	2.40	
Net Profit	Rs. 2,60,000		Rs. 2,85,000		Rs. 2,40,000

Alternative B which yields the highest net profit is recommended. It will be seen that compared to alternative A, alternative B would give an additional profit of Rs. 25,000 only after an investment in machinery and equipment is made, increasing the fixed cost by an equivalent amount per year. This would be worth while only if the demand for the product in the domestic market increases in the future or if the additional machines and equipment can otherwise be gainfully deployed.

Example 17

Alfa Engineering Works Ltd. had the following annual budget for the current year ending June 30:

Product Capacity	*60%*	*80%*
Costs (Rs. lakhs)		
Direct material	9.60	12.80
Direct labour	7.20	9.60
Factory expenses	7.56	8.04
Administrative expenses	3.72	3.88
Selling and distribution expenses	4..08	4.32
Total	32.16	38.64
Profit	4.86	10.72
	37.02	49.36

Owing to adverse trading conditions, the company has been operating during July and September of this year at 40% capacity realising budgeted selling prices.

Owing to acute competition , it has become inevitable to reduce prices by 25% even to maintain the sales at the existing level. The directors are considering whether or not their factory should be closed down until the trade recession has passed. A market research consultant has advised that in about a year's time there is every indication that sales will increase to 75% of normal capacity and that the revenues to be produced for a full year at that volume could be expected to be Rs. 40 lakh.

If the directors decide to close down the factory for a year it is estimated that:

(*a*) the present fixed costs would be reduced to Rs. 6 lakh per annum;

(*b*) closing down costs (redundancy payments, etc.) would amount to Rs. 2 lakh;

(*c*) necessary maintenance of plant would cost Rs. 50,000 per annum and

(*d*) on re-operating the factory, the cost of overhauling the plant, training and engagement of new personnel would amount to Rs. 80,000.

Prepare a report for the directors, making your recommendations.

Solution:

Decision analysis (continue or shut down the factory)

(Amount in Lakhs)

Particulars	*Operate the factory*	*Shut-down the factory*	*Differential revenues and costs*
Sales revenue	18.51	—	(18.51)
Costs:			
Direct material	6.40	—	(6.40)
Direct labour	4.80	—	(4.80)
Factory expenses (variable)	0.96	—	(0.96)
Administrative expenses (variable)	0.32	6.00	(0.12)
Administrative expenses (fixed)	3.24	—	(3.24)
Selling and distribution expenses (variable)	0.48	—	(0.48)
Selling and distribution expenses (fixed)	3.36	—	(3.36)
Closing down costs:			
Redundancy payments	—	2.00	2.00
Maintenance of plant	—	0.50	0.50
Overhauling costs	—	0.80	0.80
Total costs	25.68	9.30	(16.38)
Differential revenues favouring the decision to operate the plant.			

Example 18

The profit for the year of Push on Ltd. works out to 12.5% of the capital employed and the relevant figures are as under:

Sales	Rs. 5,00,000
Direct Materials	Rs. 2,50,000
Direct Labour	Rs. 1,00,000
Variable Overheads	Rs. 40,000
Capital Employed	Rs. 4,00,000

The new sales Manager who has joined the company recently estimates for next year a profit of about 23% on capital employed, provided the volume of sales is increased by 10% and simultaneously there is an increase in Selling Price of 4% and an overall cost reduction in all the elements of cost by 2%.

Find out by computing in detail the cost and profit for next year, whether the proposal of the Sales Manager can be adopted.

Solution:

Push On Limited
Statement Showing Cost and Profit for the Next Year

Particulars	*Existing volume, etc.*	*Volume, costs, etc. after 10% increase*	*Estimated Sales. Cost, Profit, etc., for the next year after increase in selling price @ 4% and overall cost reduction by 2%*
	Rs.	*Rs.*	*Rs.*
Sales	5,00,000	5,50,000	5,72,000
Direct Materials	2,50,000	2,75,000	2,69,500
Direct Labour	1,00,000	1,10,000	1,07,800
Variable Overheads	40,000	44,000	43,120
Marginal Cost	3,90,000	4,29,000	4,20,420
Contribution	1,10,000	1,21,000	1,51,580
Fixed Cost	60,000	60,000	58,800
Profit	50,000	61,000	92,780
Percentage Profit on Capital Employed	12.5%	—	$\frac{92,780}{4,00,000} \times 100 = 23.19\%$

Since the profit of Rs. 92,780 is more than 23% of the capital employed, the proposal of the sales manager can be accepted.

Example 19

The costs per unit of the three products. A, B & C of a Company are given below:

Products	*A*	*B*	*C*
	Rs.	*Rs.*	*Rs.*
Direct Materials	20	16	18
Direct Labour	12	14	12
Variable	8	10	6
Fixed Expenses	6	6	4
	46	46	40
Profit	18	14	12
Selling Price	64	60	52
No. of units produced	10,000	5,000	8,000

Production arrangements are such that if one product is given up, the production of the others can be raised by 50%. The directors propose that C should be given up because the contribution from that product is the lowest. Present suitable analysis of the data indicating whether the proposal should be accepted.

Solution:

Fixed Expenses:	*Units Rate*	*Amount*
A	10,000 × Rs. 6 =	Rs. 60,000
B	5,000 × Re. 6 =	Rs. 30,000
C	8,000 × Rs. 4 =	Rs. 32,000
	Total	Rs. 1,22,000

Productwise Contribution

	Products		
	A Rs.	*B* Rs.	*C* Rs.
Selling price	64	60	52
Marginal Cost	40	40	36
Contribution per unit	24	20	16
Total Contribution	2,40,000	1,00,000	1,28,000

(a) Total Profit if A given up:

	A Rs.	B Rs.	C Rs.	*Total* Rs.
Units	—	5,000	8,000	
Addl. Units	—	2,500	4,000	
Total: -	—	7,500	12,000	
Contribution (Rs)	—	1,50,000	1,92,000	3,42,000
Less: Fixed cost				1,22,000
Total Profit				2,20,000

(b) Total Profit if B is given up:

Units	10,000	8,000	
Addl. Units	5,000	4,000	
Total:	15,000	12,000	
Contribution (Rs)	3,60,000	1,92,000	5,52,000
Less: Fixed cost			1,22,000
Total Profit:			4,30,000

(c) Total Profit if C is given up:

Units	10,000	5,000	
Addl. Units	5,000	2,500	
Total:	15,000	7,500	
Contribution (Rs)	3,60,000	1,50,000	5,10,000
Less: Fixed Cost (Rs)			1,22,000
Total Profit			3,88,000

If Product B is given up, the profit is the maximum since the total contribution of B is lowest. The proposal to give up Product C is therefore not advisable.

Example 20

A company manufacturing a consumer product and working through its network of 400 depots all over the country is considering closing down the depots and reporting to dealership arrangement. The total turnover of the company is Rs. 200 crores p.a. The average turnover costs in respect of a depot is given below:

Annual Turnover	Rs. 50 lakh
Average inventory	Rs. 5 lakh
Administration expenses	Rs. 50,000 p.a.
Staff and salary	Rs. 80,000 p.a.

The inventory carrying cost is 16% p.a. which is the rate for working capital finance. Marketing through dealers would involve engaging dealers for each area. The dealers will assure a minimum sale for each area. This would result in increasing the capacity utilisation from 75% as at present to 90%. The company's P/V ratio at present is 10% and the BEP is 50% of the capacity. The current profit is Rs. 150 lakh.

Marketing through dealers would involve payment of a commission of 5% on sales. But 50% of the existing depot staff will have to be absorbed in the company. The dealers will deposit Rs. 5 crore with the company on which interest at 12% p.a. will be paid.

(*i*) You are required to work out the impact on profit ability of the company by accepting the proposal and

(*ii*) What will be your reaction, if the commission to dealers is 4% on sales.

Solution:

Comparative Profit Statement

(in crores)

	Existing	*Through Dealers*	
		5%	4%
Sales	200.00	240.00	240.00
Cost of goods sold (90% of sales)	180.00	216.00	216.00
Contribution	20.00	24.00	24.00
Expenses:			
Administration expenses (Rs. 5.000 × 400)	2.00	—	—
Staff salaries (80,000 × 400)	3.20	1.60	1.60
Inventory Carrying Cost (16%)	3.20	—	—
Other fixed costs	10.10	10.10	10.10
Commission Sales	—	12.—	9.60
Total expenses	18.50	23.70	21.30
	1.50	0.30	2.70
Add: Saving on account of interest on deposit 4% (16% - 12%)	—	0.20	0.20

The above analysis shows that proposal A will reduce the profit from Rs. 1.50 crore to Rs. 50 crore only. On the other hand, if proposal II is accepted (4% Commission), the net profit will increase to Rs. 2.90 crore. The second proposal, therefore should be accepted.

Notes:

1. When marketing is done through dealers, 50% of the staff will be retained by the company.
2. Turnover at 90% capacity utilisation will be Rs. 240 crore i.e. Rs. 200 crores × 90/75.
3. The total fixed costs are Rs. 18.50 out of which administrative expenses, staff salaries, inventory carrying costs amount to Rs. 8.40 crore hence to other fixed cost will be Rs. 10.10 crore.

4. The rate of interest for working capital finance is 16% p.a. while the rate of interest on dealers deposits is 12%. Thus the company saves 4% interest p.a. on a sum of Rs. 5 crore, if the marketing is done through dealers. This will result in a net saving of Rs. 20 lakh.

THEORY QUESTIONS

1. Discuss the nature of short-run and long-run decisions.
2. What are the steps in a managerial decision-making process.
3. What do you mean by differential analysis. Explain the concept of differential revenue and differential costs.
4. What are relevant costs. What are its characteristics?
5. Explain how do qualitative factors influence a manager's decision. Give examples.
6. Explain the nature of the following differential analysis decisions:
   (*a*) Make or Buy
   (*b*) Add or drop a product
   (*c*) Sell or process further
   (*d*) Operate or shutdown..
   (*e*) Special orders and
   (*f*) Replace or retain
   Also, discuss what relevant information is used in making the above decisions.
7. What is incremental cost. Does incremental cost mean the same thing as variable cost.
8. Give examples of how incremental costs are used in decision-making.
9. A departmental store is thinking of eliminating one of its departments because the accountant using the total cost basis to profitability analysis, says the department is operating at a loss. What should be investigated before the final decision is made.
10. Explain the basic characteristics of costs involved in decision-making.
11. How would you go about determining the point at which a manufacturing company that is facing a period of operating losses should shut down assuming that profitability of operations is the only point to be considered.
12. Why is the contribution that a product makes towards the recovery of non-escapable costs a better measure of its profitability than the profit or loss reported on its sale after it has been charged with its fair share of all costs.
13. In the very long-run, all costs are differential. Explain.
14. Explain the uses of differential accounting in decision making.
15. Distinguish between variable costs and differential costs and highlight the importance of differential costs in non-routine decisions.
16. Describe the steps in the decision making process. In which steps does the management accountant play major roles.
17. Rajan, owner of several small local business, said recently: "The general rule I follow in making short-run decisions is that variable costs are almost always relevant and fixed costs are almost always irrelevant." Do you agree. Why. Why not?
17. In deciding to add or to delete a line of business, what version of profitability should be used. Explain.
18. Although a special order would have contributed Rs. 1,00,000 to profits and the company has excess capacity, management rejected the order. What are the possible reasons for management's action.
19. What do you mean by relevant cost and relevant revenue.

PROBLEMS

1. Maxmillian Steel Refinery can sell the iron it refines as ingots, semi-finished steel or as finished steel. Additional refining requires no special facilities, and all additional refining costs are variable. Estimated costs for producing 10,000 ingot tons are Rs. 40,000. Additional refining would yield 9,360 tons of semi-finished steel at an additional cost of Rs. 30,000. An additional Rs. 25, 000 is required to transform the product to 8,470 tons of finished steel. The market price for ingots is Rs. 96 per ton, Rs. 105 for semi-finished steel, and Rs. 130 for finished steel. Fixed costs are Rs. 6,00,000. What should Maxmillan Steel produce.

Ans: Net operating profit:
Alternative 1 - Sell ingots only Rs. 3,20,000
Alternative 2 - Sell Semifinished Steel only Rs. 3,12,800
Macmillan Steel should produce Finished Steel.

2. Timeless Products, a clock manufacturer, is operating at capacity. Constrained by machine time, the company has decided to drop the most unprofitable of its three product lines. The accounting department came up with the following data from last year's operations:

	Manual	*Electric*	*Quartz*
Machine Time per Unit	0.4 hour	2.5 hours	5.0 hours
Selling Price per unit	Rs. 20	30	50
Less Variable Costs Per Unit (Rs.)	(10)	(14)	(28)
Contribution Margin (Rs)	10	16	22

Which line should Timeless Product drop.

Ans: Timeliness Products should drop the Quartz.

3. A factory is currently working at 50% capacity and produces 10,000 units of product P, the unit cost of which is Rs. 180, comprised as follows:

	Rs.
Direct Material	100
Direct Labour	30
Factory Overhead	30 (40% Fixed)
Administration Overhead	20 (50% Fixed)

The selling price per unit is Rs. 200.

If the capacity is increased to 60%, the raw material cost will increase by 2% and selling price falls by 2%. At 80% capacity, raw material cost increases by 5% and selling price falls by 5%.

You are required to work out the total costs and profit for the three capacity levels and prepare a brief note for the management on the profitability at these levels of performance with your recommendation.

Ans: Profit at 50%, Rs. 2,00,000, at 60%, Rs. 2,12,000, at 80% , Rs. 2,12,000. It is advisable to run the factory at 60% capacity level. The total amount of profit at 60% and 80% capacity is the same. In fact, it will be preferable to use the surplus capacity over 60% for some other purpose.

4. A firm is selling X product, whose variable cost per unit is Rs. 10 and fixed cost is Rs. 6,000. It has sold 1,000 articles during one month at Rs. 30 per unit. Market research shows that there is a great demand for the product if the price can be reduced. If the price can be reduced to Rs. 12.50 per unit, it is expected that 5,000 articles can be sold in the expanded market. The firm has to take a decision whether to produce and sell 1,000 units at the rate of Rs. 20 or to produce and sell for the growing demand of 5,000 units at the rate of Rs. 12.50. Give your advice to the management in taking a decision.

Ans: Profit (*a*) 100 units, Rs. 4000 (*b*) 5000 units, Rs. 6500

Proposal to manufacture and sell 5000 units is preferable.

5. On the basis of the following information in respect of an engineering company, what is the product-mix which will give the highest profit attainable. Do you recommend overtime working up to a maximum of 15,000 hour at twice the normal wages (overheads are ignored for the purpose of this question).

Product	*A*	*B*	*C*
Raw materials per unit (kg)	10	6	15
Labour hours per unit Re. 1 per hour	15	25	20
Sales price per unit (Rs)	125	100	200
Maximum production possible (units)	6,000	4,000	3,000

1,00,000 kg. raw materials are available at Rs. 10 per kg. Maximum production however is 1,84,000 with facility for a further 15,000 hours on overtime basis at twice the normal wage rate.

6. A manufacturing concern sells one of its products under the brand name "Utility" at Rs. 3.50 each, the cost of which is Rs. 3.00 each. After further professing which entails additional material and labour costs of Rs. 2.50 and Rs. 2.00 per number respectively, utility is converted into another product 'Ace' which is sold at Rs. 8.00 each. The concern at present produces per day 600 numbers of each of two products for which 2,500 labour hours are utilised. The factory overheads have been budgeted as under:

Labour hours	2000	2,000	3,000	3,500
Factory overheads (Rs)	700	800	900	1,000

The following alternative proposals have been put forth for varying the sales mix.

(*a*) To process the entire quantity of utility so as to convert it into 600 numbers of Ace. This will need an additional 500 labour hours.

(*b*) To contribute the present level of output of utility but double the production of Ace.

You are required to work out the incremental profit/loss involved in each of the two proposals and to offer your suggestions.

Ans. Proposal A – Loss Rs. 100;
Proposal B – Profit Rs. 200).

7. A company manufacturers three products A, B and C. There are no common processes and the sale of one product does not affect price or volume of sales of any other.

The company's budgeted profit/loss for 1986 has been abstracted as follows:

	Total	*A*	*B*	*C*
Sales	Rs. 3,00,000	Rs. 45,000	Rs. 2,25,000	Rs. 30,000
Production Cost:				
Variable	1,80,000	24,000	1,44,000	12,000
Fixed	60,000	3,000	48,000	9,000
Factory Cost	2,40,000	27,000	1,92,000	21,000
Selling and Administration Costs:				
Variable	24,000	8,100	8,100	7,800
Fixed	6,000	2,100	1,800	2,100
Total Cost	2,70,000	37,200	2,01,900	30,900
Profit	30,000	7,800	23,100	(–)900

On the basis of the above, the Board had almost decided to eliminate product C, on which a loss was budgeted. Meanwhile, they have sought your opinion. As the company's Cost Accountant, what would you advise. Give reasons for your answer.

Ans: P/V ratio, A 28.7%, B 32.4%, C 34%.

It is found that product C, though it has the highest P/V Ratio, seems to be non-profitable because it has to bear a higher percentage of fixed cost as compared to its total cost. The percentage comes about 35.9%, which in case of other products is too less. Since the surplus capacity generated by one product cannot be used for other products, there seems to be no justification for discontinuing product C till some new product is developed which will have a higher P/V ratio than product C. In the present circumstances, since C has a higher P/V ratio, and if sales continue to rise, C may start.

8. A factory produces 24,000 units. The cost sheet gives the following information:

	Rs.
Direct Material	1,20,000
Direct Wages	84,000
Variable Overheads	48,000
Semi-variable Overheads	28,000
Fixed Overheads	80,000
Total Cost	3,60,000

The product is sold at Rs. 20 per unit.

The management proposes to increase the production by 3,000 units for sales in the foreign market. It is estimated that the semi-variable overheads will increase by Rs. 1,000. But the product will be sold at Rs. 14 per unit in the foreign market. However, no additional capital expenditure will be incurred. The management seeks your advice as a cost accountant. What will you advise them.

Ans: Sales of additional 3000 units in the foreign market will give a profit of Rs. 9500. Hence the proposal should be accepted.

9. A machine tool manufacturing company sells its lathes at Rs. 36,500 each made up as follows:

	Rs.	
Direct Materials	16,000	
Direct Labour	2,000	
Variable Factory Overheads	5,000	
Fixed Factory Overheads	3,000	
Variable Selling Overheads	500	
Royalty	1,000	
Profit	5,000	32,500
Central Excise Duty		1,000
Sales tax		8,000
		36,500

There is enough idle capacity.

(a) A firm in Arabia has offered to buy 10 lathes of a company at Rs. 28,500 each. Should the company be interested in the business.

(b) It has been decided to sell 5 such lathes to an engineering company under the same management at bare cost. What price should you charge.

Ans: (a) contribution Rs. 4,000
Less: Sales Tax Rs. 2,340

Savings Rs. 1,660

Company may accept the export order.

(b) The company may charge Rs. 31000 (Rs. 36,500 – Rs. 5500 (Profit and selling overheads)

10. The budgeted results for X Co. include the following:

		Rs. in lakh	*Variable Cost as % of sales Value*
Sales:	Product A	60	50%
	Product B	50	60%
	Product C	80	65%
	Product D	40	80%
	Product E	30	70%
		260	

Fixed overheads for the period Rs. 100,00 lakh.

You are required to (a) prepare a statement showing the amount of loss expected, (b) assuming that the sale of only one product can be increased at a time, you are asked to recommend a change in the sales volume of each product which will eliminate the expected loss.

Ans: (a) Total loss Rs. 5,00 000.

Additional sales, required to break-even, assuming sales of only one product is increased at a time, to give the additional contribution of Rs. 5,00,000, is calculated as follows:

$$\text{Sales required} = \frac{\text{Under-recovery of fixed overheads}}{\text{P/V Ratio of the product}}$$

		Rs.
Product	$\frac{5,00,000}{50\%}$	10,00,000
B	$\frac{5,00,000}{40\%}$	12,50,000
C	$\frac{5,00,000}{35\%}$	14,28,571
D	$\frac{5,00,000}{20\%}$	25,00,000
E	$\frac{5,00,000}{30\%}$	16,66,667

The company should utilise the spare capacity available for Product 'A' to achieve maximum profitability as its P/C Ratio is highest. Fixed costs remaining the same at every level of production, this combination will lead to maximum profitability.

11. Quality Products Ltd., manufactures and markets a single product. The following data are available:

	Per Unit		Per Unit
Materials	Rs. 16	Dealer's Margin	Rs. 4
Conversion Costs (variable)	12	Selling Price	40

Fixed Cost: Rs. 5 lakh

Present Sales: 90,000 units

Capacity utilisation: 60 per cent

There is acute competition. Extra efforts are necessary to sell. Suggestions have been made for increasing sales:

(*a*) By reducing sales price by 5 per cent.

(*b*) By increasing dealer's margin by 25 per cent over the existing rate.

Which of these two suggestions you would recommend, if the company desires to maintain the present profit. Give reasons.

Ans: Present Profit Rs. 2,20,000.

(*a*) Units required to maintain the some profit 1,16,111 units

(*b*) Units required to maintain the same product 10,2,857 units.

Second proposal is recommended.

12. From the cost records of a company, for a specific period for product X, the information given in the first column is extracted. The second column can be ignored since it is only one of the projections of an assistant accountant; but it may be useful to you:

	This Period Account	*One of the future projections*
Sales in units	10,000	20,000
Profit (Loss) (in Rs.)	(10,000)	10,000
Fixed Cost (in Rs.)	(10,000)	10,000
Variable Cost per unit (in Rs.)	8	8

On this basis of the first column, determine:

(*a*) What increased sales volume is required to cover an extra attractive packaging cost of Rs. 1.50 per unit, to increase the sales, at the existing sale price, to yield zero profit.

(*b*) What increased sales volume is required, at the present sale price to cover an additional publicity expense of Rs. 5,000 for that period while yielding a profit of Rs. 5,000.

(*b*) What increased sales volume is required to reach a profit of Rs. 4,000 while reducing the selling price by 3% per unit.

Ans: (*a*) BEF if extra packaging cost is incurred 20,000 units,
(*b*) Additional sales required Rs. 10,0,000
(*c*) Additional sales required Rs. 94,000

13. A company follows the flexible budgeting system, and the position at 70% level of production, is as follows:

Production	40,000 units
Direct wages	60,000
Direct materials	80,000
Overhead:	
Fixed	84,000
Variable	42,000
	2,66,000

The selling price per unit is Rs. 8.65.

In the present market conditions, there is hardly any chance for selling more locally. A special export order for 8,000 units 6.50 per unit is received.

(*a*) Would it be product for the company to accept the order at this price.
(*b*) What is the price beyond which it would be profitable to accept this order.

14. Able Company has a plant capacity of 1,00,000 units per year, but the 2002 budget indicates that only 60,000 units will be produced and sold. The entire 2002 budget is as follows:

Sales revenues (60,000 units at Rs. 4)	Rs. 2,40,000	
Less: Cost of goods produced (based on production of 60,000 units):		
Materials (Variable)	Rs. 60,000	
Labour (variable)	30,000	
Variable manufacturing costs	45,000	
Non-variable manufacturing costs	75,000	
Total cost of goods produced		2,10,000
Gross margin		30,000
Less: Selling and administrative expenses:		
Selling (10% of sales)	24,000	
Administrative (non-variable)	36,000	
Total selling and administrative expenses		60,000
Loss from opérations		(30,000)

Required:

(*a*) Given the budgeted selling price and cost data, how many units would the company Able have to have produced and sell in order to break-even?

(*b*) Market research indicates that if Able were to drop its selling price to Rs. 3.80 per unit, it could sell 1,00,000 units in 2002. Would you recommend the drop in price. Indicate the new profit or loss figure.

15. Following is the income computation for a company for the year ending December 31, 19 A:

			Rs.
Sales revenue = 40,000 units, Rs. 25			10,00,000
Costs:			
	Non-variable	Variable	
Direct material	—	1,80,000	
Direct labour	—	2,00,000	
Factory overhead	1,40,000	60,000	
Selling expenses	1,00,000	60,000	
Administrative expenses	1,20,000	20,000	
	3,60,000	5,20,000	8,80,000
Net Income			

Maximum capacity of the company is 48,000 units per year; normal capacity is 80% of maximum; during 19B, the company expects to operate at 75% of maximum capacity. Normally, there are no changes in inventories.

Required: Estimate the net income to be reported at the following level:

(*i*) maximum capacity; (*ii*) normal capacity; (*iii*) what sales volume would be required to produce a net income of Rs. 1,92,000.

16. Yardley Corporation uses a joint process to produce products A, B and C. Each product may be sold at its split-off point or processed further. Additional processing costs are entirely variable and are traceable to the respective products produced. Joint production costs for 1984 were Rs. 50,000. Relevant data are as follows:

Sales Value and Additional Costs if Processed Further

Product	*Units Produced*	*Sales value at split-off*	*Sales value*	*Additional Costs*
A	20,000	Rs. 45,000	Rs. 60,000	Rs. 20,000
B	15,000	75,000	98,000	20,000
C	15,000	30,000	62,000	18,000
		Rs. 1,50,000		

Required:

To maximise profits, which products should Yardley subject to further processing. Why.

17. The Midland Company published the following income statement for the year just ended:

			Rs.
Sales (15,000 units)			1,50,000
Cost of goods sold:			
Materials		45,000	
Labour		30,000	
Overhead:			
Fixed	20,000		
Variable	15,000	35,000	
			1,10,000
Gross profit on sales			40,000

Selling expenses	5,000	
Administrative expenses	10,000	15,000
Net profit		Rs. 25,000

The High Point Company has offered to purchase 10,000 units for each of the next 10 years at a unit price of Rs. 9. This offer would have no effect on present sales. Present plant capacity is 20,000 units. The firm would have to buy new machinery in order to accept the offer and be able to continue producing the same quantity for its regular trade. The only machine available at the present time to do the job produces 20,000 units. It would cost the firm Rs. 1,00,000 and have a life of 10 years with no scrap value at that time.

Other fixed overhead is estimated to increase to Rs. 5,000 if the new offer is obtained. Variable overhead will increase proportionately to sales units. Labour costs will raise Rs. 0.50 per unit according to a recent contract signed with the Union. Suppliers of raw materials have indicated a 10% rise in prices in their latest price catalogues.

Selling and administrative expenses are expected to rise to Rs. 2000 and Rs. 3000 respectively.

Should the company accept the new offer or should it make a vigorous effort to sell the present unused capacity at the present sales price and decline the High Point Company Business.

18. A manufacturer has planned his level of operation at 50% of his plant capacity of 30,000 units. His expenses are estimated as follows, if 50% of the plant capacity is utilised.

(i) Direct Materials	Rs. 8,280
(ii) Direct Wages	11,160
(iii) Variable and other Manufacturing Expenses	3,960
(iv) Total Fixed Expenses irrespective of capacity utilisation.	6,000

The expected selling price in the domestic market is Rs. 2 per unit. Recently the manufacturer has received a trade enquiry from an overseas organisation interested in purchasing 6,000 units at a price of Rs. 1.45 per unit.

As a professional management accountant, what would be your suggestion regarding acceptance or rejection of the offer. Support you suggestion with suitable quantitative information.

19. Alpha Company has the following budgeted figures for its various products for next year:

	Products		
	A (Rs. '000)	*B* (Rs. '000)	*C* (Rs. '000)
Sales value	480	480	160
Variable costs	432	384	120
Fixed Costs (allocated)	24	36	50

The company is concerned about Product *C* and several alternatives are being considered:

Alternative-1

Cut *C*'s selling price by 10%. It is estimated that this will increase *C*'s unit sales by 40%.

Alternative-2

Substitute a new product *D* for *C*. Estimated sales are Rs. 1,40,000 in the first year. Variable costs are estimated at 55% of sales. Fixed cost directly attributable to *C* of Rs. 10,000 will be eliminated but Rs. 16,000 additional fixed costs directly attributable to *D* will be incurred.

Alternative-3

Eliminate *C* entirely. This will reduce the fixed costs attributable to *C* by Rs. 10,000.

Alternative-4

Convert *C* into special finish by adding additional treatments, which will secure a price increase of 20%. The additional costs incurred will be 10% of the new increased price.

Management wants to know the effect of each alternative on the profit of the company and their ranking in order of preference.

Answer:

The four alternatives have no relationship with products *A* and *B*. It can be assumed that these products will continue to make contribution whatever they are currently making. Therefore, there is no need to examine products *A* and *B* profitability.

For Product *C*, the following ranking of alternatives is applicable:

Bank 1 – Alternative 2 – Increases profit by Rs. 17,000

Bank 2 – Alternative 4 – Increases profit by Rs. 12,800

Bank 3 – Alternative 1 – Increases profit by Rs. 9,600

Rank 4 – Alternative 3 – Reduces profit by Rs. 30,000

20. The Spring Manufacturing Company is considering accepting a special order of 50,000 mattresses which it received form a large chain of department stores. The order specified a price of Rs. 30 per unit. This compared unfavourably to the company's regular price of Rs. 33 per unit. The accounting department prepared the following analysis in an attempt to show that there would be cost saving resulting from the additional sales:

	Cost per Unit without the Additional Sales (1,00,000 units)	*Cost per unit with Additional Sales (1,50,000 units)*
Variable Costs (Rs.)	20	20
Fixed Costs (Rs.)	9	6
	29	26

No additional fixed costs from would be incurred because there was excess capacity. In as much as the average cost per unit will be reduced from Rs. 29 to Rs. 26, the President of the firm believes he would be justified in reducing the price by Rs. 3 to sell to the department store chain.

Required:

Should the order for the 50,000 units at a price of Rs. 30 be accepted. Which factor not included in the accounting department's analysis should be considered in arriving at a decision.

21. Pontalba Manufacturing Company Ltd. is considering dropping the activities of Department 18. During the last year, the department produced sales totalling Rs. 1,90,000. The gross profit of the department averages about 27 per cent of the sales.

Operating expenses directly associated with the department are as follows:

	Rs.
Salaries	31,000
Supplies	7,000
Maintenance	1,000
Other costs	8,000

Operating expenses allocated to the department for general overhead and administration total Rs. 9,400. All the cost of the goods sold is considered escapable.

On the basis of the above information, you are required to prepare a report for use of the Board of Directors showing the impact of dropping the activities of Department 18.

❑❑❑

Chapter 7

BUDGETING

CONCEPT OF BUDGETING

On of the primary objectives of management accounting is to provide information to the management for planning and control. Budgeting acts as a tool of both planning and control. Budgeting is a formal process of financial planning using estimated financial and accounting data. The institute of Cost and Management Accountants (UK) defines a budget as "a financial and/or quantitative statement, prepared and approved prior to a defined period of time, of the policy to be pursued during that period for the purpose of attaining a given objective. It may include income, expenditure and the employment of capital."

Budgeting and Forecasting

Sometimes the terms "budgeting" and "forecasting" are used interchangeably. Both terms have some similarities. For example, both relate to future events and involve prediction of something. The basic difference between budgeting and forecasting lies in the degree of sophistication involved in the predictions used by them. According to the National Association of Accountants (USA) "forecasting is a process of predicting or estimating a future happening." Forecasting is an essential part of the budgeting process. Forecasting is estimating future events and their effects on the budget. Forecasting comes to an end after mere estimating. Budgeting is a process of preparing budgets and further control aspects are involved in its procedure. Besides, forecasting can be made by a firm for purposes other than budgeting, such as a forecast of general business conditions. Such forecasts are sometimes not used in budgeting.

In a large business there are a number of factors which could have an impact on the future of the business. These factors may be external as well as internal or both. External factors mainly concern changes in business environment over which a business enterprise has no control. Internal changes occur within a firm and affect the profit which is forecast in advance. Thus budgeting is not merely forecasting of a particular event. It is not simply an estimation or prediction; it is a plan. In simple terms, budgeting is an attempt, at the beginning of the year (or at any other period), to plan the profit and loss account for the year and to aim for a definite balance sheet at its end, instead of relying upon chance.

Concept of Budgetary Control

Budgetary control is a control measure in which the actual state of affairs is compared with the budget so that appropriate action may be taken with regard to any deviations before it is too late. Budgeting is thus merely part of budgetary control. The Institute of Cost and Management Accountants (UK) defines budgetary controls as "the establishment of budgets relating the responsibilities of executives to the requirements of a policy and the continuous comparison of actual with budgeted results either to secure by individual action the objective of that policy or to provide a basis for its revision." Briefly, the use of a budget to control a firm's activities is known as budgeting control. Budgetary control has the following main objectives:

1. To provide an organised procedure for planning. It provides a detailed plan of action for a business over a definite period of time.
2. To coordinate all the activities of various departments of a business firm in such a manner that maximum profit will be achieved for minimum use of resources.
3. To provide a means of determining the responsibility for all deviations form the plan (budget), and to supply information on the basis of which necessary corrective action may be taken. Thus, budgetary control has the objective of controlling cost.

Objectives and Functions of Budgeting

An effective budgeting system is vital to the success of a business firm. Without a fully coordinated budgeting system, management cannot know the direction business is taking. Budget is needed in organisations to perform the following functions: (*i*) planning, (*ii*) coordination, (*iii*) communication and (*iv*) control and performance evaluation.

Planning

Almost all business activities require some planning to ensure efficient and maximum use of scarce resources. The first step in planning is defining a company's broad aims and objectives. After the broad objectives have been defined, strategies to achieve the desired goals are formulated and tentative schedules set up. The budget is a detailed schedule of the proposed combination of the various factors of production which is the most profitable for the ensuing period. A budget incorporates expected performance and presents managerial targets. These targets guide the business operations and help in overcoming problems and analysing the future. Budgeting influences strategies which tend to change if conditions or managerial objectives change such as changing product lines. Thus, budgeting influences the formulation of all business strategies and subsequently assists business managers in executing such strategies. In this way it cultivates forced planning among managers and contributes to the achievement of overall business objectives.

Coordination

Coordination is a managerial function under which all factors of production and all departmental activities are balanced and integrated to achieve the objectives of the organisation. The individual managers working for their objectives of the organisation. The individual managers working for their individual interests (targets) also work for the benefit of the organisation as a whole. For example, to achieve to organisation's objectives, management must coordinate the activities of the production, marketing and finance departments. The budgeting process provides the basis for individuals in all parts of the organisation to exchange ideas on how best to achieve these objectives. There is a need for coordination between the production and sales departments. A production department should ensure adequate production to meet the anticipated demand of the sales department. Sufficient materials, labour and other facilities should be made available to facilitate higher production. If need be, production capacity must be increased. In turn the finance manager has to ensure adequate cash to meet greater output requirements.

Budgeting ensures coordination in the absence of which different departments in an organisation may act in a manner which is beneficial only to their individual departments, but not to the objectives of the firm as a whole. A sales department may sell more than the production department can produce or vice-versa. Similarly, the specific interests of different departments may be in conflict. The sales department may think only in terms of price, the production manager may be concerned only with quality, the purchasing manager may aim to buy in large quantities to avail of the advantages of discount, the finance manager has to take care of meeting obligations and make arrangements for funds to meet increasing business requirements. The budgeting process helps in removing inconsistencies among the goals and actions of each department and reconciles their differences so that each department contributes towards the overall objectives of the organisation.

Communication

It is necessary in an efficient organisation that all people be informed about the objectives, policies, programmes and performances. They should have a clear understanding of the aim and objectives and the part they are to play in goal attainment. This is made possible through their participation in the budgeting process. Budgets inform each manager of what others have agreed to do. They also inform managers of the resources available to achieve objectives and targets.

Control and Performance Evaluation

Budgeting enters into control at three points:

1. When a budget is being formulated, departments analyse their plans for the future and submit estimates as per their requirements, justifying each of their demands by demonstrating a need.
2. After budgets of different departments have been reviewed and approved they become targets that set desirable limits on sending.
3. At the end of the budget period, a comparison of actual expenditures with budget expenditure is made as a means of judging performances and fixing responsibility for deviations.

Budgets are the basis of performance evaluation in an organisation as they reflect realistic estimates of acceptable and expected performance. Most managers are interested to know what is expected of them so that they may monitor their own performance. It is more accurate, reliable and reasonable to measure current performance against a budget rather than against a vague expectation or against results of previous year when conditions might have changed. The sales department should be evaluated against that was reasonable to expect rather than against what was achieved in the previous year. As a basis for judging actual results, budgeted performance is generally considered a better criterion than past performance. A major weakness of using historical (past) data for judging performance is that inefficiencies may be buried in the past performance. Furthermore, the usefulness of comparisons with the past may be hampered by intervening changes in technology, personnel, products, competition, and general economic conditions.

Advantages of Budgeting

Budgeting plays an important role in the effective use of resources and achieving overall organisational goals. It helps management's in the allocation of responsibility and authority, and analysis of variances between budgets and actual results so that corrective action may be taken. It has the following advantages:

1. Budgeting compels and motivates management to make an early and timely study of its problems. It generates a sense of caution, care, and adequate study among managers before decisions are made by them.
2. Budgeting provides a valuable means of controlling income and expenditure of a business as it is a "plan for spending." It regulates the spending of money and shows up losses, waste and inefficiency emerging from performance, thus making it possible for corrective action to be taken promptly.
3. Budgeting provides a tool through which managerial policies and goals are periodically evaluated, tested and established as guidelines for the entire organisation.
4. Budgeting helps in directing capital and other resources into the most profitable channels. 4. It provides a means of ensuring that capital employed is kept at a minimum level consistent with

the level of activity planned and that it is usefully employed; at the same time it ensures that maximum output is obtained.

5. Budgeting coordinates and correlates all business activities. It enables management to decentralise responsibility without losing control of the business. It reveals weaknesses, inefficiencies and deviations in the organisation very promptly which can be checked immediately to achieve a desired goal.
6. The use of budgeting in an organisation develops an attitude of "cost consciousness," stimulates the effective use of resources, and creates an environment of profit-mindedness throughout the organisation. It emphasises how much should be spent to achieve a goal. The budgeting system does much to make clear the basic policies of top management and the objectives of the firm to lower levels in an organisation.
7. It provides a norm, basis or yardstick for measuring performance of departments and individuals working in organisations. Individual managers can evaluate their own decisions and achievements and take suitable steps to improve their performances.
8. Budgeting encourages and gives a sense of purpose to each individual in the organisation. All these positive factors lead to higher output and increase employee productivity.
9. Budgeting provides a systematic and disciplined approach to the solution of problems in the organisation.
10. Budgeting, if executed in nearly very enterprise, helps the total national economy by providing stability of employment, economic use of resources and effective prevention of waste.

In conclusion, the budgeting system although highly involved and conceptual, is basically only a managerial tool. It can make the task of managing more systematic, more effective and more rewarding. It can be applied so as to impart a high degree of flexibility in the management process. It is a relatively complex and sophisticated tool, not in the procedural or mechanical sense but in a conceptual sense. There is clear evidence that a management seriously committed to a budgeting system very rapidly raises its level of conceptual sophistication, and as a consequence there is significant elevation of the long-range profit potentials in an enterprise.

LIMITATIONS OF BUDGETING

While budgeting has many advantages that are vital to an organisation, it has certain limitations which require careful consideration:

1. Planning, budgeting or forecasting is not an exact science; it uses approximations and judgement which may not be cent per cent accurate. At best, a budget is an estimate; no one knows precisely what will happen in the future. Budgets need to be revised from time to time for any change in plans, operating conditions, technology etc.

2. The success and utility of budgeting depends on the cooperation and participation of all members of management. All persons should direct their efforts according to the plan. The top management also should adhere to the budget and provide cooperation. Many a time budgeting has failed because executive management has paid only lip service to its execution.

3. A budget is only a tool and does not eliminate nor take over the place of management. A budget cannot be substituted for management but should only be used by management for accomplishing managerial functions. Executive generally feel "circled in" by a budget and its related figures. They fail to understand that budget is meant to provide detailed information, goals and targets which may help them in achieving the company objectives.

4. The establishment of a budgeting process takes time. Also, sometimes too much is expected from a budget and in case expectations are not fulfilled, the blame is put on the budget. An efficient budgeting programme requires that responsible persons should understand the philosophy, objectives and essentials of budgeting.

5. Excessive emphasis on budgeting may result in attempts by lower level management and employees to buck the system by providing inaccurate estimates of future costs and revenues, and by failing to take advantage of changes in the environment because to do so would result in a deviation from plan, they would be considered as operating contrary to the budget. Under an imbalanced budget programme, employees will tend to overestimate costs and underestimate revenues, thus creating budget slack. As the end of budget period approaches and employees realise that actual expenses have not been as great as allowed by the budget, there may be a temptation to spend excessive amounts in order to "use up" the budget allowance. Such activities result in sub-optimal profits for the company.

BUDGETING PROCEDURES

The budgeting procedure or programme varies widely from one organisation to another. Differences in management style, organisation objectives, structure of competition and similar factors affect the procedures companies adopt in budget preparations. However, there are a set of guidelines (procedures) which are used in the budgeting process by a large number of organisations. These common steps can be listed as follows:

1. Obtaining estimates of sales, production levels, expected costs, and availability of resources from each sub-unit/division/department: The departmental heads or managers are required to provide estimates of future conditions and activities that will have an impact on the company. The discussion and participation may be in the form of informal discussions and/or detailed written reports of plans which will be submitted to the budget committee for approval.

2. Coordinating estimates: In many organisations, the budget committee evaluates the different plans submitted by various organisational units to determine the potentiality of plans in the overall interest of the company and to estimate what resources are available and can be fairly allocated among the various units of the organisation. A suggestion by a department that an advertisement programme should be increased by 25% should be evaluated in the light of the existing sales programme, availability of resources to meet extra advertising expenditures and the anticipated benefits resulting from additional sales efforts.

3. Communicating the budget to responsible managers and the concerned departments. After individual budget plans have been approved in the light of organisational goals and availability of resources, the budgets should be communicated to departments and responsible managers. Changes and modifications incorporated in the final budget should be made known to managers to obtain their cooperation and support for the budgets. Most managers will accept changes in budgets if the changes are found reasonable and necessary. But sometimes changes or revisions are made by the budget committee without studying and understanding the requirements and conditions prevailing in departments. Budgeting requires effective communication to convince the departmental manager about changes in the budget.

4. Implementing the budget plan: The final budget is presented to the managers concerned and adopted as the plan of operation for the coming budget period. The various service units in a business enterprise are required to provide the necessary materials, labour, facilities and other resources to carry out the budget.

5. Reporting Interim progress towards budgeted objectives: As a feedback in the budgeting process, performance reports are prepared to inform departmental managers and top management about the performances achieved in terms of budgeted figurers. Such an investigation may call for a need to revise the budget during the year. For example, it is advisable to reduce production when sales are low than to continue with high production levels. This feedback of information can also be used as a basis for preparing the next year's budget. Also, a comparison between planned and actual performances may highlight changes that are required in organisational objectives or in the budgets for the coming period.

ORGANISATION FOR BUDGETING (THE BUDGET COMMITTEE)

Responsibility for budget direction and execution is usually placed in the hands of a Budget Committee which reports directly to top management. In large companies the budget committee is composed of executive in charge of major functions of the business and includes the sales manager, personnel manager, finance manager, the production manager, the chief engineer, the treasurer and the chief accounts officer. One member of the budget committee is the budget director who is in-charge of preparing a budget manual of instructions and accumulating the proposed budget data. In large companies, the position may be a full-time job; in smaller companies, the post may be assigned to the finance manager or chief accounts officer or some other officer who acts as budget director on a part-time basis.

The principal functions of the budget committee are to:

1. decide the company's general policies and objectives;
2. receive and review individual budget estimates concerning different departments/units/divisions;
3. suggest changes, modifications in accordance with organisational objectives.
4. approve budgets which act as an authority/target for departmental action;
5. receive and analyse performance reports regarding the implementation of budgets;
6. suggest corrective action to improve efficiency and achieve budgetary goals.

THE BUDGET PERIOD

The budget period is an important factor in developing a comprehensive budgeting programme. This is the period for which forecasts can reasonably be made and budgets formulated. The length of the budget period depends on the type of business, the length of the manufacturing cycle from raw material to finished product, the ease or difficulty of forecasting future market conditions and other factors. However, a business enterprise generally prepares a Short-range budget, and a Long-range budget.

Short-range Budget

Short-range budgets may cover periods of three, six or twelve months depending upon the nature of the business. Most manufacturing firms use one year as the planning period. Wholesale and retail firms usually employ a six-month budget which is related to their selling seasons. In determining the period of the short-range budget, the following factors should be considered:

1. The budget period should be long enough to cover complete production of various products.
2. For business of a seasonal nature, the budget period should cover at least one entire seasonal cycle.
3. The budget period should be long enough to allow for the financing of production well in advance of actual needs. It should provide adequate time to arrange the funds for production and other purposes.
4. The budget period should coincide with the financial accounting period to compare actual results with budget estimates and thus to facilitate better interpretation of the performance.

Long-range Budget

A long-range budget or planning is defined as a systematic and formalised process for purposefully directing and controlling future operations toward a desired objective for periods extending beyond one year. Long-range budgets or plans are not described in precise terms, nor are they expected to be completely coordinated future budgets. They cover specific areas, such as future sales, future production, long-term capital expenditures, extensive research and development programmes, financial requirements, profit forecast. They evaluate the future implications associated with present decisions and help management in making present decisions and select the most profitable alternative. Long-range budgeting does not eliminate risk altogether: it only reduces the risk to a level which does not hamper the production and achievement of company objectives. A business enterprise through budgeting is prompted to take a greater but manageable risk.

There are many factors which are duly considered while preparing long-term budgets, such as market trends, economic factors, growth of population, consumption pattern, industrial production, national income, government economic and industrial policy. Quantitative sales can be budgeted for a three to five years period. After forecasting sales, a budgeted profit and loss account can be prepared relating anticipated sales to corresponding cost and thus net operating profit can be forecasted. Likewise, a balance sheet for many years can be prepared to forecast cash, inventory levels, accounts receivable, accounts payable, liabilities etc. The forecasted profit and loss account and balance sheet for a long-range is a very useful tool in accomplishing the objectives of the organisation as a whole.

There are advantages and disadvantages in both long-term and short-term budgeting, and the choice must be made judiciously. Short-term budgeting has the advantage of accuracy in budgeted figures which relate to future activity. Long-term budgeting may be less reliable as predictions for a longer period are relatively inaccurate. On the other hand, short-term budgeting has some limitations. One of the objectives of budgeting is anticipating problems long before they appear so that sufficient time is available for satisfactory solutions. This objective is difficult to achieve in short-term budgeting. Therefore, it is necessary for a business firm to prepare both long-term and short-term budgets.

BUDGET CENTRES

An organisation is usually broken down into different budget centres for administrative and control purposes. A budget centre is the lowest level in an organisation for which detailed costs are budgeted, separately from those of other budget centres. The Institute of Cost and Management Accountants (U.K.) defines a budget centre as "a section of the organisation of an undertaking defined for the purposes of budgetary control." The main factor in setting up budget centres is one of fixing responsibility for action and inaction. To ensure adequate cost control, the budget centres should fulfil the following conditions:

1. The budget of a particular budget centre should specify precisely the costs controllable by the person responsible for that centre.
2. Costs for which responsibility is joint, e.g., work carried out by a maintenance department, should be kept separate from costs which can be controlled be one manager.
3. Costs that are apportioned between two or more budget centres should also be controlled and for such costs one person should be made responsible.

LIMITING OR PRINCIPAL BUDGET FACTORS

When budgets are made, there is invariably some factor which governs or sets a limit to the quantity which can be made or sold. This is known as the limiting or principal budget factor. The Institute of Cost and Management Accountant (U.K.) defines a principal budget factor as "the factor, the extent of whose influence must first be assessed in order to ensure that the functional budgets are reasonably capable of fulfillment." In the field of sales the limiting factor is customer demand which is influenced by many factors, such as price and quality of the product, competition, the general purchasing power of the public, advertising, etc. In the field of production, the principal budget factor may be plant capacity, the supply of labour of the right quality, or the availability of scarce materials. Sometimes, management itself may impose limiting factors, e.g., management may control production to maintain a definite price level or management may not decide to purchase plant and machinery and thus maintain the same plant capacity.

The limiting or principal budget factors must be carefully considered while preparing the budget. If not properly taken into account, budgets may not be realistic and become difficult to achieve. Co-ordination among different departments will be lacking. The principal budget factors can be eliminated by taking suitable measures, for example, the plant capacity can be increased by purchase of an additional plant.

FIXED AND FLEXIBLE BUDGETING

Fixed Budgeting

The Institute of Costs and Management Accountants (U.K.) defines a fixed budget as "the budget which is designed to remain unchanged irrespective of the level of activity actually attained." It is a based on a single level of activity. A fixed budget performance report compares data from actual operations with the single level of activity reflected in the budget. It is based on the assumption that the company will work at some specified level of activity and that a stated production will be achieved. It suggests that the budget is not adjusted. It acts as a target for the forthcoming period. It represents a point fixed in advance with which actual results are compared. Fixed budgets do not change when production level changes.

However, in practice, fixed budgeting is rarely used. The main reason is that actual output is often significantly different from the budgeted output. In such a case the budget cannot be used for the purpose of cost control. The performance report may be misleading and will not contain vary useful information. For example, if actual production is 12,000 units in place of the budgeted 10,000 units the costs incurred cannot be compared with the budget which relates to different levels of activity. Since, in fixed budgeting, units are overlooked, a cost to cost comparison without considering the units may give misleading results. The performance report prepared under fixed budgeting merely discloses whether actual costs were higher or lower than budgeted costs. Therefore, the fixed budget is unable to provide useful information when actual output differs significantly from expected or budgeted output. The fact that costs and expenses are affected by fluctuations in volume limits the use of the fixed budget. If budgeted costs are compared with the actual costs at the end of the year, it will be difficult to infer how successful a business firm has been in keeping expenses within the allowed limits. Clearly, the idea of comparing performance at one activity level with a plan that was developed at some other activity level is nonsense from the viewpoint of judging how efficiently the manager has produced any given output.

A fixed budget can be usefully employed when budgeted output is close enough to the actual output. If output can be estimated within close limits, the fixed budget can be a good basis for performance measurement. Maximum managerial control may be exercised by making comparisons with actual operating figures. It is also important to note that budget levels should be determined on the basis of what is likely to happen in the future rather than on the basis of what happened in the past. Past information is useful in future planning. But budgeting on the basis of a rule of thumb such as "last year's figure plus 20%" is not beneficial. The most appropriate and logical approach is first to determine what needs to be done and then to decide how it is to be done. The budgeting process may then be adopted to estimate costs for the specific tasks that have been identified.

Flexible Budgeting

A flexible budget is defined in the terminology of cost accounting, issued by the Institute of Cost and Management's Accountants (UK) as "a budget which, by recognising the difference between fixed, semi-fixed and variable costs, is designed to change in relation to the level of activity attained."

A flexible budget is a budget that is prepared for a range, i.e., for more than one level of activity. It is a set of alternative budgets to different expected levels of activity. The flexible budget is also known by other names, such as variable budget, dynamic budget, sliding scale budget, step budget, expense formula budget and expenses control budget. The underlying principle of a flexible budget is that every business is dynamic, ever-changing and never static. Thus, a flexible budget might be developed that would apply to a "relevant range" of production, say 8,000 units to 12000 units. Under this approach, if actual production slips to 9000 units from a projected 10,000 units, the manager has a specific tool (i.e., the flexible budget) that can be used to determine budgeted cost at 9,000 units of output. The flexible budget provides a reliable basis for comparisons because it is automatically geared to changes in a production activity.

The flexible budget provides information to managers for multiple levels of output in case actual output is different from the expected level. The performance reports at the end of the accounting period are compared with a budget based on the actual output attained during that period. A flexible budget has the following important features:

1. It covers a range of activity (output).
2. It is flexible, i.e., easy to change with variation in production levels and
3. It facilitates performance measurement and evaluation.

Planning or budgeting for a range of activity rather than for a single level of activity is always preferable due to the uncertainty involved in forecasting future events accurately. Flexible budgeting assumes that uncertainty is likely to bring in fluctuations in the activity level. This budgeting aims to provide information about the effects of changes in activity levels and thus helps managers in making more effective decisions. In flexible budgeting, that range of activity is selected which is likely to occur. Activity levels, not likely to occur, are not included. Most often, one activity level at each extreme of the activity range is selected, with one or more in between. Among different activity levels the most likely activity level is made the basis for planning business operations. Flexible budgeting makes it easy to adjust plans to changing production levels without any delay. The flexibility involved in this budget makes a very useful decision making tool for management. Perhaps, the most important point in favour of flexible budgeting is that it provides the most accurate and reliable base for measuring performance and efficiency of the departments and individuals working in the organisation. A flexible budget performance report uses a budget based on the actual output level achieved. Budgeted costs are based on the actual activity level. This not only provides a better measure of efficiency as compared to a fixed budget is a compulsory requirement in any system of effective control and decision-making.

Steps in Flexible Budgeting

The following steps (stages) are involved in developing a flexible budget:

1. Deciding the range of activity to which the budget is to be prepared.
2. Determining the cost behaviour patterns (fixed, variable, semi-variable) for each element of cost to be included in the budget.
3. Selecting the activity levels (generally in terms of production) to prepare budgets at those levels.
4. Preparing the budget at each activity level selected by associating the activity level with corresponding costs. The corresponding costs to be attached with each activity level are determined in terms of their behaviour, i.e., fixed, variable, semi-variable.

Advantages of Flexible Budgeting

Flexible budgeting is budgeting that is automatically tailored to any level of activity. It provides a better evaluation of efficiency (the relation of inputs to outputs). Although it is most often associated with the control of overhead, a flexible budget may also include direct materials and direct labour.

In general, flexible budgeting has the following important advantages:

1. Accurate budgeting: The use of flexible budgets may result in the preparation of more accurate budgets. Flexible budgeting techniques require that consideration is to be given to the output factor in budget preparation. The basic idea underlying flexibility is that budgets are established for various levels of activity. Since all costs do not behave in the same manner (as some costs rise faster than others when production increases) a budget giving consideration to the volume (output) factor is bound to be more accurate than one where volume is not considered.

2. Accurate performance measurement: The flexible budgeting technique incorporates changes in activity level and compares actual results with the budget in terms of output achieved. This facilitates more meaningful comparison and evaluation between actual and budgeted data as comparable data are compared. The deviations resulting from the comparison are reliable and helpful to management in cost control and decision-making.

3. Coordination: Flexible budgeting results in coordination between all activities/departments of a business. Production is planned in relation to expected sales; materials and labour are acquired to meet expected production requirements. Facilities are provided to achieve budgetary goals, and funds are made available for the investments necessary to have higher output.

4. Control tool: Flexible budgeting is an effective management control tool. Business operations are conducted more efficiently and losses are avoided or reduced. Comparisons between the budgeted costs (at the actual production level) and actual costs form the basis for analysing cost variances and fixing responsibility for the same.

Infact, managers themselves feel motivated in controlling costs for which they are responsible. The flexible budget provides cost goals or targets based on scheduled activity or output before the decisions point, i.e., before the cost is incurred. This contributes to cost control throughout the organisation.

Example:

Prepare a flexible budget from the following information

Possible levels of Activity	*Upto 1,40,000 units*	*1,40,000 units to 1,60,000 units*	*1,60,000 units to 2,00,000 units*
Sales price	(Rs.) 1.05	1.00	0.90
Variable unit costs:			
Material	0.50	0.45	0.35
Labour	0.20	0.20	0.20
Overhead	0.10	0.10	0.10
Fixed costs	30,000	30,000	35,000

Solution:

Flexible Budget for the Period...

Level of activity (in units)	1,40,000	1,60,000	2,00,000
Sales price per unit	1.05	1.00	0.90
Estimated revenue	1,47,000	1,60,000	1,80,000
Variable costs: Material	70,000	72,000	70,000
Labour	28,000	32,000	40,000
Overhead	14,000	16,000	20,000
Fixed costs	30,000	30,000	35,000
	1,42,000	1,50,000	1,65,000
Budgeted profit	5,000	10,000	15,000
	1,47,000	1,60,000	1,80,000

From the above example, it is clear that flexible budgets primarily disclose the profits which will be earned from each level of activity. Also, for the purpose of controlling costs, it is necessary to relate the budget to the actual output achieved at the end of the budget period. If the firm has produced 1,80,000 units in a period, the budget would be changed incorporating the following figures and the differences would then be investigated:

Production level	1,80,000 units
Variable costs:	
Material	1,80,000 × 0.35 = 63,000
Labour	1,80,000 × 0.20 = 36,000
Overhead	1,80,000 × 0.10 = 18,000
	1,17,000
Fixed costs	35,000
Total costs	1,52,000

TYPES OF BUDGETS

Budgets are the end product of the budgeting process. The numbers and types of budgets in a business enterprise depend on the size and nature of the business. However, in a manufacturing concern, the following budgets are generally prepared:

(A) Operating and functional budgets:

1. Sales budget
2. Production budget
3. Production cost budget
   - (*i*) Direct materials budget
   - (*ii*) Direct labour budget
   - (*iii*) Factory overhead budget
4. Ending inventories budget
5. Cost of goods sold budget
6. Selling expense budget
7. Administrative expense budget
8. Budgeted income statement

(B) Financial Budgets:

1. Capital expenditure budget
2. Research and development budget
3. Cash budget
4. Budgeted balance sheet
5. Budgeted statement of changes in financial position

Sales Budget

The most important budget, which all other budgets are contingent upon, is the sales budget. All budgets, such as production budget, inventory budget, personnel budget, administrative budget, selling and distribution budget and others are all affected by the sales budget and are dependent upon the revenue derived from sales. Therefore, the sales budget is the starting point in preparing other functional budgets. Developing a sales budget requires forecasting future sales levels. Figure 7.1 presents a specimen of a sales budget.

A B C Company Ltd.

Sales Budget for the Year Ending December 31, 1994

Products	*Budgeted sales units*	*Budgeted sales price (Rs.)*	*Total (Rs.)*
A	70,000	80.000	56,00,000
B	80,000	1,20.000	96,00,000
	1,50,000		1,52,00,000

Fig. 7.1 Specimen of Sales Budget.

Forecasting Sales

The three main factors that should be considered by management in forecasting sales are: (*a*) information concerning past performance, (*b*) information about present conditions within the individual company and in each sales territory, and (*c*) data concerning the industry and general business conditions.

The information about past performance is the starting point for sales forecasting. The sales record for past years, and particularly for the year just ending should be available to management in minute detail. The accounting department or sales department or sales department should furnish reports showing sales of the last and preceding years in terms of classes of products, territory, branch or location.

The second essential step in forecasting sales is the accumulation of data regarding conditions within the company and in each sales territory. The management can obtain a good picture of sales prospects through information sent to the head office by salesmen, dealers, and sales officers of different territories. A survey may be conducted in sales territories about sales possibilities prior to the beginning of the fiscal year. Also, regular reports, monthly or more frequently, regarding business conditions, may be obtained. Many business firms have periodic market surveys to make proper evaluation of present sales conditions and future sales prospects. These surveys help in the determination of sales estimates by territories, especially when new products are being marketed. The market analysis or survey covers three fields: products, markets, and methods of distribution. The survey about the product covers the information about characteristics, its present uses, the possibility of creating new demands, main selling centres, and suggestions as to improvements in the appearance of package, trade-mark, or the product itself.

The survey about market and sales territories explains many factors, such as nature of the market; nature of consumers' demand for the product; consumers (both existing and prospective) characteristics, such as their age, religion, per capita income, group; competition; availability of substitutes in the market; product price, credit policies, discount facilities, sales promotion policies, sales trends, seasonal products, changes in buying habits and modes of living.

Information about general business conditions are known as 'business barometers' and they should be considered in preparing a sales forecast. The following are important business indicators:

1. Gross national product, which is the total market value of output of goods and services produced in the entire economy.
2. Personal income and purchasing power of the population.
3. Unemployment conditions.
4. Government crop reports.
5. Steel, coal and oil production.
6. Wholesale price indices.
7. Business failures.

8. Industrial production index.
9. Governmental policies.
10. Cyclical phases of the country's economy.

Sales Analysis

After collecting all relevant information for a sales forecast, a sales analysis or budget is prepared. The sales budget is usually prepared on the lines of (*i*) product, (*ii*) territory, and (*iii*) customer.

Sales budget by product: This budget is prepared in terms of quantities of the various classes of products. This further helps in the preparation of the production budget which is always in terms of units to be manufactured by the production departments. The production department should know the sales policies and demands for the product so that it can plan production and accumulate resources to meet the production target. However, when production is according to customer requirements, it is difficult to prepare a sales budget in terms of quantities. In such a case, a sales budget will normally be in terms of sales value for different products.

Sales budget by territory or area: Sometime products are sold in different geographical areas or territories. This requires that the sales budget be prepared for each territory as a means of fixing separate targets for different salesmen representing different territories. The differences between sales targets and sales achievement for each may help in determining accountability and giving proper incentives for target performance. A sales budget by territory also helps in preparing the distribution cost budget for different areas. A business firm, after comparing sales and corresponding distribution costs for each territory, can assess the profitability of doing business in that area.

Sales budgets (prepared on product and territory basis both) in terms of quantity and value are further broken down into monthly sales figures so that sales quotas can be fixed for salesmen. This also ensures coordination between production, sales, purchasing and stores departments.

Sales budget by customer: A sales budget prepared on either basis may be further classified as to the type of customers. Customer classification will indicate sales to wholesalers, retailers, jobbers, institutions, government agencies, educational institutions, foreign business, etc. This analysis reveals the contribution of each type of customer to total sales of the business firm. This may also point out that certain potential customers are not being given proper attention by the sales manager. This budget becomes a useful means of finding out new sales outlets. It also helps in locating factors responsible for decline in sales to various customer classes, thus assisting management in taking remedial measures to improve the position.

Production Budget

After preparing the sales budget, the production budget is prepared. A production budget is stated in physical units. It specifies the number of units of each product that must be produced to satisfy the sales forecasts and to achieve the desired level of closing finished goods inventory. Essentially, the production budget is the sales budget adjusted for inventory changes as follows:

Units to produce = Budgeted sales + Desired closing inventory of finished goods –
Beginning inventory of finished goods.

A specimen production budget in given in Fig. 7.2.

ABC Company
Total Production Budget for the month of December 1994

	Products	
	A	*B*
Budgeted sales (units)	70,000	80,000
Add: Desired closing finished goods inventory	20,000	30,000
	90,000	1,10,000
Less: Beginning finished goods inventory	40,000	50,000
Units to be produced	50,000	60,000

Fig. 7.2: Production Budget

The production budget deals with the scheduling of operations, the determination of volume and the establishment of maximum and minimum quantities of raw materials and finished goods inventory. Its summaries and details provide the basis for preparing the budgets of materials, labour and factory overheads.

The production budget, like other budgets, is detailed by months or quarters along with a tentative annual budget. Further, budgets are prepared for every production centre for comparison with actual production. The production budget contributes to planning, coordination and control. A production budget tends to reveal weaknesses and sources of potential trouble which can then be avoided by timely management action. Even more significant perhaps is the coordination that can result from an effective production budget. The production budget is the primary basis for planning raw material requirements, labour needs, capital and cash requirements and factory costs. Therefore, the production budget becomes the foundation for factory planning in general. It gives the factory executives something tangible upon which to base operational decisions.

Production Cost Budget

A production cost budget summarises the materials budget, labour budget, the factory overheads budget and may be expressed and analysed by departments and/or products. A production cost budget, also known as a manufacturing budget is made up of three budgets: (*i*) materials, (*ii*) labour and (*iii*) factory overhead.

Direct Materials Budget

A direct materials budget indicates the expected amount of direct materials required to produce the budgeted units of finished goods. This budget specifies the cost of direct materials used and the cost of the direct materials purchased. Fig. 7.3 explains the calculation of the direct materials budget. The usage part of the direct materials budget determines the cost of purchases of direct materials.

The direct materials budget is useful in the following ways:

1. It helps the purchasing department to prepare a schedule to ensure delivery of materials when needed.
2. It helps in fixing minimum and maximum levels of inventories in the stores department.
3. It helps the finance manager to determine the financial requirements to meet production targets.

The materials budget usually deals with direct materials only. Supplies and indirect materials are generally included in the factory overheads budget.

A B C Company
Direct Materials Budget for the Year Ending December 1994

A. Usage Budget

	Products		*Total*
	A	*B*	
Budgeted production in units	50,000	60,000	
Direct materials requirements			
Product 45 kg per unit	× 5		
Product B 8 kg per unit		× 8	
Direct materials usage (kg)	2,50,000	4,80,000	
Cost per kg	Rs. 100	Rs. 1.50	
Cost of direct materials used	Rs. 2,50,000	Rs. 7,20,000	Rs. 9,70,000

B. Purchase Budget

	Direct Materials (in kg.)		*Total*
	A	*B*	
Direct materials usage	2,50,000	4,80,000	
Budgeted closing direct materials inventory	+ 50,000	+ 75,000	
Total requirements	3,00,000	5,55,000	
Beginning direct materials inventory	70,000	1,00,000	
Purchase of direct materials	2,30,000	4,55,000	
Cost per kg.	× Rs. 1000	× Rs. 1.50	
Cost of purchase	Rs. 2,30,000	Rs. 6,82,000	Rs. 9,12,000

Fig. 7.3 Direct Materials Budget

Direct Labour Budget

The labour budget estimates the labour, adequate in number and grades, to enable the production budget to be achieved. It is generally preferable to prepare a separate direct labour budget and to include indirect labour in the factory overhead budget. The labour budget for direct and indirect labour helps the personnel or employment department in determining the number and types of workers needed. If additional workers are not needed, the task of the personnel department is easy. However, when workers are to be recruited, the personnel department has to make plans in advance. Any difficulties in getting a proper labour force is referred to the budget committee which can modify the sales budgets accordingly. The labour budget prepared must disclose the following information: (i) the number of each type of grade of worker required in each period to achieve the budgeted output, (ii) budgeted cost of such labour in each period, and (iii) period of training necessary for different types of workers.

Figure 7.4 illustrates the preparation of a direct labour budget.

A B C Company
Direct Labour Budget for the Year Ending December 1994

	Products		*Total*
	A	*B*	
Budgeted production requirements	50,000	60,000	
Direct labour hours per unit	3	2	
Total direct labour hours	1,50,000	1,20,000	2,70,000
Direct labour cost per hour	Rs. 5.00	Rs. 5.00	Rs. 5.00
Total direct labour cost (Rs.)	7.50,000	6,00,000	13,50,000

Fig. 7.4 Direct Labour Budget

Factory Overhead Budget

The factory overhead budget is prepared on the basis of the chart of accounts which reflects different expense accounts and which properly classifies expense accounts and details the cost centres or departments. Although expenses can be classified in different manners such as natural classification and variability, the preparation of the factory overhead budget requires that expenses should be classified by departments since expenses are incurred by various departments. In this way, departmental heads should be held accountable for expenses incurred by their departments. Generally, the department heads prepare budgets for their respective departments for the budget period. However, they need considerable help and advice from the budget director in order to achieve production budget. After review by the budget committee, the departmental managers are asked to review and comment on any revisions before the budget is made final.

Figure 7.5 depicts the factory overhead budget wherein overhead costs have been classified into fixed and variable components.

A B C Company
Factory Overhead Budget for the Year Ending December 1994
(based on budgeted capacity of 2,70,000 direct labour hours)

Items	*Direct labour hours (Rs.)*	*Rate per direct labour hour (Rs.)*	*Total cost*
Variable factory overhead:			
(*i*) Supplies	2,70,000	1.00	2,70,000
(*ii*) Repairs	2,70,000	0.50	1,35,000
(*iii*) Indirect labour	2,70,000	1.00	2,70,000
(*iv*) Others	2,70,000	0.40	1,08,000
Total variable factory overhead cost			7,83,000
B. Fixed factory overhead cost:			
(i) Supervision		Rs. 4,00,000	
(ii) Depreciation		5,50,000	
(iii) Property tax		2,50,000	
(iv) Others		1,77,000	
Total variable factory overhead cost			13,77,000
Total factory overhead cost			21,60,000

$$\text{Predetermine overhead rate} = \frac{\text{Rs. } 21{,}60{,}000}{2{,}70{,}000 \text{ hours}}$$

= Rs. 8.00 per direct labour hour

Fig. 7.5 : Factory Overhead Budget

Ending Inventories Budget

An inventory budget can be prepared to find out the values of direct materials and finished goods inventory as shown in Fig. 7.6.

A B C Company

Ending Inventory Budget for the Year Ending December 1994

	Rs.
Direct materials inventory	
Product A 50,000 kg. × Rs. 1.00 per kg.	50,000
Product B 75,000 kg. × Rs. 1.50 per kg.	1,12,500
	1,62,500
Finished goods inventory	
Product A 20,000 units × Rs. 25.00	5,00,000
Product B 30,000 units × Rs. 30.00	9,00,000
	14,00,000

Fig. 7.6 Ending Inventories Budget

Cost of Goods Sold Budget

After preparing direct materials, direct labour, factory overhead and ending inventory budgets, the cost of goods sold budget can be prepared. The cost of goods sold budget summarises all the above budgets as shown in Fig. 7.7.

A B C Company

Cost of Goods Sold Budget for the Year Ending Dec. 31,1994

	Rs.	*Rs.*
Direct materials:		
Beginning inventory	2,00,000	
Purchases	9,12,500	
	11,12,500	
Less: Closing inventory	1,62,500	
Cost of direct materials used		9,50,000
Direct labour		13,50,000
Factory overhead		21,60,000
Total factory cost		44,60,000
Beginning finished gods inventory		25,00,000
Total goods available for sale		69,60,000
Closing finished goods inventory		14,00,000
Cost of goods sold		55,60,000

Fig. 7.7 Cost of Goods Sold Budget

Selling Expenses Budget

Closely related with the sales budget is the selling and distribution cost budget which shows the budgeted costs of promoting sales for the budget period. It is also known as the *marketing expenses budget.* The selling cost budget is made up of a number of cost items, some of which are fixed and some variable. The principal fixed expenses are salaries and depreciation; the principal variable expenses are commissions, travel, advertising and bad debts. The variable expenses vary directly with sales. A selling expense budget consists mainly of the following major items:

(*i*) Sales representative (salaries, commissions, entertaining and travelling).
(*ii*) Sales office (office supplies, salaries, postage, telephone rent and rates)
(*iii*) Publicity office (salaries, office costs, press, journals, television, cinema, samples, sundries) and
(*iv*) Warehousing, packing and despatch (salaries, packing wages, drivers wages, vehicle costs, sundries).

Figure 7.8 exhibits an annual selling expense budget classified according to fixed and variable expenses. The annual budget should be broken down on a monthly basis so that actual expenses can be compared with the budget monthly. Also, separate budgets for each of these expenses may be prepared especially in the case of a large company.

A B C Company

Selling Expenses Budget for the Year Ending December 31, 1994

Items	*Costs (Rs.)*	*Total costs (Rs.)*
(A) Variable selling expenses:		
(*i*) Sales commission	35,000	
(*ii*) Salary and wages	40,000	
(*iii*) Advertising	15,000	
(*iv*) Travelling	22,000	1,12,000
(B) Total variable selling expenses:		
(*i*) Warehousing	60,000	
(*ii*) Advertising	30,000	
(*iii*) Marketing manager's salary	60,000	
(*iv*) Depreciation	27,000	1,77,000
Total selling expenses		2,89,000

Fig. 7.8 Selling Expenses Budget

Administrative Expense Budget

The administrative expense budget covers the administrative costs for non-manufacturing business activities. Budgeting administrative expense is often difficult. Perhaps the first difficulty is in classifying certain costs as production or administrative. For example, costs like purchasing, engineering, personnel,

A B C Company

Administrative Expense Budget for the Year Ending December 31, 1994

Items	*Amount (Rs.)*	*Amount (Rs.)*
(A) Variable administrative expenses:		
(*i*) Supplies	35,000	
(*ii*) Clerical wages	60,000	95,000
Total variable administrative expenses		
Fixed administrative expenses:		
(*i*) Directors' remuneration	1,20,000	
(*ii*) Legal charges	20,000	
(*iii*) Depreciation	25,000	
(*iv*) Salaries	30,000	
(*v*) Rent	60,000	
(*vi*) Postage, telephone etc.	32,000	
Total fixed administrative expenses		2,87,000
Total administrative expenses		3,82,000

Fig. 7.9: Administrative Expenses Budget

research and development can be administrative as well as production. Unless such and other expenses are properly classified, their proper budgeting and subsequent control cannot be exercised. The second difficulty is in determining the persons responsible for the incurrence and control of these costs. However, in order to accomplish the purpose of cost control in cost accounting, it is necessary that each item of cost should be under the jurisdiction and control of a responsible person who is accountable for incurring the cost.

The administrative expense budget contains expenses like directors' remuneration, legal charges, audit fees salaries, rent, office expenses, interest, property taxes, postage, telephone, telegraph etc. These expenses should be properly classified under different headings to determine the responsibility of cost incurrence and control. For example, these expenses can be classified into different categories such as company administration, general accounting, general office etc. Fig. 7.9 presents an administrative expense budget.

Budgeted Income Statement

A budgeted income statement summarises all the individual budgets, i.e. sales budget, cost of goods sold budget, selling budget and administrative expense budget. No new estimates are made; figures are taken from budgets previously prepared. This budget determines income before taxes. If the tax rate is available, net income after taxes can also be computed. Fig. 7.10 exhibits a budgeted or projected income statement.

A B C Company

Budgeted Income Statement for the Year Ending December 1994

		(Rs.)
Sales		
Cost of goods sold		1,52,00,000
		55,60,000
Gross margin		96,40,000
Selling expenses	2,89,000	
Administrative expenses	3,82,000	6,71,000
Income before taxes		89,69,000
Income taxes (assuming 50%)		44,84,500
Net Income		44,84,500

Fig. 7.10 Budgeted Income Statement

Capital Expenditure Budget

The budgeting of capital expenditure is one of the most important areas of managerial decisions. Large sum of money and long periods of time are often involved in this budget which therefore require utmost care and sound judgement. Changes and adjustments in the routine and current manufacturing operations can be done without much difficulty. But capital expenditures represent long-term commitments. Also, the benefits of capital expenditure spread over a long period of time. Generally, capital expenditures are relatively large in comparison with operating expenditures and have a long-term impact on the organisation and the achievement of its goals. Therefore, any errors in this budgeting decision may prove very critical to the business firm. The capital expenditure budget aims at minimising errors while making capital expenditure decisions. It is necessary that business firms should establish definite procedures and methods for evaluating the merits of a project before funds are committed. The effective control of capital expenditures is exercised in advance by requiring that each proposed project be evaluated in terms of its merits. After alternative capital expenditure projects have been investigated regarding expected sales, manufacturing costs, marketing costs, etc., the most profitable alternative should be selected. Further, the investments that have been made should also be reviewed.

Capital expenditure budgets are prepared for both short and long-range projects depending on the requirements of the business firm. Short-range projects are implemented during the current accounting periods;

therefore, these provisions should be made in the current budget. Long-range projects are not executed in the current period, they are expressed only in general terms. They become budget commitments only when the time for their implementation approaches. Timing is very important in achieving the most profitable results in long-term capital expenditure budgeting which involves significant investment. This is the reason why the top management has the responsibility of translating long-term capital projects into budget commitments.

Research and Development Budget

Research has now become a continuous activity in many industries. Research and development programmes should be identified and their corresponding cost should be budgeted. The research and development budget is the most important tool for planning and controlling research and development cost. It compels the management to think in advance about the fairness of these expenses both in total amounts and in each field of a research programme. It helps in coordination with the company's other plans and projects. Since the research and development programmes compete with other desirable activities in allocation of funds, coordination is needed to balance financially immediate and long-term company plans. Also, this budget guides the research and development department to plan correctly the staff and equipment requirements and special facilities needed for the work.

The preparation of research and development budgets should be based on reasonably accurate estimates and should be flexible. Research projects should be planned and evaluated and then grouped into long-term and short-term projects. A short-term research programme is needed to earn a satisfactory rate on return of the funds invested. A long-term research programme is developed to ensure that the research programmes are in line with future market trends, and demand and research costs are in conformity with budgeted financial position. Research and development is discretionary cost and therefore in case of decline in operating income and financial position of the business, some research programmes may be curtailed or postponed.

Cash Budget

A cash budget contains detailed estimates of cash receipts (cash inflows) and disbursements (cash outflows) for the budget period or some other specific period. Cash budgeting is extremely important since business operations require adequate cash to acquire materials, and meet various expense and loan obligations. Therefore, planning cash flows is very useful for all types of organisations. The preparation of a cash budget has the following objectives:

(*i*) It indicates the effect on the cash position of seasonal requirements, large inventories, unusual receipts and delay in collecting receivables.

(*ii*) It indicates the cash requirements needed for a plant or equipment expansion programme.

(*iii*) It points up to the need for additional funds from sources such as bank loans or sale of securities and the time factors involved. In this connection, it might also exert a cautionary influence on plans for plant expansion leading to a modification of capital expenditure decisions.

(*iv*) It indicates the availability of cash taking advantage of discounts.

(*v*) It assists in planning the financial requirements of bond retirements, income tax instalments, and payments to pensions and retirement funds.

(*vi*) It shows the availability of excess funds for short-term or long-term investments.

Thus, a cash budget is a useful tool in the cash management of organisations as it reveals potential cash shortages as well as potential periods of excess cash. It brings equilibrium between available cash and the cash demanding activities – operations, capital expenditures, etc. A cash budget which reveals the cash position may indicate: (*i*) the need for additional financing to meet projected cash deficits or (*ii*) the need to put excess cash to profitable use not allowing it to lie idle in the cash account. This budget aims at optimising cash balances, that is, having adequate cash to cover liquidity needs and not having so much cash that profitability is sacrificed.

The cash budget is closely related to the sales budget, and operating expenses budget. But these budgets themselves do not automatically determine an optimum cash position. This is because of the difference in the nature of the cash budget and other budgets. The cash budget is concerned with and determines the timing of cash inflows and outflows on a cash basis, whereas the other budgets are concerned with and determines the timing of cash inflows and outflows on a cash basis, whereas the other budgets are concerned with and determine the timing of the basic transaction on an accrual basis. A cash budget includes no accrual items.

Period of Cash Budget

The period of time covered by a cash budget depends on the type of business, management planning needs, and cash position. A cash budget may generally be related to the following time periods:

(*i*) *Operational cash planning:* Cash budgets may be prepared monthly, weekly or even daily to meet informational requirements of management. This type of cash budgeting is primarily meant for dynamic control of cash balances to minimise interest cost on loans and opportunity cost deriving from idle cash in the business.

(*ii*) *Short-range:* Short-range cash budgeting is prepared annually and is in correspondence with the annual profit plan. It indicates cash inflows and outflows as generated by the annual profit plan. It helps in determining short-term credit needs and controlling cash during the year.

(*iii*) *Long-range:* Long-range budgeting does not disclose detailed estimates of revenue and expenses. Its purpose is to determine whether cash can be generated through working capital growth and at what times funds are needed. The effects of business expansion and long-term trends are incorporated in long-range cash budgeting. Long-range cash projection is in accord with (*i*) the timing of the capital expenditure projects and (*ii*) the timing of the long-range profit plan (usually five years).

Projection of long-range cash inflows (primarily from sales and services) and long-range cash outflows (primarily from expenses and capital expenditures, including expansion projects) is vital for making financing decisions and developing long-term credit needs.

Preparation of a Cash Budget

A cash budget may be prepared by following either of the three generally accepted procedures:

(*i*) The receipts and disbursements method.

(*ii*) The adjusted profit and loss or adjusted net income method and

(*iii*) Balance sheet method.

In the first method, all anticipated cash receipts are carefully forecasted such as cash sales, cash collections from debtors, dividends, interest on investments, proceeds from sale of assets, royalties, bank loans, etc. Likewise, cash disbursements for materials purchases, supplies, salaries, repayment of loans, dividends, taxes, expenses, purchases of plant or equipment are also determined. The preparation of a cash budget according to this method requires the use of the following budgets: (*a*) sales budget, (*b*) direct materials budget (*c*) direct labour budget, (*d*) factory overhead budget, (*e*) selling and administrative expense budget, (*f*) capital expenditure budget, (*g*) research and development budget, (*h*) finance budget regarding dividends, loans, income taxes, etc. This method is useful for short-range cash projection but is not appropriate for long-term cash budgeting. This method is in accordance with the annual profit plan.

The second approach is the profit and loss cash flow method or adjusted net income method. The starting point in this approach is budgeted profit reflected in the income statement. Basically, projected profit is converted from an accrual basis to a cash basis. That is, the budgeted profit of a period is adjusted for non-cash transactions and expected cash-oriented changes in asset and liability accounts not affected by profit calculations. Using the budgeted profit for a period as a starting point, various non-cash transactions are added back to net profit for the period. Non-cash items are depreciation, bad and doubtful accounts, expired insurance premiums, expenses, and income tax accruals. After this, anticipated decrease in assets or increase in liabilities are further added and anticipated increases in assets or decreases in liabilities are deducted. The budgeted cash at the end of a period is the cash balance at the beginning of the period plus the net cash increase (or minus the net cash decrease) as indicated in the analysis of the adjusted profit method. This method is especially appropriate for making long-range cash projections, but it is not useful in planning and control of cash as compared to the receipts and disbursement method. The reason is that the adjusted profit method does not contain detailed cash receipts and disbursement items; rather it shows only aggregate cash flows.

The third approach is the balance sheet method. In this approach, closing balances of all (budgeted) balance sheet items except cash and bank balances are found and put in a budgeted balance sheet. If the total of liabilities side items is more than the total of asset side items, the balancing figure will be cash/bank balance. On the contrary, if the total of assets side items is more than the total of liabilities side items, the balancing figure will be bank overdraft or shortage in cash. Budgeted figures of closing balance sheet items can be found after adjusting the opening balance sheet items with the transactions anticipated for the year.

Budgeted or Projected Balance Sheet

A projected balance sheet represents the expected financial position at a particular date. The projected balance sheet is prepared from the budgeted balanced sheet at the beginning of the budget period and the expected changes in the account balances reflected in the operating budgets, capital expenditure budgets, and cash budget. If any of the accounts or relationships among the accounts appearing on the projected balance sheet are not according to management's requirements and objectives, the operating plan might have to be changed. For example, if a bank or financial institution requires a business firm to maintain a certain minimum current ratio and debt-equity ratio, the operating plan would have to be changed if these ratios are indeed too low. Furthermore, unfavourable ratios may decrease the value of company shares in the stock exchange and lower the creditability of the firm in the investment market. The projected balance sheet also automatically determines the arithmetical accuracy of other budgets since they are used in preparing the forecasted balance sheet.

Budgeted Statement of Changes in Financial Position

The projected statement of changes in financial position is usually prepared from data in the budgeted income statement and changes between the projected balance sheet at the beginning of the budget period and projected balance sheet at the end of the budget period. This projected statement is very useful to management in the financial planning process.

Master Budget (or Comprehensive Budget)

A master budget sometimes called a comprehensive budget, is the summary or total budget package for a business firm. A comprehensive budget is a set of financial statements and other schedules showing the expected or proforma results for a future period. A comprehensive budget normally contains an income statement, a balance sheet, a statement of cash receipts and disbursements and schedules of production, purchases and fixed asset acquisitions. The budget package might have other components depending on the needs of the firm. A comprehensive budget is the end product of the budget-making process. A master budget is a tool for coordinating all the individual budgets of an organisation into an acceptable effective plan. It shows the budgeted profit and loss account for the budget period and the budgeted balance sheet at the end of the period. It reveals the top management's goals of revenues, expenses, net income, cash flows and financial position. The other budgets prepared by a business firm are specific, i.e. they deal with separate distinct activities of the organisation such as sales, production, selling and distribution and administrative activities. They incorporate plans and budgetary goals for a small segment of a business enterprise. However to achieve business objectives, it is necessary to have coordination among different budgets reflecting diverse activities of a business firm. For example, there should be coordination between sales and production departments and the goals of the production department should match the goals of the sales department. In the absence of coordination among the budgets, a business firm may have problems, such as surplus inventory, shortage of stock, non-availability of raw materials and other resources, employees' dissatisfaction etc. A master budget takes the macro (aggregate) view of the business enterprise and coordinates sales with production, raw materials, manpower, machinery and other resources with production targets and the like. The coordination and cohesiveness among different budgets helps management in making better predictions of profitability, cash flow, financial position and the firm's capacity to overcome challenges. The master budget is an integrative tool that cuts across divisional boundaries in order to coordinate the firms' diverse activities. While master budgets provide plans for an entire system, operating budgets provide plans for the organisation's sub-system, that is, operating budgets constitute the building blocks used to complete the master budget.

Whether a business firm prepares specific operating budgets or a complete master budget depends on a number of factors. The primary reason is the need of management at a particular time. For example, management may be more concerned with a single or specific aspect at a time, such as adequacy of the cash position. If the cash budget reveals that all is well, it may be the only budget needed to be prepared for management's use. If the cash budget reveals an inadequate or poor cash position, then other budgets making up the master budget will have to be prepared. In this situation, new budgets or forecasts will continue to be prepared, unless management finds an acceptable set of budgets.

REVISION OF BUDGETS

As stated earlier in the chapter, successful budgets should have adequate flexibility to meet changing business conditions. Since budgets are used for planning, operation, coordination and control, they should be revised if changes occur in the environment. Revision of budgets may be necessary due to the following factors, some of which might have been considered earlier in the development of budgets:

1. Errors committed in preparing the budgets which may subsequently be known.
2. Emergence of unforeseen and unanticipated situations which may cause the budget to be revised.
3. Changes in internal factors, e.g. production, forecast, sales forecast, capacity utilisation, etc.
4. Changes in internal factors, e.g. market trends, nature of the economy, prices of inputs and resources, consumers' tastes and fashions.

Changes in the above factors do not affect a firm's budgets if they are of minor significance. Some changes, however, considerably affect budgets and in this situation management is faced with two problems:

1. Whether only individual budgets should be changed and
2. Whether the master budget be changed.

Regarding the first problem, most business firms are in agreement and suggest that specific individual budgets should be changed. For instance, if there is likely to be a significant change in expected sales (increase or decrease), production and purchasing departments should be informed about this to avoid over-stocking or under-stocking. Failure to inform them would break down coordination and subsequently affect the budget goals.

A revision of the master budget is debatable and sometimes is opposed mainly on two counts: (*i*) the master budget process is highly complex and expensive; (*ii*) the evaluation process may take care of these changes if the changes take place. The second argument is more or less on middle ground. While it argues for revision when changes do occur, it focusses on actual effects rather than projected changes. It is felt that this avoids making small changes in the plan that are of little consequence and keeps the management from trying to outguess random fluctuations in their forecast. Those who support the revision of the master budget argue that the revised budget is a better and more effective basis for performance evaluation and control. By revising budget, all members of the organisation come to know of the expectations and standards for which they will be accountable.

Example 1

For production of 10,000 electrical automatic irons, the following are the budgeted expenses:

	Per unit (Rs.)
Direct materials	60
Direct labour	30
Variable overheads	25
Fixed overheads (Rs. 1,50,000)	15
Variable expenses (direct)	5
Selling expenses (10% fixed)	15
Administration expenses (Rs. 50,000 rigid for all levels of production)	5
Distribution expenses (20% fixed)	5
Total cost of sale per unit	160

Prepare a budget for production of 6,000; 7,000 and 8,000 irons, showing distinctly marginal cost and total cost.

Solution:

Flexible Budget of Electrical Automatic Irons

Production	*6,000 unit*		*7,000 units*		*8,000 units*	
	Total (Rs.)	*per unit (Rs.)*	*total (Rs.)*	*per unit (Rs.)*	*total (Rs.)*	*per unit (Rs.)*
Direct material	3,60,000	60.00	4,20,000	60.00	4,80,000	60.00
Direct labour	1,80,000	30.00	2,10,000	30.00	2,40,000	30.00
Direct variable Expenses	30,000	5.00	35,000	5.00	40,000	5.00
Variable overheads:						
Production	1,50,000	25.00	1,75,000	25.000	2,00,000	25.00
Selling	81,000	13.50	94,500	13.50	1,08,000	13.50
Distribution	24,000	4.00	28,000	4.00	32,000	4.00
Marginal cost	8,25,000	137.50	9,62,500	137.50	11,00,000	137.50
Fixed production Overheads	1,50,000	25.00	1,50,000	21.43	1,50,000	18.75
Administration overheads	50,000	8.33	50,000	7.14	50,000	6.25
Selling overheads	15,000	2.50	15,000	2.14	15,000	1.88
Distribution overheads	10,000	1.67	10,000	1.43	10,000	1.25
Fixed cost	2,25,000	37.50	2,25,000	32.14	2,25,000	28.13
Total cost (Marginal cost plus fixed cost)	10,50,000	175.00	11,87,500	169,54	13,25,000	165.63

Working notes:

	Selling expenses	*Distribution expenses*
Total for 10,000 units	1,50,000	50,000
Variable: 90% and 80% respectively	1,35,000	40,000
Variable expenses per unit	13.50	4.00
Fixed expenses 10% and 20% of total, respectively	15,000	10,000

Example 2

The following data are available in a manufacturing company for a yearly period.

	Rs. (lakhs)
Fixed expenses:	
Wages and salaries	9.5
Rent, rates and taxes	6.6
Depreciation	7.4
Sundry administrative expenses	6.5
Semi-variable expenses (at 50% of capacity):	
Maintenance and repairs	3.5
Indirect labour	7.9
Sales department salaries, etc.	3.8
Sundry administrative salaries	2.8
Variable expenses (at 50% of capacity):	
Materials	21.7
Labour	20.4
Other expenses	7.9
	98.0

Assume that the fixed expenses remain constant for all levels of production: semi-variable expenses remain constant between 45% and 65% of capacity, increasing by 10% between 65% and 80% capacity and by 20% between 80% and 100% capacity.

Sales at various levels are:	*Rs. (lakhs)*
50% capacity	100
60% capacity	120
75% capacity	150
90% capacity	180
100% capacity	200

Prepare a flexible budget for the year and forecast the profit at 60%, 75%, 90% and 100% capacity.

Solution:

Flexible Budget for the Period.....

Capacity level	*50%* *100*	*60%* *120*	*75%* *150*	*90%* *180*	*100%* *200*
Fixed expenses:					
Wages and salaries	9.5	9.5	9.5	9.5	9.5
Rent, rates and taxes	6.6	6.6	6.6	6.6	6.6
Depreciation	7.4	7.4	7.4	7.4	7.4
Sundry administrative expenses	6.5	6.5	6.5	6.5	6.5
(A) Total fixed costs	30.0	30.0	30.0	30.0	30.0
Semi-variable expenses:					
Maintenance and repairs	3.5	3.5	3.8	4.2	4.2

Indirect labour	7.9	7.9	8.7	9.5	9.5
Sales department salaries	3.8	3.8	4.2	4.6	4.6
Sundry administrative expenses	2.8	2.8	3.1	3.3	3.3
(B) Total semi-variable costs	18.0	18.0	19.8	21.6	21.6
Variable expenses:					
Materials	21.7	26.0	32.5	39.0	43.4
Labour	20.4	24.5	30.6	36.7	40.8
Other expenses	7.9	9.5	11.9	14.3	15.8
(C) Total variable cost	50.0	60.0	75.0	90.0	100.0
(D) Total cost (A) + (B) + (C)	98.0	108.0	124.8	141.6	151.6
(E) Sales	100.0	120.0	150.0	180.0	200.0
(F) Profit (E – D)	20	12.0	25.2	38.4	48.4

Example 3

A department of Company X attains sale of Rs. 6,00,000 at 80% of the normal capacity and its expenses are given below:

	Rs.
Administration costs:	
Office salaries	90,000
General expenses	2% of the sales
Depreciation	7,500
Rates and taxes	8,750
Selling costs:	
Salaries	8% of the sales
Travelling expenses	2% of the sales
Sales office	1% of the sales
General expenses	1% of the sales
Distribution costs:	
Wages	15,000
Rent	1% of the sales
Other expenses	4% of the sales

Draw up a flexible administration, selling and distribution costs budget, operating at 90%, 100% and 110% of normal capacity.

Solution:

Flexible Budget of Department.... of Company X

		Level of Activity			
Items	*Basis*	*80%* Rs.	*90%* Rs.	*100%* Rs.	*110%* Rs.
Sales		6,00,000	6,75,000	7,50,000	8,25,000
Administrative costs					
Office salaries	fixed	90,000	90,000	90,000	90,000
General expenses	2% of sales	12,000	13,500	15,000	16,500
Depreciation	fixed	7,500	7,500	7,500	7,500
Rates and taxes	fixed	8,750	8,750	8,750	8,750
Total administrative costs		1,18,250	1,19,750	1,21,250	1,22,750

Selling costs					
Salaries	8% of sale	48,000	54,000	60,000	66,000
Travelling expenses	2% of sales	12,000	13,500	15,000	16,500
Sales office expenses	1% of sales	6,000	6,750	7,500	8,250
General expenses	1% of sales	6,000	6,750	7,500	8,250
Total selling costs		72,000	81,000	90,000	99,000
Distribution costs					
Wages	fixed	15,000	15,000	15,000	15,000
Rent	1% of sales	6,000	6,750	7,500	8,250
Other expenses	4% of sales	24000	27000	30000	33000
Total distribution costs		45,000	48,750	52,500	56,250
Total administration, selling and distribution costs		2,35,250	2,49,500	2,63,750	2,78,000

Notes: In the absence of information it has been assumed that office salaries, depreciation, rates and taxes and wages remain the same at 110% level of activity also. However, in practice, some of these costs many change if present capacity is exceeded.

Example 4

The budget manager of Jaypee Electricals Ltd. is preparing a flexible budget for the accounting year commencing from 1st April 1993. The company produces one product, component – Peekay. Direct material costs Rs. 7 per unit. Direct labour average Rs. 2.50 per hour and requires 1.60 hours to produce one unit of Peekay.

Salesmen are paid a commission of Re. 1 per unit sold. Fixed selling and administration expenses amount to Rs. 85,000 per year.

Manufacturing overhead has been estimated in the following amounts under specified conditions of volume:

Volume of production (in units)	1,20,000	1,50,000
Expenses:	Rs.	Rs.
Indirect material	2,64,000	3,30,000
Indirect labour	1,50,000	1,87,500
Inspection	90,000	1,12,500
Maintenance	84,000	1,02,000
Supervision	1,98,000	2,34,000
Depreciation- Plant & Equipment	90,000	90,000
Engineering services	94,000	94,000
Total manufacturing overhead	9,70,000	11,50,000

Normal capacity of production of the company is 125000 units.

Prepare a budget of total cost at 1,40,000 units of output.

Solution:

Flexible Budget for the year April 1993 to March 1994

Production Volume 140000 units

Items of cost	*Fixed Costs (Rs.)*	*Variable cost (Rs.) Per unit*	*Variable cost (Rs.) Total*	*Total Cost (Rs.)*
Direct materials	—	7.00	9,80,000	9,80,000
Indirect labour	—	4.00	5,60,000	5,60,000
Indirect materials	—	2.20	3,08,000	3,08,000
Indirect labour	—	1.25	1,75,000	1,75,000
Inspection	—	0.75	1,05,000	1,05,000
Maintenance	12,000	0.60	84,000	96,000
Supervision	54,000	1.20	1,68,000	2,22,000
Depreciation-plant & Equipment	90,000	—	—	90,000
Engineering services	94,000	—	—	94,000
Sales commission	—	1.00	1,40,000	1,40,000
Fixed selling and distribution expenses	85,000	—	—	85,000
Total	3,35,000	18.00	2,52,000	28,55,000

Working Notes:

Segregation of semi-variable costs into fixed and variable components:

Fixed and variable components:

$$\text{Variable cost per unit} = \frac{\text{Difference in cost}}{\text{Difference in output}}$$

$$\text{Fixed cost} = \text{Total cost} - \text{Variable cost}$$

(*i*) Maintenance – Variable cost per unit $= \dfrac{\text{Rs. }1,02,000 - 84,000}{1,50,000 - 1,20,000}$

$$= \frac{\text{Rs. }18,000}{30,000 \text{ units}} = 60 \text{ p.}$$

$$\text{Fixed cost} = \text{Rs. } 84,000 - (12,000 \times .60)$$

$$= 84,000 - 72000$$

$$= 12,000$$

Variable cost $= 14000 \times .60 =$ Rs. 84000

(*ii*) Supervision

$$\text{Variable cost per unit} = \frac{\text{Rs. }2,34,000 - 1,98,000}{1,50,000 - 1,20,000}$$

$$= \frac{\text{Rs. }36,000}{30,000 \text{ units}}$$

$$= \text{Rs. } 1.20 \text{ per unit}$$

Fixed cost = Rs. 1,98,000 – (1,20,000 × 1.20)
= 1,98,000 – 144000
= 54,000
Variable cost = 1,40,000 units × Rs. 1.20
= Rs. 1,68,000

(*iii*) Indirect materials, Indirect labour and Inspection are fully variable costs. This can be proved by taking these elements of costs and following the above method of segregation. For instance, as an example, indirect materials is taken.

Indirect materials

$$\text{Variable cost per unit} = \frac{\text{Rs. } 3,30,000 - 2,64,000}{1,50,000 - 1,20,000}$$

$$= \frac{\text{Rs. } 66,000}{30,000}$$

= Rs. 2.20 per unit

Fixed cost = Rs. 2,64,000 (12,000 × 2.20)
= 2,64,000 – 2,64,000
= No fixed cost

Example 5

Gemini Steel Ltd. manufacturers a single product for which market demand exists for additional quantity. Present sales of Rs. 60,000 per month utilises only 60% capacity of the plant. Marketing Manager assures that with the reduction of 10% in the price, he would be in a position to increase the sale by about 25% to 30%.

The following data are available:

(*i*) Selling price Rs. 10 per unit
(*ii*) Variable cost Rs. 3 per unit
(*iii*) Semi-variable cost Rs. 6,000 fixed + 50 paise per unit
(*iv*) Fixed cost Rs. 20,000 at present level estimated to be Rs. 25,000 at 80% output.

You are required to prepare the following statements:

(1) The operating profits at 60%, 70% and 80% levels at current selling price, and

(2) The operating profits at proposed selling price at the above levels.

Solution:

Statement Showing Operating Profit At Current Prices

	Capacity levels		
	60%	*70%*	*80%*
Output and Sales (Units)	6,000	7,000	8,000
	Rs.	Rs.	Rs.
1. Sales	60,000	70,000	80,000
2. Cost:			
Variable cost	18,000	21,000	24,000

Semi-variable cost	9,000	9,500	10,000
Fixed cost	20,000	20,000	24,000
Total costs	47,000	50,500	58,000
3. Profit (Loss) (1)-(2)	13,000	19,500	22,000

Note: The fixed cost at 70% level has been taken as Rs. 20,000, presuming that it will increase only at 80% capacity and not earlier.

Statement Showing Operating Profits At Proposed Selling Price

	Capacity Levels		
	60%	*70%*	*80%*
Output Sales (units)	6,000	7,000	8,000
1. Sales @ Rs. 9 per unit	54,000	63,000	72,000
2. Costs:			
Variable costs	18,000	21,000	24,000
Semi-variable costs	9,000	9,500	10,000
Fixed costs	20,000	20,000	24,000
Total costs	47,000	50,000	58,000
3. Profit (1) – (2)	7,000	12,500	14,000

Example 6

A B C Ltd. manufactures a single product for which market demand exists for additional quantity. Present sale of Rs. 60,000 p.m. utilises only 60% capacity of the plant. Sales manager assures that with a reduction of 10% in the price, he would be in a position to increase the sale by about 25% to 30%.

The following data are available:

(*a*) Selling price — Rs. 10 per unit

(*b*) Variable cost — Rs. 3 per unit

(*c*) Semi variable cost — Rs. 6,000 fixed plus for 0.50 per unit

(*d*) Fixed cost — Rs. 20,000 at present level estimated to be Rs. 24,000 at 80% output.

You are required to submit the following statements to the board showing:

(1) The operating profits at 60%, 70% and 80% levels at current selling price and at proposed selling price.

(2) The percentage increase in the present output which will be required to maintain present profit margin at the proposed selling price.

Solution:

(1) Operating Statement

Capacity utilization	60%	70%	80%
	Rs.	*Rs.*	*Rs.*
Sales	60,000	70,000	80,000
Variable cost	18,000	21,000	24,000
	3,000	3,500	4,000
Total variable cost	21,000	24,000	28,000
Marginal contribution	39,000	45,500	52,000
Fixed element of semi-variable cost	6,000	6,000	6,000
Fixed cost	20,000	20,000	24,000
Operating profit	13,000	19,500	22,000

Proposed Selling price = Rs. 10 – 10% of Rs. 10 = Rs. 9 per unit;

The variable cost is Rs. 3.5 per unit and the fixed cost remains constant.

The operating profits at the proposed selling price will thus be:

	60%	70%	80%
Sales	Rs. 54,000	Rs. 63,000	Rs. 72,000
Variable cost	21,000	24,500	28,000
Fixed cost	26,000	26,000	30,000
Total cost	47,000	50,500	58,000
Operating profit	7,000	12,500	14,000

(2) Sale Value = Variable cost + Fixed cost + Profit

If x be the number of units produced and sold at the proposed selling price of Rs. 9 per unit to maintain the present level of profit of Rs. 13,000.

Then 9 x = 35 × 26000 + 13,000, where x = 7091 units

$$\text{Percent increase in the present output} = \frac{7{,}091 - 6{,}000}{6{,}000} = 18.18\%$$

Example 7

Bala Company expects to sell 84,000 units of finished goods over the next 3 months period. The company currently has 44,000 units of finished goods on hand and wishes to have an inventory of 48,000 units at the end of the 3 – month period. To produce 1 unit of finished goods requires 4 unit of raw materials. The company currently has 2,00,000 units of raw materials on hand and wishes to have an inventory of 2,20,000 units of raw materials on hand at the end of the 3-month period.

How many units of raw materials must the Bala Company purchase during the 3-month period?

Solution:

Material Requirements

Finished Units to be produced	= (84,000 Units) to be sold	+ (48,000 Units in) Ending Inventory	– (44, 000 Units) Beginning Inventory

Units to Be Produced = 88,000

Units of Raw Materials to Be Used = 4 units of Raw Materials per Finished Unit × 88,000 Units = 3,52,000

Units of Raw Materials to be purchased	= 3,52,000 Units to be used	+ 2,20,000 Units desired ending Inventory	– 2,00,000 units in Beginning inventory

= 3,72,000 units

Example 8

The following details apply to an annual budget for a manufacturing company:

Quarter	1st	2nd	3rd	4th
Working days	65	60	55	60
Production (units per working day)	100	110	120	105
Raw material purchases (by weight of annual to all)	30%	50%	20%	—
Budgeted purchase price (per kg.)	Re. 1	1.05	1.125	—

Quantity of raw material per unit of production: 2 kg. Budgeted opening stock of raw material – 4,000 kg. (cost Rs. 4,000).

Budgeted closing stock of raw material: 2,000 kg. Issues are priced on FIFO basis.

Calculate the following budgeted figures:

(*a*) Quarterly and annual purchases of raw material, by weight and value.

(*b*) Closing quarterly stocks by weight and value.

Solution:

Basic Calculations

		kg.
	Annual Consumption	
	1st Qtr. 65 × 100 × 2	= 13,000
	2nd Qtr. 60 × 110 × 2	= 13,200
	3rd Qtr. 55 × 120 × 2	= 13,200
	4th Qtr. 60 × 105 × 2	= 12,600
		52,000
	Annual Purchases	kg.
	Consumption	52,000
Add:	Budgeted closing stock	2,000
	Annual requirements	54,000
Less:	Opening stock	4,000
	Purchases	50,000

(a) Raw Materials Purchase Budget

Quarter Quantity	*Kg.*	*Rate*	*Amount*
1st 50,000 × 30/100 =	15,000	Re. 1	15,000
2nd 50,000 × 50/100 =	25,000	1.05	26,250
3rd 50,000 × 20/100 =	10,000	1.125	11,250
Annual purchases	50,000		52,500

Statement of Quarterly Budgeted Closing Stock

Particulars	*1st Quarter*			*2nd Quarter*			*3rd Quarter*			*4th Quarter*		
	(Qty.) (kgs.)	*Rate Rs.*	*Amt. Rs.*	*Qty. (kgs)*	*Rate Rs.*	*Amt. Rs.*	*Qty (kgs)*	*Rate Rs.*	*Amt. Rs.*	*Qty. (kgs)*	*Rate Rs.*	*Amt. Rs.*
Op. Stocks	4,000	1	4,000	6,000	1	6,000	17,800	1.05	18,690	14,600	16,080	
Purchases	15,000	1	15,000	25,000	1.05	26,250	10,000	1.125	11,250	—	—	
	19,000	1	19,000	31,000		32250	2800	—	29,940	14,600	16,080	
Consumption	13,000	1	13,000	13,200		13560	13200	1.05	13,860	12,600	13,830	
	6,000		6,000	17,800		18690	14,600		16,080	2,000	2,250	

6,000 × Re. 1, 7, 2,000 × 1.05 = 13,560

4,600 × Rs. 1.05 + 8,000 Rs. 1.125 = 13,830

Example 9

Gama Engineering Company Limited manufactures two products X and Y. An estimate of the number of units expected to be sold in the first seven months of 1994 is given below:

	Product X	*Product Y*
January	500	1,400
February	600	1,400
March	800	1,200
April	1,000	1,000
May	1,200	800
June	1,200	800
July	1,000	900

It is anticipated that:

1. there will be no work-in-progress at the end of any month and
2. finished units equal to half the anticipated sales for the next month will be in stock at the end of each month (including December 1993). The budgeted production and production costs for the year ending 31st December 1994 are as follows:

	Product X	*Product Y*
Production (units)	11,000	12,000
Direct materials per unit (Rs.)	12	19
Direct wages per unit (Rs.)	5	7
Other manufacturing charges		
Apportionable to each type of product (Rs.)	33,000	48,000

You are required to prepare:

(*a*) A production budget showing the number of units to be manufactured each month.

(*b*) A summarised production cost budget for the six-month period, i.e. January to June 1994.

Solution:

Gama Engineering Company Limited

Production Budget (in units) for the Six Months Ending 30th June, 1994

	Jan.	*Feb.*	*March*	*April*	*May*	*June*
Product X:						
Closing stock	300	400	500	600	600	500
Sales	500	600	800	1,000	1,200	1,200
	800	1,000	1,300	1,600	1,800	1,700
Less: Opening stock	250	300	400	500	600	600
Production (in units)	550	700	900	1,100	1,200	1,100
Product Y:						
Closing stock	700	600	500	400	400	450
Sales	1,400	1,400	1,200	1,000	800	800
	2,100	2,000	1,700	1,400	1,200	1,250
Less: Opening stock	700	700	600	500	400	400
Production (in units)	1,400	1,300	1,100	900	800	850

(c) Summarised Production Cost Budget for the Six Months Ending 30th June, 1994

Production (in units)	*5550 X*		*6350 Y*	
	Unit cost	*Total cost*	*Unit cost*	*Total cost*
Direct materials	Rs. 11	Rs. 66,600	Rs. 19	Rs. 1,20,650
Direct wages	5	27,750	7	44,450
Manufacturing charges	3	16,650	4	25,400
	20	1,11,000	30	1,90,500

Note: Manufacturing charges have been presumed to be variable costs in the absence of any other information. They could, however, be presumed to be fixed charges also for the whole year. In such a case they will be taken as 50% of the annual charges for the first six months in each case.

Example 10

As a cost accountant of Modern Manufacturing Company, you are asked to prepare a quarterly production budget and direct materials purchase budget for the accounting year, 1st July 1981 to 30 June 1982.

The following information is relevant:

(*i*) The company manufactures only two products A and B

(*ii*) Sales volume forecast (in units):

1981-82	*A*	*B*
Quarter I	1,500	2,000
Quarter II	1,000	2,500
Quarter III	1,000	2,000
Quarter IV	1,500	2,500
1982-83		
Quarter I	1,500	2,500

(*iii*) Raw materials requirement forecast: The standard quantities of the two raw materials, X and Y which should be used in the manufacture of the two products and the prices of these raw materials have been estimated as follows:

Standard quantities:

Raw material X – 2 units for each unit of Product A

Raw materials Y – 3 units for each unit of Product B

Estimated Cost:

Raw material X – Rs. 10 per each unit of X

Raw material Y – Rs. 6 for each unit of Y

Usage variance:

5% is provided to cover spoilage and scrap in the case of material X and 4% in the case of material Y.

(*iv*) Stock forecasts:

Estimated opening stock:

Product A 750 units

Product B 1,250 units

Raw material X	1,578 units
Raw material Y	3,900 units

It is planned that the closing stock level at the end of each quarter should be maintained at a level equal to half the expected sales for the next quarter for both the products and the raw materials stocks at the end of each quarter should be held accordingly.

Solution:

Production Budget

	Qr. I		*Qr. II*		*Qr. III*		*Qr. IV*		*Total*	
Units	*A*	*B*	*A*	*B*	*A*	*B*	*A*	*B*	*A*	*B*
Sales Forecast	1,500	2,000	1,000	2,500	1,000	2,000	1,500	2,500	5,000	9,000
(+) Closing stock	50	1,250	500	1,000	750	1,250	750	1,250	2,500	4,750
(–) Opening stock	750	1,250	500	1,250	500	1,000	750	1,250	2,500	4,750
Production Units	1,250	2,000	1,000	2,250	1,250	2,250	1,500	2,500	5,000	9,000

Material Purchase Budget

	Qr. I		*Qr. II*		*Qr. III*		*Qr. IV*		*Total*	
Units	*X*	*Y*	*X*	*Y*	*X*	*Y*	*X*	*Y*	*X*	*Y*
Standard Consumption	2,500	6,000	2,000	6,750	2,500	6,750	3,000	7,500	10,000	27,000
(+) Usage variance	125	240	100	270	125	270	150	300	500	1,080
(+) Closing stock	1,000	3,750	1,000	3,000	1,500	3,750	1,500	3,750 }	5,250	14,820
(+)	50	150	50	120	75	150	75	150 }		
(–) Opening stock	1,575	3,900	1,050	3,900	1,050	3,120	1,575	3,900	5,250	14,820
Purchase Units	2,100	6,240	2,100	6,240	3,150	7,800	3,150	8,800	10,500	28,080
	X	X	X	X	X	X	X	X	X	X
	10	6	10	6	10	6	10	6	10	6
Purchase Value (Rs.)	21,000	37,440	21,000	37,440	31,500	46,800	31,500	52,800	1,50,000	1,68,480
Total purchase (Rs.)	58,440		58,440		78,300		73,300		2,73,480	

Example 11

A limited company is engaged in the business of manufacturing standard toys. It has prepared a six-monthly budget, which shows the following particulars:

Sales	80,000 unit @ Rs. 20 per unit
Variable costs:	Rs. 6 per unit
Manufacturing	Re. 1 per unit
Selling	Re. 1 per unit
Distribution	Re. 0.25 per unit
Semi-variable costs:	
Manufacturing	Rs. 60,000
Selling	Rs. 30,000
Administration	Rs. 16,000
Fixed costs:	
Manufacturing	60,000
Selling	40,000
Administration	80,000

It is decided to provide a plastic tray along with the sale of toys. It is estimated that this gesture on the part of the company will boost up sales from 80,000 units to 1,00,000 units.

The above proposal would involve an additional expenditure estimated as under:

Semi-variable costs:	
Manufacturing	4,000
Selling	4,000
Administration	2,000
Fixed costs:	
Manufacturing	10.000

You are required to prepare a statement showing (*i*) comparative cost of production and (*ii*) profitability. Also state the factors which the management should take into account at the final decision.

Solution:

Statement Showing Comparative Cost of Production and Profitability

	Present budget units (80,000) Rs.	*Proposed budget units (1,00,000)* Rs.
Variable costs:		
Manufacturing @ Rs. 6 per unit	4,800,000	6,00,000
Selling @ Re. 1 per unit	80,000	1,00,000
Administration @ Re. 0.25 per unit	20,000	25,000
Semi-variable costs:		
Manufacturing	60,000	64,000
Selling	30,000	34,000
Administration	16,000	18,000
Fixed costs:		
Manufacturing	60,000	70,000
Selling	40,000	40,000
Administration	80,000	80,000
Total cost	8,66,000	10,31,000
Sales	16,00,000	20,00,000
Profit	7,34,000	9,69,000

Example 12

You are requested to prepare a sales overhead budget from the estimates given below:

Advertisement		Rs. 2,500
Salaries of the sales department		5,000
Expenses of the sales department		1,500
Counter salesmen's salaries and dearness allowance	6,000	
Commission to counter salesmen at 1% on their sales		
Travelling salesmen's commission at 10% on their sales and expenses at 5% on their sales		

Sales during the period were estimated as follows:

	Counter sales	*Travelling salesmen*
	Rs. 80,000	Rs. 10,000
	1,20,000	15,000
	1,40,000	20,000

Solution:

Sales Overhead Budget for The Period Ending ...

	Estimated Sales		
	Rs. 90,000	Rs. 1,35,000	Rs. 1,60,000
Fixed Overheads:			
Advertisement	2,500	2,500	2,500
Salaries of sales department	5,000	5,000	2,500
Expenses of sales department	1,500	1,500	,500
Counter salesmen's salaries and DA	6,000	6,000	,000
	15,000	15,000	15, 00
Variable overheads:			
Counter Salesmen's commission @ 1% on sales	800	1,200	1,4 0
Travelling salesmen's commission @ 10@	1,000	1,500	2,000
Expenses@5%	500	750	1,000
Total sales overheads	17,300	18,450	19,400

Example 13:

A company normally collects cash from credit customers as follows:

50 per cent in the month of sale, 30 per cent in the first month after sale, 18 per cent in the second month after sale, and 2 per cent are never collected. Sales, all on credit, are expected to be as follows:

	Rs.
January	5,00,000
February	6,00,000
March	4,00,000
April	5,00,000

(*a*) Calculate the amount of cash expected to be received from customers during March.

(*b*) Calculate the amount of cash expected to be received from customers during April.

Solution: Rs.

(*a*) Budgeted cash collection in March:	
From January Sales (.18 × 5,00,000)	90,000
From February Sales (.30 × 6,00,000)	1,80,000
From March Sales (.50 × 4,00,000)	2,00,000
Total Budgeted Collections in March	4,70,000
(*b*) Budgeted cash collections in April:	
From January Sales (.18 × 6,00,000)	1,08,000
From February Sales (.30 × 4,00,000)	1,20,000
From March Sales (.50 × 5,00,000)	2,50,000
Total Budgeted Collections in April	4,78,000

Example 14

The January 1 cash balance of Jay Company is Rs. 5,000. Sales for the first four months of the year are expected to be as follows: January, Rs. 65,000; February, Rs. 54,000; March, Rs. 66,000 and April, Rs. 63,000. On January 1, collected amounts for November and December of the previous year are Rs. 13,500 and Rs. 39,150 respectively; Collections from customers follow this pattern; 55% in the month of sale, 30% in the month following the sale, 13% in the second month following the sale and 2% non-collection.

Materials purchase for December were Rs. 10,000. Forecast purchases for the coming year are: Rs. 12,500; February, Rs. 16,500; March Rs. 13,000; and April Rs. 14,000. Purchases are usually paid by the 10th of the month following the month of purchase. Other cash expenditures of Rs. 41,000 are forecasted for each month.

Calculate:

(*i*) Expected cash collections during February
(*ii*) Expected cash balance, February 1
(*iii*) Expected cash balance, February 28.

Solution:

Cash Budget of Jay Company For Months of January and February

	January	*February*
Opening Balance	5,000	27,550
Receipts-From customers	73,550	60,510
(A)	78,550	88,060
Payments		
For purchases	10,000	12,500
Other expenditure	41,000	41,000
Total Payments (B)	51,000	53,500
Closing Balance (A) – (B)	37,550	34,560

Thus:

(*i*) Expected cash collections during February = Rs. 60,510
(*ii*) Expected cash balance – February 1 = Rs. 27,550
(*iii*) Expected cash balance – February 28 = Rs. 34,560

Working Note

Collections on account of Sales

January

For November arrears 13,500 × 13/15	=	Rs. 11,700
For December arrears $\frac{39,150}{45} \times 30$	=	Rs. 26,100
For January Sales 65,000 × 55/100	=	Rs. 35,750
		Rs. 73,550

February

For December arrears $\frac{39,150 \times 13}{45}$	=	Rs. 11,310
For January sales 65,000 × 30/100	=	Rs. 19,500
For February sales 54,000 × 55/100	=	Rs. 29,700
		Rs. 60,510

Example 15

ABC Co. wished to arrange overdraft facilities with its bankers during the period April to June 1980 when it will be manufacturing mostly for stock. Prepare a Cash Budget for the above period from the following data, indicating the extent of the bank facilities the company will require at the end of each month:

(*a*)

	Sales Rs.	*Purchases* Rs.	*Wages* Rs.
February	1,80,000	1,24,800	12,000
March	1,92,000	1,44,000	14,000
April	1,08,000	2,43,000	11,000
May	1,74,000	2,46,000	10,000
June	1,26,000	2,68,000	15,000

(b) 50 per cent of the credit sales are realised in the month following the sales and the remaining 50 per cent in the second month following. Creditors are paid in the month following of the month purchase.

(c) Cash at Bank on 1.4.80 (estimated) Rs. 25,000.

Solution:

A B C Co.
Cash Budget for April to June 1980

	April Rs.	*May* Rs.	*June* Rs.
Opening Balance (Overdraft)	25,000	56,000	(47,000)
Receipts:			
Collections from Debtors	1,86,000	1,50,000	1,41,000
	2,11,000	2,06,000	94,000
Payments:			
Payments to creditors	1,44,000	2,43,000	2,46,000
Wages	11,000	10,000	15,000
Closing Balance (Overdraft)	56,000	(47,0000)	(1,67,000)
	2,11,000	2,06,000	94,000

The overdraft facilities required by ABC Co. for different months are as under:

(*i*) In May 1980 Rs. 47,000

(*ii*) In June 1980 Rs. 1,67,000

Working notes

Collections From Debtors

April 1980	Rs.
Sales for February 1,80,000 × ½	90,000
Sales for March 1,96,000 × ½	96,000
	1,86,000

May 1980	
Sales for March 1,92,000 × ½	96,000
Sales for April 1,08,000 × ½	54,000
	1,50,000
June 1980	
Sales for April 1,08,000 × ½	54,000
Sales for May 1,74,000 × ½	87,000
	1,41,000

Example 16

A newly started company wishes to prepare cash budget from January. Prepare a cash budget for the first six months from the following estimated revenues and expenses:

Months	*Total sales*	*Materials*	*Wages*	*Production*	*Selling & Distribution*
January	20,000	20,000	4,000	3,200	800
February	22,000	14,000	4,400	3,300	900
March	24,000	14,000	4,600	3,300	800
April	26,000	12,000	4,600	3,400	900
May	28,000	12,000	4,800	3,500	900
June	30,000	16,000	4,800	3,600	1,000

Cash balances on 1st January was Rs. 10,000. A new machine is to be a installed at Rs. 30,000 on credit to be repaid by two equal installments in March and April.

Sales Commission @ 5% on total sales is to be paid within the month following actual sales.

Rs. 10,000 being the amount of 2nd call may be received in March. Share premium amounting to Rs. 2,000 is also obtainable with the 2nd call.

Period of credit allowed by supplies – 2 months

Period of credit allowed to customers – 1 months

Delay in payment of overhead – 1 month

Delay in payment of wages – ½ month

Assume cash sales to be 50% of total sales.

Solution:

Cash Book
For the Period January to June

	Particulars	*January* Rs.	*Feb.* Rs.	*March* Rs.	*April* Rs.	*May* Rs.	*June* Rs.
A	Balance b/d	10,000	18,000	29,800	20,000	6,100	8,800
B	Receipts:						
	Cash Sales (50%)	10,000	11,000	12,000	12,000	14,000	15,000
	Debtors			11,000	13,000	13,000	14,000
	Capital		10,000	10,000			
	Share Premium	—	—	2,000	—	—	—
	A + B Total	20,000	39,000	64,800	45,000	33,100	37,800

C Payments:						
Materials	—	—	20,000	14,000	14,000	12,000
Wages	2,000	2,000	2,200	2,300	2,300	2,400
		2,200	2,300	2,300	2,400	2,400
Production Overhead	—	3,200	3,300	3,300	3,400	3,500
Selling and Distribution	—	800	900	800	900	900
Commission	—	1,000	1,100	1,200	1,300	1,400
Machine	—	—	15,000	15,000	—	—
Total	2,000	9,200	44,800	38,900	2,4300	22,600
Balance c/d	18,000	·29,800	20,000	6,100	8,800	15,200

Example 17

SM Ltd. furnishes the following forecast for the quarter ending 31st March, 1981.

Sales: January	Rs. 12,00,000
February	Rs. 11,00,000
March	Rs. 14,00,000

During the month of December last, the company made a sale of Rs. 10,00,00 and computed the cost of sales as under:

Raw material	Rs. 3,50,000
Wages (variable)	Rs. 1,75,000
Overheads (variable)	Rs. 1,75,000
Overheads (fixed)	Rs. 1,50,000

The fixed overheads include depreciation of Rs. 40,000.

One-fifth of sales is for cash on which a cash discount of 11/2% is allowed. Of the remaining portion 50% is collected in the same month and the balance in the next month. Raw material suppliers allow a credit of one month. Wages are paid on the last working day of the month to which they relate. While variable overheads are paid in the next month, fixed overhead expenses are met in the same month.

The percentage of contribution to sales as obtained in December last is expected to be maintained during the forthcoming quarter also. The cash balance on 1st January 1981 is Rs. 50,000. The company has to pay a sum of Rs. 60,000 an installment of arrears of wages in March 1981 and the bank will debt quarterly interest of Rs. 4,00,000 on drawings in March 1981.

Solution:

Sales and cost of sales:

	Dec. '80	*Jan. '81*	*Feb. '81*	*Mar. '81*
Cash sales	2,00,000	2,40,000	2,20,000	2,80,000
Credit sales	8,00,000	9,60,000	8,80,000	11,20,000
Total sales	10,00,000	12,00,000	11,00,000	14,00,000
Cost of sales:				
Raw materials	3,50,000	4,20,000	3,85,000	4,90,000
Wages	1,75,000	2,10,000	1,95,000	2,45,000
Overheads variable	1,75,000	2,10,000	1,92,000	2,45,000
Depreciation	40,000	40,000	40,000	40,000
Overheads fixed	1,10,000	1,10,000	1,10,000	1,10,000

Cash Budget

	Jan. '81 (Rs.)	Feb '81 (Rs.)	March '81 (Rs.)
Receipts:			
Opening Balance	50,000	(–) 28,600	1,75,600
Debtors (for last month)	4,00,000	4,80,000	4,40,000
Debtors (for this month)	4,80,000	4,40,000	5,60,000
Cash sales less discount	2,36,400	2,16,700	2,75,800
Total	11,66,400	11,08,100	14,51,400
Payments:			
Raw materials	3,50,000	4,20,000	3,85,000
Wages	2,10,000	1,92,500	2,45,000
Overheads variable	1,75,000	2,10,000	1,92,500
Overheads fixed	1,10,000	1,10,000	1,10,000
Arrears of wages	—	—	60,000
Interest on term loan	3,50,000	—	—
Bank interest	—	—	4,00,000
Total	11,95,000	9,32,500	13,92,500
Deficit (carried over) (to be met by loan or overdraft)	28,600	—	—
Surplus carried over (after Liquidation of loan or overdraft)	—	1,75,600	58,900

In framing the cash budget, a provision will be made for meeting the deficit in January 1981 to the extent of Rs. 28,600 by loan or overdraft. If we assume that the loan/draft is paid back in February 1981, the closing balances at the end of February and March, 1981 will be Rs. 1,75,600 and Rs. 58,900 respectively.

Example 18

A glass manufacturing company requires you to calculate and present the budget for the next year from the following information:

Sales:

Toughened glass	Rs. 3,00,000
Bent toughened glass	Rs. 5,00,000
Direct material cost	60% of sales
Direct wages	20 workers @ Rs. 150 per month
Factory overheads:	
Indirect labour:	
Works manager Rs. 500 per month	
Foreman Rs. 400 per month	
Stores and spares	21/2% on sales
Depreciation on machinery	Rs. 12,600
Light and Power	Rs. 5000
Repairs and maintenance	Rs. 8000
Other sundries	10% on direct wages
Administration, selling and distribution expenses.	Rs. 14,000 per year

Solution:

Master Budget for the Period Ending on...

			Rs.
Sales (as per sales budget)			
Toughened glass.. units @ Rs..			3,00,000
Bent toughened glass.units @ Rs.			5,00,000
			8,00,000
Less: Cost of production (as per cost of production budget)			
Direct materials (.. units @ Rs...)	Rs. 4,80,000		
Direct wages	36,000		
Prime cost		5,16,000	
Factory overhead:			
Variable:			
Stores and spares (2 ½% of sales)	20,000		
Light and power	5,000		
Repairs and maintenance	8,000	33,000	
Fixed:			
Works manager's salary	6,000		
Foreman's salary	48,000		
Depreciation	12,600		
Sundries	3,600	27,000	
Works cost			5,76,000
Gross profit			2,24,000
Less: Administration, selling and Distribution overheads			14,000
Net profit			2,10,000

Example 19

A limited company is formed to take over a running business. It has been decided to raise Rs. 55 lakhs by issuing equity shares, and the balance of capital required in the first six months is to be financed by a financial institution against an issue of Rs. 5 lakh 8% debentures (interest payable annually) in its favour.

Initial outlay consist of:

Freehold premises	Rs. 25 lakh
Plant and machinery	Rs. 10 lakh
Stock	Rs. 6 lakh
Vehicles and other items	Rs. 5 lakh

Payments on the above items are to be made in the month of incorporation. Sales during the first six months ending on June 30 are estimated as under:

January	Rs. 14 lakh	April Rs. 25 lakhs
February	Rs. 15 lakh	May Rs. 26.50 lakhs
March	Rs. 18.50 lakh	June Rs. 28 lakhs

Lag in payment:

Debtors	2 month
Creditors	1 month

Other information:

(*a*) Preliminary expenses: Rs. 50,000 (payable in February)

(*b*) General expenses: Rs. 50,000 per month (at the end of each month).

(*c*) Monthly wages and salaries (payable on the 1st day of the next month):

Rs. 80,000 for the first three months

Rs. 95,000 thereafter.

(*d*) Gross profit rate is expected to be 20% on sales.

(*e*) The shares and debentures are to be issued on 1st January

(*f*) The stock level throughout is to be the same as the outlay.

Prepare a cash budget, a projected trading, and profit and loss account for the six months ending June 30 and the projected balance sheet as on that date.

Solution:

Co. Ltd.,
Cash Budget for the Six Months Ending June 30, 19...

(in lakhs of rupees)

Receipts	*Jan.*	*Feb.*	*March*	*Apr.*	*May*	*June*	*Total*
	(Rs.)	*(Rs.)*	*(Rs.)*	*(Rs.)*	*(Rs.)*	*(Rs.)*	*(Rs.)*
Opening balance	—	13.50	1.30	2.80	2.50	0.50	-
Receipts:							
Shares	55.00	—	—	—	—	—	55.00
8% debentures	5.00	—	—	—	—	—	5.00
Sales	—	—	14.00	15.00	18.50	25.50	72.50
Total receipts	60.00	13.50	15.30	17.80	21.00	25.50	132.50
Payments:							
Fixed assets:							
Freehold premises	25.00	—	—	—	—	—	25.00
Plant and machinery	10.00	—	—	—	—	—	10.00
Vehicles	5.00	—	—	—	—	—	5.00
Preliminary expenses	—	0.50	—	—	—	—	0.50
Wages	—	0.80	0.80	0.80	0.95	0.95	4.30
General expenses	0.50	0.50	0.50	0.50	0.50	0.50	3.00
Purchases	6.00	10.40	11.20	14.00	19.05	20.25	80.90
Total payments	46.50	12.20	12.50	15.30	20.50	21.70	128.70
Closing balance	13.50	1.30	2.80	2.50	0.50	3.80	3.80
Total receipts	60.00	13.50	15.30	17.80	21.00	25.50	132.50

Projected Trading and Profit, and Loss Account for the Six Months Ending June 30,19...

(in lakhs of Rs.)

To purchases	Rs. 102.35	By Sales	Rs. 127.00
To Wages and salaries	Rs. 5.25	By closing stock	Rs. 6.00
To Gross profit (20% on sales)	Rs. 25.40		
	Rs. 133.00		133.00

To Expenses	Rs. 3.00	By Gross profit b/d	25.40
To Debentures interest (6 months)	0.20		
To Net profit (subject to depreciation)	22.20		
	25.40		25.40

Projected Balance Sheet as on June 30,19

Liabilities	*Rs.*	*Assets*	*Rs.*
Equity share capital	55.00	Freehold premises	25.00
Profit and loss account	22.20	Plant and machinery	10.00
8% Debentures	5.00	Vehicles etc.	5.00
Interest due	0.20	Stock	6.00
Wages and salaries outstanding	0.95	Debtors	54.50
		Preliminary expenses	0.50
Trade creditors	21.45		
	104.80		104.80

Working notes:

(*i*) *Purchases:* gross profit ratio is 20% on sales. Therefore, purchases will be equivalent to 80% of sales less wages. For example, in June, sales are Rs. 28 lakhs and 80% thereof Rs. 22.40 lakhs. The amount of purchases for this month therefore will be 21.45 lakhs (i.e., Rs. 22 lakhs less Rs. 0.95 lakhs for wages). The same method has been followed for other months.

(*ii*) *Depreciation on fixed assets:* In the absence of any information, no depreciation has been charged on the fixed assets.

ZERO BASE BUDGETING (ZBB)

Zero Base Budgeting (ZBB) is a method of budgeting whereby all activities are revaluated each time a budget is formulated and every item of expenditure in the budget is fully justified. That is, ZBB involves starting from scratch or zero.

In traditional budgeting, departmental managers need to justify only increases over the prior year's budget (known as incremental budgeting). This implies that what is already being spent is automatically sanctioned. Under the ZBB concept, each department's functions are reviewed completely and all expenditures, rather than only the increases, must be approved. Also, in some departments, ascertainment of budgeted costs is easier than other departments. For example, in production departments, it is easier to determine costs of inputs to achieve a level of budgeted output. But, in other departments such as accounts, personnel, research and development, it is difficult to even identify the output, and therefore equally greater difficult to determine the cost of input to sustain (unidentifiable) output. Consequently, the budgets of previous years tend to be subjectively increased as the next year's budgeted expenditure. However, the previous year's budgets may be inefficient and adjusting merely next year's budgets to the previous year's budget may result in wastages. ZBB overcomes this problem, to a certain extent. It rejects the traditional view of annual budgeting as an incremental process which takes into account current expenditure plus an estimate of next year's expenditure to arrive at the next budget. Instead, the projected expenditure for existing programmes should start from base zero with each year's budgets being compiled as if the programs were being launched for the first time.

Application of ZBB

ZBB involves the following stages:

(1) Each separate activity of the organisation is identified and called a *decision package*. A decision package is a document that identifies and describes a specific activity in such a manner that management can (*i*) evaluate it and rank it against other activities competing for limited resources, and (*ii*) decide whether to approve or disapprove it.

(2) Each decision package must be justified *i.e.,* it should be enquired into whether a decision package promotes the goals of an enterprise.

(3) If justified, then the cost of minimum efforts needed to sustain each decision package is determined.

(4) Alternatives for each decision package are considered in order to select better and cheaper options for the package.

(5) Incremental decision packages are also justified and costed in the above manner. These incremental packages describe the costs and benefits of additional work that could be done above that required by the base package for the minimum amount of work needed to carry out the activity.

(6) Managers rank their decision packages in order of priority for resource allocation.

(7) Resources are allocated to the packages.

Advantages of ZBB

(1) It represents a move towards allocation of resources by need and benefit and thus results in more efficient allocation of resources.

(2) It identifies and eliminates wastages and absolute operations.

(3) It ensures that the best possible methods of performing jobs are used and that new ideas emerge.

(4) It creates a questioning attitude rather than one which accepts that current practices represent value for money.

(5) It leads to increased staff involvement which may lead to improved motivation and greater interest in the job.

(6) It increases communication and coordination within the organisation.

(7) Managers become more aware of the costs of inputs which helps them to identify priorities.

(8) The documentation of decision packages provides management with a deep, coordinated knowledge of all the organisation's activities.

(9) It is useful especially for service departments where it can be difficult to identify output.

Disadvantages of ZBB

(1) The costs involved in preparing a vast number of decision packages in a large form are very high.

(2) It is very time-consuming and a large amount of additional paper work is involved.

(3) Managers develop fear and feel threatened by ZBB and therefore may oppose new ideas and changes.

(4) The ranking of decision packages and allocation of resources is subjective to a certain degree, which can result in departmental conflict.

(5) Administration and communication of ZBB process may become critical problems because more managers become involved in this process than in most budgeting and planning procedures and these problems are further compounded in large organisations.

THEORY QUESTIONS

1. Define budget and budgetary control.
2. Explain the relationship between planning and control process and budgeting.
3. List the major components of a planning and control process.
4. Explain how an organisation can benefit from budgeting.
5. What is the meaning of operating budget, financial budget and master budget.
6. Explain the role of a sales forecast in budgeting. What is the difference between sales forecast and a sales budget.
7. What is participative budgeting. How does it help in creating positive behaviour among the people in an organisation.
8. Discuss the differences between fixed and flexible budgeting. Why are flexible budgets considered superior to fixed budget.
9. How does budgeting help management in the discharge of its functions.
10. What is a cash budget. How is it prepared.
11. How does budgeting serve as an instrument of control.
12. What are the advantages arising out of the budgetary system. What do you think are the essentials of an effective budgetary control system.
13. Discuss the objectives and limitations of budgeting.
14. Define budgeting and discuss the objectives of introducing a budgetary system in an organisation.
15. Explain the differences between a forecast and a budget. Give examples to illustrate the differences between:
    (*a*) Fixed budget.
    (*b*) Flexible budget and
    (*c*) Functional budget.
16. What are functional budgets. Which functional budgets are most commonly used by management.
17. Define budgetary control and distinguish it from standard costing. Discuss the inter-relationship between budgetary control and the standard costing system.
18. Discuss briefly the procedure for the preparation of a sales budget.
19. Describe briefly the fundamental functions of business budgets.
20. Explain the concept of a flexible budget. How is it prepared.
21. Point out the benefits that may be derived from budgetary control by a manufacturing concern.
22. What is Zero Base Budgeting (ZBB). What are the steps in ZBB.
23. Discuss the advantages and disadvantages of Zero Base Budgeting.

PROBLEMS

1. A factory engaged in manufacturing plastic toys is working at 40% capacity and produces 10000 toys per month. The present cost break-up for one toy is as under:

Material	Rs. 10
Labour	Rs. 3
Overhead	Rs. 5 (60% fixed)

The selling price is Rs. 20 per toy. If it is decided to work the factory at 50% capacity, the selling price falls by 3%. At 90% capacity, the selling price falls by 5% accompanied by a similar fall in the price of material. You are required to prepare a statement showing profit at 50% and 90% capacity.

Ans: Profit 40% capacity Rs. 20,000, 50% capacity Rs. 25,000, 90% capacity Rs. 71250.

2. Prepare a flexible budget for overheads on the basis of data given below. Ascertain the overhead rates at 50,60 and 70 per cents capacity.

	At 50% Capacity Rs.	At 60% Capacity Rs.	At 70% Capacity Rs.
Variable Overheads:			
Indirect material	6,000		
Indirect labour	18,000		
Semi-variable overheads:			
Electricity (40% fixed, 60% variable)	30,000		
Repairs and maintenance (80% fixed 20% variable)	3,000		
Fixed Overheads:			
Depreciation	16,500		
Insurance	4,500		
Salaries	15,000		
Total overheads	93,000		
Estimated direct labour hours	1,86,000		

Ans:

Overhead rates
Capacity level 50% Rs. 0.55
Capacity level 60% = Rs. 0.50
Capacity level 70% = 0.46

3. The budgeted cost of a factory specialising in the production of a single product at the optimum capacity of 6,400 units per annum amounts Rs. 1,76,048 as detailed below:

Fixed cost		Rs. 20,688
Fixed cost		
Variable costs:		
Power	Rs. 1,440	
Repairs etc.	Rs. 1,700	
Miscellaneous	Rs. 540	
Direct material	Rs. 49,280	
Direct labour	1,02,400	1,55,360
		1,76,048

Having regard to possible impact on sales turnover by market trends, the company decided to have a flexible budget with a production target of 3,200 and 4,800 units (the actual quantity proposed to be produced being left to a later date before commencement of the budget period). Prepare a flexible budget for production levels at 50% and 75% capacity.

Assume selling price per unit is maintained at Rs. 40 as to present, indicate the effect on net profit.

Administration, selling and distribution expenses continue at Rs. 3,600.

Ans.: Net profit (*a*) 100% Rs. 75,352

(*b*) 75% Rs. 51,192

(*c*) 50% Rs. 26,032

4. Draw up a flexible budget for overhead expenses on the basis of the following data and determine the overhead rates at 70%, 80% and 90% plant capacity levels.

	At 80" capacity
	Rs.
Variable Overheads:	
Indirect labour	12,000
Indirect material	4,000
Semi-variable Overheads:	
Power (30% fixed, 70% variable)	20,000
Repairs & Maintenance (60% fixed, 40% variable)	2,000
Fixed Overheads:	
Depreciation	11,000
Insurance	3,000
Others	10,000
Total overheads	62,000
Estimated direct labour hours	1,24,000 hours

Ans: Overhead rate per direct labour hour

(*a*) 70%	Re. 0.5359
(*b*) 80%	Re. 0.5000
(*c*) 90%	Re. 0.4720

5. Draw a material procurement budget (quantitative) from the following information:

Estimated sales of a product 40,000 units. Each unit of the product requires 3 units of material A and 5 units of material B.

Estimate opening balances at the commencement of the next year:

Finished product	5,000 units
Material A	12,000 units
Material B	20,000 units
Material on order:	
Material A	7,000 units
Material B	11,000 units

The desirable closing balances at the end of the next year:

Finished product	7,000 units
Material A	15,000 units
Material B	25,000 units
Material on order:	
Material A	8,000 units
Material B	10,000 units

Ans: Units to be procured A 1,30,000 B, 2,14,000

6. From the following information relating to 2001 and conditions expected to prevail in 2002, prepare a budget for 2002.

State the assumptions you have made.

2001 Actuals

	Rs.	
Sales	1,00,000	(40,000 units)
Raw materials	53,000	
Wages	11,000	
Variable overheads	16,000	
Fixed overheads	10,000	

2002 prospects		
Sales	1,50,000	(60,0000 units)
Raw materials	5%	Price increase
Wages	10%	Increase in wage rate
Additional plant	5%	Increase in productivity One lathe, Rs. 25,000 One drill, Rs. 12,000

Ans: Budget for 2002 - Rs. 11,539

7. Prepare a production budget for each month and a summarised production cost budget for the six-month period ending 31st December, 1994 from the following data of product X.

(*i*) The units to be sold for different months are as follows:

July 1994	1,100
August	1,100
September	1,700
October	1,900
November	2,500
December	2,300
January1995	2,000

(*ii*) There will be no work-in-progress at the end of any month.

(*iii*) Finished units equal to half the sales for the next month will be in stock at the end of each month (including June 1994)

(*iv*) Budgeted production and production cost for the year ending 31st December 1994 are as follows:

Production (units)	22,000
Direct material per unit	10.00
Direct wages per unit	4.00
Total factory overhead apportioned to product	88,000

Ans: Total production cost Rs. 1,98,900.

8. A factory is currently working to 50% capacity and the product cost is Rs. 180 per unit as below:

Material	100
Labour	30
Factory overhead	30 (40% fixed)
Administrative overhead	20 (50% fixed)

The product is sold at Rs. 200 per unit and the factory produces 10,000 units at 50% capacity. Estimate profit if the factory works to 60% capacity. At 60% working, raw material cost increased by 20% and selling price falls by 20%.

9. The cost of an article at a capacity level of 10,000 units is given under A below. For a variation in capacity above or below this level, the individual expenses vary as indicated in B below:

	A (Rs.)	B
Material cost	50,000	100% varying
Labour cost	30,000	100% varying
Power	3,000	80% varying
Repairs and maintenance	3,500	80% varying
Stores	2,000	80% varying
Inspection	800	25% varying
Depreciation	10,000	100% varying
Administrative overhead	3,600	25% varying
Selling overhead	4,500	50% varying
Total	1,07,400	
Cost per unit	10.74	

Find out the unit cost of the product under each individual expense at production levels of 8,000 units and 12,000 units.

Ans: Cost per unit Rs. 10.91; Rs. 10,626.

10. The expenses budgeted for the production of 10,000 units in a factory one as under:

	Per unit *Rs.*		*Per unit* *Rs.*
Materials	70	Variable expenses (direct)	5
Labour	25	Selling expenses (10% fixed)	13
Variable overheads	20	Distribution expenses fixed	7
Fixed overheads (Rs. 1,00,000)	10	Administrative expenses	5
			155

Prepare a budget for production of:

(*i*) 8,000 units

(*ii*) 6,000 units

Administration overheads are fixed for all levels.

11. A company is manufacturing two products X and Y. A forecast about the number of units to be sold in the first seven months is given below:

Month	*Product X*	*Product Y*
January	10,000	28,000
February	12,000	28,000
March	16,000	24,000
April	20,000	20,000
May	24,000	26,000
June	24,000	16,000
July	20,000	18,000

It is anticipated that:

(*i*) there will be no work-in-progress at the end of any month:

(*ii*) finished units equal to half the sales for the next month will be in stock at the end of each month (including December of previous year).

Budgeted production and production costs for the year ending 31st December are as follows:

	Product X	*Product Y*
Production (Units)	2,20,000	2,40,000
Direct materials per unit	12.5	19
Direct Wages per unit (Rs.)	4.5	7
Total factory overheads to each type of Product (Rs.)	66,000.	96,000

Prepare for six months ending 30th June, production budget and a summarised cost of production budget.

(*Ans:* Production Budget total = 2,38,000 units; Total cost of production = Rs. 1,16,00,000).

12. Prepare a cash budget in respect of 6 months from July to December from the information given in the table as under:

Month	*Credit Sales*	*Material*	*Wages*	*Overheads*				
				Production	*Administration*	*Selling*	*Distribution*	*Research and Development*
	000 Rs.	*000 Rs.*	*000 Rs.*	*000 Rs.*	*ration Rs.*	*Rs.*	*Rs.*	*Rs.*
April	100	40	10.0	4.4	3,000	1,600	800	1,000
May	120	60	11.2	4.8	2,900	1,700	900	1,000
June	80	40	8.0	5.6	3,000	1,500	700	1,200
July	100	60	8.0	4.6	2,900	1,400	900	1,200
August	120	70	10.0	5.6	3,000	1,900	1,100	1,200
September	140	80	10.0	5.4	3,000	2,000	1,200	1,400
October	160	90	10.0	5.8	3,100	2,250	1,250	1,600
November	180	100	11.0	6.0	3,100	2,150	1,250	1,500
December	200	110	11.6	6.4	2,200	2,300	1,500	1,600

Cash balance on July 1 was expected to be Rs. 1,50,000.

Expected Capital Expenditure:

Plant and Machinery to be installed in August at a cost of Rs. 40,000 will be payable on September 1. Extension to Research and Development Department amounting to Rs. 10,000 will be completed on August 1, payable Rs. 2000 per month from completion date. Under a hire-purchase agreement, Rs. 4,000 is payable to each month.

Cash sales of Rs. 2,000 per month are expected. No commission is payable.

A sales commission of 5 per cent on (credit) sales is to be paid within the month following the sales.

Period of credit allowed by suppliers	3 months
Period of credit allowed to customers	2 months
Delay in payment of overheads	1 month
Delay in payment of wages	1 month

Income-tax of Rs. 1,00,000 is due to be paid on October 1. Preference share dividend of 10 per cent on Rs. 2,00,000 is to be paid on November 1.

Ten per cent calls on ordinary share capital of Rs. 4,00,000 is due on July 1 and September 1.

Dividend from investments amounting to Rs. 30,000 expected on November 1.

Ans: Balance July Rs. 2,44,000, Aug. Rs. 2,36,000, September Rs. 2,63,000, October Rs. 1,89,000, November Rs. 2,33,000, Dec. Rs. 2,75,000.

13. From the information given below, prepare a cash budget of the Jaipur Refrigerators (P) Ltd. for the quarter January-March 1994:

	Dec. '93	*Jan.' 94*	*Feb. '94*	*March '94*	*April '94*
(*a*) Sales budget unit	60	60	65	75	80
(*b*) Selling price per unit Rs.	1,000	1,000	1,000	1,000	1,000
(*c*) Off-season discount	20%	20%	10%	-	-
(*d*) End of month inventory units	10	12	15	25	25

(*e*) Half the sales proceeds are collected in the month of sale and the other half in the month following.

(*f*) Materials amounting to Rs. 300 per unit manufactured are purchased one month in advance of manufacture and paid for in cash, earning 5% cash discount on half of the material purchased.

(*g*) Direct labour budget was Rs. 50 per unit and variable overheads Rs. 100 per unit.

(*h*) Indirect labour budget was Rs. 6,000 per month.

(*i*) Depreciation was provided uniformly at Rs. 3,000 per month.

(*j*) The fixed overheads budget was Rs. 6,000 per month during off season and Rs. 7,000 during the season. Out of this, the quarterly premium for fire insurance amounting to Rs. 600 was payable in the first month of each quarter.

(*k*) Dividends for the year 1993 amounting to Rs. 20,000 were expected to be declared in March 1994 and payments were to be spread between March and April.

(*l*) A machine was sold for Rs. 10,000 in December 1993 on 3 month's credit.

(*m*) The company had overdraft arrangements with the State Bank of Jaipur and Bikaner upto Rs. 50,000.

Ans: Balance January Rs. 6410.

February Rs. 12797.50

March Rs. 30,597.50.

❑❑❑

Chapter 8

RESPONSIBILITY ACCOUNTING

DECENTRALISATION

In small organisations, decision making and management of the business are often done by a single individual. However, in large organisations, especially organisations engaged in manufacturing or undertaking multiple products and activities, successful management of it by the top management becomes more difficult. In order to overcome this difficulty, the large organisation may be decentralised or divisionalised. When the decision authority is delegated to managers, they in turn are held responsible for the consequences of their decision-making. The process of delegating decision authority and responsibility in an organisation is known as *decentralisation.* In any organisation, infact, some authority can be found delegated to the lower level management. In this way almost every organisation can be said to be 'decentralised.' However, decentralisation is found in case of companies producing multiple products. Divisions in companies mean different things in different companies. In some companies, divisions are organised on the basis of product lines whereas in some decentralised companies, divisions may be created on the basis of geographical areas. Also, the term decentralisation or divisionalisation refers to those situations where individual managers of decentralised subunits are given responsibility for profit and not just costs or revenues. In decentralised organisations, the top management handles broad corporate policies, establishes long range plans, raises capital and conducts other coordinating activities.

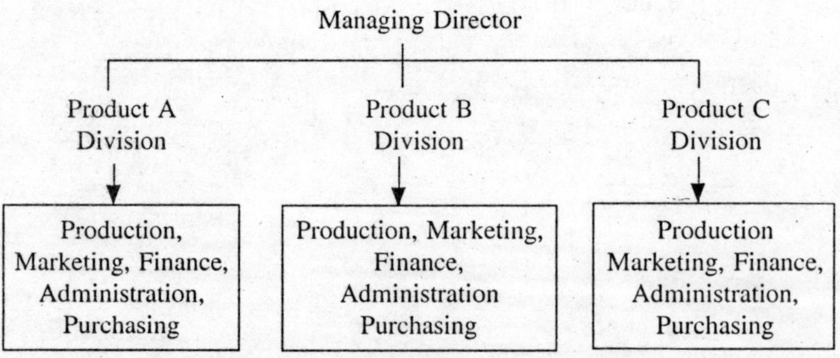

Fig. 8.1: Divisionalised Organisational Structure

An example of divisionalised (decentralised) organisational structure is displayed in Fig. 8.1. It can be noticed that different divisions have been created in terms of products made in each division in this particular decentralised company and these divisions are responsible for all the operations relating to their respective products. Divisional managers will have decision-making authority for their divisions and thus may be free to set selling prices, choose which market to sell in, make product mix and output decisions and make purchasing decisions. Some functions (activities) like research and development, industrial relations and general administration may be centralised with the top management which may have a responsibility for providing services to all of the divisions.

FUNCTIONAL ORGANISATIONAL STRUCTURE

A functional organisation structure is one in which all functions of a similar type within an organisation are placed under the control of a departmental head or manager. Such departmental managers have responsibility to perform only a part of the overall functions. An example of a functional organisational structure is shown in Fig. 8.2. Here it is shown that the company has five separate departments e.g. production,

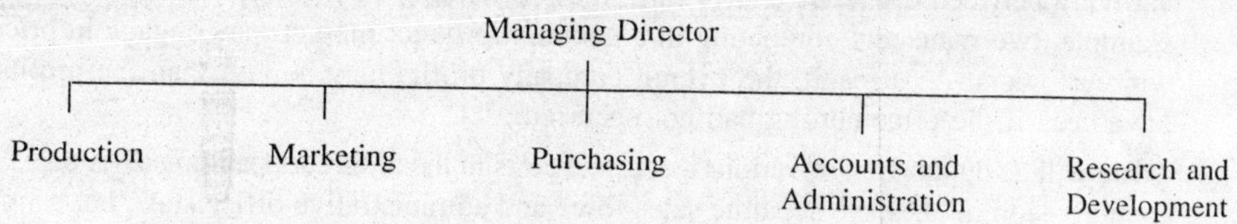

Fig. 8.2: Functional Organisational Structure

marketing, purchasing, account and administration, research and development. In this manufacturing company, the manager of each department (or activity) is a part of the process of purchasing the raw materials, using raw materials to make finished products, selling finished products to customers, administering accounts and administration, and finally supervising research and development activities. For example, the purchasing department is responsible for purchasing raw materials and supplies for all products at a minimum cost, reasonable quality and within proper time so that production requirements can be fulfilled without any difficulty. The production department has the responsibility for the manufacture of all products and the marketing department performs the selling function and is responsible for creating sales revenue for the company. In a functional or centralised organisation, and all decisions like pricing, production, product mix are made by the top management and therefore functional managers or departmental heads in a centralised organisation enjoy for less independence and autonomy than the divisional managers in a decentralised or divisionalised organisation. For example, the production manager in a functional organisation (Fig. 8.2) has no control over sources of supply selling prices and does not make production and product mix decisions.

Advantages of Divisionalisation

A number of advantages are found with divisionalisation/decentralisation of an organisation:

(*i*) Top management becomes free from detailed involvement in day-to-day operations and enables them to devote their time and efforts to strategic planning, policy formulation, overall coordination and direction.

(*ii*) It improves the decision making process and leads to more informed decisions in the organisation because the managers who are directly involved in the day-to-day running of business and are familiar with the situation, make decisions.

(*iii*) Speedier decisions can be made as decisions can be taken on the spot by the manager without any need of sending to/getting information from the top management.

(*iv*) Managers can rapidly respond to changes in the market, competition, opportunities available, due to non-existence of administrative bottlenecks in their organisation which can increase the profitability of the overall company.

(*v*) Experience of decision-making at the divisional level provides the divisional managers better career training.

(*vi*) Decentralisation enhances motivation and efficiency of the divisional managers as they find their status increased with wider responsibilities and greater freedom to manage their activities and more control over the factors which determine their performances and

(*vii*) Divisionalisation may be more helpful in building good labour-management relations as the divisional managers will be able to maintain personalised contact with the employees.

Disadvantages of Divisionalisation

There are some disadvantages of divisionalisation. They are listed as follows:

(*i*) Different divisions are likely to compete unreasonably and they make take action which may increase their profits but only at the expense of other divisions. This may adversely affect cooperation and harmony between divisions and in turn, the profitability of the entire company may suffer. For example, two managers competing in a common product market may engage in price cutting to win customers. As a result, the overall company profits may be less than the profits that could have been if the price cutting had not occurred.

(*ii*) There will be duplication of various assets and costs in the different operating divisions. For example, each division might have separate sales force and administrative office staff, but centralisation of these personnel could save money. Further, the costs of gathering and processing information in a divisionalised organisation might be greater than if such information were gathered and processed centrally. If top management of a decentralised company is going for divisionalisation, it is important that they assess whether the additional benefits will exceed the additional costs and

(*iii*) A further argument against divisionalisation is that the top management loses some control by delegating decision making to the divisional manager. It is argued that a series of control reports is not as effective as detailed knowledge of a company's activities.

RESPONSIBILITY CENTRE

A responsibility centre may be defined as an area of responsibility which is controlled by an individual. A responsibility centre is an activity such as a department over which a manager exercises responsibility. Responsibility areas may be departments (drilling or maintenance department), product lines (chemicals or fertilisers), territories (North or South) or any other type of identifiable unit or combination of units. The specific types of responsibility areas depend on the nature of the firm and its activities. It is relatively easy to identify activities with specific managers. A plant manager is in charge of a plant and is usually responsible for producing budgeted quantities of specific products within budgeted cost limits. A sales manager is responsible for getting orders from customers, and so on. In most cases, it is relatively easy to identify activities with specific managers. However, in some cases it is not a simple task to isolate the responsibilities of managers.

It should be noted that effective planning and control systems are structured around the implicit or explicit areas of responsibility within the organisation. Further, to be held accountable for performance, managers must have clearly defined areas of responsibility activities they control.

Types of Responsibility Centres

Responsibility centres can be classified by the scope of responsibility assigned and decision-making authority given to individual managers. The following are the four common types of responsibility centres:

1. *Cost Centre*

A cost of expense centre is a segment of an organisation in which the managers are held responsible for the cost incurred in that segment but not for revenues. Responsibility in a cost centre is restricted to cost. For planning purposes, the budget estimates are cost estimates; for control purposes, performance evaluation is guided by a cost variance equal to the difference between the actual and budgeted costs for a given period. Cost centre managers have control over some or all of the costs in their segment of business, but not over revenues. Cost centres are widely used forms of responsibility centre. Also, a marketing department, a sales region or a single sales representative can be defined as a cost centre. Cost centres may vary in size from a small department with a few employees to an entire manufacturing plant. In addition, they may exist within other cost centres. For example, a manager of a manufacturing plant organised as a cost centre may treat individual departments within the plant as separate cost centres, with the department managers reporting directly to the plant manager. Cost centre managers are responsible for the costs that are controllable by them and their subordinates. However, which costs should be charged to cost centres, is an important question in evaluating cost centre managers.

2. *Revenue Centre*

A revenue centre is a segment of the organisation which is primarily responsible for generating sales revenue. A revenue centre manager does not possess control over cost, investment in assets, but usually has control over some of the expenses of the marketing department. The performance of a revenue centre is evaluated by comparing the actual revenue with budgeted revenue, and actual marketing expenses with budgeted marketing expenses. The Marketing Manager of a product line or an individual sales representative are examples of revenue centres.

3. *Profit Centre*

A profit centre is a segment of an organisation whose manager is responsible for both revenues and costs. Managers of Profit Centres have control over both costs and revenues. In a profit centre, the manager has the responsibility and the authority to make decisions that affect both costs and revenues (and thus profits) for the department or division. The main purpose of a profit centre is to earn profit. These managers aim at both the production and marketing of a product. The performance of the profit centre is evaluated in terms of whether the centre has achieved its budgeted profit. A division of the company which produces and markets the products may be called a *profit centre*. Such a divisional manager determines the selling price, marketing programmes and production policies. Profit centres make managers more concerned with finding ways to increase the centre's revenue by increasing production or improving distribution methods. The manager of a profit centre does not make decisions concerning the plant assets available to the centre. For example, the manager of the sporting goods department does not make the decision to expand the available floor space for the department.

Mostly profit centres are created in an organisation in which they (profit divisions) sell products or services outside the company. In some cases, profit centres may be selling products or service within the company. For example, repairs and maintenance department in a company can be treated as a profit centre if it is allowed to bill other production departments for the services provided to them. Similarly, the data processing department may bill each of the company's administrative and operating departments for providing computer-related services.

An example of a profit centre in a department store having different retail departments is displayed in Fig. 8.3.

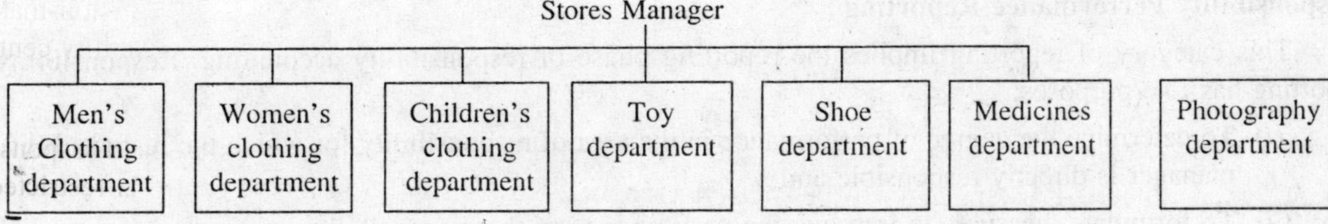

Fig. 8.3: Profit Centre

4. Investment Centre

An investment centre is responsible for both profits and investments. The investment centre manager has control over revenues, expenses and the amounts invested in the centre's assets. He also formulates the credit policy which has a direct influence on debt collection, and the inventory policy which determines the investment in inventory. The manager of an investment centre has more authority and responsibility than the manager of either a cost centre or a profit centre. Besides controlling costs and revenues, he has investment responsibility too. Investment on asset responsibility means the authority to buy, sell and use divisional assets.

RESPONSIBILITY ACCOUNTING

The term 'responsibility accounting' refers to the accounting process that reports how well managers (of responsibility centres) have fulfilled their responsibility. Also known as activity or profitability accounting, it is an information system that personalises control reports by accumulating and reporting cost and revenue information according to defined responsibility areas within a company. Responsibility accounting systems are tailored to the organisational structure so the revenues and costs are accumulated and reported by centres of responsibility within the organisation.

The responsibility accounting system makes the following important assumptions:

(*i*) The areas of responsibility are defined for which managers should be held responsible.

(*ii*) Managers are only charged with the items and responsibility over which they can exercise a significant degree of direct control.

(*iii*) Managers should actively participate in establishing the goals or budgets against which their performance is measured.

(*iv*) Goals defined for each area of responsibility should be attainable with efficient and effective performance.

(*v*) Control (performance) reports should contain significant information related to each area of responsibility and

(*vi*) Responsibility centre managers should try to accomplish the budgets and objectives established for their respective areas of responsibilities.

Responsibility accounting is closely related with the goal of controllability. Accordingly, in responsibility accounting, those elements in a certain area of activity are identified which are controllable and then a person is given the responsibility for managing such elements. Responsibility accounting implies that individuals in an organisation should be made responsible for only those elements which they can control. Obviously they cannot be responsible for those items which they cannot control. They should also not claim any authority over those revenues which are not the result of their actions and performances. For instance, a foreman in a production department can be held responsible only for direct material and direct labour costs, because these are the costs which are controllable by him. On the other hand, the divisional manager of the production division can be held accountable for all direct and indirect costs incurred in his division. Generally, those decision makers who are placed higher in the authority hierarchy, are held responsible for a greater number of activities and financial elements. In the long run, however, all costs are controllable by someone in the organisation.

Responsibility Performance Reporting

This category of reporting implies the reporting phase of responsibility accounting. Responsibility reporting has two purposes:

(*i*) To determine the degree of performance in the area of responsibility for which the responsibility manager is directly responsible and

(*ii*) To formulate measures to improve the performance of the responsibility centre manager.

Responsibility reporting should be suitable and relevant with respect to content, frequency of reporting and level of detail required. In order to provide relevant contents in the report, only those items that are controlled by the particular responsibility centre manager should be reported. Frequency of reporting and the quantum of details in the report can be decided in terms of requirements. Generally, in a production department of a manufacturing enterprise, detailed data on production, direct and indirect costs need to be gathered and reported to the foreman quite frequently. However, the same data is reported to the senior management in a summarised form and at less frequent intervals. The difference in the frequency of reporting in this situation is due to the fact that the foreman has direct responsibility whereas senior managers have overall responsibility for long-term and strategic decisions. Matz and Usry[1] have mentioned the following as the characteristics of responsibility reporting:

(*i*) Reports should fit the organisation chart, that is, the report should be addressed to the individual responsible for the items covered by it, who, in turn will be able to control those costs under his jurisdiction. Managers must be educated to use the results of the reporting system.

(*ii*) Report should be prompt and timely. Prompt issuance of a report requires that cost records be organised so that information is available when it is needed.

(*iii*) Reports should be issued with regularity. Promptness and regularity are closely tied up with the mechanical aids used to assemble and issue reports.

(*iv*) They should be easy to understand. Often they contain accounting terminology that managers with little or no accounting training find it difficult to understand, and vital information may be incorrectly communicated. Therefore, accounting terms should be explained or modified to fit the user. Top management should have some knowledge of the kind of items chargeable to an account as well as the methods used to compute overhead rates, make cost allocations and analyse variances.

(*v*) Reports should convey sufficient but not excessive details. The amount and nature of the details depend largely on the management level receiving the report. Reports to the management should neither be loaded with immaterial facts or so condensed that management lacks vital information essential to carrying out its responsibilities.

(*vi*) They should give comparative figures, i.e. a comparison of actual with budgeted figures or of predetermined standards with actual results and the isolation of variances.

(*vii*) Reports should be analytical. Analysis of underlying papers, such as time tickets, scrap tickets, work orders and material requisitions provide reasons for poor performance which might have been due to power failure, machine breakdown, an inefficient operator, poor quality of materials or many other similar factors.

(*viii*) Reports for operating management should, if possible, be stated in physical units as well as in terms of money since monetary information may give a foreman not trained in the language of the accountant a certain amount of difficulty and

(*ix*) Reports may tend to highlight departmental efficiencies and inefficiencies, results achieved, future goals or targets.

Responsibility Reporting for Cost Centres

A specimen of responsibility performance reporting for cost centres is given in Fig. 8.4, which has been designed to provide relevant cost information to three levels of responsibility centres in a manufacturing enterprise-Foreman, Production Manager and General Manager.

---

1. Adolph Matz and Milton F. Usry, *Cost Accounting, Planning and Control*, South Western Publishing Co. pp. 300-301.

Responsibility Report

(A) Foreman (Paint Section)

Item	*Actual Cost (Rs.)*	*Budgeted Cost (Rs.)*	*Variance (Rs.)*
Direct materials	50,000	48,400	(–) 1,600
Direct labour	31,000	34,000	(+) 3,000
Indirect labour	12,000	12,000	—
Supplies	100	1,600	(+) 600
	94,000	96,000	(+) 2,000

(B) Production Manager

Item	*Actual Cost (Rs.)*	*Budgeted Cost (Rs.)*	*Variance (Rs.)*
Paint Section	94,000	96,000	(+) 2,000
Cleaning Section	1,20,000	1,21,000	(+) 1,000
Assembly Section	1,61,000	1,58,000	(–) 3,000
	3,75,000	3,75,000	0

(C) General Manager

Item	*Actual Cost (Rs.)*	*Budgeted Cost (Rs.)*	*Variance (Rs.)*
Production department	3,75,000	3,75,000	(–)
Sales department	3,74,000	3,80,000	(+) 6,000
Office administration	1,10,000	1,10,000	(+) 2,000
Interest on loans	15,000	15,000	—
	8,74,000	8,82,000	(+) 8,000

Fig. 8.4: Responsibility Report

From the above figure, it can be found that each responsibility report contains items and information which are required by the concerned responsibility centre manager and which are within his responsibility area. For example, in the foreman's report, relevant production cost information is given. In the responsibility report prepared for the production manager, information on different sections of his department is included in an aggregated manner and for the general manager, the responsibility report contains information for different departments. It can be further noticed that responsibility reporting goes on aggregating information as the reports are prepared for higher level managers in the organisational hierarchy. That is, the amount of detail decreases as reports reach higher and higher levels of management. Managers cannot make effective use of information that is too detailed and voluminous. Departmental managers do not routinely receive reports detailing all of the costs of the work centres. Managers who want such detailed information can get it and might well seek it if they were concerned about some particular elements of cost.

Responsibility Reporting for Profit Centres

Responsibility accounting reports for profit centres are normally in the form of income statements. The principal of controllability also applies to responsibility reporting for profit centres. Fig. 8.5 gives a sample of the responsibility report for profit centres organised on the basis of product lines and geographical areas. Managers at the lowest level in the profit centre are responsible for product lines. They are subordinate to the managers of the geographical areas, who are, in turn, responsible to the Managing Director of the company.

Profit centre reporting can be prepared in a different manner to provide more detail on individual components of the appliance segment in the particular region. Fig. 8.6 shows an alternative responsibility reporting format giving information on different categories of appliances. For simplicity, budgeted figures are omitted.

Responsibility Reports for Profit Centres (Thousands of Rupees)

	Current Month		*Year to Date*	
	Budget (Rs.)	*Over (Under) (Rs.)*	*Budget (Rs.)*	*Over (Under) (Rs.)*
Report to Product Manager — Appliances, Asian Region				
Sales	122.0	1.5	387.0	3.2
Variable costs:				
Production	47.5	2.8	150.7	5.9
Selling and administrative	12.2	1.8	38.7	1.9
Total variable costs	59.7	4.6	189.4	7.8
Contribution margin	62.3	(3.1)	197.6	(4.6)
Direct fixed costs	36.0	(1.2)	98.5	(3.1)
Product margin	26.3	1.9	99.1	1.5
Report to Manager — Asian Region				
Product margins:				
Appliances	26.3	(1.9)	99.1	(1.5)
Industrial equipment	37.4	3.2	134.5	7.3
Tools	18.3	1.1	59.1	(2.0)
Total product margins	82.0	2.4	292.7	3.8
Regional expenses (common to all product lines)	18.5	0.8	61.2	(1.3)
Regional margin	63.5	1.6	231.5	5.1
Report to Executive Vice President				
Regional margins:				
Asian	63.5	1.6	231.5	5.1
European	78.1	(4.3)	289.4	(8.2)
USA	211.8	(3.2)	612.4	(9.6)
Total regional margins	353.4	(5.9)	1,133.3	(12.7)
Corporate expenses (common to all Regions)	87.1	1.4	268.5	3.1
Corporate profit	266.3	(7.3)	864.8	(15.8)

Fig: 8.5: Profit Centres Responsibility Reports

Alternative Responsibility Reporting Formal
— Report to Product Manager — Appliances, Asian Region (Thousands of Rupees)

	Total (Rs.)	*Small Home Appliances (Rs.)*	*Large Home Appliances (Rs.)*	*Commercial Appliances (Rs.)*
Sales	390.2	126.3	109.5	154.4
Variable costs:				
Production	156.6	41.1	31.2	84.3
Selling and administrative	40.6	14.2	18.1	8.3
Total variable costs	197.2	55.3	49.3	92.6
Contribution margin	193.0	71.0	60.2	61.8
Direct fixed costs	27.4	9.5	11.2	6.7
Margin	165.6	61.5	49.0	55.1
Costs common to products in the appliance line	68.0			
Product margin	97.6			

Fig. 8.6: Responsibility Reports for Individual Products

Example 1

Nicefit manufactures readymade garments by a simple process of cutting the clothes in various shapes and sewing the corresponding pieces together to form the finished products.

The Accounts Department reports the following for the last quarter of 1994:

	Budgeted	*Actual*
Bad Debt Losses	5,000	3,000
Cloth used	31,000	36,000
Advertising	4,000	4,000
Audit Fees	7,500	7,500
Credit Reports	1,200	1,050
Sales Representative		
Travelling Expenses	9,000	10,200
Sales Commission	7,000	7,000
Cutting Labour	6,000	6,600
Thread	500	450
Sewing Labour	17,000	18,400
Credit Dept. Salaries	8,000	8,000
Cutting Utilities	800	700
Sewing Utilities	900	950
Director Marketing		
Salaries & Administration Expenses	20,000	21,400
Production Engineering Expenses	13,000	12,200
Sales Management Office Expenses	16,000	15,700
Production Manager Office Expenses	18,000	17,000
Director Manufacturing		
Salaries & Administration Expenses	2,1000	20,100

Using the above data, prepare responsibility accounting reports for the Director-Marketing, the Director-Manufacturing and the Production Manager.

Solution:

Responsibility Accounting Reports

For the Production Manager

	Budgeted Rs.	*Actual Rs.*	*Variance Rs.*
Cutting Department:			
Cloth	31,000	36,000	5,000 (Unfavourable)
Cutting Labour	6,000	6,600	600 (Unfavourable)
Cutting Utilities	800	700	100 (Favourable)
Total Cutting Dept. (A)	37,800	43,300	5,500 (Unfavourable)
Sewing Department:			
Thread	500	450	50 (Favourable)
Sewing Labour	17,000	18,400	1,400 (Unfavourable)
Sewing Utilities	900	950	50 (Unfavourable)
Total Sewing Dept. (B)	18,400	19,800	1,400 (Unfavourable)
Total (A + B)	56,200	63,100	6,900 (Unfavourable)

For the Director – Manufacturing

	Rs.	*Rs.*	*Rs.*
Production Department*	56,200	63,100	6,900 (Unfavourable)
Production Engineering Expenses	13,000	12,200	800 (Favourable)
Production Manager — Office Expenses	18,000	17,000	1,000 (Favourable)
Total	87,200	92,300	5,100 (Unfavourable)

(*As per Responsibility Accounting Report for the Production Manager)

For the Director-Marketing

	Rs.	*Rs.*	*Rs.*
Sales Representative:			
Travelling Expenses	9,000	10,200	1,200 (Unfavourable)
Sales Commission	7,000	7,000	—
Total (A)	16,000	17,200	1,200 (Unfavourable)
Sales Management:			
Office Expenses (B)	16,000	15,700	300 (Favourable)
Advertising (C)	4,000	4,000	—
Credit Department			
Salaries	8,000	8,000	—
Credit Reports	1,200	1,050	150 (Favourable)
Bad Debt Losses	5,000	3,000	200 (Favourable)
Total (D)	14,200	12050	2,150
Total (A + B + C + D)	50,200	48,950	1.250 (Favourable)

Example 2

A manufacturing company has five plants A, B, C, D and E. Each plant has a forming, cleaning and packing department.

Each level of management has responsibility over costs incurred at its level.

The budget for the current year has been set up as follows:

Plant	Budgeted cost (Rs.)
A	67,500
B	61,250
C	54,200
D	67,500
E	67,500

Budgeted information for Plant C is as follows:

Plant Manager's office	Rs. 1,175
Forming department	Rs. 15,000
Cleaning department	Rs. 27725
Packing department	Rs. 10,300

Budgeted information for Plant C forming department is as follows:

Direct materials	4,167
Direct labour	7,500
Factory overhead	3,334

The following additional budgeted data are available:

President, Office	8,125
Vice-President, Marketing	10,000
Vice-President, Manufacturing Office	2,084

The following actual costs are incurred during the year:

Plant	Actual Cost
A	63,825
B	62,150
C	54,238
D	65,550
E	68,400

The actual cost for Plant C (Forming Department) were as follows.

Direct materials	Rs. 167 under budget
Direct labour	2000 under budget
Factory overhead	167 over budget

Actual costs for Plant C (Plant Manager) were:

Plant manager's office	1,238
Cleaning Department	28,750
Packing Department	11,250
Forming Department	

Actual costs for the president's level were:

President, Office	8,188
Vice-President, Marketing	14,900
Vice-President, Manufacturing	3,16,658

Prepare a responsibility report for the year showing the details of the budgeted, actual and variance amounts for the following areas:

Level 1 Forming department – Plant C

Level 2 Plant Manager, Plant C

Level 3 Vice-President, Manufacturing

Level 4 President

Solution:

Responsibility Report

	Budgeted (Rs.)	*Actual (Rs.)*	*Variance (Rs.)*
President (level 4)	8,125	8,188	63
President's office	10,000	14,900	4,900
Vice-President, Manufacturing	3,20,034	3,16,658	3,376
Total controllable costs	3,38,159	3,39,745	1,587
Vice-President, Manufacturing: (level 3)			
Vice President, Manufacturing Office	2,084	2,495	412
Plant A	67,500	63,825	(3,675)
Plant B	61,250	62,150	900
Plant C	54,200	54,238	38
Plant D	67,500	65,550	(1,950)
Plant E	67,500	68,400	900
Total controllable costs	3,20,034	3,16,658	(3,376)
Plant Manager, Plant C: (level 2)			
Plant Manager's office	1,175	1,238	63
Forming department	15,000	13,000	(2,000)
Cleaning department	27,725	28,750	1,025
Packing department	10,300	11,250	950
Total controllable costs	54,200	54,238	38
Forming department, Plant C: (level I)			
Direct materials	4,167	4,000	(167)
Direct labour	7,500	5,500	(2,000)
Factory overhead	3,334	3,500 167	
Total controllable costs	15,000	13,000	(2,000)

THEORY QUESTIONS

1. What is decentralisation. What are the advantages of decentralisation.
2. Explain the concept of responsibility accounting. What are the different types of responsibility centres.
3. Distinguish between a cost centre, a profit centre and an investment centre.

❑❑❑

Chapter 9

STANDARD COSTING AND VARIANCE ANALYSIS

Control of cost is one of the most important objectives of cost accounting which cannot be achieved without some standard against which actual can be compared. All management's are interested not only in knowing what costs are but also how satisfactory they are. The use of standard costs increases cost consciousness among management and employees and can improve business profits by providing a base for performance evaluation. Standard costing, therefore, helps managerial planning and control in a significant manner. This chapter introduces the concepts and basic procedures of standard costing and also explains the techniques used in standard cost variance analysis. However, before discussing standard costing, it will be appropriate to evaluate briefly historical cost accounting and its limitations.

Historical Cost and its Limitations

Historical cost systems are principally associated with recording of historical, or as they are commonly called, *actual costs*. Historical costing is the ascertainment of costs after they have been incurred. It indicates to the management the results of actual transactions that have taken place in an organisation during some previous period. The recording of historical costs is useful as it determines the cost of resources used towards achieving organisational objectives. Historical costs, however, have the following limitations:

(*i*) Historical costs are collected after they have been incurred and therefore are ineffective in cost control. The costs have been incurred, they cannot be undone and no steps can be taken to correct inefficiencies.

(*ii*) They are not helpful in cost reduction since they contain no standards or goals towards which employees can work.

(*iii*) They do not provide reliable guides to the management in the tasks of budgeting, planning, and decision-making. Historical costs reflect a situation in a previous period. But the company, infact, may be working under conditions different from those prevailing during that previous period. Therefore, historical costs are not useful in budget making, performance evaluation, detecting above or below standard performance.

Definition of Standard Cost, Standard Costing

A standard cost is a planned cost for a unit of product or service rendered. Standard costs are highly detailed, scientifically predetermined costs of material, labour and overheads chargeable to a product or service. Standard costs represent excellent target costs that should be obtained. The Institute of Cost and Management

Accountants (UK) defines standard costs as *"a predetermined cost which is calculated from management's standards of efficient operation and the relevant necessary expenditure. It may be used as a basis for price fixing and for cost control through variance analysis."* Standard cost expresses what costs should be under attainable good performance. They are projections of what actual costs should be under an assumed set of conditions. The term "standard" has been called by different names in accounting e.g., "a norm", "a mode or example or comparison," "a measure of comparison," "a criterion of excellence," "a yardstick", "a benchmark," "an index of waste or potential savings, "a sea level from which to measure cost altitudes," "a gauge." *A standard may be a norm or a measure of comparison in terms of specific items such as pounds or kilograms of materials, labour hours required, hours of plant capacity used.*

Standard costing is the setting of predetermined cost estimates in order to provide a basis for comparison with actual costs. The Institute of Cost and Management Accountants (UK) defines standard costing as "the preparation and use of standard cost, their comparison with actual cost and the analysis of variances to their causes and points of incidence. Although the terms budgeted and standard cost are sometimes used interchangeably, budgeted costs normally describe the total planned costs for a number of products.

STANDARD COSTS AND ESTIMATED COSTS

The term Standard Costs should not be confused with "Estimated Costs." Both these costs differ in the following respects:

First, estimated costs are frequently less accurately determined. These costs are developed from projections using averages of past data regarding performance. Standard costs are predetermined realistically and much more scientifically through the use of time and motion studies, engineering estimates and specifications, selected measures of plant capacity and cost behavior patterns. Thus the fundamental difference between an estimated cost and a standard cost is depth of analysis, prediction techniques and amount of effort used to develop cost information.

Second, estimated costs are not helpful to the management in accomplishing managerial functions as they are not scientifically predetermined costs. But standard costs involve more sophistication, operation analysis and evaluation and comprehensive review of internal and external factors. They become reliable measures for product costing, product pricing, planning, coordination and cost control purposes.

Third, estimated cost emphasises on actual cost with which it is compared at the end of the accounting period. If the estimated costs are found higher or lower than actual costs, they are revised for use in the next accounting period. Revisions in estimated costs are made in accordance with changes in actual cost conditions which are expected to continue during the next accounting period. *In standard costing, the emphasis is on standard costs, i.e., what cost of material, labour and overheads should be incurred if the factory is to be operated as a highly efficient unit with each manager, foreman, worker, plant and machine functioning as an efficient part of the production process.* Under standard costing, actual costs are ascertained only to facilitate their comparison with standard costs.

Standard Costs and Budgets

Standard costs and budgets are both vital tools in planning, operation and control of a business enterprise. Both differ in the following respects:

1. A standard costing system can operate without any comprehensive budgeting system. But budgets in the absence of standard costs will only be fair estimates and cannot provide a reasonable base against which the actual results can be compared.
2. The objectives of budgeting are different from standard costing. A budget is a profit plan reflecting anticipated financial inflows and outflows. It is comprehensive in nature and covers several business activities, such as production, purchase, selling and distribution, research and development. Budgets include both income and expenditure, but standards are set usually for expenses only. Standard

costs are developed only for the production and related manufacturing costs. Also, standard costs reflect planned costs under assumed efficient operating conditions, capacity level and operation.

3. Budgets project the volume of business and levels of costs which should be maintained. That is, they reflect cost ceilings which should not be exceeded if the budgeted profits is to be attained. If the expenses go up, the profit will be reduced. Standard costs emphasise, the cost levels to which cost should be reduced. If costs reach this level, profit will be increased. Standards are minimum targets which are to be attained by actual performance at specific efficiency.
4. Budgets covering the entire business present the forecasted profit and loss account and sometimes balance sheet also. Therefore, budgets act as guides for operating the business on a definite course of action. Standards are frequently used only in labour operation and do not represent expected costs but the cost that should be in certain assumed conditions of performance.
5. Budgets if achieved by the organisation do not usually involve much variance analysis. The achievement of budget targets point out the efficiency attained and therefore no analysis on a large scale is needed unless circumstances have considerably changed. Under standard costing, detailed variance analysis is carried out to find out deviations so that corrective action may be taken.
6. Review and revision of budgets is more frequently based on the changing circumstances than those of standard costs. Standard costs are more static and subject to less change.
7. Budgets are equally important for planning, organisation, coordination and control functions of management. Standard costs contribute relatively more to the control function than other managerial function although standards are used for all business function.
8. Budgeting may be applied in such businesses which are of a jobbing nature, but standard costing is difficult to apply because of the dissimilar nature of difficult jobs. Jobs are better controlled through predetermined budget and costs for different jobs are ascertained historically. In those businesses where manufacturing is done under conditions of continuous processing or under mass production methods, standard costing is applied.

Inspite of the above differences, there are some similarities between standard costing and budgeting. Both have in common the establishment of predetermined measures of performance and the comparison of actual and planned performance so as to disclose deviations which are used for the purpose of cost control. Both have the same objective of managerial control and are therefore inter-related and cannot function independently. Both help in the preparation of reports which compare actual costs and predetermined costs for management planning and control. Standards are almost indispensable to the work of establishing and operating a budget. A study made by the National Association of Accountants (USA) concludes that standard costs are especially valuable in developing the cost side of the budget because they provide a reliable and convenient source of data for converting the budgeted production schedule into requirements for raw materials, labour and services.

ADVANTAGES OF STANDARD COSTING

Standard costing is a system of cost accounting which facilitates the performance of the entire managerial process — planning, organisation, coordination and control. Among the many advantages generally attributed to standard costing, the most important may be listed as follows:

1. Managerial planning: Planning is a process of using all resources in such a manner that maximises business profits. Management must plan for efficient and economic operations for standard costs to be effective. The standard costs, carefully determined, will disclose inefficiencies in operations, which can be thoroughly investigated and remedial action taken. Standard costs are more convenient than actual costs for budget preparation because the standard costs at different production levels and for different product mixes are readily built up into total costs as called for by the budget. On the other hand, using actual costs requires a great deal of analysis and adjustment when extensive changes in product volume or product-mixes take place. Furthermore, actual costs are influenced by many temporary or random influences which make it difficult to predict the future behaviour of unstandardised costs.

2. Coordination: The establishment of standards coordinates all functions-manufacturing, marketing, engineering, research and accounting towards the achievement of a common goal. Setting standards involves defining and communicating targets so that they can work towards the attainment of the goal.

3. Cost control: Cost control and cost reduction are probably the most important aims of any costing system; and standard costing gives due recognition to this fact. Cost control has the objective of production of the required quality at the lowest cost attainable under existing conditions. Effective control requires detailed standards, to show how much of each material should be used, how much labour should be required for each operation, and what facilities and services will be needed, Standards enable management to make periodic comparison of actual costs with standard costs in order to measure performance and to take action to maintain control over costs. Standard costs help management in cost control through the principle of exception i.e., highlighting only those activities which fail to come up to standard or which exceed the standard. The off standard conditions can be investigated and proper action can be taken before they continue for a long time. Standards help develop cost conscious attitudes, because it makes cost variances clearly observable by the management. Cost consciousness tends to reduce costs and encourage economies in all phases of the business and guides management towards improvement.

4. Economical means of costing and record-keeping: The use of standard costs can reduce clerical labour and expenses by avoiding the detailed record-keeping which is necessary when actual costs alone are used. The following benefits are derived which reduce the cost of record-keeping:

(*i*) By carrying inventory at standard cost, store ledgers can be kept in terms of quantities only. This eliminates much clerical time in pricing and balancing items on the stores ledger. Total standard cost of inventory can readily be obtained at any time by multiplying the quantity in stock by the standard unit cost.

(*ii*) When standard costs are used, requisition or bills for materials to be put into production can be written and priced more rapidly than when the goods must be priced at actual cost. Infact materials requisitions, labour time tickets and production cost cards can be prepared in advance of production.

(*iii*) The standard cost of goods finished can be obtained immediately upon completion since it is necessary to multiply the quantity by the unit standard cost. Simple and economical costing methods can be used in place of elaborate costing methods.

(*iv*) The time required to prepare reports which are used by management can be reduced. Since most reports are useful in proportion to their timeliness, standard costing helps management to take remedial action promptly by providing useful and timely reports of variances.

(*v*) The time which must be devoted by management to the study and analysis of cost reports is much reduced when standard costs are used. Standard costs tend to eliminate unnecessary details and focus on those aspects which acquire management attention and thus bring economies and effectiveness in management reporting.

(*vi*) The time required to assemble cost data for budget preparation or special cost studies such as pricing is reduced because it is not necessary to devote so much time to the analysis and collection of past actual costs.

5. Formulating price and production policies: Standard costs as compared to actual costs can be used for estimating selling prices. When standard unit costs are available, expected costs and sales prices can be computed on the basis of standard costs. Standards already established can easily be modified to reflect current conditions and changes in material prices or labour rates and the price of the product can be determined on a realistic basis. Also, the problem of absorption of fixed overheads is better tackled and simplified by using standard costs. Standard costs are predetermined costs which help management in the decision process by providing standard unit costs for various levels of activity. These costs are thus useful to management in determining price policies, preparing bids for prospective others, planning production of new products and new methods and furnishing cost estimates for all managerial decisions.

Actual costs, on the other hand, may reflect excessive usage of material, abnormal labour times or an inequitable charge for overheads. Actual overhead cost per unit at any given time may be so influenced by temporary fluctuations in production levels as to make actual cost entirely unusable for pricing. Standard costs, on the contrary, are based upon carefully determined and planned usages of material, labour and overhead facilities and thus are free from accidental and temporary distortions caused by excessive spoilage, reoperation, abnormal factors, etc.

Necessary adjustments in standards to incorporate changing conditions can be done without any difficulty whenever required. Standard overhead rates are determined upon a normal production or activity level and therefore, provide an acceptable base for determining product prices which will recover full overhead costs in the long run.

6. Standards as incentives to employees: If standards are reasonable and attainable, they act as incentives to employees to improve their performances and to maintain the quality of the product. Each worker performs his job with advance knowledge of the standard set for the particular job; he knows that if his work is less than the standard, he is responsible for the variance. Standards motivate workers, supervisors and foremen to work more efficiently in the accomplishment of their respective standards. Many incentives like cash bonus, individual and group bonus, prizes, vacation time and promotions can be given for equalling or surpassing standards. Similarly, the management can decide upon action to be taken for below standard performance.

DIFFERENT TYPES OF STANDARDS

The two principal considerations affecting the classification of standards are: (*i*) attainability of standards, that is, the ease with which it is possible to achieve the standards, and (*ii*) frequency with which the standards are revised. On the basis of these two factors, it is possible to classify standards as ideal, normal, basic, current or expected actual standards.

Ideal, Perfect, Maximum Efficiency or Theoretic Standards

Ideal standards (costs) are the standards which can be attained under the most favourable conditions possible. The level of performance under ideal standards would be achieved through the best possible combination of factors — the most favourable prices for materials and labour, highest output with best equipment and layout and maximum efficiency in the utilisation of the production resources – in other words, maximum output at minimum cost. Such standards reflects only goals or targets without any hope of performance being currently achieved. These standards are extremely tight and does not provide for waste and inefficiency in any form; no material is wasted; no units are spoiled; there are no idle hours; operator's work at predetermined speeds, the available capacity is fully utilised. The ideal standard represents the ultimate goal to strive for, but its attainment is impossible over sustained periods. It sets its sights on the stars.

Normal Standards

Normal standards are the average standards which (it is anticipated) can be attained during a future period of time, preferably long enough to cover one business cycle. Standards are set on a normal capacity basis which represent a volume that average out the company' peak and slack periods. Constant unit costs are employed throughout the cycle, regardless of changes in current costs or selling prices. These standards are not revised until the cycle has run its full course. This generally results in an incorrect valuation of inventories and consequent errors in the profit disclosed as the inventories are understated in periods of high prices, and overstated when prices are low. Normal standards are mainly used as a device to solve the problem of absorbing fixed overheads rather than in connection with material cost and wages. Since these standards do not reflect the goals to be attained, they are not often used.

Basic Standards

The Institute of Cost and Management Accountants (UK) defines a basic standard as the standard which is established for use unaltered for an indefinite period which may be a long period of time. Basic standards are seldom revised or updated to reflect current operating costs and price level changes. Basic standards representing a fixed base are used primarily to measure trends in operating performance. Although useful basic standards must be adjusted before they can be used for performance evaluation purposes, they can be based upon any capacity level that is selected initially to develop the standards.

Currently Attainable or Expected Actual Standards

Current standards are standards which are established for use over a short period of time, and are related to current conditions. They represent current costs to be expected from efficient operations. These standards do not anticipate ideal performance; they are difficult but possible to achieve. Currently attainable standards are formulated after making allowance for the cost of normal spoilage, cost of idle time due to machine breakdowns and the cost of other events which are unavoidable in normal efficient operations. They take the place of actual cost and are recorded in account books and financial statements. Any deviation from these standards reflect inefficiencies in the production activities, unless the variances have occurred due to uncontrollable factors. Currently attainable standards are revised to reflect changes in methods and prices. Much effort and costs are involved in developing these standards. Based on engineering estimates, currently attainable standards are the most expensive of the four types of standards. But these standards are most accurate and very useful to the management in product costing, inventory valuations; estimates, analysis, performance evaluation, planning, employee motivation and for managerial decision making and external financial reporting.

HOW TIGHT SHOULD STANDARD BE?

The establishment of standards or standard cost is decided by the use to be made of them. It can be rightly said that a single standard may not be suitable for all purposes. For the purposes of cost control, tight standards need to be established. The attainable (good) performance standards are useful for purposes of inventory valuation, product costing and income determination. Realistic standards are needed for pricing decisions and capital expenditure decisions.

High Standards

A high standard helps in cost reduction and motivating employees to try to reach the targets established. High standards represent the best possible performance and if achieved, raise the level of performance and efficiency as compared to poor or loose standards. High standards being unattainable in practice may not be good for the employees. Employees may not seriously accept them because they know that they are unattainable and impossible to achieve. Employees will always have an opportunity to explain away or excuse the failure to reach them. They are also not realistic and therefore cannot be used in product costing, inventory, valuation, financial statement, planning and capital investment decisions.

Law (Loose) Standards

A standard which is low or loose can be attained by poor performance. However, it defeats the purpose of standard costing and fails to disclose inefficiencies. Similarly, standards set in terms of average past performance expect too little. Since jobs on which performance is poor are likely to be more numerous than are jobs on which performance is exceptionally good, average past performance standards are usually considerably looser. Such standards do not help the management in cost control as they are not accurate measures to compare actual results.

In conclusion, it can be said that accountants generally seem to favour currently attainable standards which are most appropriate for performance appraisal, accounting purposes, cost control and decision-making. Such standards produce good performance, promote employee motivation and include unavoidable elements, such as spoilage, lost time and capacity not utilised in setting standards.

Variance Analysis

The function of standards in cost accounting is to reveal variances between standard costs which are allowed and actual costs which have been recorded. The Institute of Cost and Management Accountants (UK) defines variance as the difference between a standard cost and the comparable actual cost incurred during a period. Variance analysis can be defined as the process of computing the amount of, and isolating the cause of variances between actual costs and standard costs. Variance analysis involves two phases:

(*i*) Computation of individual variances and

(*ii*) Determination of the cause(s) of each variance.

First, we concentrate on the computation of material, labour and factory overhead variances. Analysis of causes, reporting variances to managers and accounting disposition of variances conclude the study of standard costing.

MATERIAL VARIANCES

The following variances constitute material variances:

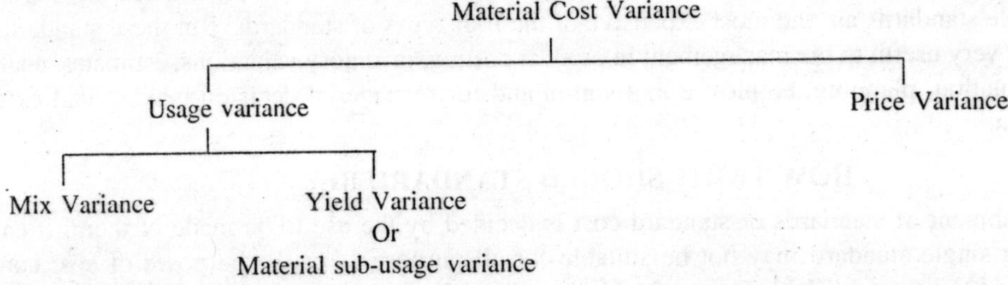

Material Cost Variance

Material cost variance is the difference between the actual cost of direct materials used and standard cost of direct materials specified for the output achieved. This variance results from differences between qualities consumed and quantities of materials allowed for production and from differences between prices paid and prices predetermined. This can be computed by using the following formula:

Material cost variance = $(AQ \times AP) - (SQ \times SP)$

When AQ = Actual quantity

AP = Actual Price

SQ = Standard quantity for the actual output and

SP = Standard Price

Material Usage Variance

The material quantity or usage variance results when actual quantities of raw materials used in production differ from standard quantities that should have been used to produce the output achieved. It is that portion of the direct materials cost variance which is due to the difference between the actual quantity used and standard quantity specified. As a formula this variance is shown as:

Materials quantity variance = (Actual quantity – Standard Quantity) × Standard Price

A material usage variance is favourable when the total actual quantity of direct materials used is less than the total standard quantity allowed for the actual output.

Example:

Compute the materials usage variance from the following information:

Standard material cost per unitMaterials issued		
Material A – 2 pieces @ Re. 1.00 =	2.00	Material A 2,050 pieces
Material B – 3 pieces @ Rs. 2.00 =	6.00	Material B 2,980 pieces
	Rs. 8.00	
Units completed	1,000	

Solution:

Materials usage variance = (Actual quantity – Standard Quantity) × Standard Price.

Material A = (2,050 – 2,000) × Rs. 1.00 = Rs. 50 (Adverse or unfavourable)

Material B = (2.980 – 3,000) × Rs. 2 = Rs. 40 (Favourable)

It should be noted that the standard rather than the actual price is used in computing the usage variance. Use of an actual price would have introduced a price factor into a quantity variance. Because different departments are responsible, there two factors must be separate.

Materials Price Variance

A materials price variance occurs when raw materials are purchased at a price different from standard price. It is that portion of the direct materials which is due to the difference between actual price paid and standard price specified and cost variance multiplied by the actual quantity.

Expressed as a formula,

Materials price variance = (Actual price – Standard Price) × Actual quantity.

Materials price variance is unfavourable when the actual price paid exceeds the predetermined standard price. It is advisable that materials price variance should be calculated for materials purchased rather than materials used. Purchase of materials is an earlier event than the use of materials. Therefore, a variance based on quantity purchased is basically an earlier report than a variance based on quantity actually used. This is quite beneficial from the viewpoint of performance measurement and corrective action. An early report will help the management in measuring the performance so that poor performance can be corrected or good performance can be expanded at an early date.

Example:

Assuming in Example 1 that material A was purchased at the rate of Re. 1.00 and material B was purchased at the rate of Rs 2.10, the material price variance will be as follows:

Materials price variance = (Actual Price – Standard Price) × Actual Quantity

Material A = (1,00 – 1.00) × 2,050 = Zero

Material B = (2.10 – 2.00) × 2,980 = 298 (Unfavourable)

Total Material price variance = Rs. 298 (Unfavourable)

The total of materials usage variance and price variance is equal to materials cost variance.

Materials Mix Variance

The materials usage or quantity variance can be separated into mix variance and yield variance.

For certain products and processing operations, material mix is an important operating variable. Specific grades of materials and quantity are determined before production begins. A mix variance will result when materials are not actually placed into production in the same ratio as the standard formula. For instance, if a product is produced by adding 100 kg. of raw material A and 200 kg of raw material B, the standard material mix ratio is 1:2. Actual raw materials used must be in this 1:2 ratio, otherwise a materials mix variance will be found. Material mix variance is usually found in industries, such as textiles, rubber and chemicals, etc. A Mix variance may arise because of attempts to achieve cost saving, effective resources utilisation and when the needed raw materials quantities may not be available at the required time.

Materials mix variance is that portion of the materials quantity variance which is due to the difference between the actual composition of a mixture and the standard mixture. It can be computed by using the following formula:

Material mix variance = (standard cost of actual quantity of the actual mixture – standard cost of actual quantity of the standard mixture)

Or

Materials mix variance = (Actual mix – Revised standard mix of actual input) × Standard price.

Revised standard proportion is calculated as follows:

$$\frac{\text{Standard mix of a particular material} \times \text{Actual input}}{\text{Total standard quantity}}$$

Example:

A product is made from two raw materials, materials A and materials B. One unit of finished product requires 10 kg of materials. The following is standard mix:

Materials A – 20%	2 kg @ Rs. 2.00 =	Rs. 4.00
Materials B – 80%	8 kg @ Rs. 1.00 =	Rs. 8.00
100%	10 kg. Rs.1.20	Rs. 12.00

During a period one unit of product was produced at the following costs:

Material A –	8 kg @ Rs. 2.00 =	Rs.16.00
Material B –	4 kg @ Rs. 1.25 =	Rs. 5.00
	12 kg Rs. 1.75	Rs. 21.00

Compute the materials mix variances.

Solution:

Materials mix variance = (Actual proportion – Revised standard proportion of actual input) × Standard price.

Revised standard proportion

$$\frac{\text{Standard proportion of a particular mix} \times \text{Actual input}}{\text{Total standard quantity}}$$

Revised standard proportion:

Material A = 2/10 × 12 = 2.40 kg.

Material B = 8/10 × 12 = 9.60 kg.

Materials Mix Variance:

Material A = (8 kg. – 2.40 kg.) × 2.00 = 5.60 × 2.00

= 5.60 × 2.00 = Rs.11.20 (Unfavourable)

Material B = (4 kg. – 9.60) × 1.00

= 5.60 × 1.00 = Rs. 5.60 (Favourable)

Total mix variance = Rs 5.60 (Unfavourable)

Materials Yield Variance

Materials yield variance explains the remaining portion of the total materials quantity variance. It is that portion of materials usage variance which is due to the difference between the actual yield obtained and standard yield specified (in terms of actual input) . In other words, yield variance occurs when the out put of the final product does not correspond without that could have been obtained by using the actual inputs. In some industries like sugar, chemicals, steel etc. actual yield may differ from expected yield based on actual input resulting into yield variance.

The total of materials mix variance and materials yield variance equals materials quantity of usage variance . When there is no materials mix variance the materials yield variance equals the total material mix variance the material yield variance equals the total materials quantity variance. Accordingly mix and yield variances explain distinct parts of the total materials usage and are additive. The formula for computing yield variance is as follows:

Yield variance + (Actual yield – Standard yield specified) × Standard cost per unit

Example:

Standard input = 100 tonnes, standard yield = 90 tonnes, standard cost per tonne of output = Rs. 20 Actual input 200 tonnes, actual yield 182 tonnes. Compute the yield variance.

Solution:

Standard yield for the actual input = $\frac{90}{100} \times 200 = 180$ tonne

Yield variance = (Actual yield – Standard yield for the actual input) × standard cost per unit

= 182 – 180 × Rs. 20

= 2 × 20 =40 (favourable)

The above yield variance can be computed by using another formula also, *e.g.*, Yield variance = (Actual loss – Standard loss on actual input) × Standard cost per unit.

= (18 tonnes – 20 tonnes) × Rs. 20

= Rs. 40 (Favourable)

In this example, there is no mix variance and therefore e, the materials usage variance will be equal to the materials yield variance.

The above formula uses output or loss as the basis of computing the yield variance which can also be computed on the basis of input factors only. The fact is that loss in input equals loss in output. A lower yield simply means that a higher quantity of input has been used and the anticipated or standard output (Based on Actual inputs) has not been achieved. Yield, in such a case, is known as sub-usage variance (or revised usage variance) which can be computed by using the following formula:

Sub-usage or revised usage variance = (Revised Standard Proportion of actual input – standard quantity) x Standard cost per unit of input

Example:

Standard material and standard price for manufacturing one unit of a product is given below:

	Standard material	*Standard Price*
Material A	5 kg	@ Rs. 4
Material B	3 kg	@ Rs. 6

The actual production of the product is 400 units

The actual material A 2500 kg @ Rs 3,90

B 1000 kg @ Rs. 6.25

Calculate the materials sub-usage variance

Solution:

Revised standard proportion of actual input

Material A = 5/8 × 3500 = 2187.5 kg

Material B = 3/8 × 3500 = 1312.5 kg

Material sub usage variance:

(Revised standard proportion of actual input –standard quantity) x SP

Material A = (2187.5 – 2.000) × 4 =187.5 × 4 = Rs. 7450 (Unfavourable)

Material B = (1,312.5 – 1,200) × 6 = 112.5 × 6 = Rs. 675 (Unfavourable)

Total materials sub usage variance = Rs. 1,425 (unfavourable)

$$\text{Or } (3{,}500 - 3{,}200) \times \text{Rs. } \frac{15,200}{3,200}$$

$$= 300 \times \frac{15,200}{3,200} = \text{Rs. } 1{,}425 \text{ (unfavourable)}$$

Materials yield variance always equals sub-usage variance. The difference lies only in terms of calculation. The former considers the output or loss in output and the latter considers standard input and actual input used for the actual output. Mix and yield variance both provide useful information for production control, performance evaluation and review of operating efficiency.

Example 1

From the following particulars, compute: (*a*) materials cost variance; (*b*) materials price variance and (*c*) materials usage variance:

Quantity of materials purchased	3,000 units
Value of materials purchased	Rs. 9,000
Standard quantity of materials required per tonne of output	30 Units
Standard rate of materials	Rs. 2.50 per unit
Opening stock of materials	Nil
Closing Stock of materials	500 units
Output during the period	80 tonnes

Solution:

Materials consumed = 3,000 – 500 = 2,500 units

Actual rate of material = Rs. $\frac{9,000}{3,000}$ = Rs. 3 per unit

Standard quantity for actual output = 30 × 80 = 2,400 units

Materials cost variance = Actual cost – Standard Cost

= (Actual price × Actual quantity) – (SP × Standard quantity)

= Rs. 3 × 2,500 – Rs. 2.50 × 2,400 = 7,500 – 6,000 = Rs. 1,500 (Adverse)

Materials price variance = Actual quantity (Actual price – Standard price)

= Rs. 2,500 (Rs. 3 – Rs. 2.50)

= Rs. 1,250 (Adverse)

Materials usage variance = (AQ – SQ) × SP

= (2,500 – 2,400) × Rs. 2.50

= Rs. 250 (Adverse)

Example 2

The standard materials cost to produce a tone of a chemical is:

300 kg. of material A @ Rs. 10 per kg.

400 kg. of material B @ Rs. 5 per kg.

500 kg. of material C @ Rs. 6 per kg.

During a period, 100 tonnes of mixture x was produced from the usage of:

35 tonnes of material A at a cost of Rs. 9,000 per tonne

42 tonnes of material B at a cost of Rs. 6,000 per tonne

53 tonnes of material C at a cost of Rs. 7,000 per tonne

Calculate the price, usage and mix variances

Solution:

Material	*Standard*			*Actual*		
	Qty. (kg)	*Rate (Rs.)*	*Amount (Rs.)*	*Qty. (kg)*	*Rate (Rs.)*	*Amount (Rs.)*
A	30,000	10	3,00,000	35,000	9	3,15,000
B	40,000	5	2,00,000	42,000	6	2,52,000
C	50,000	6	3,00,000	53,000	7	3,71,000
	1,20,000		8,00,000	1,30,000		9,38,000

(1) Materials cost variance = Actual cost – Standard cost for actual output = Rs. 9,38,000 – Rs. 8,00,000 = Rs. 1,38,000 (Adverse)

(2) Materials price variance = Actual quantity × (actual price- standard price)

A = 35,000 × (9 – 10) = Rs. 35,000 (F)
B = 42,000 × (6 – 5) = Rs. 42,000 (A)
C = 53,000 × (7 – 6) = Rs. 53,000 (A)

Total Rs. 60,000 (A)

(3) Material usage variance = Standard price × Actual quantity – Standard quantity for actual output)

A = Rs. 10 × (35,000 – 30,000) =Rs. 50,000(A)
B = 5 × (42,000-40,000) = Rs. 10,000 (A)
C = 6 × (53,000 –50,000) = Rs. 18,000 (A)

Total: Rs. 78,000 (A)

(4) Materials mix variance = standard price × (Actual quantity – Revised Standard Quantity)

A = Rs. 10 × (35,000 – 32,500)
= 10 × 2,500 = Rs. 25,000 (A)

$$B = 5 \times \left(42,000 - \frac{1,30,000}{3}\right)$$

$$= 5 \times \frac{4,000}{3} = \text{Rs. } 6,667 \text{ (F)}$$

$$C = 6 \times \left(53,000 - \frac{1,62,500}{3}\right)$$

$$= 6 \times \frac{3,500}{3} = 7,000\ (F)$$

Total: 11,333 (*A*)

Working notes:

$$\text{(1) Revised standard quantity} = \frac{\text{Standard quantity of a mix} \times \text{Total actual quantity}}{\text{Total standard quantity of mixture}}$$

$$A = \frac{30,000}{1,20,000} \times 1,30,000 = 32,500 \text{ kg.}$$

$$B = \frac{40,000}{1,20,000} \times 1,30,000 = \frac{1,30,000 \text{ kg}}{3}$$

$$C = \frac{50,000}{1,20,000} \times 1,30,000 = \frac{1,62,500}{3} \text{ kg.}$$

$$\text{(2) Std. cost per unit of output} = \frac{\text{Total standard cost}}{\text{Total standard output}}$$

$$= \frac{\text{Rs.}8,00,000}{100} = \text{Rs. } 8,000 \text{ per tonnes}$$

(3) Standard Output for actual mix = $\dfrac{\text{Standard output}}{\text{Standard mix}}$ × Actual mix

$$= \frac{100 \times 1{,}30{,}000}{1{,}20{,}000}$$

$$= \frac{1{,}300 \text{ tonnes}}{12}$$

(4) Materials yield variance (although not asked for in the question would be calculated as follows:

Materials yield variance = (Actual output – standard output for actual mixture) × Standard cost per unit of output

$$= \left(100 - \frac{1{,}300}{12}\right) \times \text{Rs. } 8{,}000$$

$$= 100/12 \text{ x Rs. } 8{,}000$$

$$= \text{Rs. } 66{,}667 \text{ (Adverse)}$$

Example 3:

The standard cost card for product SLMCO reveals:

Standard materials	
2 kg of A Rs. 2 per kg	4.00
1 kg. of B Rs. 6 per kg	6.00
Direct labour (3 hours @ Rs. 6 per hour)	18.00
Variable Overheads (3 hour @ Rs. 4 per direct labour hour	12.00
Total Standard Cost per unit	40.00

It is proposed to produce 10,000 unit of SIMCO in the month of March and budgeted cost based on the information contained in the standard cost card are as follows:

	Rs.
Direct Materials	
A 20,000 kg @ Rs. 2 per kg.	40,000
B 10,000 kg Rs. 6 per kg.	60,000
Direct Labour (30,000 hours @ Rs. 6 per hour)	1,80,000
Variable overhead (30,000 hours @ Rs. 4 per direct labour)	1,20,000
Total	4,00,000

The actual results are:

Direct Material	
A 19,000 kg @ Rs. 2.20 per kg.	41,800
B 10,000 kg @ Rs. 5.60 per kg.	56,560
Direct labour (28,500 hour @ Rs. 6.40 per hour)	1,82,400
Variable overheads	1,04,000
	3,84,760

Actual production was 9,000 units

From the above, calculate the following variance:

(*a*) Materials: Price and usage

(*b*) Labour: Wage rate and labour efficiency

(*c*) Variable overhead total and overhead expenditure variance

Solution:

Materials Price Variance = Actual Qty. × (Actual Rate – Standard Rate)

A =	19,000 × (2.20 – 2)	Rs. 3,800 (A)
B =	10,100 × (5.60 – 6)	Rs. 4,040 (F)
		Rs. 240 (F)

Materials usage variance = Standard Rate × (Actual Quantity – Std. Qty. for Actual output)

A =	2 × (19,00 – 18,000)	Rs. 2,000 (A)
B =	6 × (10,000 – 9,000)	Rs. 6,600 (A)
		Rs 8,600 (A)

Labour Rate Variance = Actual time × (Actual Rate – Standard Rate)

= 28,500 × (6.40 – 6) = Rs. 11,400 (A)

Labour efficiency variance = Standard Rate × (Actual time – Standard time for actual output)

= 6 × (28,500 – 27,000) = Rs. 9,000(A)

Total Variable overhead variance = Actual Variable Overheads – Standard Variable overheads

= 1,04,000 – 9,000 × 12

= 1,04,000 – 1,08,000 = Rs. 4,000 (F)

Overhead (Variable)

Expenditure variance = Actual Variable Overheads – Std. Variable overheads

= 1,04,000 – 28,500 × Rs. 4

= 1,04,000 – 1,14,000 = Rs. 10,000 (F)

Example 4

A company manufacturing 'distempers' operates a costing system. The standard cost of one of the products of the company shows the following standards:

Materials	*Quantity*	*Standard price per kg*	*Total*
Rs.	*Rs.*		
A	40 kg.	75	3,000
B	10 kg.	50	500
C	50 kg.	20	1,000
Material cost per unit (total)			4,500

The standard input mix is 100 kg. and the standard output of the finished product is 90 kg..

The actual results for the period are:

Material Used

A = 240,000 kg. @ Rs. 80/kg.

B = 40,000 kg. @ Rs. 52/kg.

C = 220,000 kg.@ Rs. 21 kg.

Actual output of the finished product = 4,20,000 kg..

You are required to calculate the material price, mix and yield variance.

Solution:

Material	Standard Qty/kg.	Standard Rate	Standard Amount	Actual Qty	Actual Rate	Actual Amount
A	2,00,000	75	1,50,000	2,40,000	80	1,92,00,000
B	50,000	50	25,00,000	40,000	52	20,80,000
C	2,50,000	20	50,00,000	2,20,000	21	46,20,000
	5,00,000		2,25,00,000	5,00,000		2,59,00,000

Standard output 4,50,000
Actual out put 4,20,000

Materials Cost Variance = (Actual cost – Standard cost of actual output)
= 2,59,00,000 – 4,20,000 × 50
= Rs. 49,000,000 (A)

Materials price variance = Actual quantity. × (Actual rate – standard rate)

A = 2,40,000 × (80 – 75) = 12,00,000 (A)
B = 40,000 × (52 – 50) = 80,000 (A)
C = 2,20,000 × (21 – 20) = 2,20,000 (A)
= 15,00,000

Materials usages variance = standard rate × (Actual qty – Standard quantity for actual output)

A = 75 × (2,40,000 – 2,00,000 × 42/45) = 40,000,000 (A)
B = 50 × (40,000 – 50,000 × 42/45) = 3,33,333 (F)
C = 20 × (2,20,000 – 2,50,000 × 42/45) = 2,166,667 (F)
34,00,000 (A)

Material Mix Variance + Standard rate × (Actual quantity – Revised standard quantity)

A = 75(2,40,000- 2,00,000) = 30,00,000 (A)
B = 50 (40,000 – 50,000) = 5,00,000 (F)
C = 20 (2,20,000 – 2,50,000) = 6,00,000 (F)
19,00,000

Material yield

Variance = Standard cost per unit × (Actual output – Standard output for actual mix)
= 50(4,20,000 – 4,50,000)
= Rs. 15,00,000 (A)

Example 5

One kilogram of product 'K' requires two chemicals A and B. The following were the details of product 'K' for the month of June 1987.

(*a*) Standard mix chemical 'A' 50% and chemical 'B' 50%

(*b*) Standard price per kilogram of chemical 'A' Rs. 12 and chemical 'B' Rs. 15.

(*c*) Actual input of chemical 'b' 70 kilograms.

(*d*) Actual price per kilogram of chemical 'A' Rs. 15.

(*e*) Standard normal loss 10% of total input

(*f*) Materials cost variance total Rs. 650 adverse.

(*g*) Materials yield variance total Rs. 135 adverse.

You are required to calculate:

1. Materials mix
2. Materials usage variance total.
3. Materials price variance total
4. Actual loss of actual input
5. Actual input of chemical 'A' and
6. Actual price per kilogram of chemical 'B'.

Solution:

Working Notes:

1. In the question actual output has not been given. It has been presumed that the actual output is 90 kgs. In case actual output is presumed to be different, the resultant variance will also be different.
2. The standard input for actual output has been worked out as follows:

   Total Mix = 90 × 100/90 =100 kg.

   Since the proportion of A and B in total mix is equal, the standard input of material A and B will be 50 kg. each.
3. Material cost variance total is Rs. 650 (A). It means the actual cost of material is Rs. 2,000 (i.e., (50 × 12 + 50 × 15) + 650)
4. Material yield variance is Rs. 135 (A). The standard output for actual mix has been ascertained as follows:

   Material yield = Standard cost per unit × (Actual output – Standard output for actual mix)

$$135\ (A) = \frac{1{,}350}{90} \times (90 - x)$$

$$\text{or } 135(A) = 15\ (90) - x)$$

$$135 = 1{,}350 - 15x$$

$$15x = 1{,}350 = 135 = 1{,}485$$

$$x = 99$$

The standard output for actual mix is 99 kg. The actual input should therefore be 99 x 100/ 99= 110 kg.

(5) Total actual mix is 110 kg. out of which 70 kg. is that of material B. Hence, the input of material A should be 40 kg.

(6) The total,actual cost of material A is Rs. 600 (i.e., 40 × 15), while the total actual cost of output is Rs. 2,000. The total actual cost of material B is therefore Rs.1,400 (i.e. 2,000 – 600). The rate per kg of material B comes to Rs. 20 per kg. From the above details the following table can be prepared;

Chemical	Standard			Actual		
	Qty.	*Rate*	*Amount*	*Qty.*	*Rate*	*Amount*
A	50	12	600	40	15	600
B	50	15	750	70	20	1,400
	100		1,350	110		2,000

Standard output for actual mix: 99 kg;

Actual output for actual mix: 90 kg

The information desired by the question can now be ascertained as follows:

1. Material Mix Variance = Standard Rate × Actual Quantity – Revised Quantity)

$$A = 12 \times \left(\frac{40 - 50 \times 100}{100}\right)$$

$$= 12 \times (40 - 55) = 180 \text{ (F)}$$

$$B = 15 \times \left(\frac{70 - 110 \times 50}{100}\right)$$

$$= 15 \times (70 - 55) = 225 \text{ (A)}$$

Total: 45 (A)

2. Material usage variance = Standard Rate × (Actual quantity – Standard quantity) for actual output

A = 12 × (40 – 50) = 120 (F)
B = 15 × (70 – 50) = 300 (A)
180 (A)

3. Material Price Variance = Actual quantity × (Actual Rate – Standard Rate)

A = 40 × (15 – 12) = 120 (A)
B = 70 × (20 – 15) = 350 (A)
470 (A)

4. Actual Loss of Actual Input:

Actual Input	110
Actual Output	90
Loss	20

Example 6

The standard material cost for a normal mix of one tonne of chemical X is based on:

Chemical	*Usage*	*Price per kg.*
A	240 kg	Rs. 6
B	400	12
C	640	10

During a month, 6.25 tonnes of X were produced from:

Chemical	*Consumption (Tonnes)*	*Cost (Rs.)*
A	1.6	11,200
B	2.4	30,000
C	4.5	47,250
	8.5	88.450

Analyse the variances.

Solution:

(*a*) Total Materials cost variance = (Actual Cost – Standard cost for actual output)
= Rs. 88,450 – Rs 79,000
= Rs. 9,450 (Adverse)

Standard materials cost for 6.25 tonnes of X:

	Quantity (Tonne)	*Rate (Rs. per tonne)*	*Cost (Rs.)*
A	$\frac{240}{1000} \times 6.25 = 1.5$	6,000	9,000
B	$\frac{400}{1,000} \times 6.25 = 2.5$	12,000	30,000
C	$\frac{6,400}{1,000} \times 6.25 = 4.0$	10,000	40,000
	8.0	9,875	79,000

(*b*) Materials price variance = Actual quantity × (Actual price – Std. price)
= A 1.6 × (7000 – 6000) = 1,600 (a)
= B 2.4 × (12,500- 12,000) = 1,200 (A)
= C 4.5 × (10,500 – 10,000) = 2,250 (A)
Total =Rs. 5,050 (A)

(*c*) Material usage variance = Standard rate × (Actual quantity – Standard quantity for actual output
A = 6,000 × (1.6 – 1.5) = Rs. 600 (A)
B = 12,000 × (2.4 – 2.5) = Rs. 1,200 (F)
C = 10,000 × (4.5 – 4.0) = Rs. 5,000 (A)
Total Rs. 4,400 (Adverse)

(*d*) Materials mix variance = Standard rate × (Actual quantity – Revised standard quantity)

$$A = 6,000 \times \left(\frac{1.6}{1} - \frac{12.75}{8}\right) = 37.5 \text{ (A)}$$

$$B = 12,000 \times \left(\frac{2.4}{1} - \frac{21.25}{8}\right) = 3,075 \text{ (F)}$$

$$C = 10,000 \times \left(\frac{4.5}{1} - \frac{34}{8}\right) = \quad 2,500 \text{ (A)}$$

537.50 (F)

$$\text{Revised standard quantity} = \frac{\text{Actual mix} \times \text{Standard quantity}}{\text{Standard mix}}$$

A $\frac{8.5}{8} \times 1.5 = \frac{12.75}{8}$

B $\frac{8.5}{8} \times 2.5 = \frac{21.25}{8}$

C $\frac{8.5}{8} \times 4 = \frac{34}{8}$

(*e*) Yield variance = Standard Cost per tonne × (Actual output – Standard output for actual mix)

$$= \text{Rs. } 12,640 \times \frac{6.25}{8} \times (6.25 - 850)$$

= Rs. 4,937.5 (Adverse)

$$= \frac{79,000}{6.25} = \text{Rs. } 12.640$$

Standard cost is Rs. 7900.

Example 7

SV. Ltd. manufacture BXE by mixing three raw materials for every batch of 100 kgs of BXE, 1255 kgs of raw material are used. In February 1986, 60 batches were prepared to produce output of 5,600 of BXE. The standard and actual particulars for February 1986 are as under:

Raw Material	*Mix%*	*Standard price per kg Rs.*	*Mix %*	*Actual price per kg Rs.*	*Quantity of Raw Materials purchased kg Rs.*
A	50	20	60	21	5,000
B	30	10	20	8	2,000
C	20	5	20	6	1,200

Calculate:

(*i*) Material Cost Variance (*ii*) Material Price Variance (*iii*) Material Mix Variance and (*iv*) Material yield variance).

Solution:

Raw	Standard Kg	Standard Rate	Standard Amount	Actual Kg	Actual Rate	Actual Amount
Material						
A	3,750	20	75,000	4,500	21	94,500
B	2,250	10	25,000	1,500	8	12,000
C	1,500	5	7,500	1,500	6	9,000
	7,500		1,05,000	7,500		1,15,500

Material Cost

Variance = (Actual Cost – Standard Cost for Actual output)
= 15,500 – 1,05,000/6,000 × 5,600
= 1,15,500 – 98,000 = 17,500 (A)

Material price = Actual quanity × (AR – AR)
Variance A = 4,500 × (21 – 20) = 4,500 (A)
B = 1,500 × (8 – 10) = 3,000 (F)
C = 1,500 × (6 – 5) = 1,500 (A)
3,000 (A)

Material Usage Variance = Standard rate × (Actual Qty – Std. Qty for actual output)

Variance A = $20 \times (4{,}500 - \frac{3{,}750}{6{,}000} \times 5{,}600)$
= 20 × (4,500 – 3,5000) = 20,000 (A)

B = $10 \times (1{,}500 - \frac{2{,}250}{6{,}000} \times 5{,}600)$
= 10 × (1,500 – 2,100) = 6,000(F)

C = $5 \times (1{,}500 - \frac{1{,}500}{6{,}000} \times 5{,}600)$
= 5 × (1,500 – 1,400) = 500 (A)
14,500 (A)

Material Mix Variance = Standard Rate × (Actual Qty – Revised Std. Qty)
A = 20 × (4,500 – 3,750) = 15,000 (A)
B = 10 × (1,500 – 2,250) = 7,500 (F)
C = 5 × (1,500 – 1,500) —
7,500 (A)

Since the Standard Mix and Actual Mix are the same, the Standard Quantity and Revised Standard Quantity will also be the same.

Material yield variance = Standard cost per unit × (Actual output – Standard output for actual mix)

$= \frac{1,05,600}{6,000} \times (5,600 - 6,000)$

$= 17.5 \times 400 = 7,000$ (A)

The Material Yield Variance is equal to Material Sub-usage Variance calculated as follows:

Material = SR × (Revised Standard quantity – Standard Quantity for actual output)

Sub-usage Variance

A = 20 × (3,750 – 3,500) =	5,000 (A)
B = 10 × 2 (2,250 – 2,100) =	1,500 (A)
C = 5 × (1,500 – 1,400) =	500 (A)
	7,000 (A)

Note: The question gives quantity of raw materials purchased and not quantity actually used. It has been presumed that total quantity used was 7,500 kg. In case of material C, purchase amounts to 1,200 kgs. only and hence opening stock has been presumed of 3000 units at Rs. 6 per unit.

Alternative Solution — In case quantity purchased is taken as quantity actual used, the various variances will be as follows:

(*i*) Material

Price variance = Actual quantity × (Actual Rate – Standard Rate)

A = 5,000 × (21 – 20) =	5,000 (A)
B = 2,000 × (8 – 10) =	4,000 (F)
C = 1,200 × (6 – 5) =	1,200 (A)
	Total 2,200 (A)

(*ii*) Material Usage Variance = Standard rate × (Actual quantity– Standard rate)

$A = 20 \times (5,000 - \frac{3,750}{6,000} \times 5,600)$

$= 20 \times (5,000 - 3,500)$

$20 \times 1500 = 30,000$ (A)

$B = 10 \times (2,000 - \frac{2,250}{6,000} \times 5,600)$

$= 10 \times (2,000 - 2,100)$

$= 10 \times 100 =$ 1,000 (F)

$C = 5 \times (1,200 - \frac{1,500}{6,000} \times 5,600)$

$= 5\ (1200 - 1,400)$

$= 5 \times 200 =$ 1,000 (F)

Total 28,000 (A)

Material Mix Variance = Standard rate × Actual quantity – Revised Standard Quantity)

$$\text{Revised Standard Quantity} = \frac{\text{Actual total mix}}{\text{Standard mix}} \times \text{Standard Quantity}$$

$$A = \frac{8,200}{7,500} \times 3,50 = 4,100$$

$$B = \frac{8,200}{7,500} \times 2,250 = 2,460$$

$$C = \frac{8,200}{7,500} \times 1,500 = 1,640$$

A = 20 (5,000 – 4,100) =	18,000 (A)
B = 10 × (2,000 – 2460) =	4,600 (F)
C = 5 (1200 – 1640) =	2200 (F)
Total	11,200 (A)

Material Yield Variance = Standard cost per unit x (Actual output – Standard output actual mix)

$$= \frac{1,05,000}{6,000} \left(5,600 - \frac{6,000}{7,500} \times 8,200\right)$$

$= 17.5 \times (5,600 - 6,650)$

= 16,800 (A)

Material yield variance is equal to material sub-usage variance which can be ascertained as follows:

Material Sub-usage variance = Standard Rate × (Revised standard quantity – Standard quantity for actual output)

A = 20 × (4,100 – 3,500) = 20 × (600) =	12,000 (A)
B = 20 × (2,460 –2,100) = 10 × (360) =	3,600 (A)
C = 5 × (1,640 – 1,400) = 5 × (240) =	1,200 (A)
Total	16,800 (A)

Example 8

Vinak Ltd. produces an article by blending two raw materials. It operates a standard costing system and the following standards have been set for raw materials:

Materials	*Standard mix*	*Standard price per kg*
A	40%	Rs. 4.00
B	60%	Rs. 3.00

The standard loss in processing is 15%.

During April 2002, the company produced 1700 kg of finished output. The position of stock and purchases for the month of April 1980 is as under:

Material	*Stock on 1.4.80 (kg.)*	*Stock on 30.4.80 (kg.)*	*Purchased during April 1980 (kg.)*	*Cost (Rs.)*
A	35	5	800	3,400
B	40	50	1,200	3,000

Calculate the following variances:

(*i*) Material price variance
(*ii*) Material usage variance
(*iii*) Material yield variance
(*iv*) Material mix variance and
(*v*) Total materials cost variance.

Solution:

Standard cost of standard mix

Type of Material	*Standard quantity of material required*	*Standard price per kg*	*Standard quantity*
A	800	Rs. 4	Rs. 3,200
B	1,200	Rs. 3	Rs. 3,600
Total	2,000		6,800

Notes:

1. The loss being 15% to produce 85 kg of articles, the standard quantity of material required is 100 kg. Therefore, to produce 1,700 kg of the article, the standard quantity of material required is 100/85 x 1,700 kg or 2,000 kg.
2. Out of 2,000 kg. of material used, 40% is type A and 60 % is type B, i.e. 800 kg of A and 1,200 kg of B are the standard quantities.

Actual cost

Type of material	*Actual quantity of material used kg.*	*Actual price per kg*	*Actual quantity × Actual price Rs.*
A	830	4.25	3,518.75
B	1,190	2.50	2,995.00
Total	2,020		6,513.75

*Actual quantity of material A is 830 kg: out of this 35 kg is available at the standard price of Rs. 4 per kg and remaining 795 kg at Rs. 4.25 per kg.

Actual quantity of material B used is 1,190 kg; out of this 40 kg is available at the standard price of Rs. 3 per kg and remaining 1,150 kg at Rs. 2.50.

(*i*) Material price variance = Actual quantity × (Actual price – Standard price)

A. Standard price of 8.30 Units @ 4	3,320.00	
Actual price of 35 units @ Rs. 4	140.00	
795 unit @ Rs. 4.25	3,378.75	3,518.75
		198.75 (A)
B. Standard price of 1,190 units @ Rs. 3		3,3570.00
Actual price of 40 units @ Rs. 3	120 .00	
1,150 unit @ Rs. 2.50	2,875.00	2,995.00
		575.00 (F)
		376.75 (F)

(*ii*) Materials (Total) Usage Variance = Standard price x (Actual Quantity – Standard quantity)

A : 4 × (830-800)	120.000(A)
B : 3 × (1,190 – 1,200)	30.00 (F)
	90.00(A)

(*iii*) Material yield variance = Standard rate × (Actual yield – standard yield)

$$\text{Standard rate} = \frac{\text{Total standard cost}}{\text{Yield}} = \text{Rs.}\ \frac{6,700}{1,700} = \text{Rs. 4 per kg}$$

Yield variance = 4 (1,700 – 1,717) or Rs. 68 (A)

* By using 2,000 kg of material, standard yield is 1,700 kg. Therefore, the standard yield by using 2,020 kg of material will be $\left(\frac{1,700}{2,000}\right) \times 2,020$ or 1,71 kg.

(*iv*) Material Mix Variance = Actual quantity × (per unit standard cost of standard mix – per unit standard cost of actual mix)

$$= 2,020\left(\frac{6,800}{2,000} - \frac{6,890}{2,2020}\right)$$

= 2,020 (3.4 – 3.410) or Rs. 22 (A)

(*v*) Materials Cost Variance = (Actual cost – Standard cost)

= Rs. 6513.75 – 6800

= Rs. 286.25 (F)

Example 9

The following details relating to the product 'X' during the month of March 1989 are available. You are required to compute the material and labour cost variance and also to reconcile the standard and the actual cost with the help of such variances:

Standard cost per unit:

Material 50 kg	@ Rs. 40 per kg
Labour 400 hours	@ Rs. 1 per hour

Actual cost for the month:

Material 4,900 kg	@ Rs. 42 per kg
Labour 39,600 hours	@ Rs. 1.10 per hour

Actual production = 100 units

Solution:

Material Cost Variance = Actual cost – Standard cost for actual output

= (4900 × 42) – (100 × 50 × 40)

= (2,05,800 – 2,00,000)

= Rs. 5,800 (Adverse)

Material Price Variance = Actual quantity × (Actual Rate – Standard Rate)

= 4,900 × (42 – 40) = Rs. 9,800 (Adverse)

Material Usage = Standard Rate × (Actual quantity – Standard Quantity for actual output

= 39,600 × 1.10 – 100 × 400 × 1

= 43,560 – 40,000 = Rs. 3,560 (Adverse)

Labour Rate Variance = Actual time × (Actual rate – Standard rate)
= 39,600 × (1.10 – 1) = Rs. 3,960 (Adverse)

Labour efficiency = Std. Rate × (Actual time – Standard for actual output)
Variance = 1 × (39,000 – 40,000) = Rs. 400 (Favourable)

Total Standard cost of 100 units:

Direct Material Cost	Rs. 2,00,000
Direct Labour Cost	Rs. 40,000
	Rs. 2,40,000

Total Actual cost of 100 units:

Direct Material Cost	Rs. 2,05,800
Direct Labour Cost	Rs. 43,560
	Rs. 2,49,360

Reconciliation of Standard and Actual Cost

Standard cost		Rs. 2,40,000
Add: Material Cost Variance:		
MPV	9,800 (A)	
MUV	4,000 (F)	5,800 (A)
Add: Labour cost variance		
LRV	3,960 (A)	
LEV	400 (F)	3,560(A)
Actual cost		2,49,360

Example 10

From the data given below, calculate:

(*a*) Individual material price variance for materials X and Y assuming that price variance are calculated at the time of purchase;

(*b*) Individual material usage variances for materials X and Y assuming that the was no work-in – progress either at the commencement or at the end period.

	X		*Y*	
	Qty kg	*Value* Rs.	*Qty* Kg.	*Value*
Raw Material	2,000	4,000	5,000	6,250
Issues to works	2,150		3,950	
Works stocks of materials				
Opening	300	—	1,000	
Closing	200	—	1,250	

Standard price : Material X: Rs. 1.90 kg
Material Y: Rs 1.30 per kg

Standard usage:	Material X	Material Y
Product A	1kg	1 kg
Product B	0.1 kg	1kg

Output during the period:

Product A 1,130 units

Product B: 2,550 units

Solution

(*a*) Material price variance (At the time of purchase):

Actual Quantity purchased × (Actual rate – Standard Rate)

Material X: 2,000 × (2 – 1.90)

Rs. 200 (Adverse)

Material Y: 5,000 × (1.25 – 1.30)

: Rs. 250 (Favourable)

(*b*) Direct Material actually consumed:

		Material X	*Material Y*
	Opening stock of material in works 300 kg.	1,000 kg.	
	Issuers to works	2,150 kg.	3,950 kg.
Less:	Closing stock with manufacture	200kg.	1,250 kg.
	Material consumed in manufacture	2,250 kg.	3,700 kg.

Out put during the period: A: 1,130 Units

Product: B 2,250 units

Standard Usage of direct material:

	Material X kg.		*Material Y kg.*
Product A: 1,130kg × 1 kg	1,130	1,130 × 1 kg.	1,130
Product B : 2,550 × 0.5kg	1,275	2,550 × 1 kg.	2,550
Total:	2,405 kg.		3,680 kg.

Material price variance = Standard rate × (Actual quantity – Standard quantity for actual output)

Material X = 1.90 × (2,250 – 2,405) = Rs. 294.5 (Favourable)

Material Y = 1.30 × (3,700 – 3,680) = Rs. 26 (Adverse)

LABOUR VARIANCES

Direct labour variances arise when actual labour costs are different from standard labour costs. In analysing labour costs, the emphasis is on labour rates and labour hours. Labour variances constitute the following:

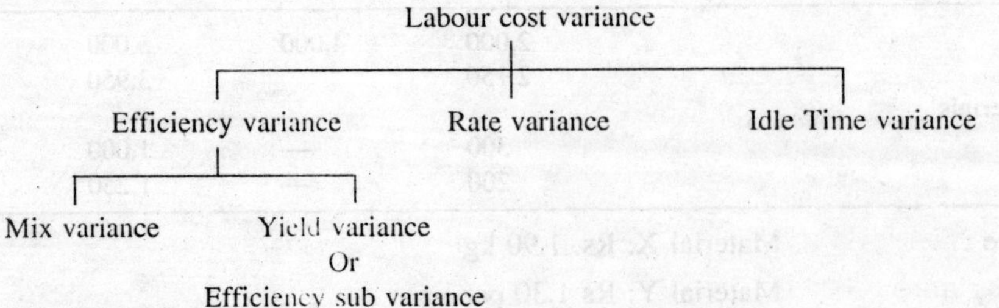

1. Labour Cost Variance

Labour cost variance denotes the difference between the actual direct wages paid and the standard direct wages specified for the output achieved. This variance is calculated by using the following formula:

Labour cost variance = (AH × AR – SH × SR)

Where AH = Actual hours
AR = Actual rate
SH = Standard hours
SR = Standard rate

2. Labour Efficiency Variance

The calculation of labour efficiency or usage variance follows the same pattern as the computation of materials usage variance. Labour efficiency variance occurs when labour operations are more efficient or less efficient than standard performance. If actual direct labour hours required to complete a job differ from the number of standard hours specified, a labour efficiency variance result it is the difference between actual hours expended and standard labour hours specified multiplied by the standard labour rate per hour. Labour Efficiency Variance is completed by applying the following formula:

Labour efficiency variance = (Actual hour – standard hours for the actual output) × Standard Rate per hour.

Assume the following data

Standard labour hour per unit	=	5 hours
Standard labour rate per hour	=	Rs 3.00
Units completed	=	1,000
Labour cost recorded	=	5,050 @ Rs. 3.05
Labour Efficiency Variance	=	(5,050 – 5,000) × Rs. 3
	=	Rs. 150 (unfavourable)

It may be noted that the standard labour hour rate and not the actual rate is used in computing labour efficiency variance. If quantity variances are calculated, changes in prices /rates are excluded, and when price variances are calculated, standard quantities are ignored.

3. Labour Rate Variance

Labour rate variance is computed into the same manner as material price variance. When actual direct labour hour rates differ from standard rates, the result is a labour rate variance. It is that portion of the direct wages variance which is due to the difference between the actual rate paid and standard rate of pay specified. The formula for its calculation is Labour Rate Variance = (Actual rate – Standard rate) × Actual hours.

Using data from the example given above, the labour rate variance is Rs. 252.50.

Labour Rate Variance = (3.05 – 3.00) × 5050 hours
= 0.5 × 5050
= Rs. 252.50 (unfavourable)

The number of actual hours worked is used in place of the number of the standard hours specified because the objective is to know the cost difference due to changes in labour hour rate and not hours worked. Favorable rate variances arise whenever actual rate are less than standard rate; unfavourable variances occur when actual rates exceed standard rate.

4. Labours Mix Variance

Labour mix variance is computed in the same manner as materials mix variance. Manufacturing or completing a job requires different types or grades of workers and production will be competed if labour is mixed according to standard promotions. Standard labour mix may not be adhered to under some circumstances and substitution will have to be adhered to under some circumstances and substitution will have to be made. There may be changes in the wage rates of some workers, there may be a need to use more skilled or expensive types of labour e.g., employment of men instead of women sometimes workers and operators may be absent These lead to the emergence of a labour mix variance which is calculated by using the following formula:

Labour mix variance = (Actual labour mix – Revised standard labour mix in terms of actual total hours × Standard rate per hour

To take an example, suppose the following were the standard labour cost dates per unit in factory:

Class	*Proportion*			
A	50% 3 hours	@ Rs. 4.00	=	Rs .12
B	50% 3 hours	@ Rs. 2.00	=	Rs. 6
	100% 6 hours	@ Rs. 3.00	=	Rs. 18

In a period, many class B workers were absent and it was necessary to substitute class B workers Since class A workers were less experienced with the job, more labour hours were used. The recorded costs of a unit were:

Class	*Production*		*Costs*
A	75%	6 hours @ Rs. 4.00	Rs. 24.00
B	25%	2 hours @ Rs. 2.00	Rs. 4.00
	100%	8 hours @ Rs. 3.50	Rs. 28.00

Labour mix variance will be calculated as follows:

Labour mix variance = (Actual proportion – Revised standard proportion of actual total hours) × standard rate per hour

Revised standard proportion:

$$\text{Class A} = \frac{3}{6} \times 8 = 4 \text{ hours}$$

$$\text{Class B} = \frac{3}{6} \times 8 = 4 \text{ hours}$$

Applying the formula:

Class A = (6 – 4) × Rs. 4 = 8 (Unfavourable)

Class B = (2 – 4) × Rs. 2 = Rs. 4 (Favourable)

Total labour mix variance = Rs. 4 (Unfavourable)

Labour Yield Variance

The final product cost contains not only material cost but also labour cost. Therefore, gain or loss (higher or lower output than the standard output) should take into account labour yield variance also. A lower output simply means that final output does not correspond with the production units that should have been produced from the hours expended on the inputs. It can be computed by applying the following formula:

Labour yield variance = (Actual output – Standard output based on actual hours)

Or

Labour yield variance = (Actual loss-standard loss on actual hours) × Average standard labour rate per unit of output

Labour yield variance is also known as labour efficiency sub-variance which is computed in terms of inputs, i.e. standard labour hour efficiency sub-variance is computed by using the following formula:

Labour efficiency sub-variance (Revised standard mix –standard mix) x standard rate

Example 11

Standard labour hours and rate for production of one unit of Article A is given below:

	Per unit (hr)	*Rate per Hours (Rs.)*	*Total (Rs.)*
Skilled worker	5	1.50	7.50
Unskilled worker	8	0.50	4.00
Semi-skilled worker	4	0.75	3.00
Total			Rs. 14.50

Actual data	Rate per hour (Rs.)	Total (Rs.)
Articles produced 1,000 units		
Skilled worker 4,500 hr.	2.00	9,000
Unskilled worker 10,000 hr.	0.45	4,500
Semi-skilled workers 4,200 hr.	0.75	3,150
		Rs. 16,650

Calculate: (*i*) Labour cost variance
(*ii*) Labour rate variance
(*iii*) Labour efficiency variance
(*iv*) Labour mix variance
(*v*) Labour yield variance
(*vi*) Labour efficiency sub-variance

Solution:

(*i*) Labour cost variance: (AH × AR) – (Standard hour for actual production × SR)
Skilled worker (4,500 × 2 – 5,000 × 1.50)
9,000 – 7,500 = Rs. 1,500 (Adverse)
Unskilled worker (10,000 × 0.45 – (8,000 × 0.50)
4,500 – 4,000 = Rs. 5,000 (Adverse)
Semi-skilled worker (4,000 × 0.75) – 4,000 × 0.75)
3,150 – 3,000 = Rs. 150 (Adverse)
Total labour cost variance = Rs. 2,150 (Adverse)

(*ii*) Labour rate variance: (AR – SR) × AH
Skilled worker (2.00 – 1.50) × 4,500 = Rs. 2,250 (A)
Semi-skilled worker (0.75 – 0.75) × 4,200 = Nil
Unskilled worker (0.45 – 0.50) × 10,000 = Rs., 500(F)
Total labour rate variance = Rs. 1,750 (A)

(*iii*) Labour efficiency variance:
Skilled (4,500 – 5,000) × 1.50 = Rs. 750 (F)
Unskilled (10,000 – 8,000) × 0.50 = Rs. 1,000 (A)
Semi –skilled (4,200 – 4,000) x 0.75 = Rs. 1.50 (A)
Total labour efficiency variance = Rs. 400 (A)

(*iv*) Labour-mix variance: First, revised standard hours should be calculated by using the following formula:

$\frac{\text{Standard labour mix}}{\text{Total standard hours}} \times \text{Total actual hours}$

Skilled worker = $\frac{5,000}{17,000} \times 18,700 = 5,500$ hours

Unskilled worker = $\frac{8,000}{17,000} \times 18,700 = 8,800$ hours

Semi-skilled worker = $\frac{4,000}{17,000} \times 18,700 = 4,400$ hours

Labour mix variance = (Actual labour mix-Revised standard labour mix of actual hours) × Standard rate

Skilled worker (4,500 – 5,500) × 1.50 = Rs. 1,500 (F)
Unskilled worker (1,000 – 8,800) × 0.50 = Rs. 600 (A)
Semi-skilled worker (4,200 – 4,400) × 0.75 = Rs. 150 (F)
Total labour mix variance Rs. 1,050(F)

(*v*) Labour yield variance:
(Actual production – Standard production on actual hours) × Average standard labour rate per unit
(1,000 – 1,100) × 14.50 = Rs. 1,450 (Unfavourable)

(*vi*) Labour efficiency sub-variance:
(Revised Standard hours – Standard hours for actual production) × standard rate
Skilled worker (5,500 – 5.000) × 1.50 = Rs. 750 (A)
Unskilled worker (8,800 – 8,000) × 0.50 = Rs. 400 (A)
Semi-skilled worker (4,400 – 4,000) × 0.75 = Rs. 300 (A)
Total efficiency sub variance = Rs. 1,450(A)

Idle Time Variance

Idle time variance occurs when workers are not able to do the work due to some reason during the hours for which they are paid. Idle time can be divided according to causes responsible for creating idle time, e.g., idle time due to breakdown, lack of materials or power failures Idle time variance will be equivalent to the standard labour cost of the hours during which no work has been done but for which workers have been paid for unproductive time. Suppose, in a factory 2000 workers were idle because of a power failure. As a result of this loss of production of 4,000 units of product A and 8,000 units of product B occurred. Each employee was paid his normal wage (a rate of Rs. 2 per hour). A single standard hour is needed to manufacture four units of product A and eight units of product B. Idle time variance will be computed in the following manner:

Standard hours lost:

Product A = $\frac{4,000}{4}$ = 1,000 hours

Product B = $\frac{8,000}{8}$ =1,000 hours

Total hours lost = 2,000 hours

Idle time variance (power failure)

2,000 hours @ Rs. 2 per hour = Rs. 4,000 (Adverse)

Example 12

Standard hours for manufacturing two products M and N are 15 hours per unit and 20 hours per unit respectively. Both products require identical kind of labour and the standard wage rates per hour is Rs. 5. In the year 1994, 10,000 units of M and 15,000 units of N were manufactured. The total of labour hours actually worked were 4,50,000 and the actual wage bill came to Rs. 23,00,000. This includes 12,000 hours paid for @ Rs.7 per hour and 9,400 hours paid for @ Rs. 7.50 per hour, the balance having been paid at Rs.5 per hour. You are required to compute the labour variances:

Solution:

Labour cost variance = (Actual labour cost – Standard labour cost for actual output)

Standard cost:

For Product M = 10,000 units × 15 hrs. × 5 = 7,50,000
For Product N = 15,000 units × 20 hrs. × 5 = 15,00,000
Total standard cost 22,50,000
Total actual labour cost = Rs. 23,00,000
Labour cost variance = Rs.23,00,000 – Rs. 22,50,000
= Rs. 50,000 (Adverse)

Labour rate variance = Actual hours × (Actual rate – Standard Rate)
= 12,000 × (Rs. 7 – Rs. 5) = Rs. 24,000 (A)
= 9,400 × (Rs. 7.50 - Rs. 5) = Rs. 23,500 (A)
= 4,28,600 × (Rs. 5 - Rs. 5) = —
Total: Rs. 47,500 (A)

Labour efficiency variance = Standard Rate × (Actual time – Standard Time)
= Rs. 5 × (4,50,500 – 4,50,000)
= Rs. 2,500 (Adverse)

Example 13

A group of workers normally consists of 30 men, 15 women and 10 boys. They are paid at standard hourly rates as under:

Men	0.80
Women	0.60
Boys	0.40

In a normal working week of 40 hours, the group is expected to produce 2,000 units of output.

During the week ending 31st December, 1987 the gang consisted of 40 men, 10 women and 5 boys. The actual wages paid were @ Rs. 0.70, Rs. 0.65 and Rs. 0.30 respectively; four hours were lost due to abnormal idle time and 1,600 units were produced.

Calculate: (*i*) wage variance, (*ii*) wage rate variance, (*iii*) labour efficiency variance, (*iv*) group composition variance (*i.e.*, labour mix variance) and (*v*) labour idle time variance.

Solution:

Workers	Standard			Actual		
	Hours	Rate	Amt.	Hours	Rate	Amt.
Men	1,200	0.80	960	1,600	0.70	1,120
Women	600	0.60	360	400	0.65	260
Boys	400	0.40	160	200	0.30	60
	2,200		1,480	2,200		1,440

Labour cost variance = (Actual labour cost – Standard Labour cost for actual output)

$$1{,}440 - \frac{1{,}480}{2{,}000} \times 1600$$

= Rs. 256 (Adverse)

Wage rate variance = Actual hours paid × (Actual rate – Std. Rate)

Men = 1,600 × (0.70 – 0.80) = R 160 (F)

Women = 400 × (0.65 – 0.60) = Rs. 20 (A)

Boys = 200 × (0.30 – 0.40) = Rs. 20 (F)

Total labour efficiency variance = Standard Rate × (Actual hours paid – Standard Hours for actual output)

Men $= \text{Rs. } 0.80 \times (1{,}600 - 1{,}600 \times \frac{1{,}200}{2{,}000}$

= Rs. 0.80 × (1,600 – 960) = 512(A)

Women $= \text{Rs. } 0.60\ (400 - 6000 \times 400 \left(\frac{6{,}000 \times 1{,}600}{2{,}000}\right)$

= Rs. 0.60 × (400 – 480) = 48(F)

Boys $= \text{Rs. } 0.40 \times \left(200 - \left(\frac{400 \times 1{,}600}{2{,}000}\right)\right.$

= Rs. 0.40 × (200 – 320) = 48 (F)

= Rs. 416 (A)

Total labour efficiency variance may be sub-divided into (*i*) labour efficiency variance and (ii) idle time variance

Idle Time Variance = (Standard Labour Rate × Hours Lost)

Men = 0.80 × 160 = 128

Women = 0.60 × 40 = 24

Boys = 0.40 × 20 = 8

Rs. 160 (A)

Labour efficiency variance (after excluding idle time variance) Standard rate × (Actual time taken – Standard time for actual output)

Men = Rs. 0.80 × (1,440 – 960) =384 (A)

Women = Rs. 0.60 × (360-480) = 72 (F)

Boys = 0.40 × (180 –320) = 56 (F)

256 (A)

Total labour efficiency variance may also be classified into: (i) mix variance, and (ii) yield variance. Mix variance can be calculated as follows:

Mix variance = Standard Rate × (Actual time worked – Revised standard Time)

Total actual time worked = 1440 + 360 + 180

= 1980 hours

$$\text{Men} = \text{Rs.}0.80 \times 1{,}440 - \frac{1{,}980 \times 1{,}200}{2{,}200}$$

Rs. 0.80 × (1,440 – 1,080) = Rs. 288(A)

$$\text{Women} = \text{Rs. } 0.60 \times \left(\frac{360 - 1{,}980 \times 600}{2{,}200}\right)$$

Rs. 0.60 × (360 – 540) = Rs. 108 (F)

$$\text{Boys} = \text{Rs. } 0.40 \times \left(180 - \frac{1{,}980 \times 400}{2{,}200}\right)$$

Rs. 0.40 × (180 – 360) = Rs. 72 (F)

Total = Rs. 108 (A)

Yield Variance = Standard cost per unit × (Actual output – Standard Output for actual time worked)

= Rs. 0.74 × (1,600 – 1,800)

= Rs. 148 (Adverse)

Actual time worked = 2,200 – 220

= 1980

$$= \frac{1980 \text{ hrs.} \times 2000 \text{ units}}{2200 \text{ hours}}$$

= 1,800 units

Example 14

The standard labour component and the actual labour component engaged in week for a job are as under:

	Skilled workers	*Semi-skilled workers*	*Unskilled workers*
(A) Standard number of workers in the gang	32	12	6
(B) Standard wage rate per hour (Rs.)	3	2	1
(C) Actual number of workers employed in the gang during the week	28	18	4
(D) Actual wage rate per hour (Rs.)	4	3	2

During the 40-hour working week, the group produced 1,800 standard labour hours of work.

Calculate:

(i) Labour efficiency variance

(ii) Labour mix variance

(iii) Rate of wages variance

(iv) Total labour cost variance

Solution:

Category of workers	Standard Hrs	Standard Rate	Standard Amount	Actual Hrs	Actual Rate	Actual Amount
Skilled	1,280	3	3,840	1,120	4	4,480
Semi- skilled	480	2	960	720	3	2,160
Unskilled	240	1	240	160	2	320
	2,000		5,040	2,000		6,960

Labour Cost Variance =

= Actual cost – Standard cost for actual output

= Rs. 6,960 – Rs. 4,536

= Rs. 2,424 (Adverse)

Labour Rate Variance =

= Actual time × (Actual rate – standard rate)

Skilled = Rs. 1,120 × (4 –3)

= 1,120 (A)

Semi-skilled =Rs. 720 × (3 – 2)

= Rs. 720 (A)

Unskilled = Rs.160 × (2 – 1)

= Rs. 160 (A)

Total = Rs. 1,120 (A) + Rs. 720 (A) + Rs. 160 (A)

= 2,000 (Adverse)

Labour Efficiency Variance

= Standard rate × (Actual time – Standard time for actual output)

Skilled = 3 × (1,120 – 1,152)

= Rs. 96 (F)

Semi skilled =2 × (720 – 432)

= Rs. 576 (A)

Unskilled = 1 × (160 – 216)

= Rs. 56 (F)

Total = Rs. 96 (F) + Rs. 576 (A) + Rs. 56 (F)

= Rs. 424 (A)

Labour Mix Variance (DIMV)

= Standard rate × (Actual time – Revised standard time)

Skilled = 3 × (1,120 – 1,280)

= Rs. 480 (F)

Semi-skilled = 2 × (720 – 480)

= Rs. 480 (A)

Unskilled = 1 × (160 – 240)

= Rs. 80 (F)

Total = Rs. 480 (F) = Rs. 480 (A) + Rs. 80 (F)

= Rs. 80 (Favourable)

Labour Yield Variance =

= Standard cost per hour of work × (Actual output – Standard output for actual mix)

= 2.52 × (1,800 – 2,000)

= Rs. 504 (Adverse)

Working notes:

1. Standard cost for actual output = $\frac{5,040}{2,000}$ × 1,800

2. Standard time for actual output:

   Skilled = $\frac{1,800}{2,000}$ × 1,280 = 1,152 hours

   Semi-skilled = $\frac{1,800}{2,000}$ × 480 = 432 hours

   Unsullied = $\frac{1,800}{2,000}$ × 240 = 216 hrs

3. Revised standard time = $\frac{\text{Actual mix}}{\text{Standard mix}}$ × Standard time

   Since, standard Mix and Actual mix are the same, the standard time will also be the revised standard time.

   Standard Cost per hour of standard work:

   = $\frac{\text{Total Standard cost}}{\text{Total Standard hours of work}}$

   = $\frac{5,040}{2,000}$

   = Rs. 2.52

Example 15

The standard material and labour cost for two products X and Y are:

Materials (same for both)	*X*		*Y*	
	5 kg	Rs. 50	3kg	Rs. 30
	10 hrs	Rs. 5	8 hr	Rs. 4
		Rs. 55		Rs. 34

500 units of X and 200 units of Y were manufactured in a period against total material cost and labour cost as under:

Material:	Product X: 2,700 kg material Product Y: 700 kg material	Rs. 37,400
Labour:	Product X: 6,000 hours Product Y: 2,000 hours	Rs. 3,600

Reconcile the standard prime cost and actual prime cast for the production of 500 units of X and 200 units of Y.

Solution:

Material price per kg = Rs. 37,400/3,400 kg = Rs. 11

Labour rate per hour = 3,600/8,000 = 0.45

Material price variance = (AP – SP) × AQ

X = (11 – 10) × 2,700 = 2,700 (A)
Y = (11 – 10) × 700 = 700 (A)

3400 (A)

Material Usage Variance = (AQ – A) × SP

X = (2,700 – 2,500) × 40 = 2,000 (A)
Y = (700 – 600) × 10 = 1,000 (A)

3,000 (A)

Labour Rate Variance = (AR – SR) × AH

X = (0.45 – 0.50) × 6,000 = 300 (F)
Y = (0.45 – 0.50) × 2000 = 100 (F)

400 (F)

Efficiency Variance = (AH – SH) × SR

X = (16,000 – 5,000) × 0.50 = 500 (A)
Y = (2,000 – 1,600) × 0.50 = 200 (A) 700 (Unfavourable)

= Rs. 700 (A)

Reconciliation Statement:

Std. Prime cost for X = Rs. 55 × 500 = 27,500
Std. Prime cost for Y = Rs. 34 × 200 = 6,800

34,300

Actual prime cost

X - 2,700kg @ Rs. 11 =	29,700		
6,000 hr @ Rs.)45 =	2,700		
		32,400	
Y – 700 kg. @ Rs. 11 =	7,700		
2,000 hr @ Rs. 0.45 =	900		
		8,600	
			41,000
Prime cost variance (–)			6,700 (A)

Example 16

The following standards have been set to manufacture a product:

Direct Materials

2 Units of A at Rs. 4 per unit	8.00
3 Units of B at Rs. 3 per unit	9.00
15 units of C at Rs. 1 per unit	15.00
	32.00
Direct labour 3 hrs @ Rs. 8 per hour	24.00
Total Standard Prime Cost	56.00

The company manufactured and sold 6,000 units of the product during the year. Direct Material Costs were as follows:

12,500 units of A at Rs. 4.40 per unit

18,000 units of B at Rs. 2.80 per unit

88,500 units of C at Rs. 1.20 per unit

The company worked 17,500 direct labour hours during the year. For 2,500 of these hours, the company paid at Rs. 12 per hour while for the remaining, the wages were paid at the standard rate. Calculate materials price and usage variances and labour rate and efficiency variances.

Solutions:

Output 6,000 units

	Standard			*Actual*		
	Qty. Units	*Rate Rs.*	*Amount Rs.*	*Qty. Units*	*Rate Rs.*	*Amount Rs.*
A	12,000	4.00	48,000	12,500	4.40	55,000
B	18,000	3.00	54,000	18,000	2.80	50,400
C	90,000	1.00	90,000	88,500	1.20	1,06,200
Total	1,20,000		1,92,000	1,19,000		2,11,600

Material Price Variance = Actual Quantity. × (Actual rate – Standard Rate)

Material	A = 12,500 × (4.40 – 4) =	5,000 (A)
	B = 11,000 × (2.80 – 3) =	3,600 (F)
	C = 88,500 × (1.20 –1) =	17,700 (A)
	Total	Rs. 19.100 (Adverse)

Material Usage Variance = Standard Rate × (Actual – Standard Quantity for actual output)

Material	A = A × (12,500 – 12,000) =	2,000	(A)
	B = 3 × (18,000 – 18,000) =	Nil	
	C = 1 × (88,500 – 90,000) =	1,500	(F)
Total		Rs. 500	(Adverse)

Labour Rate Variance = Actual × (Actual Rate – Standard Rate)

(*i*)	= 2,500 × (12 – 8) =	10,000	(A)
(*ii*)	= 15,000 × (8 – 8) =	Nil	
	Total	Rs. 10,000	(Adverse)

Labour Efficiency Variance = Standard Rate × (Actual time – Standard time for actual output)
= 8 × (17,500 – 16,000 × 3)
= Rs. 4,000 (Favourable)

Example 17

From the following data of A and Co. Ltd. relating to budgeted and actual performance for the month of March 1987, compute the Direct Material and Direct Labour Cost Variances.

Budgeted data for March:		
Units to be manufactured		1,50,000
Units of Direct Material required (based on std. Rates)		4,95,000
Planned purchase of Raw Material (Units)		5,40,000
Average unit cost of direct material		Rs. 8
Direct Labour Hours per unit of finished goods		3/4 hr.
Direct Labour Cost (Total)	Rs.	29,92,500
Actual data at the end of March		
Units actually manufactured	Rs.	1,60,000
Direct Material Cost (Purchase cost based on units actually issued)	Rs.	43,41,900
Direct Material Cost (purchase cost based on units actually purchased)	Rs.	45,10,000
Average unit cost of Direct Material	Rs.	8.20
Total Direct Labour hours for March	Rs.	1,25,000
Total Direct Labour cost for March	Rs.	33,75,000

Solution:

Direct Material Variances:

MCV = Actual material cost – Standard material cost of actual output
= 43,41,900 – 1,60,000 × 3.3 × 8
= 43,41,900 – 42,24,000
= 1,17,900 (Adverse)

MPV = Actual Quantity × (Actual Rate – Standard Rate)
= 5,29,500 × (8.20 – 8)
= Rs. 1,05,900 (Adverse)

MUV = Standard Rate × (Actual Quantity – Standard Quantity for actual output)
= 8 × (5,29,500 – 1,60,000 × 3.30)
= 8 × (5,29,500 – 5,28,000)
= Rs. 12,000 (Adverse)

Direct Labour Variances

LCV = Actual labour cost – Std. labour cost for actual output
= 33,75,000 – 1,60,000 × 3/4 × 26.60
= 33,75,000 – 31,92,000
= Rs. 1,83,000 (Adverse)

LRV = Actual time × (Actual Rate – Standard Rate)
= 1,25,000 × (27 – 26.60)
= Rs. 50,000 (Adverse)

LEF = Standard Rate × (Actual time – Standard Time for actual output)
26.60 × (1,25,000 – 1,60,000 × 3/4)
= 26.60 × (1,25,000 – 1,20,000)
= Rs. 1,33,000 (Adverse)

Working Notes:

(*i*) Standard Units of Direct Material required per unit of output:

$$= \frac{4,95,000}{1,50,000} = 3.30 \text{ Units}$$

(*ii*) Total Actual quantity of Direct Materials used

$$= \frac{43,41,900}{8.20} = 5,29,500 \text{ Units}$$

(*iii*) Standard Direct Labour cost per hour

$$= \frac{29,92,500}{1,50,000 \times 3/4} = \frac{29,92,500}{1,12,500} = \text{Rs. } 26.50$$

(*iv*) Actual Direct Labour cost per hour

$$= \frac{33,75,000}{1,25,000} = \text{Rs. } 27$$

OVERHEAD VARIANCES

The analysis of factory overhead variances is more complex than variance analysis for direct materials and direct labour. There is no standardisation of the terms or methods used for calculating overhead variances. For this reason it is necessary to be familiar with the different approaches which can be applied in overhead variances. Generally, the computation of the following overhead variances are suggested:

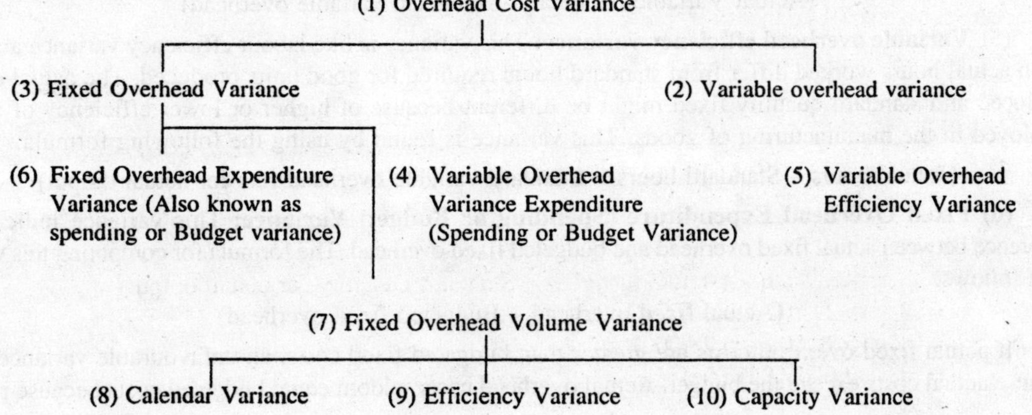

Total Overhead Cost Variance

This overall overhead variance is the difference between the actual overhead cost incurred and the standard cost of overhead for the output achieved. This can be computed by applying the following formula:

Actual overhead incurred – (Standard hours for the actual output × Standard overhead rate per hour)

Or

Actual overhead incurred – (Actual output × standard overhead rate per unit)

To illustrate the overall overhead variance, assume that the actual overhead for a department amounts to Rs. 10,000 for the month of January 2002 and standard (or allowed) hours for work performed (Actual output) total 4,500 hours, while actual hours used are 5,000. If overhead rate is Rs. 2 per hour, the overall overhead variance will be the following:

Actual department overhead	Rs. 10,000
Overhead charged to production (4,500 hours × Rs. 2)	Rs. 9,000
Overall or net overhead variance (Unfavorable)	Rs. 1,000

Variable overhead Variance: It is the different between actual variable overhead cost and standard variable overhead allowed for the actual output achieved. The formula for computing this variance is as follows:

Actual overhead cost – Actual output × Variable overhead rate

Or

Actual overhead cost – (Standard hours for actual output) × Standard overhead rate per hour.

Fired Overhead Variance: This variance indicates the difference between the actual fixed overhead cost and standard fixed overhead cost allowed for the actual output. This variance is found by using the following formula.

Fixed overhead variance = Actual overhead cost – Fixed overhead absorbed)

Or

Actual overhead cost – (Actual output × Fixed overhead rate per unit)

Or

Actual overhead cost – (Standard Hours for actual output × Standard Fixed overhead rate per hour)

(4) Variable Overhead Expenditure (Spending or Budget) Variance: This variance indicates the difference between actual variable overhead and budgeted variable overhead based on actual hours worked. This variance is found by using the following formula:

(Actual Variable overhead – Budgeted variable overhead)

(5) Variable overhead efficiency variance: This variance is like labour efficiency variance and arises when actual hours worked differ from standard hours required for good units produced. The actual quantity produced and standard quantity fixed might be different because of higher or lower efficiency of workers employed in the manufacturing of goods. This variance is found by using the following formula:

(Actual hours – Standard hours × Standard variable overhead rate for actual output)

(6) Fixed Overhead Expenditure (Spending or Budget) Variance: This variance indicates the difference between actual fixed overhead and budgeted fixed overhead. The formula for computing this variance is as follows:

(Actual fixed overhead – Budgeted fixed overhead)

If actual fixed overhead costs are greater than budgeted fixed costs, an unfavourable variance results because actual costs exceed the budget. Actual overhead costs seldom equal budgeted costs because property tax rates may change, insurance premiums may increase or equipment changes may affect depreciation rates. As an illustration, assume that a company completed 36,000 units (equal to 18,000 standard productive hours) in 18,500 hours at the recorded fixed cost of Rs. 75,100. The standard fixed cost rate per hour is Rs. 4. Therefore,

Expenditure variance = (Actual overhead costs – Budgeted overhead costs)

That is = (75,100 – 18,500 × 4)

= (75,100 – 74,000)

= Rs. 1,100 (Unfavourable)

The expenditure or budget variance provides management with information, which helps in controlling costs. The budget variance is usually prepared on a departmental basis and the factors that cause the budget variance are, therefore, controllable by departmental managers.

(7) Fixed Overhead Volume Variance: Volume variance relates to only fixed overheads. This variance arises due to the difference between the standard fixed overhead cost allowed (absorbed) for the actual output and the budgeted fixed overhead based on standard hours allowed for actual output achieved during the period. The variance shows the over-or-under-absorption of fixed overheads during a particular period. If the actual output is more than the standard output, there is over-absorption and variance is favourable. If actual output is less than the standard output, the volume variance is unfavourable. The formula for computing this variance is as follows:

(Budgeted overhead applied to actual output – Budgeted fixed overhead based on standard hours allowed for actual output)

or

(Actual Production – Budgeted production) × Standard fixed overhead rate per unit

Volume variance is further sun-divided into three variances.

(8) Fixed Overhead Calendar Variance: It is that portion of volume variance, which is due to the difference between the number of actual working days in the period to which the budget is applicable and budgeted number of days in the budget period.

If actual working days is more than the budgeted working days, the variance is favourable as work has been done on days more than budgeted or allowed and vice-versa. The formula is as follows:

(No. of actual working days – No. of Budgeted working days) × Standard fixed overhead rate per day

Calendar variance can be computed based on hours or output.

Then the formula are:

Hours Basis

Calendar Variance = (Revised Budget Capacity hours – Budget Hours) × Standard fixed overhead rate per hour

If revised budgeted capacity hours are more than the budgeted hours, the variance will be favourable. In the reverse situation, the Variance will be unfavourable.

Output Basis

Calender Variance = (Revised budgeted quantity in terms of actual number of days worked – Budgeted quantity) × Standard fixed overhead rate per unit

If revised budgeted quantity is more than the budgeted quantity; the variance is favourable; if revised budgeted quantity is less, the variance will be unfavourable.

(9) Fixed Overhead Efficiency Variance: It is that portion of volume variance which arises when actual hours of production used for actual output differ from the standard hours specified for that output. If actual hours worked are less than the standard hours, the variance is favourable and when actual hours are more than the standard hours, the variance is unfavourable. The formula is:

Fixed Overhead Efficiency Variance = (Actual hours – Standard hours for actual production) × Fixed overhead rate per hour

Or

Fixed Overhead Efficiency Variance = (Actual production – Standard production as per actual time available) × Standard fixed overhead rate per unit

(10) Fixed Overhead Capacity Variance: It is that part of fixed overhead volume variance which is due to the difference between the actual capacity (in hours) worked during a given period and the budgeted capacity (expressed in hours).

The formula is:

Capacity Variance = (Actual Capacity Hours – Budgeted Capacity) × Standard fixed overhead rate per hour

This variance represents idle time also. If actual capacity hours are more than the budgeted capacity hours, the variance is favourable and if actual capacity hours less than the budgeted capacity hours, the variance will be unfavourable.

In case actual number of days and budgeted number of days are also given, then budgeted capacity hours will be calculated in terms of actual number of days and it will be known as revised budgeted capacity hours, i.e. budgeted hours in actual days worked. In this situation, the formula for calculating capacity variance will be as follows:

Capacity = (Actual Capacity hours – Revised Budgeted Capacity hours × Standard fixed overhead rate per hour

In the above formula, the variance will be favourable if actual capacity hours are more than the revised budgeted hours. However, if actual capacity hours are lesser than the revised budgeted hours, the variance will be adverse as lesser hours means that lesser actual hours have been worked, taking the actual days utilised into account.

Two-way, Three-way and Four-way Variance Analysis

The above overhead variances are also classified as two-way, three-way and four-way variance. The different variances under these categories are listed below. The formulae for commuting these variances are similar to as explained in the preceding section:

(A) Two-way Variance Analysis

(1) Controllable Variance (Budget Variance)

(2) Volume Variance (Uncontrollable variance)

(B) Three-way Variance Analysis

(1) Expenditure Variance (Spending Variance)

(2) Capacity variance and

(3) Efficiency variance

(C) Four-way Variance Analysis

(1) Expenditure Variance (Spending Variance)

(2) Variable Overhead Efficiency Variance

(3) Fixed Overhead Efficiency Variance and

(4) Capacity Variance

Example 18

Budgeted hours for month of March 1990 = 180 hours

Standard rate of article produced per hour = 50 units

Budgeted fixed overheads Rs. 2,700

Actual production = 9,200 units

Actual hours for production = 175 hours

Actual fixed overhead costs = Rs. 2,800

Calculate Overhead Cost Variances.

Solution:

1. **Overhead Cost Variance:**

(Actual Overhead Cost – Standard Overhead of actual output)

(2,800 – 9,200 units × 30)

(2,800 – 2,760) = Rs. 40 (Unfavourable)

$$\text{Standard Overhead rate per unit} = \frac{2{,}700}{180 \text{ hours} \times 50} = \frac{2{,}700}{9{,}000} = \text{Rs. } 0.30\text{p.}$$

2. **Overhead Expenditure Variance**

(Actual Overhead – Budgeted Overhead)

(2,800 – 2,700 = Rs. 100 Unfavourable

3. **Overhead Volume Variance:**

(Budgeted Overhead for actual output – Budgeted fixed overhead)

(30P × 9200 units – 2,700)

(2,760 – 2,700) = Rs. 60 (Favourable)

It can be calculated in the following manner also:

(Actual Production – Budgeted Production) × Standard Rate per unit

(9,200 – 9,000) × .30 P = Rs. 60 favourable

Or

(Budgeted hrs for actual production – Budgeted hours) × Standard rate per hour

(*184 hours – 180) × Rs. 15

$$\frac{\text{Rs. } 2{,}700}{180 \text{ hours}} \text{ Rs. } 15$$

4 × 15 = Rs. 60 (Favourable)

For 9,000 units standard hours required = 180 hours

$$\text{For 9,200 units standard hours } \frac{9{,}200 \times 180}{9{,}000} = 184 \text{ hours}$$

Example 19

From the following data, calculate overhead variances:

	Budgeted	*Actual*
Output	15000 units	16000 units
No. of working days	25	27
Fixed overheads	Rs. 30,000	Rs. 30,500
Variable overheads	Rs. 45,000	Rs. 47,000

There was an increase of 5 % in capacity.

Solution:

1. **Total Overhead Cost Variance:**
(Actual overhead cost – Actual units × Standard Rate)
(Rs. 30,500 + 47,000 – 16,000 × Rs. 5)
Rs. 77,500 – Rs. 80,000 = Rs. 2,500 (Favourable)

$$\text{Standard rate} = \frac{\text{Standard overhead}}{\text{Standard output}}$$

2. **Variable Overhead Variance**
(Actual variable cost – Actual units × Standard Rate)
(47,000 – 16,000 × Rs. 3)
Rs. 47,000 – Rs. 48,000 = Rs. 1,000 (Favourable)
3. **Fixed Overhead Variance**
Actual fixed overhead cost – (Actual units × Standard Rate of fixed overhead)
30,500 – (16,000 × 2)
30,500 – 32,000 = Rs. 1,500 (Favourable)
4. **Volume Variance**
Actual units × Standard Rate – Budgeted fixed overheads
16,000 × Rs. 2 – Rs. 30,000 = Rs. 2,000 (Favourable)
(Actual production – Budgeted production) × Fixed overhead rate per unit
= (16000 – 15000) × Rs. 2 = Rs. 2000(F)
5. **Expenditure Variance:**
Actual fixed overheads – budgeted fixed overheads
Rs. 30,500 – 30,000 = Rs. 500 unfavourable
6. **Capacity Variance:**
St. Rate (Revised budget units – Budgeted units)
Revised budgeted units = Budgeted units + Increase in incapacity

$$= 15{,}000 + \frac{5}{100} \times 15{,}000 = 15{,}750 \text{ units}$$

= Capacity Variance =
Rs. 2(15,750 units – 15,000 units)
Rs. 2 × 750 = Rs. 1,500 (Favourable)

7. **Calender Variance:**
Increase or decrease in production due to more or less working days × Standard Rate per unit
Within 25 days, Standard production with increased capacity = 15,750 units, within 2 days (27,25),

Production will be increased by = $\frac{15,750 \times 2}{25}$ = 1260 units

Calender variance = 1,260 units × Rs. 2
= Rs. 2,520 (Favourable)

8. Efficiency Variance:

Standard Rate (Actual Production – Standard Production)

Standard production:

Budgeted production = 15,000 units

Production increased due to increase in capacity	=	750 units
Production increased due to 2 more working days	=	1,260 units
	=	17,010 units

Efficiency Variance = Rs. 2(16,000 units – 17,010 units)

Rs. 2 (– 1,010 units) = Rs. 2020 (Unfavourable)

Example 20

	Budget	*Actual*
Output (in units)	6,000	6,500
Hours	3,000	3,300
Overhead cost: Fixed	Rs. 1,200	1250
Variable	Rs. 6,000	6,650
	Rs. 7,200	7,800
Number of days	25	27

Compete and analyse the overhead variances.

Solution:

Overhead cost variance = (Actual overheads – Recovered overhead)
= 7,900 – 6,500 × 1.20
= 7,900 – 7,800 = Rs.100 (Adverse)

Variable overhead cost variance = Actual overheads – Reconsed overheads
= 6650 – 6,500 × Rs. 15
= Rs. 150 (Adverse)

Fixed overhead cost variance = Actual overheads – Recovered overheads
= 1,250 – 0.20 × 6,500
= 1,250 –1,300
= Rs. 50 (Favourable)

Verification

Overhead cost variance = Fixed overhead cost variance + Variable overhead cost variance
= Rs. 150 (Adverse) + Rs. 50 (Favourable)
= Rs. 100 (Adverse)

Fixed overhead variance may further be classified into:

Expenditure variance = Actual overheads – Budgeted overheads

Fixed overhead volume variance = (Actual production – Budgeted production) × Std. Overhead rate per unit

= (6,500 – 6,000) × .20 = Rs. 100(F)

= Rs. 1,250 – Rs. 1,200

= Rs. 50 (Adverse)

Fixed Overhead volume variance = Recovered overheads – Budgeted overheads

= 1,300 – 1,200

= Rs. 100 (Favourable)

Recovered overheads = 6,500 units × Rs.1,200/6,000 units = Rs. 1300

Or6,500 units × 120 = Rs. 1300

Verification

Fixed overhead cost variance = Expenditure variance = volume variance

= Rs. 50 (A) + Rs. 100 (F)

= Rs. 50 (Favourable)

Fixed overhead volume variance may further be classified into:

Efficiency variance = Recovered overheads – Standard overheads

= (Standard Rate per unit × Actual output – Standard Rate per unit × Std. Output for actual time)

= (0.20 × 6,000) – (0.20 × 6,480)

= 1,300 – 1,296

= Rs. 4 (Favourable)

Verification

Fixed Overhead volume variance = Efficiency variance + Capacity variance

= Rs. 4 (F) + Rs. 96 (F)

= Rs. 100 (favourable)

Example 21:

In a factory the standard units of Production for the year were fixed at 1,20,000 units and overhead expenditures were estimated to be:

Fixed	Rs. 12,000
Variable	Rs. 6,000
Semi-variable	Rs. 1,800

Actual production during April of the year was 8,000 units.

Each month has 20 working days.

During the month in question, there was one statutory holiday.

The actual overheads amounted to:

Fixed overhead	Rs. 1,190
Variable	Rs. 480

Semi-Variable Rs. 192

Semi-variable charges are considered to include 60% expenses of a fixed nature and 40% of variable character.

Find out the expenditure, volume and calendar variances.

Solution:

Total overhead cost variance = Actual overheads – Recovered overheads

= 1,862 – 1,320 = Rs. 542.00 (Adverse)

(*a*) Expenditure Variance:

Variable overheads = Actual variable overheads-Standard variable overheads absorbed

= Rs. 556.80 – Rs. 448 = 108.80 (Adverse)

Fixed overheads = Actual fixed overheads – Budgeted fixed overheads

= 1,305.20 – 1090 = 215.20 (A)

Total overhead expenditure variance = 324.00 (Adverse)

(*b*) Volume Variance:

For fixed overheads = Recovered overheads – Budgeted overheads

= Rs. 872 – 1,090 = 218.00 (Adverse)

Total 542.00 (Adverse)

(*c*) Calendar Variance (included in the volume variance):

= Fixed overhead to be absorbed per day

$$= \text{Rs. } \frac{13{,}080}{240} = \text{Rs. } 54.50$$

= Loss due to one day Rs. 54.50 (Adverse)

Working notes:

1. (A) Standard rate of absorption per unit:

$$\text{Fixed overheads: } \frac{\text{Budgeted fixed overheads}}{\text{Budget output}}$$

$$= \frac{12{,}000}{1{,}20{,}000} \qquad \text{Re. } 0.10$$

Fixed overheads element in semi-variable overheads *i.e.,* 60% of Rs. 1,800

$$\frac{1{,}080}{1{,}20{,}000} \qquad \text{Re. } 0.009$$

Standard rate of absorption of fixed overheads per unit.	Re. 0.109
Fixed overhead for 8000 units	
8000 × Re 0.109 =	Rs. 872

(B) Budgeted variable overheads:	Rs. 6,000
Add: Variable element in semi-variable overheads 40% of Rs. 1,800	Rs. 720
Total budgeted variable overheads	Rs. 6,720

Standard variable cost per unit $\dfrac{6,720}{1,20,000}$

Variable overheads for 8,000 units @ Rs. 0.056 Rs. 448

2. Budgeted annual fixed overheads are
Rs. 12,000 = 60% of Rs.1,800 = 13,080

Budgeted monthly fixed overheads are $\dfrac{13,080}{12}$ = Rs. 1.090

3. Actual fixed overheads are Rs. 1,090 = 60% of Rs. 192 = Rs. 1,305.20
4. Actual variable overheads are Rs. 480 + 40% of Rs. 192 = Rs. 556.80

Example 22

A manufacturing company operates a costing system and showed the following data in respect of the month of November.

Actual No. of working days	22
Actual man-hours worked during the month	4,300
Number of products produced	425
Actual overhead incurred (Rs.)	1,800

Relevant information from the company's budget and standard cost data is as follows:

Budgeted number of working days per month	20
Budgeted man hours per month	4,000
Standard man hours per product	10
Standard overhead rate per man-hour	50p

You are required to calculate for the month of November:

(*a*) the overhead variance;
(*b*) the calender variance and
(*c*) the volume variance.

Solution:

(*a*) Overhead cost variance:
Actual overhead cost – Standard overhead cost of actual production
Rs, 1800 – Rs.2,125 = Rs. 325(F)

(*b*) Overhead calendar variance:

(*i*) Where standard overhead rate per unit is given:
Revised budgeted quantity, (i.e. budgeted quantity on the basis of actual no of working days – Budgeted quantity) × Standard rate per unit.
= (440 – 400) × 5
= 40 × 5 = Rs. 200 (F)

(*ii*) Where standard rate per hour is given:
(Possible number of hours – Budgeted hours) × Standard overhead rate per hour
(4,400 – 4,000) × Rs.0.50
400 × Rs. 0.50 = Rs. 200(F)

(c) Overhead volume variance:

(i) Where standard rate per unit is given:
(Actual production – Budgeted production) × Standard overhead rate per unit
(425 – 400) × Rs.5
25 × Rs.5 = 125 (F)

(ii) Where standard rate per hour is given:
(Standard hours for actual production – Budgeted hours) × Standard ovehead rate per unit
(4,250 – 4,000) × 0.50
250 × 0.50 = Rs. 125(F)

Working notes:

1. Standard cost per unit
0.50 × 10 hr. = Rs. 5 per unit
2. Standard overhead cost of actual production
425 unit × Rs.5 per unit = Rs. 2,125
3. Revised budgeted quantity:
If there are 20 working days, standard production is 400 units,
If there are 22 working days, standard production is

$$\frac{400}{20} = 440 \text{ units}$$

4. Possible hours:
In 20 working days the standard hours are 4,000. Therefore, in 22 working days, the standard hours are:

$$\frac{4{,}000 \times 22}{20} = 4{,}400 \text{ hours}$$

5. Standard hours for actual production:
Actual production × Standard hours per unit
425 × 10 = 4,250 hour.

Example 23:

In department A, the following data is submitted for the week ending 31st October:

Standard output for 40 hours per week	1,400 units
Standard fixed overhead	Rs. 1,400
Actual output	1,200 units
Actual hours worked	32 hours
Actual fixed overhead	Rs. 1,500

Prepare a statement of variance.

Solution:

Basic calculations:

Budgeted overhead	Rs. 1,400
Actual overhead	Rs. 1,500
Standard output (in units)	Rs. 1,400
Actual output (in units)	Rs. 1,200
Standard hours	Rs. 40
Actual hours	Rs. 32

1. Standard production per standard hour $= \dfrac{\text{Standard output}}{\text{Standard hours}}$

$= \dfrac{1,400}{40} = 35$ units

2. Standard fixed overhead rate per units $= \dfrac{\text{Standard fixed overhead}}{\text{Standard units produced}}$

$= \dfrac{\text{Rs.}1,400}{1,400} = \text{Rs. } 1.00$

3. Standard fixed overhead rate per hour $= \dfrac{\text{Standard fixed overhead}}{\text{Standard hours worked}}$

$= \text{Rs. } \dfrac{1,400}{40} = \text{Rs. } 35$

Statement of fixed overhead variances of Department A:

A. Expenditure variance:
(Actual overhead – Budgeted overhead)
Rs. 1,500 – Rs. 1,400 =Rs.100 (Adverse)

B. Volume variance:
Standard Fixed overhead rate per unit × (Actual output – Budgeted output)
Rs. (1,200 – 1,400 = Rs. 200 (Adverse)

C. Total overhead cost variance
(Actual overhead – Overhead recovered by actual output)
Rs. 1,500 – Rs. 1,200 = Rs. 300 (Adverse)

(*a*) Efficiency variance:
Standard Fixed overhead rate per unit × (Actual production – Standard production for actual hours)
Rs. 0.1 (1,200 – 32 × 35) = Rs. 80 Favourable

(*b*) Capacity variance:
Standard fixed overhead rate per hour (Actual hours – Standard hours)
Rs. 35 (32 – 40) = Rs. 280 (Adverse)

Example 24

S.V. Ltd. has furnished you with the following data:

	Budget	*Actual*
No. of working day	25	27
Production in units	20,000	22,000
Fixed Overheads	Rs. 30,000	31,000

Budgeted fixed overhead rate is Rs. 1.00 per hour.

The actual hours worked were 31,500.

Calculate the following variances:

(*i*) Total overhead variance

(*ii*) Expenditure variance

(*iii*) Volume variance

(*iv*) Efficiency variance

(*v*) Capacity variance and

(*vi*) Calendar variance

Solution:

	Budgeted data		Actual data
Budgeted overhead	Rs. 30,000	Actual overhead	Rs. 31,000
Budgeted output (Units)	20,000	Actual output (units)	22,000
Budgeted days	25	Actual days	27
Budgeted hours	30,000	Actual hours	31,500
Budgeted overhead rate per hour Rs. 1			
Standard time per unit of output	1.5 hour		
Standard rate per unit	Rs. 1.50		
Budgeted hours worked per day	1,200 hours		

(*i*) Overhead cost variance:
Actual overhead cost – (Standard hours for actual output × Standard overhead rate)
(31,000 – 33,000 × 1) = Rs. 2,000 (F)

(*ii*) Overhead expenditure variance
(Actual overhead – Budgeted overhead)
(31,000 – 30,000) = Rs. 1,000 (A)

(*iii*) Volume variance:
Standard rate per unit × (actual output – Budgeted output)
Rs. 1.50 × (22,000 – 20,000) = Rs. 3,000 (F)

(*iv*) Efficiency variance:
Standard rate per unit × (Actual production – Standard production for actual hours)
Rs. 1.5 (22,000 – 21,000) = Rs. 1,500 (F)

(*v*) Capacity variance:
Standard rate per hour (Actual hours – Standard hours)
Re. 1 (31,500 – 32,400) = Rs. 900 (A)

(*vi*) Calender variance
(Actual No. of working days – Standard No. of working days)

$$\times \frac{\text{Standard overhead}}{\text{Standard number of days}}$$

$$(27 - 25)\frac{30,000}{25} = \text{Rs. } 2,400(F)$$

Example 25

The following information was obtained from the records of a manufacturing unit using standard costing system:

	Standard	Actual
Production	4,000 units	3,800 units
Working Days	20	21
Fixed overhead	40,000	39,000
Variable overhead	12,000	12,000

You are required to calculate the following overhead variances:

(*a*) Variable overhead variance

(*b*) Fixed overhead variance

(*i*) Expenditure variance

(*ii*) Volume variance

(*iii*) Efficiency variance

(*iv*) Calendar variance

(*c*) Also prepare a Reconciliation Statement for the standard fixed expenses worked out at standard fixed overhead rate and the Actual Fixed Overhead.

Solution:

Basic Calculation	*Budgeted Data*	*Actual Data*
Variable Overhead (Rs)	12,000	12,000
Fixed Overhead (Rs)	40,000	39,000
Production (Units)	4,000	3,800
Working (Days)	21	20

$$\text{Standard variable overhead rate per unit} = \frac{12{,}000}{4{,}000 \text{ units}} = \text{Rs. } 3$$

Standard production per day = 200 × Rs. 10 = Rs. 2,000.

(*a*) Variable overhead cost variance = Actual Variable overhead – Recovered Variable overhead

= 12,000 – 3,800 × 3

= 12,000 –11,400 = Rs. 600 (A)

(*b*) Fixed Overhead variance = (Actual Fixed Overheads – Recovered Fixed Overheads)

= 39,000 – 38,000 = Rs. 1,000 (A)

(*i*) Fixed Overhead Expenditure Variance = Actual Overheads – Budgeted Overheads Expenditure

= 39,000 – 40,000 = Rs. 1,000 (F)

(*ii*) Fixed Overhead Volume Variance = Recovered Overhead – Budgeted Overheads

= 38,000 – 40,000 = Rs. 2,000 (A)

(*iii*) Fixed Overhead Efficiency Variance= Standard Fixed overhead rate per day (Actual days – Budgeted days)

= 2,000 × (21 – 20)

= Rs. 2,000(F)

Or

= Standard fixed overhead rate per day × Extra days/Deficit worked

= 2,000 × 1= 2,000(F)

(*c*) Reconciliation Statement

Standard Fixed Overheads (3,800 × 10)		Rs. 38,000
Less: Fixed Overhead Expenditure Variance 1000(F)		
Less: Fixed Overhead Calendar Variance	2,000(F)	Rs. 3,000 (F)
		35,000
Add: Fixed overhead efficiency variance (A)		4,000
Actual Fixed overheads		39,000

SALES VARIANCES

Sales variance is the difference between the actual value of sales achieved in a given period and budgeted value of sales. There are many reasons for the difference in actual sales and budgeted sales such as selling price, sales volume, sales mix. Sales variance can be calculated by using any one of the following two methods:

A. Sales variance based on turnover and

B. Sales Variance based on Margin (i.e., contribution margin or profit).

The first approach, sales variance based on turnover, accounts for difference in actual sales and budgeted sales. The sales variances using margin approach account for differences in actual profit and budgeted profit. In the margin method, it is assumed between actual costs of production and standard cost of production. The reason for this assumption is that cost variances are calculated separately to analyse the difference between actual cost and standard cost of production. Therefore, cost side of the sales variance is assumed constant under the margin method. Sales variances computed under these two methods show different amounts of variance.

The different sales variances under these two approaches and their formulae are given below:

(A) Sales Variances Based on Turnover:

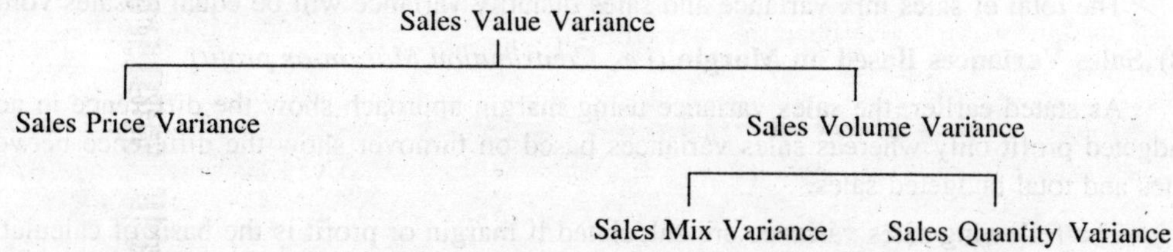

(*i*) *Sales value variance* – also know as sales variance, this variance shows the difference between actual sales value and budgeted sales value. The formula is Sales value Variance = (Actual value of sales – Budgeted value of sales)

Actual sales = Actual quantity sold × Actual selling price
Budgeted sales = Standard Quantity × Standard selling price
Sales value variance = (Actual Quantity × Actual selling price – (Standard quantity × Standard selling price)

If actual sales are more than the budgeted sales, there is favourable variance and if actual sales is less than the budgeted sales, unfavourable variance arises.

(*ii*) *Sales Price Variance* – This variance is due to the difference between actual selling price and standard or budgeted selling price. The formula is:

Sales Price Variance = (Actual selling price – Budgeted selling price) × Actual quantity

If actual selling price is less than the budgeted selling price, variance is favourable and if actual selling price is more than the budgeted selling price, there will be unfavourable sales price variance.

(*iii*) *Sales volume variance* – Sales volume variance arises when the actual quantity sold is different from the budgeted quantity. If actual sales quantity exceeds the budgeted sales quantity, there is a favourable sales volume variance and if actual quantity sold is less than the budgeted quantity, the variance is unfavourable. The formula is:

Sales Volume Variance = (Actual quantity – Budgeted quantity) × Budgeted selling prices

Sales volume variance is divided into two variances:

(*iv*) Sales Mix Variance and

(*ii*) Sales quantity variance.

(i) Sales Mix Variance: Sales mix variance is one part of overall sales volume variance. This variance shows the difference between actual mix of goods sold and budgeted mix of goods sold. The formula is

Sales Mix Variance = (Actual Mix of quantity sold – Actual quantity in standard proportion) × Standard selling price

Sales Mix Variance = (Budgeted price per unit of actual mix – Budgeted price per unit of budgeted mix) × Total actual quantity.

If actual mix sales are more than the actual mix sales in standard or budgeted proportion, the variance is favourable and if actual mix sales are less than the standard mix (of actual sales), the variance is unfavourable. Similarly, If budgeted price per unit of actual mix is more than the budgeted price per unit of budgeted mix, favourable variance will arise. In the reverse situation, variance will be unfavourable.

(v) Sales quantity variance: This variance is also a part of overall volume variance. This variance shows the difference between total actual sales quantity and total budgeted sales quantity. If total actual quantity is more than the total budgeted quantity less than the total budgeted quantity, there will be unfavourable sales quantity variance. The formula is sales quantity variance = (Total actual quantity – Total budgeted quantity) × Budgeted price per unit of budgeted mix.

The total of sales mix variance and sales quantity variance will be equal to sales volume variance.

(B) Sales Variances Based on Margin *(i.e., Contribution Margin or profit)*

As stated earlier, the sales variance using margin approach show the difference in actual profit and budgeted profit only whereas sales variances based on turnover show the difference between total actual sales and total budgeted sales.

The following sales variance are calculated if margin or profit is the basis of calculation:

Sales Variances Based on Margin or profit:

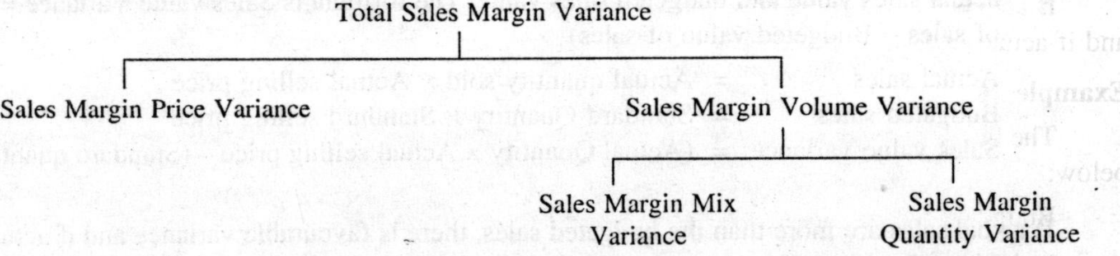

(i) Total Sales Margin Variance: This variance indicates the aggregate of total variance under the margin method. This variance shows the difference between actual profit and budgeted profit. The formula is:

Total sales margin variance = Actual profit – Budgeted profit

If actual profit is more than the budgeted profit, variance will be favourable and if actual profit less than the budgeted profit, unfavourable variance will arise.

(ii) Sales Margin Price Variance: This variance is one part of the total sales margin and arises due to the difference between actual margin per unit and budgeted margin per unit. It is significant to note that, assuming the cost of production being constant, the difference in the actual margin and budgeted margin will only be because of the difference between actual selling price and budgeted selling price. The formula for calculating sales price variance is

Sales Margin Price Variance = (Actual Margin per unit – Budgeted Martin per unit) × Actual quantity

If actual margin per unit is more than the budgeted margin per unit, favourable variance will be found and if actual margin is less than the budgeted margin, variance will be unfavourable.

(ii) Sales Margin Volume Variance: This variance shows the difference between actual sales units and budget sales unit.

The formula is:

Sales Margin Volume Variance = (Actual quantity – Budgeted quantity) × Budgeted Margin per unit

If actual sales units are more than the budgeted sales units, variance will be favourable and if actual sales units are less than the budgeted sales unit, unfavourable variance will arise.

Sales margin volume variance can be calculated using another formula which is:

Sales margin volume variance = (Standard profit on actual quantity of sales – Budgeted profit)

If standard profit exceeds budgeted profit, variance will be favourable and if standard profit is less than the budgeted profit, unfavourable variance will emerge.

Sales margin volume variance consists of (*i*) sales margin mix variance and (*ii*) sales margin quantity variance.

(iii) Sales Margin Mix Variance: This variance shows the difference between actual mix of goods and budgeted (standard) mix of goods sold. The formula is:

Sales Margin Mix Variance= (Actual sales mix – Standard proportion of actual sales mix) × Budgeted margin per unit.

If budgeted margin per unit on actual sales mix is more than the budgeted margin per unit on budgeted mix, variance will be favourable. In the reverse situation, unfavourable variance will arise.

(v) Sales Margin Quantity Variance: This variance will be found when the total actual sales quantity in standard proportion is different from the total budgeted sales quantity. The formula is:

Sales Margin Quantity Variance= (Actual sales in standard proportion – Budgeted sales) × Budgeted margin per unit on budgeted mix

If actual sales (in standard proportion) are more than the budgeted sales, variance will be favourable and if actual sales are less than the budgeted sales, unfavourable variance will arise.

Example 26

The budgeted and actual sales of a concern manufacturing and marking a single product are furnished below:

Budgeted Sales	10,000 units at Rs. 4 per unit
Actual sales	5,000 units at Rs. 3.50 per unit and
	8,000 units at Rs. 4 per unit

Calculate: (*a*) sales price variance and

(*b*) sales volume variance

Solution:

(A) Sales price variance = Actual sales – Standard sales

Standard sales = Standard price × Actual quantity

= Rs. 4 × 13,000

= Rs. 52,000

Actual sales = Actual price × Actual quantity

= Rs. 3.50 × 5,000 + Rs. 4 × 8,000

= Rs. 17,500 + Rs. 32,000

= Rs. 49,500

Sales Price variance = Rs. 49.500 – Rs. 52,000

= Rs. 2,500 (Adverse)

(*c*) Sales volume variance = Standard sales – Budgeted sales

= Rs. 52,000 – 40,000

= Rs. 12,000 (Favourable)

Sales value variance = Actual sales – Budgeted sales

= Rs. 49,500 – Rs. 40,000

= Rs. 40,000 – Rs. 49,500

= Rs. 9,500 (Favourable)

Example 27:

	Standard			*Actual*		
	Qty.	*Sale price Rs.*	*Total Rs.*	*Qty.*	*Sale price Rs.*	*Total Rs.*
Product X	500	5	2,500	500	5.00	2,500
Product Y	400	6	2,400	600	6,25	3,750
Product Z	300	7	2,100	400	6.75	2,700

Calculate: (*i*) Sales value variance, (*ii*) Sales price variance, (*iii*) Sales mix variance and (*iv*) Sales sub-volume variance.

Solution:

		Rs.
(*i*)	Sales Value variance:	
	Formula: (Actual Quantity × AP) – (SQ – SP)	
	Product X (500 × 5) – (500 × 5)	1,350 (F)
	Product Y (600 × 6.25) – (400 × 6)	
	Rs. 3,750 – 2,400	
	Product Z (400 × 6.75) – (300 × 7)	
	2700 – 2100	600 (F)
	Total sales value variance	1,950 (F)
(*ii*)	Sale price variance:	
	Formula: (AP – SP) × Actual quantity	
	Product X (Rs. 5-5) × 500	Nil
	Product Y (6.25 – 6) × 600	150 (F)
	Product Z (Rs. 6.75 – 7) × 400	100 (A)
	Total sales price Variance	50 (F)
(*iii*)	Sales mix variance:	
	Formula (Actual proportion – Revised standard mix of actual total sale) × SP	
	Product X (500 – 625) × 5	625 (A)
	Product Y (600 – 500) × 6	600 (F)
	Product Z (400 – 375) × 7	175 (F)
	Total sales mix variance Rs.	150 (F)

(*v*) Sales Sub-volume variance:

Formula: (Revised standard mix – Standard mix) × SP

Product X (625 –500) × 5	625 (F)
Product Y (500 – 400) × 6	600 (F)
Product Z (375 – 300) × 7	525 (F)
Total sales sub-volume variance Rs.	1,750 (F)

Check:

Sale price variance = Sales mix variance + Sales sub-usage = Sale value variance.

Rs. 50 (F) + Rs. 150 (F) + Rs. 1,750 (F) = Rs. 1,950 (F)

Working notes:

Revised standard mix

If 1,200 units are total sales, Product A sold = 500

$$\text{Product A If } 1{,}500 = \frac{\text{Standard units of product} \times \text{AQ}}{\text{Total standard units}}$$

$$= \frac{500 \times 1{,}500}{1{,}200} = 625 \text{ units}$$

$$\text{Product B} \quad = \frac{400 \times 1{,}500}{1{,}200} = 500 \text{ units}$$

$$\text{Product C} \quad = \frac{300 \times 1{,}500}{1{,}200} = 375 \text{ units}$$

Disposition of variance:

Variance may be disposed off in either of the following ways:

1. Inventories and the cost of goods sold may be adjusted to reflect the actual costs.
2. Variances may be transferred to the profit and loss account. Under the first method, all variances are allocated between the inventory accounts and cost of goods sold account. This method, in fact, converts the accounts balances from standard costs to actual historical costs. The following arguments are given in support of this method:
   - Only actual costs should be recorded in the cost of goods sold account and inventory accounts. The supporters of this method do not favour standard costs as true costs or costs suitable for use in the profit and loss account but as merely guides in factory management. Actual costs are facts and therefore, should be used in the financial statements.
   - Variances from the standard are costs and not losses and therefore should be reflected in the inventory valuations and cost of goods sold and
   - If the variances are large, standard costs do not represent the actual costs and therefore are not good measures to determine the costs of goods sold and inventory.

Under the second method, the variances are considered as profit or loss items in the period in which they occurred. The work-in-process, finished goods inventory and cost of goods sold are stated at standard costs. Unfavourable cost variances are deducted from the gross profit at standard costs. Favourable cost variance are added to the gross profit calculated at standard cost. The treatment of the cost covariances under this method is shown month income statement as given below:

ABC Company

Income Statement for the year Ending December 31.....

	Rs.	*Rs.*
Sales revenue		5,00,000
Cost of sales (Standard)	3,00,000	
Selling and administrative expenses (Standard)	1,50,00	4,50,000
Net Income (Standard)		50,000
Deduct unfavourable variance from standard costs:		
Material price	200	
Material usage	800	
Labour efficiency	900	
Overhead:		
Volume	2,000	
Budget	1,100	5,000
Net income (actual)		45,000

The second method has the following arguments in its favour:

(*i*) Standard costs helps in the preparation of statements at an early date; actual cost delays the determination of inventory costs and cost of goods sold.

(*ii*) Standard costs avoid the inclusion of costs due to wastage, losses, inefficiencies, excessive overheads from low production volume. Standard costs represent normal costs and therefore inventory figures are conservative and acceptable for income determination and other purposes.

(*iii*) In a multi-product company, it may be difficult to determine accurately how much variance should be distributed to each product.

(*iv*) In taking corrective action, managers may find it more useful when variances are depicted in the profit and loss account. Managerial attention is usually hampered when variances are combined with cost of goods manufactured.

Accountants who support this method believe that only standard costs should be considered the true costs. Variances are not treated as increases or decreases in manufacturing costs but as deviations from contemplated costs, due to abnormal inactivity, extravagance, inefficiencies or efficiencies or other changes in business conditions. This viewpoint leads to the closing of all variance to the income summary account, which is an acceptable procedure as long as standards are reasonable representatives of what costs ought to be.

It is difficult to suggest which method should be followed in accounting for variances. If the variances are large and significant, the first method, i.e. distribution of variances to the respective accounts appears to be appropriate for financial reporting tax and job and contract pricing purposes. The second method may be preferable when the variances are insignificant. Thus, the treatment of variance depends on many factors such as (*i*) size of variance, (*ii*) accuracy of standard costs, (*iii*) causes of variances such as incorrect standard costs, (*iv*) timing of variances, e.g. caused by seasonal fluctuation, (*v*) types of variances-material, labour and overheads.

MANAGERIAL USES OF VARIANCES

Determination of variance is only the first step in the process of standard cost variance analysis. Mere computation of material labour and overhead variance is useless for cost control and performance evaluation. The final objective of variance analysis is to determine the person(s) responsible for each variance and to pinpoint the cause(s) for incurrence of these variances. Properly used, standard cost variances are useful tools in achieving effective cost control. and control. That is, before the management can take effective action for improving control over costs, it needs to know not only the amount of variances, but also where the variance originated, who was responsible for them and what caused them to arise. Analysis of standard cost variance is, therefore, necessary by responsibilities and causes.

Analysis of variance by Responsibilities

Control over cost must be applied at the place and time where the cost originates. Variances must be identified with the manager responsible for the costs incurred who should be held responsible for that cost. The cost factors which are directly controllable by operating supervision must be separated from those costs factors for which executive management is responsible.

Specific titles of individuals who are responsible for each type or variance differ among business enterprises. Generally speaking, the following personnel are held accountable for variances noted against them:

Responsibility for Cost Variances

Variance	*Personnel Responsible*
(*i*) Materials price variance	Purchasing agent or purchasing manager
(*ii*) Materials quantity variance	Plant superintendent, departmental supervisors, machine operators, quality control department and material handlers
(*iii*) Labour rate standard	Personnel (employment) department manager, departmental supervisor and plant superintendent.
(*iv*) Labour efficiency variance	Plant superintendent, departmental supervisors, production scheduling department, quality control department, material handlers and machine operators.
(*v*) Overhead expenditure variance	Variable portion is the responsibility of the individual foreman or supervisor, they are expected to keep actual expenses within the budget. Fixed portion of the responsibility of top manager.
(*vi*) Overhead efficiency variance	Same personal who are responsible for labour efficiency variance.
(*vii*) Overhead volume variance	Top management and production schedulers.

Analysis of Variances by Causes

Variance reflect the effect on costs which certain events or conditions have produced. Before the management can decide whether or not action is called for and if so, what should be done, it is necessary to know what caused the variance to arise. Reasons for the variance should determine a plan for necessary corrective action made either by discussing possible causes with the supervisors or by examining underlying data and records. The analysis of variance by cause is therefore an important aspect of the use of standard costs to attain effective cost control. For any standard cost variance, there are many possible causes. The following list is not all inclusive but does indicate causes responsible for variances.

Possible causes of Standard Cost Variance

Materials Price Variance

1. Recent changes in purchase price of materials.
2. Failure to purchase anticipated quantities when standards were established resulting in higher prices owing to non-availability of quantity purchase discounts.
3. Not taking cash discounts anticipated at the time of setting standards resulting in higher prices.
4. Substituting raw material differing from original materials specifications.
5. Freight cost changes and changes in purchasing and storekeeping costs if these are debited to the material cost.

Materials Quantity Variance

1. Poor material handling
2. Inferior workmanship by machine operator.
3. Faulty equipment.
4. Cheaper, defective raw material causing excessive scrap.
5. Inferior quality control inspection
6. Pilferage and
7. Wastage due to inefficient production method.

Labour Rate Variance

1. Recent labour rate change within industry
2. Employing a man of a grade different from the one laid down in the standard.
3. Labour strike leading to utilisation of unskilled help.
4. Labour lay-off causing skilled labour to be retained at higher rates, so as to prevent resignations and job switching.
5. Employee sickness and vacation time.
6. Paying a higher overtime allowance than provided for in the standard.

Labour Efficiency Variance

1. Machine breakdown, use of defective machinery and equipment.
2. Inferior raw materials.
3. Poor supervision.
4. Lack of timely material handling.
5. Poor employee performance.
6. Inefficient production scheduling-delays in routing work, materials, tools and instructions.
7. Inferior engineering specifications.
8. New inexperienced employees.
9. Insufficient training of workers and
10. Poor working conditions-inadequate or excessive heating, lighting, ventilation etc.

Overhead Volume Variance

(Factors causing either idle time or overtime of plant and facilities)

1. Failure to utilise normal capacity.
2. Lack of sales order
3. Too much idle capacity
4. Inefficient or efficient utilisation of existing capacity.
5. Machine breakdown
6. Defective materials
7. Labour troubles and
8. Power failures

Overhead Efficiency Variance

These included all causes which are listed under labour efficiency variance.

Analysis of Variances by Products

Since the management usually wants current true costs when decisions are to be made with respect to pricing and related questions, variances are often analysed by products in order to arrive at current product costs. Companies producing non-standard goods according to customer's specifications may also help analyse variances by job orders. The analysis of variances by causes is useful in deciding whether or not cost variances should be allocated to products in arriving at product costs for pricing. Standard product costs should be reviewed periodically and revised when it is found that the standard product costs in use are no longer useful for the purpose.

VARIANCE REPORTS TO MANAGEMENT

Variance reports basically aim to inform managers responsible for the operation when actual performance differs from the standards.

To be effective, the report must be timely, accurate and clearly understood by the recipients.

Control of production and costs is a matter of timing; the effectiveness of the control is often in direct proportion to the speed with which variances are reported. Timely reporting often requires daily and weekly reporting of performance information. Therefore, it is important to focus managerial attention on off-standard conditions immediately following each shift, day or week, rather than to accumulate and summarise variances from standards each month. A month, and generally even a week, is too long a period for many off-standard conditions to remain unchecked and uncorrected, because the time interval may prevent positive identification of employees who are responsible for the unsatisfactory work. Prompt review of variances can disclose conditions needing managerial attention and can also provide the management with information which contributes to the making of sounder decisions with respect to the future.

Variance analysis reports are primarily control reports. In developing and reporting the variances, it should be remembered that the results must (*i*) deal with relevant distinctions, (*ii*) be understandable, (*iii*) measure with reasonable accuracy what they are supposed to measure, (*iv*) be presented and explained concisely, (*v*) be timely and (*vi*) provide the amount of details needed by different persons at each level of management.

Limitations of Standard Costing

Standard costs are not without their shortcomings. Standards and standard costing are essential parts of the system of cost control, revealing deviations from a plan and indicating where responsibility lies so that corrective action may be taken. However, standard costs have some limitations which should be kept in mind before using them.

The first limitation is regarding the predetermined nature of standard costs. The accuracy of standard costs is bounded by the knowledge and skill of the people who created them and they contain the prejudices of their makers. Such badly conceived standard costs do not enjoy the confidence of the users of the system.

Secondly, it is difficult to select a type of standard (ideal, currently attainable, normal, etc.) which can help in cost control and achieve other managerial purposes. If standards are too low, they defeat the objective of standard costing and bring the operating efficiency down. If they are too high, they can create ill-will and encourage employees to beat the system by fair means or foul. There is also a dispute as to what level of standards should be used for external financial reporting and internal management purposes.

Thirdly, a good programme of standard costing requires that both management and operating personnel should have full confidence in it and standards should be fair and workable. Educating employees is necessary in this regard. However, lack of acceptability, education and communication is a major difficulty in operating a standard costing system. There is the problem of human relation to add to the problems of setting up and operating the system, and sometimes this aspect is more involved in standard costing than the mechanics of the system itself.

Inspite of the above limitations, standard costing has developed into an extraordinary and very useful tool and has contributed much in providing different finds of cost data for so many different purposes.

THEORY QUESTIONS

1. Identify the role of standard costs in the budgetary control process.
2. Discuss briefly the use of standard costs in the following management activities: cost reductions, operating performance, evaluation, product pricing decisions and providing incentive.
3. Compare and contrast the usefulness of ideal standards, basic standards and currently attainable standards.
4. "Standard costs are bases for a proper managerial control of manufacturing operation". Define standard cost and explain the above statement.
5. What is standard costing and how would you distinguish it from budgetary control.
6. What are the points of similarity and difference between budgeted and standard costs.
7. "Variance analysis is an integral part of standard cost accounting." Explain this statement.
8. By purchasing low-grade materials, a company reports favourable material price variance, but it consistently experiences unfavourable material quantity variances. What relationship may exist between these conditions. Is the price variance really favourable.
9. What are the shortcomings of historical costs for managerial uses.
10. What is the difference between an estimated cost and a standard cost.
11. Describe briefly how standard costs are set for (*a*) material and (*b*) labour.
12. Briefly explain the meaning of each of the following variançes: material prices, material usages, labour efficiency, and labour rate.
13. Discuss some of the problems that might be created by standards which are set too high and by standards which are too loose.
14. What are the advantages and limitations of standard costing.
15. Discuss briefly some of the limitations of standard costs.
16. Explain why overhead variances are generally treated as period costs.
17. Discuss the information which a well-designed cost report should give to management from the point of view of production and control. How should such information be given.
18. How does standard costing improve the control function.
19. Explain why the materials price variance is often computed at the point of purchase rather than at the point of issuance.
20. A standard cost sheet is a key component of a standard cost system. Describe a standard cost sheet and explain why it is significant.
21. Explain the significance of overhead variances with suitable illustrations.
22. "The variance analysis, the key element in standards costing, essentially consists of the application of the principle of management by exception" Elucidate.

PROBLEMS

1. The standard quantity and standard price of raw material required for one unit of product A are given as follows:

	Quantity	*Selling price*
Material X	2 kg.	Rs. 3 per kg.
Material Y	4 kg.	Rs. 2 per kg.
	6 kg.	

The actual production and relevant data are as follows:

Output 500 units of Product A

Material	*Total quantity for 500 units*	*Total cost (RS)*
X	1,100 kg.	3,410
Y	1,800 kg.	3,960

Calculate the variances.

(*Ans.* Material cost variance Rs. 370 (A): usage variance Rs.100 (F); Material price variance Rs. 470 (A))

2. From the data given below, calculate the materials price variance, the materials usage variance and materials mix variance. Consumption per 100 units of product:

Raw material	*Standard*	*Actual*
A	40 units @ Rs. 50 per unit	50 units @ Rs. 50 per unit
B	6- units @ Rs. 40 per unit	60 units @ Rs. 45 per unit

(*Ans.* Material Price Variance Rs. 300 (A); Mix Variance Rs.60 (A); Usage Variance Rs 500(A))

3. The standard material cost for 100 kg. of chemical D is made up of:

Chemical A – 30 kg. @ Rs. 4 per kg.

Chemical A – 40 kg. @ Rs. 5 per kg.

Chemical A –80 kg. @ Rs. 6 per kg.

In a batch, 500 kg of chemical D was produced from a mix of:

Chemical A –140 kg. at a cost of Rs. 588

Chemical A – 220 kg. at a cost of Rs. 1,056

Chemical A – 440 kg. at a cost of Rs. 4 per kg.

How do the yield, mix and price factors contribute to the variance in the actual cost per 100 kg. of chemical D over the standard cost.

(*Ans.* Material cost variance Rs. 100.80 (A)

Material price variance Rs. 40.80 (A)

Material nix variance Rs. 6.67(A)

Material sub-usage variance Rs. 53.33(A)

Material usage variance Rs. 60(A)

4. XY Ltd. manufacturers of product P, use a standard cost system. Standard product and cost specifications for 1,000 kg of product P are as follows:

Ingredients	*Quantity kg.*	*Price Rs. per kg.*	*Cost*
A	800	2.50	2,000
B	200	4.00	800
C	200	1.00	200
Input	1,200		3,000 = Rs. 2.50 per kg.
Output	1,000		3,000 = Rs. 3.00 per kg.

Material records indicate:	*Consumption in January*
A	1,57,000 kg. @ Rs. 2.40
B	38,000 kg. @ Rs. 4.20
C	36,000 kg. @ Rs. 1.10

Actual finished production for the month of January is 2,00,000 kg. Calculate:

1. Material price variance
2. Material mix variance
3. Material yield variance

(*Ans.* Rs. 4,500 (F); Rs.3,000 (A); 22,500 (F))

5. The following data relates to a firm:

Material	*Standard* *Qty. (kg.)*	*Price*	*Total*	*Material* *Qty.(kg.)*	*Actual* *Price*	*Total*
A	500	6	3,000	400	6	2,400
B	400	3.75	1,500	500	3.60	1,800
C	300	3.00	900	400	2.80	1,120
	1,200			1,300		
Less: Actual loss				220		
10% loss	120					
	1,080		5,400	1,080		5,320

Calculate: (*i*) Materials cost variance

(*ii*) Materials price variance

(*iii*) Material mix variance

(*vi*) Material yield and

(*v*) Total material usage variance.

(*Ans:* (*i*) Rs. 80 (A) (*ii*) Rs. 155(F), (*iii*) Rs. 375 (F) (*iv*) Rs. 450 (A) (*v*) Rs. 75 (A).

6. The standard cost of a certain chemical mixture is:

   40% Material A at Rs. 200 per tonne

   60% Material B at Rs. 300 per tonne

   A standard loss of 10% is expected in production. During a period materials used are:

   90 tonnes Material A at the cost of Rs. 180 per tonne.

   110 tonnes Material Bat the cost of Rs. 340 per tonne.

   The weight produced is 182 tonnes of good production.

Calculate and present:

(*i*) Material price variance

(*ii*) Material usage variance

(*iii*) .Material mix variance and

(*iv*) Material yield variance

(*Ans.* (*i*) Rs. 2,600 (A) (*ii*) Rs. 1,577.77 (F) (*iii*) Rs. 1,000 (F) and (*iv*) Rs. 5,77,777 (F)

7. The standard cost of a certain chemical mixture is: 40% material A @ Rs. 20 per tonne; 60% material B @ Rs. 30 per tonne. A standard loss of 10% is expected in production. During a period of one month, 90 tonnes of material A @ Rs. 18 per tonne and 110 tonnes of material B @ 34 per tonne were used to produce 182 tonnes of good production.

Calculate the (*a*) materials price variance (*b*) Materials mix variance, and (*c*) materials yield variance.

(*Ans:* (*a*) Rs. 260 (A); (*b*) Rs. 100(F); (*c*) Rs.57.78(F)

8.(*a*) The standard set for material consumption was 100 kg @ Rs. 2.25per kg.

In a cost period; Opening stock was	100kg @ Rs. 2.25 per kg.
Purchase made	500 kg @ Rs. 2.15 per kg. and
Consumption	110 kg

Calculate:

(*a*) Usage variance.

(*b*) Price variance: (*i*) when variance is calculated at point of purchase; (*ii*) when variance is calculated at point of issue on FIFO basis; and (*iii*) when variance is calculated at point of issue on LIFO basis.

(c) What is the effect on closing stock valuation when materials are charged out to cost on basis (*ii*) and (*iii*) above.

(*Ans.* (*a*) Usage variance Rs. 22.50 (A)

(*b*) (*i*) Rs. 50 (F) (*ii*) Re. 1 (F), (*iii*) Rs. 11 (F).

9. From the data given below, calculate labour variances for the two departments:

	Dept. A	*Dept. B*
Actual gross wages (Direct)	Rs. 2,000	Rs. 1,800
Standard hours produced	8,000	6,000
Standard rate per hour	30 paise	35 paise
Actual hours worked	8,200	5,800

	Dept. A	*Dept. B*
(*Ans.* Labour cost variance	Rs. 40(F)	Rs. 300 (F)
Labour rate variance	460 (F)	230 (F)
Labour efficiency variance	60 (A)	70 (F)

10. The details regarding composition and the weekly wage rates of labour force engaged on a job scheduled to be computed in 30 weeks are as follows:

Category of workers	*Standard* No. of labourers	*Standard* Weekly rate	*Actual* No of labourers	*Actual* Weekly wage
Skilled	75	60	70	70
Semi-skilled	45	40	30	50
Unskilled	60	30	80	20

The work is actually completed in 32 weeks. Calculate the various labour variances.

[*Ans.* Labour cost variance. Rs. 13,000(A) Rate variance Rs. 6,400(A), Labour efficiency 6,600(A), Mix variance Rs. 9,600(F), Labour sub-efficiency Rs. 16,200(A)].

11. A chemical company gives you the following standard and actual data of its Chemical No. 1456. You are required to calculate variances.

Standard data (*kg.*)	*Total* *Rs.*	*Actual data* *Rs.*		*Total* *Rs.*
450 of material A @ 20 per kg.	9,000	450 kg @ 19 per kg.	8,550	
360 of material B @ 10 per kg.	3,600	360 kg@11 per kg.	3,960	12,510
810	12,600	810		
2,400 skilled hours @ Rs. 2 per hour	4,800	2,400 hour @ 2.25		5,400
1,200 unskilled hours @ Re. 1 per hour	1,200	1,200 hrs. @ 1.25		1,500
90 Normal loss		50 kg. Actual loss	760	19,410

(*Ans.* Material cost variance Rs. 790(F), Material price variance Rs. 90(F) Material yield Rs. 700(F), Labour cost Rs. 566.67(A) Labour rate 900(A), Labour yield 333.33(F).

12. The following data is supplied to you:

Standard					*Actual*			
Input	*Material*	*Rs. per kg.*	*Rs.*	*Total Rs.*	*Input kg.*	*Rs. per kg.*	*Rs.*	*Total Rs.*
400	A	50	20,000		420	45	18,000	
200	B	20	4,000		240	25	6,000	
100	C	15	1,500	25,500	90	15	1,350	25,250
700								
Labour								
100 man hours @ Rs. 2 per hr.			200		120 hr. @ Rs. 2.50 per hour		300	
200 women hrs. @ R. 1.50 per hr.			300	500	240 hours @ Rs. 1.60 per hour		384	684
25 kg. Normal loss					75 kg. Actual loss			
675 kg.				26,000	675 kg.			26,934

From the above information calculate variances.

(*Ans.* Material cost 750(A), Material price 900(F), Material mix 171.43(F), Material yield 1,821.43(A), Labour cost 184(A), Labour mix 64,29(A), Labour yield 35.71(A), Labour rate 84(A).

13. The records of Conwest Engineering Corporation indicate the following for the month of April 1992:

Standards	*Factors*	*Units cost*
Direct materials	4 gallons @ Rs. 1.20	Rs. 4.80
Direct labour	3 hours @ Rs. 1.80	Rs. 5.40
Factory overhead	Re. 0.60 @ per labour hr.	Rs. 1.80
Total manufacturing cost		Rs. 12.00

Month of April Activity

(*i*) Production during the month of April 1992 has been 6,500 units with no beginning or ending work-in-progress inventories.

(*ii*) *Materials:*

Purchased 32,000 gallons @ Rs. 1,18 per gallon

Used in production 25,600 gallons

(*iii*) *Labour:*

Hours worked 20,000

Average hourly wage rate Rs. 1.75

(*iv*) Factory overheads:

Total overhead cost incurred Rs. 12,500

Calculate material variances, labour variances and only total variance for factory overheads.

(*Ans.* Material price variance Rs. 512 (Favourable)

Material usage variance Rs. 480 (Favourable)

Material Cost Variance Rs. 992 (Favourable)

Labour rate variance Rs. 1,000 (Favourable)

Labour Time Variance Rs. 900 (Adverse)

Labour Cost variance Rs. 100 (Favourable)

total overhead variance Rs. 800 (Adverse)

14. | | | |
|---|---|---|
| No. of working days | 20 | 22 |
| Man hours per day | 8,000 | 8,400 |
| Output per manhour in unit | 1.0 | 0.9 |
| Overhead cost (Rs.) | 1,60,000 | 1,68,000 |

Calculate overhead variances such as:

(*i*) Overhead cost variance
(*ii*) Overhead efficiency variance
(*iii*) Overhead capacity variance
(*iv*) Overhead calendar variance

(*Ans.* (*i*) Rs. 1,680(A) (*ii*) Rs. 18,480 (A) (*iii*) Rs. 24,800(F) (*iv*) Rs. 1,600(F)

15. Vinak Ltd. has furnished you the following information for the month of August, 2002:

	Budget	*Actual*
Output (Units)	30,000	32,500
Hours	30,000	33,000
Fixed overhead	Rs. 45,000	50,000
Variable overhead	Rs. 60,000	68,000
Working days	25	26

Calculate the variances.

(*Ans.* Total overhead cost variance Rs. 4,250(A)
Variable overhead cost variance Rs. 3,000(A)
Fixed overhead cost variance Rs. 1,250(A)
Expenditure variance Rs. 750(A)
Capacity Variance Rs. 4,500(A)
Calendar variance Rs. 1,800(F)

16. From the following data for a factory for the month of January 1991, compute overhead variances under Four-Way Analysis:

	Standard	*Actual*
Number of units produced	15,000	8,000
Capacity (hours)	30,000	17,000
Variable Overheads	30,000	15,500
Fixed overheads	45,000	46,300

(*Ans.* (*i*) Spending variance Rs. 200(F)
(*ii*) Variable efficiency Rs. 13,000(F)
(*iii*) Fixed efficiency Rs. 19,500(A)
(*iv*) Idle capacity Rs. 19,500(A)
(*v*) Net variance Rs. 13,200(F)

17. Alliance Francisė Ltd. operates a small business with wide seasonal fluctuation. Budgeted overhead is Rs. 12,000 per month plus rs. 2 per direct labour hour at the normal volume of 1,000 units. The standard labour cost per unit of production is 3 hours at Rs. 5 per hour. During March 1988, 800 units were produced which required 2,500 direct labour hours at a total labour cost of Rs. 12,000. Actual overhead amounted to Rs. 17,200, of which Rs. 5,500 were variable.

Compute the following variances:

(*i*) Labour efficiency variance
(*ii*) Variable overhead efficiency variance
(*iii*) Variable overhead spending variance
(*iv*) Fixed overhead spending variance and
(*v*) Fixed overhead volume variance.

Ans: (*i*) Rs. 500(A) (*ii*) Rs. 200(A) (*iii*) Rs. 500(A) (*iv*) Rs. 1,700(A) (*v*) Rs. 2,400(A)

18. Herdelia Chemical Company produces a petro-product using the following proportion of materials:

	Pounds	*Cost per Pound Rs.*	*Amount Rs.*
Material A	50	5.00	250
Material B	40	6.00	240
Material C	60	3.00	180
	150	4.4667	670
Standard shrinkage (33$^1/_3$%)	50		
Net weight and costs	100	6.70	670

A recent production run yielding 100 output pounds requires input of:

	Pounds	*Per Pound Rs.*
Material A	40	5.20
Material B	55	6.00
Material C	65	2.60

Calculate materials price, mix and yield variances.

Ans. Material Mix Variance Rs. 10.33(A)
Material Price Variance Rs. 18.00(F)
Yield Variance Rs. 44.67(A)
(or usage variance)
Net material cost variance Rs. 37.00(A).

19. Pioneer Plastics Limited operates a budgetary control and standard costing system. From the following data calculate:

(*i*) Sales Variance

(*ii*) Sales Volume Variance

(*iii*) Sales Price Variance

Product	*Std. selling price per unit*	*Std. cost price per unit*	*Budget*		*Actual*	
			Units to be sold	*Sales value*	*Units sold*	*Sales volume*
A	10.00	12.00	100	1,200	100	1,100
B	9.40	12.00	50	600	50	600
C	7.50	9.00	100	900	200	1,700
D	4.00	6.00	75	450	50	300
Total	—	—	325	3,150	400	3,700

(*Ans.* Sales value variance Rs. 550(F), Sales price variance Rs. 200(A), Sales volume variance Rs. 750(F).

20. The budgeted sales for one month and the actual results achieved are as under:

		Budget			Actual	
Product	*Quantity*	*Rate*	*Amount Rs.*	*Quantity Nos.*	*Rate Rs.*	*Amount Rs.*
A	1,000	100	1,00,000	1,200	125	1,50,000
B	700	200	1,40,000	800	150	1,20,000
C	500	300	1,50,000	600	300	1,80,000
D	30	500	1,50,000	400	600	2,40,000
	2,500		5,40,000	3,000		6,90,000

Calculate in respect of each product the sales variances.

(*Ans.* Sales value Rs. 1,50,000(F); Sales price Rs. 30,000(F) and Sales volume Rs. 1,20,000(F).